CINEMA AT THE END OF EMPIRE

CINEMA AT

DUKE UNIVERSITY PRESS ✳ *Durham and London* ✳ *2006*

PRIYA JAIKUMAR

THE END OF EMPIRE

A Politics of Transition in Britain and India

© 2006 Duke University Press ∗ All rights reserved
Printed in the United States of America on acid-free paper ⊛
Designed by Amy Ruth Buchanan
Typeset in Quadraat by Tseng Information Systems, Inc.
Library of Congress Cataloging-in-Publication Data and permissions
information appear on the last printed page of this book.

For my parents

MALATI AND JAIKUMAR

*

*

As we look back at the cultural archive, we begin to reread
it not univocally but *contrapuntally*, with a simultaneous
awareness both of the metropolitan history that is narrated
and of those other histories against which (and together
with which) the dominating discourse acts.

—Edward Said, *Culture and Imperialism*

CONTENTS

ILLUSTRATIONS

ACKNOWLEDGMENTS

With each year that I worked on this manuscript, I accrued new debts of grati-tude. For access to documents, films, and film stills, I am thankful to the helpful staff at the National Film Archive of India in Pune; the Maharash-tra State Archives in Mumbai; the Nehru Memorial Library and the National Archives in New Delhi; the British Film Institute, the Public Records Office, and the British Library in London; and the University of Southern California (USC) Cinema-Television Library in Los Angeles. Generous grants sponsored my bicontinental archive crawl. Of particular assistance were the American Institute of Indian Studies Junior Research Fellowship, Northwestern Uni-versity's Dissertation Year Fellowship, travel grants from the Center for Inter-national and Comparative Studies and the University Research Grants Com-mittee, travel funds from the English Department at Syracuse University, and a sabbatical from USC's Critical Studies Division.

Friends and family—particularly Arundhathi Subramaniam and Vikram Kapadia in Mumbai; Anuradha Nayar, Rajeev Nayar, and Sanjay Suri in Lon-don; the Vartaks and the Mukherjees in Pune; and my parents in New Delhi—sustained me with their hospitality, food, drink, and conversation as I worked my way through files and films. Navigating the voluminous holdings of the

India Office Library would have been no fun without the help of my friend and fellow film-enthusiast Kaushik Bhaumik. And thanks are due to Arjun Mahey for introducing me to Joseph Conrad in his inimitable way, many years ago.

Several people offered invaluable feedback as I went through drafts of this book. I am particularly grateful to Tom Gunning, Madhu Dubey, Mimi White, Steve Cohan, Sarah Street, Marsha Kinder, Dana Polan, Urmi Bhowmik, Alex Lykidis, and to Syracuse University's English Faculty Reading Group for helping me clarify the project. Gunning is wholly responsible for turning my interest in cinema into a passion and a profession; I would not have written this book without him. Dubey's take-no-prisoners attitude toward what she calls "lazy cultural-studies jargon," kept me honest, and Noël Burch's interest in my work spurred me on at a crucial moment. Roopali Mukherjee wrote her book as I wrote mine, and it was immeasurably helpful to go through the process together. I can only hope that our long phone conversations about books, theorists, and the point of it all were as indispensable to her as they were to me. Tom Holden reminded me to stick to deadlines and take breaks, often treating me to dinners and road trips. His close reading of sections of this book helped me to streamline the project and, more important, to conclude it. The love, friendship, and intelligence of these people and of my family equipped me for the luxuries and labors of academic writing.

I am incredibly fortunate to have had the experienced and astute guidance of Ken Wissoker, Courtney Berger, and the staff at Duke University Press for the publication of my first book, which is so much better because of their careful and inspired work and their enthusiastic support. Anonymous reviewers for the press suggested changes that also vastly improved the text's quality and readability. Revised versions of three previous articles are included in the book, and I thank *Cinema Journal*, *Screen*, and *The Moving Image* for granting me permission to reprint the material. The British films discussed here are still in circulation, and a few that are not (like *The Great Barrier* and *The End of the River*) can be found at the British Film Institute in London. The Indian films analyzed in the final chapter can be viewed at the National Film Archive of India in Pune.

Never had a larger area of the globe been under the
formal or informal control of Britain than between the
two world wars, but never before had the rulers of Britain
felt less confident about maintaining their old imperial
superiority.

—Eric Hobsbawm, *The Age of Extremes*

INTRODUCTION

We must abandon the rubric of national cinemas if we are to consider the
multiple, conjunctural pressures applied by decolonization on the political
entities of an imperial state and its colony. Declining British imperialism, increasing U.S. hegemony, and internal nationalist factions implicated Britain
and India in each other's affairs, shaping state policies, domestic markets,
and emergent cinemas in both regions. A parallel narration of their inter-
twined histories clarifies the global function of cinema during late colonialism by interrogating the consequences of a redistribution of political power
in plural and linked cultural contexts.

In 1931 Winston Churchill spoke to the Council of Conservative Associates
in Britain, explaining his resistance to granting India dominion status. "To
abandon India to the rule of Brahmins would be an act of cruel and wicked
negligence. . . . These Brahmins who mouth and patter the principles of Western Liberalism . . . are the same Brahmins who deny the primary rights of
existence to nearly sixty million of their own countrymen whom they call 'untouchable' . . . and then in a moment they turn around and begin chopping
logic with Mill or pledging the rights of man with Rousseau."[1] In castigating

Hindu Brahmins for their adherence to oppressive social practices despite a competent knowledge of Western liberalism, Churchill exposed the ineffable qualifications in his own rationale for Britain's continued control over India. His suggestion was that although Britain *also* denied sovereignty to well over sixty-million people, it did not patter on about liberalism but grasped the true essence of that political philosophy. Two kinds of commercial British and Indian film from the 1930s responded directly to this line of argument. The first recreated similarly paternalistic defenses of empire, with films like *Sanders of the River* (1935) and *The Drum* (1938), both produced by Churchill's friend and confidant Alexander Korda. The second, against Churchillian condemnation, imagined an alternative Indian society.

Nitin Bose's *Chandidas*, a popular 1934 film produced by the Calcutta-based film studio New Theaters, opens with the declaration that it is "based on the life problems of the poet Chandidas—A problem India has not been able to solve." [2] The film tells the melodramatic tale of a young poet (K. L. Saigal) and his beloved Rani (Uma Shashi), a lower-caste woman, through a narrative and a musical soundtrack that continually link the romantic tribulations of these young lovers to contemporary social issues. Chandidas fights the Brahmin taboo against washerwoman Rani *dhoban*'s entry into a Hindu temple, weighing the arguments for humanity (*manushyata*) over religious conduct (*dharma*). By the film's conclusion, a coalition of commoners supports the transgressive couple's vision of an egalitarian future for India.

Popular British and Indian films of the 1930s foresee decolonization in utopian visions of realigned power, holding dystopic predictions at bay. In so doing, their content and form negotiates the anxiety and exhilaration of impending sociopolitical changes in the imperial metropolis and its colony. Extending Ella Shohat's and Robert Stam's observation that cinema's beginnings coincided with "the giddy heights" of imperialism, I argue that cinema's late colonial period embodied the ambiguities, possibilities, and fears generated by two historical paradoxes: that of colonialism's moral delegitimation *before* its political demise and that of its persistence in shaping modern postcolonial societies well *after* the end of formal empire. [3] To articulate key facets of this complex transition as it relates to cinema, the communicative terrain of negotiations surrounding film policy (part 1) and the affective, ideological domain of film aesthetics (parts 2 and 3) structure my analysis. This allows for a critical and conceptual comparativism across British and Indian regulatory texts and film forms that would be harder to achieve if I began with the category of national cinema.

The framework of national cinemas has become a dominant analytic trope in Film Studies because of the nation's function as a central axis along which films are regulated, produced, consumed, and canonized.[4] Insights about the nation's ideological production and reconstitution through cinema hold profound relevance to my analysis, but I abdicate the nation as an organizing device in order to resist the temptation of making it, in Foucault's words, a "tranquil locus on the basis of which other questions (concerning . . . structure, coherence, systematicity, transformations) may be posed."[5] The very notion of a modern nation-state was under construction in India and under reconstruction in Britain. At the territorial apogee of empire in the early twentieth century, decolonizing movements pushing for a universalization of political modernity (or bourgeois democracy)[6] challenged the legitimacy of colonialism. India's devastatingly partitioned formation threw into question its own viability as a prospective nation, even as it exposed the fragility of a British nation-state that was constituted on internally schismatic—simultaneously liberal and imperial—political philosophies. British and Indian films were part of this turbulence. One has only to think of the conclusions to Shejari/Padosi (Marathi/Hindi, Shantaram, 1941) and Black Narcissus (Powell and Pressburger, 1947) in conjunction to realize this: the spectacular drowning of a Hindu and a Muslim in Shantaram's film imparts the same disquiet as an Irish and British nun's fatal scuffle by a precipice in the latter. Each film permits a particular textual figuration of uncertainty about the political future.

The study of colonial cinemas—framed by an analysis of Eurocentrism, censorship, racism, dominant ideology, and nationalist resistance—has not adequately addressed the cultural registers of changing international power politics during the early twentieth century. The British State underwent complex negotiations to render its regime legitimate and effective in the face of anticolonial nationalisms, domestic dissent, and ascending U.S. global power. In this political landscape Indian filmmakers rebuffed imperial state initiatives while fashioning a regionally hegemonic film industry and wresting a domestic audience from Hollywood's control. To grasp these complexities, I offer an interpretation that moves between the British and Indian governments, between British and Indian cinemas in relation to their states, and between silent and sound films. Thus the operative categories in this book—state policy and film aesthetics—indicate related areas of contention between a fragmenting empire and a nascent nation, as well as within them.

Film policies and film texts also present parallels and counterpoints as types of discourses. The regulatory debates and film aesthetics of this period are both shot through with contradictions between the languages of imperialism and anticolonialism, making them linked expressions of a political transformation.[7] But the British State treated film as a generic commodity in order to create a comprehensive film policy applicable to Britain's imperium, although in reality a British film had appeals and market-potentialities quite distinct from those of an Indian, Canadian, or Australian film. In the latter sections of this book I examine particular British and Indian films of radically divergent national, economic, and aesthetic agendas to expose the fallacy of the British State's universalist assumptions about cinema discussed in part I.

*

My narrative opens in 1927, the year after a watershed imperial conference that marked the British State's official acknowledgment of its changing status in relation to its colonies and dominions. Resolutions passed at Britain's Imperial Conference of 1926, which closely preceded the Brussels International Congress against Colonial Oppression and Imperialism, resulted in concessions to dominion separatism and colonial self-governance.[8] The term *commonwealth* began to replace *empire*, and the British State reoriented itself to a new political collective.[9] A key debate in Britain, echoing controversies from 1903, surrounded the creation of "imperial preference."[10] Eventually ratified at the Imperial Conference of 1932, imperial preference involved agreements between territories of the British Empire to extend tariff concessions to empire-produced goods. The British State hoped that reinvigorating the imperial market would assist Britain in counteracting its new rivals in trade (the United States) and ideology (the Soviet Union). Rebelling colonies and nearly sovereign dominions could still transform "Little England" into "Great Britain," it was suggested, if only Britain could appeal to the idea of *bilateralism* in imperial affairs. Over the next two decades, the shift in Britain was tectonic: from free trade to protectionism, from the rhetoric of dominance to admissions of vulnerability, from a posture of supremacy to concessions to the need for reciprocity in imperial relations.

In film the official re-evaluation of Britain's industrial status led to the Cinematograph Films Act of 1927, which fixed an annual percentage of British films to be distributed and exhibited within Britain. The act was meant to guarantee exhibition of British films, thus attracting investment to the nation's neglected film-production sector, which had languished while British film exhibitors and distributors (renters) benefited through trading with Hollywood. Following World War I, the dictates of profit and of booking con-

tracts had impelled British film renters and exhibitors to distribute and release Hollywood films in preference to British ones.[11] By 1924, three of the
largest distribution companies in Britain were U.S.-owned, handling about
33 percent of total films screened in Britain. Hollywood dominated British
colonial and dominion film markets as well, and a dramatic signpost of Britain's crisis came in 1924, in the month dubbed "Black November," when
British studios remained dark in the absence of domestic film production.

The Cinematograph Films Act (or Quota Act) of 1927, ostensibly initiated
to assist British films against Hollywood's prevalence in the domestic British
market, was in truth equally shaped by imperial aspirations. A trail of letters, petitions to the state, and memoranda archives the efforts of British
film producers to extend the ambit of state protectionism to the empire by
way of "Empire quotas" and "Empire film schemes." Not unlike a potential Film Europe that aimed to contest Film America in the 1920s and 1930s,
these quota initiatives and empire film schemes were attempts to persuade
colonial and dominion governments of the benefits of a porous, collaborative empire market.[12] To this end the 1927 British Quota Act extended quota
concessions not to British films exclusively but to "British Empire films," a
new term that posed a strange lexical conundrum, referring simultaneously
to *every* film produced in the British Empire (conjuring a world where films
from India, Australia, New Zealand, and Britain circulated between those
markets with ease) and *no* film (given the impossibility of finding audiences
charmed equally by all empire-produced films). As the social historian Prem
Chowdhry has shown, British films like The Drum screened to anticolonial
picketing in India.[13] There was no happy imperial collective, and therefore
no film to satisfy it.

The gap between reality and the implicit goal of such film regulations
opens new areas for investigation. First, it focuses attention on Britain's ambition to acquire a market within the empire, which underwrote emerging
regulatory definitions of the British film commodity in palpable ways. Second, regulatory language betrays material intent when we follow the state's
struggle over naming things. In speaking of "the politics of colonial society"
as "a world of performatives," Sudipto Kaviraj argues that "words were the
terrain on which most politics were done. Despite their symbolic and sub-
liminal character, the political nature of such linguistic performances should
not be ignored."[14] In 1927–28 Indian and British film industry personnel,
film trade associations, journalists, and statesmen drew on multiple kinds of
knowledge (of other cinemas, other governments) and beliefs (in alternative

political and economic practices) to launch cosmopolitan criticisms of imperial quota policies. Correspondingly, during the following ten years, British state agents desisted from legislative initiatives for British Empire films and emphasized diplomatic negotiations.

The British film industry's overtures for preferential treatment in India began to gesture increasingly toward Britain's own reciprocal openness to Indian films, as in the following 1932 memorandum sent by British filmmakers to their state.

> The British Film Industry recognizes that India, in common with all other countries, wishes to develop its own film production trade, and that certain Indian-made films, suitable to the European market, may well seek distribution in Great Britain. There is no obstacle to this at present (other than the limited demand in this country for pictures portraying mainly oriental themes) and on the contrary Indian films have exactly the same facilities for inclusion in the United Kingdom quota as films made in any part of the British Empire—including Great Britain. On the other hand, unless India wishes to reserve its home market entirely or mainly for Indian-made films, it is assumed that films of British make are likely to meet the requirements of the population better than those of foreign production.[15]

Such delicately worded imperial presumptions of bilateralism point to a new modality of power play that has been neglected by colonial film scholars.[16] Here Britain is included in the empire rather than asserted as its sovereign commander, though its films claim a greater cultural proximity to India than those of "foreign production." Clearly, applications of "soft power"—that is, attempts at apparently multilateral discussions to assert authority—accompanied the more traditional use of "hard power" through media censorship and unequal film-tariff structures in places like India, Australia, and New Zealand.[17]

The evidence lies in a flurry of administrative paperwork passing between different branches of the British government (the Customs Office, the British Board of Trade, the Dominion and Colonial Office, and the Economic and Overseas Department of Britain's India Office in particular), in which strategic shifts toward notions like "imperial preference" show a state working to transform its empire into a network of allies that would voluntarily assist British film production. What we see in action is a state adapting to its splintering control over an empire, as transformations in imperial relations, state discourse, and colonial subject-positions structure the words of emerging regulations. Writing about these changes prevents, in Michel Foucault's cinematic metaphor, the surrender of history to "a play of fixed images disappearing in turn," in which postcolonial relations seem to suddenly replace colonial ones without continuities or consequences.[18]

1947 marked Britain's official hand-over of political sovereignty to a region violently divided between India and Pakistan, and my analysis terminates with that year. Despite its apparent tidiness, this book's periodization remains questionable. Epistemological disagreements between Indian historiographers over the nature and locus of anticolonial struggles unsettle efforts to present a linear chronology of Indian nationalism. While everyone agrees that a live wire of colonial resistance ran through the Indian subcontinent by the 1920s, nationalist activism was launched on multiple and frequently nonconsonant fronts by groups like the Swarajists (proponents of self-rule who favored legislative reform), revolutionaries (who supported terrorist violence against the state), Gandhian Satyagrahis (advocates of complete civil disobedience and constructive social work), regional nationalists (like Periyar's Self-Respect Movement and the Dravidian Movement, which hailed independence from imperialism as well as from north India), members of the Muslim League, the Hindu Mahasabha, the Rashtriya Swayamsevak Sangh, the Indian Left, and peasant and tribal resistance groups, to name a few.

Challenging the view that India's nationalist movement, led by the Indian National Congress, succeeded in articulating an inclusive political vision built on civil libertarian and democratic principles, the Subaltern Studies Collective of Indian historians contend that peasant and tribal rebellions formed an autonomous domain of politics.[19] According to the subalternists' argument, excavating sociopolitical consciousness among tribal and minoritarian communities requires writing against the grain of modern India's nationalist history, which has difficulty conceptualizing revolutionary subjectivities formed outside the public realm of bourgeois politics. Breaking down unified notions of nationalism also brings forth the possibility of contradictory affiliations—such as women articulating nationalisms against indigenous and inherited patriarchies—that, though not fully defined movements, nevertheless provided an agenda for social critique and action. Additionally, histories of liberal secular nationalism can be charged with yielding inadequate analytical tools for grasping parallel developments in the politicization of religion since the formation of the Indian nation, a trend proven by the sway of Hindutva politics in India since the 1990s.[20] Beyond cataclysmic divisions between Hindus and Muslims, figureheads like Gandhi, Savarkar, Ambedkar, and C. N. Annadurai signify deep factional, ideological rifts within the nation then and now.

If a narration of India's biography becomes impossible when we question the parameters of its nationalist archive or the terms of its narration, periodizing imperialism also continues to be frustrating work. The Leninist definition of modern imperialism as the height of monopoly capitalism distinguishes it from older monarchical empires (without denying that dynastic ancien régimes accompanied the birth of capitalist adventurism). However, Britain's synchronically varied colonial pursuits across multiple possessions and colonialism's diachronic role in defining the British State's structure and policies over centuries make it difficult to pinpoint originary and concluding events of modern British imperialism.[21] The nation's "internal" colonies of Northern Ireland, Scotland, and Wales further push definitions of British imperialism to include contentious domestic politics.

Mindful of these dilemmas, I propose that the challenge for a cultural analysis of late empire lies in observing the internal heterogeneities as well as significant ruptures of its practice, and in building a conceptual framework sensitive to imperialism's historical multivalence. To construct this framework we may begin with a significant structural break in British imperialism that occurred with colonialism's "retreat" or, more appropriately, with its rationalization in the mid- to late nineteenth century. To use the anthropologist Ann Stoler's phrase, the "embourgeoisement" of empire during the period of "high" or "late" colonialism "enhanced expectations of hard work, managed sexuality, and racial distancing among the colonial agents," as the British State invented an administrative and educational machinery to discipline imperial officials as well as include colonial subjects in the work of empire-maintenance.[22] In India Thomas Babington Macaulay's educational policies exemplify this modern, bourgeois imperialism. Instituted in 1836, British India's education system was the most practical solution to maintaining British power in a place where a few governed the many; it created, in Macaulay's often quoted words, "a class who may be interpreters between us and the millions whom we govern; a class of persons, Indian in blood and colour, but English in taste, in opinion, in morals and in intellect."[23] A significant point of rupture in the practice of British imperialism may be located, then, in Britain's modernization of its imperial practices through the formation of liberal democratic institutions across colonies to facilitate imperial administration.

Cinema, coming in the late 1890s, participated in the internal contradictions of a modernized language of empire. Liberalism's impulse toward self-governance put pressure on imperialism's essential unilateralism to define the internal form and formal contradictions of British film policy and commercial film style. These contradictions were exaggerated with Britain's own experience of global vulnerability in the early twentieth century. Various geopolitical factors precipitated a crisis in British state power during the interwar period, including the active intervention of anticolonial movements, domestic debates over the empire's profitability to Britain, and the rise of new (more "efficient" and invisible, transnational and corporate) imperialisms.[24] Britain's cinematographic subjugation to the United States was only one reminder of the nation's newfound fragility, significant given the growing importance of cinema in social life and startling in view of Britain's expectation of dominance over its colonial markets.[25] Sir Stephen Tallents, Chairman of Britain's Empire Marketing Board, a state-funded organization that promoted imperial trade in various commodities from 1926 to 1933, voiced both sentiments when he claimed, "No civilised country can to-day afford either to neglect the projection of its national personality, or to resign its projection to others. *Least of all countries* can England afford either that neglect or that resignation."[26]

On the one hand, the British film industry perceived itself to be victimized by Hollywood in the manner of its own legacy of exploitation. As Britain's *World Film News* bemoaned in 1937, "The Americans, with impressive supply of Hollywood pictures, have the necessary tank power to put native [British] exhibitors to their mercy. They are using it remorselessly. . . . *So far as films go, we are now a colonial people.*"[27] On the other hand, colonialism was more than a convenient analogy. Petitions from British film producers lobbying for a quota underscored the "value of empire markets" "to counteract the great advantage held by the American producing companies through their possession of so large and wealthy a market."[28] Even as dominions and colonies acquired a new relevance for British trade in view of rising U.S. economic and territorial power, the push of dominion nationalisms meant that they could not be claimed unilaterally. These internal wrenches formative of British cinema's regulatory and aesthetic composition can be linked to two kinds of changes: the first relates to a conflict between late imperial and emerging postcolonial (and neocolonial) global politics, the second to a shift in the *representability* of imperialism.

Whereas imperialism and nationalism have coexisted as ideologies and as material practices, they have endured inverse histories as systems of signi-

fication. The overt discussion of imperialism as a modern economic practice accompanying territorial colonization has been short-lived. Edward Said
notes that during the 1860s in England "it was often the case that the word
'imperialism' was used to refer, with some distaste, to France as a country
ruled by an emperor."[29] The word "imperialism" did not enter European jour-
nalistic and political vocabulary to describe economic and state policy until
the 1890s, although most industrialized nations shared a long history of an-
nexation and colonization by that time.[30] In his 1902 book, *Imperialism*, the
British political economist J. A. Hobson aimed "to give more precision to a
term" that was poorly defined despite being "the most powerful movement in
the current politics of the Western world."[31] But already by the 1940s, popular media as well as political rhetoric in the West had grown averse to the
word. Europe faced mounting domestic and international criticism against
colonial administrative strategies and, after the horrors of European fascism,
growing support for demonstrable democratization in the governance of all
nations and races. As the nation became a prevalent political unit in the twentieth century, providing a pivot of identification for communities with aspirations for sovereignty, imperialism hid its tracks. The visibility of one necessitated the invisibility of the other, in that empire ceased to be the manifest
rationale of international policy.[32] Somewhere in the middle of the twentieth
century, empire became embarrassing.

Social theorists ranging from Hannah Arendt and Benedict Anderson to
Gyan Prakash observe an "inner incompatibility" between the constructs of
"empire" and the liberal "nation-state," because empire's predication on expansion and domination contradicts liberalism's assumption of contractual
participation and consent.[33] The onus of conceptual or linguistic inconsistencies is a small inconvenience when imperialism and liberal nationhood co-
habit in practice, producing such distinctive political and textual attitudes as
imperial nationalism, "enlightened" colonialism, or internally contradictory
prescriptions of representative government in definitions of liberal nationalism itself.[34] So it is necessary to emphasize that beyond theoretical incom-
patibilities, historical events of the early twentieth century made the exclusionary processes and internal contradictions of liberal imperial Western
democracies visible and in need of defense.

Historian John Kent points out that after World War I the British State
faced the dilemma of needing American money to underwrite postwar recuperation while trying to avoid complete financial dependence on the United
States. British strategists hoped that the empire could resolve this crisis.[35]

The state initiated efforts to increase exports to dollar-zones by creating a demand for colonial goods in the United States. This involved modernizing imperial production through colonial development funds and empire quota schemes, and negotiating with increasingly nationalist colonies and dominions.[36] If World War I exposed the extent to which imperial Britain was vulnerable to a changing global economy and polity, World War II revealed the moral anachronism of the British Empire. With the visible cruelties of German and Italian Fascism and the invisible exploitation of American finance capitalism, Britain's brand of colonialism looked awkwardly similar to the former and just plain awkward compared to the latter. Symptomatic of Britain's changing imperial status in this new century, the British State became invested in earning the approbation of an emerging international community of nations by demonstrating its moral responsibility toward its colonies. John Grierson, the founder of Britain's documentary film movement, succinctly expressed both official preoccupations—with colonial welfare and international perception—at the 1948 "Film in Colonial Development" conference. Speaking of the need to train African filmmakers, Grierson reminded his audience that "Hitler, not of pleasant memory, once used a phrase of England's colonies, that we were allowing 'cobwebs to grow in our treasure house.' I shall not say much about that, except to emphasise that international criticism is growing on how we use and develop our work in the Colonies."[37]

The two decades spanned by this book may be best measured or periodized by the divergent legitimacies granted to imperialism and nationalism, which ensured that they had varying legibilities. This variance was expressed in the language of film regulation, in the aesthetics of film form, and in their internal heterogeneities. Factions within the state and the film industries of Britain and India mobilized the appeal of nationalism, with each faction implying that its own position would best serve the needs of its respective nation. Below the apparently unifying discourse of nationalism lay divisive investments in Britain and India's political future. British factions debated questions of colonial dependence versus colonial sovereignty and of free trade versus state protectionism, even as Indians were divided over the form and function of a secular state in India's political future.

Confronting British and Indian state regulations and film texts from this period demands an agnosticism toward their avowed nationalist appeals to discern what was in fact at stake. This requires a sensitivity toward individual film productions, film-policy proposals, and their rebuttals, to read a late-colonial cultural archive built by British and Indian individuals navigating between increasingly legitimate (modern, nationalist) and delegitimized (imperialist, feudal) discourses. Though policymakers, film directors, film producers, and film actors belonged to different kinds of institutions, all were involved in this play between individual will and institutional language. And so historical agents—parliamentarians and bureaucrats no less than film stars, directors, critics, journalists, and audiences—enter my narrative as participants who modified contexts that, in turn, structured and sanctioned their realms of self-expression.

To parody a well-known saying, I shall say that a little formalism turns one away from History, but that a lot brings one back to it.
—Roland Barthes, *Mythologies*

Communities are to be distinguished, not by their falsity/genuineness, but by the style in which they are imagined.
—Benedict Anderson, *Imagined Communities*

one ✳ FILM POLICY AND FILM AESTHETICS AS CULTURAL ARCHIVES

In the 1930s British film journals worried about Hollywood's exploitation of Britain's film market, and Indian film journals complained of the lack of affordable equipment, of exploitative middlemen, and of a need for better stories.[1] Although colonialism was not a preoccupying theme, it was the pervasive condition, as changes in imperial state politics and colonial relations defined the alternatives available to British and Indian film industries confronting obstacles to their development. Everything in British India was under renegotiation: the colony's right to sovereignty, the imperial state's entitlement to colonial resources, the jurisdiction of imperial administrators, and the future of empire. These contests were etched into commercial film-policy debates and film form in both territories. With this opening chapter I look ahead to the rest of the book, and write about how the angels of culture, history, and politics danced upon a pin's head of film-policy semantics and film style.

State Form

In 1932 the British Commission on Educational and Cultural Films, funded by grants from private trusts and local authorities, published the report *The Film in National Life*. The commission had been established at a 1929 conference of "some hundred Educational and Scientific organizations" to examine sound and silent films, and to evaluate cinema as a medium of education, art, and entertainment in Britain.[2] The report is best known for its recommendations to create a national film institute, which became the template for the British Film Institute, established in 1933. Less known is the fact that the report also contained an assessment of commercial British films in the colonies. Based on its study, *The Film in National Life* concluded that the "responsibility of Great Britain is limited to what, by the production and interchange of its films, she can do in this country. The Colonies are under varying forms of control; and their Governments cannot be expected to take constructive action without a clear and firm lead from the Home [British] Government. There the responsibility of Great Britain is double, for what is done at home and for what is done overseas."[3]

The report highlights, in condensed version, three related aspects of the British State's attitude toward commercial cinema during late empire. In the 1920s and 1930s state-funded committees in Britain, the colonies, and the dominions assessed local film production, transforming a new cultural industry into manageable, organizable data. The desire to influence colonial film industries underwrote these official collations and productions of knowledge about film, which in turn guided the rationalization and regulation of British cinema within the domestic British market. At the same time, colonial and dominion film industries reacted to Britain's regulatory initiatives with varying degrees of reservation as they asserted their boundaries of cultural sovereignty. In the first part of this book I deal with the parallel operation of such domestic and imperial negotiations, which began in 1927–28 when the British State assessed both the British film industry and the Indian film market, rendering them cognate territories for potential state intervention. Subsequent to its evaluation of Britain's industry, the state resolved that British film production was a necessary industrial sector for Britain and worthy of measured domestic protection, as provided by the Quota Act (chapter 2). At the same time, the state accepted an evaluation of Indian film as a luxury industry that was best left to its own devices (chapter 3). Here was a linked state apparatus—with the government of India answerable to the British parliament and the Crown—arriving at opposing definitions of two film industries in relation to their respective domestic markets.

A series of questions become interesting in this context. What kinds of arguments and lobby groups did British film producers utilize to acquire state assistance? Why and on what terms was the Indian film market assessed? Who conducted the investigation in India, and why did the state withdraw from active intervention there? Answers to these questions demonstrate that the state's adjudication of the British film industry as essential and of the Indian film industry as inessential altered the authorized boundaries of state power with regard to cinema in both countries. A liberal state's authority derives in part from its jurisdiction over differentiating between "public" and "private" spheres, "essential" and "tertiary" industries.[4] Liberal-state rationality or "governmentality" operates through the codification of social and cultural information to generate a legitimate agenda for state intervention or restraint in relation to its populace and their governing institutions. This Foucauldian conceptualization of the state as a collective of practices operationalized through multiple points of attempted and actual regulations frames government and society in mutually constitutive terms.[5] However, for Foucault the correlative of the state's suasive power is the free (rather than the colonial) subject. Foucault's theory of the liberal state necessarily brushes up against the West's simultaneous application of nonconsensual state power in the colonies to convey the contradictory operations of Western political modernity.

The British State, constitutionally liberal at home but not in its colonies, was an agent of modernization in both domains through the twinned enactment of liberal and imperial policies. Scholarship on the colonial state in anthropology, ethnography, literary studies, and history has long offered evidence of such circuitous historical mappings by studying "the metropole and the colony as a unitary field of analysis."[6] The virtue of this analysis is that, by shifting attention to the role played by colonies in the definition of a modern British state, it moves beyond orientalist ideas of Britain as the "unconscious tool of history" that brought colonies into modernity and a capitalist trajectory.[7] The field of cinema studies has remained largely untouched by this work, owing perhaps to the specialized nature of our discipline.[8] To begin with an analysis of the British State in film history alone, considering the metropole and the colony in conjunction demands several necessary revisions to existing accounts.

First, it points to the need to re-evaluate (direct and indirect) intertwinings of British and colonial film industries in relation to a state that defined its role through presiding over *both*. Second, an analysis informed by the consonant functions of the state in relation to Britain and its colonies remedies a critical asymmetry. Scholarly discussions have been forthcoming about the impact of decolonization on postcolonial nations but reticent with regard to its significance for the industries and identities of colonizing nation-states. In film studies this has produced a curious lack of dialogue between work on postcolonial national cinemas and European national cinemas, though both have been prolific and productive areas of investigation in themselves. The bulk of available scholarship on Indian cinema focuses on the period following India's independence in 1947, examining the relationship between cinema and national identity or the Indian nation-state. This concentration of work conveys, by its definitional emphasis, the importance of decolonization to the development of a film industry in India. (Unwittingly it also reproduces the "postcolonial misery" of Partha Chatterjee's description, because the study of the region's cinema remains tethered to the end of colonialism as its primary temporal reference point.)[9] Meanwhile, the significance or insignificance of colonial and dominion markets remains largely uninterrogated by studies that emphasize the centrality of U.S., European, and domestic markets to the industrial strategies of a nation like Britain.[10]

Studying British cinema in the late 1920s and 1930s demands an acknowledgment of multiple alterities to engage Britain's extensive territorial reach during its increasing vulnerability to Hollywood. British film policies were defined by a complex set of maneuvers as the imperial nation-state adapted to an environment of colonial/dominion sovereignty, U.S. domination, and domestic factionalization. Similarly, films produced in India responded to Hollywood's cultural and Britain's political supremacy by drawing on variegated commercial, linguistic, and visual influences. By the 1930s, the colony was a center for film production and ancillary film-related businesses. So the third aspect that emerges from a dual assessment of Britain and India is the need to broaden definitions of colonial resistance, looking beyond colonial responses to British and Hollywood films to consider as well what the colony produced under political constraints. The analysis of Britain and India in tandem leads to an account of the colonial state's evaluations of the Indian film industry and simultaneously highlights the Indian film industry's stance toward the state, including the industry's development in the absence of assistance from its government.

As is well documented by scholarship on colonial cinema, the British State assessed India as a site for censorship.[11] Britain also evaluated India as a center for film production and a potential market for British films, which has received scant attention from film scholars. Surprisingly, British evaluations of India were frequently at cross-purposes. Were Indians impressionable natives to be monitored and exposed to edifying images of the West? Were their locally produced films worthy of attention? Were they an untapped market resource to be enticed for Britain's profit? An eloquent expression of this bafflement can be found in *The Film in National Life*, which conveys a firm opinion of cinema's role in an Africa strangely divested of Africans ("In Africa, [film] can aid the missionary, the trader, and the administrator" [137]) but is disjointed when talking about India: "Great Britain owes a duty to the Dominions; the Dominions to Great Britain and to each other; and India owes a duty first to herself. . . . The film can as well display the ancient dignity of the *Mahabharata* as teach the Indian peasant the elements of hygiene and sanitation" (137).

References to educational films mentioned awkwardly alongside productions based on the *Mahabharata*, a Hindu epic that served as a popular source for colonial Indian films, suggest confusion over the role of cinema in a colony with its own popular film production. "India has at once an ancient culture and an illiterate peasantry," notes the report, continuing that the nation is "midway between the two points. She is producing films which are as yet far from good, but which might become works of beauty, while many of her peasantry are as simple and illiterate as African tribes" (126). The "midway" status of India reflected, in some senses, the political liminality of India's position in relation to Britain. Dyarchy had been established in India in 1919, which meant that at the level of the provincial government, power was shared between British agencies and largely elective legislative councils. By the 1920s and 1930s, while India was not quite a colony (the executive body was accountable to the legislature, and the latter had some Indian representation), it was not a dominion either (the most important subjects were reserved for British officials; Indian representation was primarily ceded at the local and provincial rather than the central government, on a controversially communal basis; and the British parliament retained the power to legislate for India). So most British state documents refer to the territory as "the Dominions and India" or "India and the Colonies."[12]

India's own film production and its film industry's discourse from this period offer refreshing alternatives to such mystifications. The record of colonial Indian cinema, though patchy, does not merely replicate imperialist

frameworks of knowledge. To this end, the Indian Cinematograph Committee (ICC) interviews conducted by state representatives in conversation with
members of the Indian film industry between 1927 and 1928 make a thrilling document. In lively debate with the state committee on the possibility
of granting special preferences for British films in India, vocal Indian film
producers, actors, distributors, and exhibitors disabled the premises of the
state questionnaire by revealing contradictions in the committee's position.
To hear their side of the story, a discussion of Britain and India requires a turn
toward Indian films, film journals, newspapers, and state-instituted committees, and an examination of Indian cinema on its own terms (chapters 3
and 7).

The idea of autonomy in cinema or culture is a complex one.[13] My claim
is that nascent institutional forms of the Indian film industry and evolving
forms of Indian cinema laid claim to economic and aesthetic autonomy from
the state in what were perhaps the most effective ways of resisting the British
government, competing with Hollywood film imports, and defining a national imagination. Prem Chowdhry discusses the ways in which defiance of
British authority was evident in India's hostile reception of select British and
U.S. films. Without denying the significance of such mobilization, it must
be acknowledged that Indian cinema's emerging independence at the level
of commerce and film content rendered British cinema incontrovertibly in-
effectual in the colony.

Of necessity, aspirants of the Indian film industry relied on their own financial resources.[14] Indian film trade organizations emphasized the need
for the Indian industry to sustain itself without state support. Speaking at
the first Indian Motion Picture Congress (IMPC) in 1939, Chandulal J. Shah,
owner of India's Ranjit Studios noted: "It is a tragedy that we the national and
nationalist producers are not given any facilities in our country by our own
Government and States whereas the British, American, and even German
Producers have often been welcomed to make use of everything India possesses. We must end this intolerable situation by our united effort."[15] Baburao Patel, the inimitable editor of *filmindia*, a leading Bombay film magazine,
expressed similar sentiments in a characteristically provocative exchange
with F. J. Collins, publisher of the rival journal *Motion Picture Magazine*, whom
Patel accused of being "a supporter of foreign interests."[16] "The Indian film
industry never asked for a Quota Act as the Britishers did against the Americans. People in our industry never worried about the foreign competition
however intense it has been. We have always welcomed healthy competition

but we strongly object to the ungrateful and dirty insinuations which the hire-lings of these foreign interests have chosen to make against our industry and its men . . . (by) calling the Motion Picture Society of India 'a self-constituted organization with no credentials.' "[17]

Despite Patel's affronted objection, the colonial Indian film industry and its institutions could well have been described as a "self-constituted organization" struggling for credentials. In 1921 the censors endorsed 812 films, of which only 64 were of Indian origin. Over 90 percent of the imported films were from the United States. (According to Indian silent- and early-sound-film director Naval Gandhi, Universal Studios had the largest share in 1927).[18] By 1935 Hollywood and other film imports led by a narrower margin, consti-tuting a little over half of the total feature films screened in India.[19] The 1930s also witnessed the collapse of Madan Theatres, a major importer of U.S. films, and the success of Indian studios, particularly Bombay Talkies and Ranjit Movietone in Bombay, New Theaters in Calcutta, Prabhat in Pune, and United Artists Corporation in Madras.[20] Though the studios had mostly disinte-grated by the mid-1940s and dominant genres of colonial Indian cinema (in-cluding mythological, historical, devotional, and stunt films) had lost their immediate popularity, Indian films had secured a stable domestic status by 1947.[21] Historians Eric Barnouw and S. Krishnaswamy attribute this to the in-vention of sound, arguing that the Indian filmmaker "now had markets which foreign competitors would find difficult to penetrate. The protection which the Government of India had declined to give him though a quota system had now been conferred by the coming of the spoken word."[22]

To place their observation in a broader context: Indian silent cinema evolved a distinctive visual and performative idiom that was redefined and consolidated with sound and the emergence of film-related businesses (such as film journalism and song-books that bolstered the indigenous star system) to cultivate a strong domestic market for the local product by the 1930s. This was a decade of innovation and experimentation as filmmakers explored local content, learned from European and U.S. film-production techniques, and used their films to implicitly oppose the colonial government. They sought ways to simultaneously combat imports and survive with a foreign power at the nation's helm. Thus the autonomy that Indian films sought to claim from the state was not absent of a cultural interface with multiple contexts but in fact dependent on it.[23]

Tracing links between a film and its multiple formative factors reveals something of a truism: no colonial Indian film is reducible to its nationalist rhetoric, any more than a British empire film is to its imperialist discourse. An explicitly anticolonial film like *Thyagabhoomi* (Tamil, K. Subrahmanyam, 1939) may be interpreted through alternative determining matrices such as its original author "Kalki" R. Krishnamurthy's popularity as a Tamil literary figure or its actor Baby Saroja's rising stardom, both of which contributed to the film's success in South India. Seeking the various avenues of familiarity between an Indian or a British film and its domestic audience allows us to construct a context for a film's popularization of nationalist or imperial thematics. In India, for instance, such disparate examples as Zubeida's success in *Gul-e-Bakavali* (silent, Rathod, 1924) and Nurjehan's popular rendition of Naushad's song "Jawaan hai Mohabbat" in *Anmol Ghadi* (Hindi, Mehboob, 1946) fall into a continuum of a new taste-culture manufactured by a film industry that had a more-or-less improvised logic to its organization. Indian cinema fell into an order of pleasure and financial structure that drew both organically and tactically on its cultural distinctiveness. This made Indian protests against British films more a matter of anticolonial political strategy than of necessity. It also made Indian cinema's relative stylistic and institutional independence a crucial aspect of the colonial phase.

The development of the Indian film industry despite the absence of state assistance—almost outside the comprehension and purview of the imperial state—foreshadowed its postcolonial future. The Indian government constituted in 1947 brought no radical change in policy toward India's film industry, since assessments of cinema as a luxury item did not alter with independence. On the contrary, India's new government added state taxes, *octroi* taxes (for film transportation), mandatory screenings of the government's Films Division presentations (sold at a stipulated price to commercial exhibitors), and heavy, centralized censorship.[24] (Not until May 1998 did the Indian government grant formal industrial status to Indian film and television companies.) None of this is to scandalously suggest that the national government was no different from the colonial one. Certainly, at the level of content, the creation of an Indian nation-state placed different imperatives upon popular Indian films, since representing the nation on celluloid was no longer an allusive, embattled process. Yet for India's commercial film industry, the period from 1927 to 1947 intimated future governmental attitudes toward popular Indian films and underscored the commercial industry's need to flourish despite, rather than with, state assistance.[25]

Colonial India was not alone in its film productivity or in its maneuvers to deflect state interest and inquiry. Britain's attempts to initiate an imperial collaboration against Hollywood films were disrupted by other film industries in the empire, which either entered into lucrative arrangements with the United States to assist domestic production (as did Canada) or initiated their own protectionist policies (as did New South Wales). Prior to submitting its report on the Indian film industry to the British government, the ICC examined the film-industry structures of Canada, Australia, New Zealand, and the United Kingdom in detail, and read the 1927 report of the Royal Commission on the Moving Picture Industry in Australia, a body equivalent to the ICC, which investigated the possibility of a "quota" in Australia.[26] Such circuits of communication among state representatives within the empire point to a type of state activity not covered by scholarly work on colonial cinema, which focuses primarily on the repressive imperial state apparatus.

Scholarship on British and Indian cinema in relation to colonial politics can be placed in three general categories: studies that analyze hegemonic versus resistant film reception (covering the jingoistic acceptance of empire films as well as colonial protests against British films, Hollywood films, and colonial censorship); studies that analyze hegemonic and resistant film content (particularly cinematic manifestations of orientalism, racism, and Eurocentrism versus those of hybridity and diaspora); and studies that analyze hegemonic and resistant film production (including educational, documentary, trade, and propaganda films, such as those made by the British Empire Marketing Board; commercial British films about empire from the 1930s; the post-1985 Black British Film Collective; and contemporary politicizations of Britain's minorities).[27] While such oppositions of empire were certainly crucial to popular and official definitions of visual modernity in the metropolis and its colony, just as crucial was the contentiously *shared* space of imperium. Decolonization was a defining matrix for the conduct of state policy in both Britain and India. In internally divided ways, both film industries were caught in dialogic—collaborative and antagonistic—relations with their state. Simultaneous analysis of these industries allows a host of insights: into the subtle ways in which the loss of colonial markets influenced British film regulations; into empire as a material reality for British film producers rather than an exclusively ideological construct in films; into the colonial filmmakers' claims to autonomy and their critique of imperial bureaucracy that, in turn, influenced British film policy.

Demands for equivalent treatment from colonial and dominion film industries produced distinct shifts in the language of imperial policy, with the British State's claim to equivalence, distributive justice, and reciprocity in film policy becoming a necessary device of (self) redemption and (colonial) placation. Shifts in British film-policy semantics, while deceptively small, in fact form a lead to the state's emendation of official definitions of British film in consonance with cultural and political changes within the empire.

Aesthetic Form

Commitment to the arts and political fervor were closely allied in India, and Indian-film historians provide a valuable record of anticolonial campaigns in film journals, film songs that supported Indian independence, nationalist picketing against imported films, and protests against censorship.[28] In addition to being reactive, the realms of culture and politics were mutually constitutive. Colonialism was an important limiting and enabling context for the emergence of Indian cinema's thematic concerns and aesthetic modes. Indian films of the 1930s transformed censorship against the depiction of British colonialism into an erasure of colonial history (in mythic narratives) and a displacement of India's present onto a precolonial past (in historical tales).[29] British commercial films, as well as Indian productions, variously reinvented their colonial legacy to envision an impending future of radically altered state power, offering an intriguing comparative axis to measure British and Indian film aesthetics in relation to each other.

Contradictory assessments of Britain's colonial past were under way in literature, with popular British fiction on empire defending attitudes parodied within canonized texts of the 1930s. Best-selling English novels by Edgar Wallace, A. E. W. Mason, Rumer Godden, Rider Haggard, and Rudyard Kipling were adapted for the screen, while the more ambivalent, modernist, critically acclaimed counternarratives of empire—including works by Joseph Conrad, E. M. Forster, Somerset Maugham, George Orwell, Graham Greene, Joyce Cary, and Evelyn Waugh—were mostly overlooked by filmmakers and screenwriters.[30] Given that, according to the 1927 Quota Act, a film based on any original work by a British subject was eligible for quota privileges within Britain, the overwhelming preference for filming pulp and popular fiction about triumphal imperial adventures and the discrepancy between popular and serious literature on empire raise significant questions.

Robust imperial adventures were attractive to filmmakers because they were familiar stories, nationalist in character, spectacularly global in setting, and promised to "lead the exhibitor on to better business—better because bigger, and better because Imperial."[31] The film historians Jeffrey Richards and Marcia Landy argue that because commercial British imperial films were so popular in the United Kingdom and the United States, they cannot be dismissed as having been favored solely by a conservative British minority.[32] To pursue their assessment further, empire cinema's apparently pro-imperial ideology and its relationship with potentially anti-imperial literary and political concerns of the period can be engaged by posing the "revulsion" toward empire as a foil against which to assess imperial films.[33] Despite notions to the contrary, empire films were not monolithically ideological; while a certain skepticism and ironic distance may have already entrenched itself between Britain's imperial past and its present in serious literature, such positions were demonstrably in process in cinema.[34]

The forms of empire film texts, much like the negotiations of British film policy, were structurally constituted by the dilemmas of decolonization. Britain's decline in global power had created a series of disturbances: in the position of British industry with regard to imperial and global markets, in Britain's status relative to an international community of nations, and in the internal structures of local British industries. Popular empire cinema in particular was a product of the uneven development of Britain's film production, distribution, and exhibition sectors, and of its film production's subjugation to Hollywood. Put simply, Hollywood's dominance over Britain in combination with the British State's emphasis on the empire as a reinvigorating and exclusive national resource yielded the commercial film industry's investment in imperial spectaculars.

The form and content of commercial British cinema—like film policy negotiations, state-sponsored trade films, and documentaries within their specific institutional contexts—exemplified historical upheavals of an empire redrawing its political and industrial boundaries, and restructuring its capitalist base.[35] The crises of imperial breakdown, market realignment, and political revalidation strongly influenced commercial *and* noncommercial films about empire. The Empire Marketing Board (EMB), created in 1926 to revive imperial trade in all products, and the Quota Act of 1927, formed to resuscitate British film production, were both popularly understood to offer a "lead" to the commercial film industry regarding the exploitability of imperial markets and themes "for reasons of the pay-box and patriotism."[36] Though EMB films were state-commissioned, connections between EMB and commercial films were more complex than a binary division between state sponsorship and market dependence might suggest. Martin Stollery points out that with the exception of John Grierson, the EMB's creative personnel

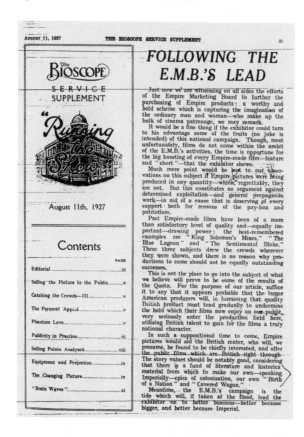

1. It was hoped that the Quota Act, like the EMB, would boost empire trade. Courtesy BFI National Library.

were "temporary, non-unionized workers nominally employed by small commercial firms contracted by the EMB and GPO for specific purposes."[37] In other words, there was a wide overlap of personnel and perspective between official and commercial productions, and the presence of (or critique of) statist ideology cannot be measured solely by tracing a film's sponsorship and source of funding.

Commercial films about empire were a competitive product serving multiple needs. Consider Alexander Korda's productions like *Sanders of the River* (1935), *Elephant Boy* (1937), *The Drum* (1938), *The Thief of Baghdad* (1940), and *The Four Feathers* (1939), which were high-quality productions that succeeded at U.K. and U.S. box offices while also qualifying for national quota privileges.[38] Their success benefited the British film producer, renter, and exhibitor, while simultaneously visualizing the redemptive ideals behind empire building. Discussing the EMB's promotion of imperial trade, England's newspaper *The Times* noted in 1934 that words like *empire* "had become tainted by unfortunate associations" until the EMB's advertising and documentary films "*re-deemed*" empire "*by art.*"[39] British film producers pushing for government support had frequently argued that commercial films could do more for Britain's imperial standing than state propaganda, because "pictures, in order to attain their object, must not be purely propaganda pictures: they must be of such a kind as to take their place naturally, and by the ordinary commercial method, on the screens of the world and this by reason of their entertainment and dramatic value."[40] Commercial filmmakers seeking a regulatory fillip clearly found it advantageous to align their arguments with the state's interest in reviving Britain's global image. Jeffrey Richards traces intriguing links between Joseph Ball of the National Publicity Bureau under Neville Chamberlain's government in 1934 and the filmmakers Alexander Korda, Michael Balcon, and Isidore Ostrer, to suggest that Ball encouraged the commercial producers to invest in salable imperial epics.[41] In addition to fielding direct state pressure, commercial filmmakers had to contend with the effects of a far-reaching official agenda to rehabilitate Britain for a new political environment. By rearticulating Britain's identity as demonstrably liberal in relation to its imperium, commercial British films participated in the visual and cultural politics of late empire.[42]

The relationship of culture to its context exists at the ingrained level of form. As Edward Said suggested, one cannot lift an argument from a work of fiction "like a message out of a bottle"; it is inscribed in the architecture of the text's narrative and images.[43] In the British empire films I explore in chapters 4 through 6, the redemptive thematics of late imperialism were enabled by at least three aesthetic forms or imaginative modes, which I characterize as the realist, romance, and modernist modes of imperial cinema. The "imaginative mode," which I adapt from Peter Brooks's work on melodrama, refers to a more-or-less internally coherent representational system that facilitated certain accounts of the imperial encounter to retrospectively justify political, social, and racial domination.[44]

Hierarchies between the imperializer and the imperialized are naturalized and reified by the realist mode of commercial empire cinema in films such as *Sanders of the River, Rhodes of Africa* (Viertel, 1936), and, with some variation, *Elephant Boy*.[45] The conflicts of interest between colonizing and colonized nation are acknowledged to a greater degree in the romance mode but are displaced onto symbolic, near-mythic narratives. This can be seen in *The Drum, The Four Feathers, King Solomon's Mines* (Stevenson, 1937), and, somewhat anomalously, *The Great Barrier* (Barkas and Rosmer, 1937). The modernist mode of imperial cinema, though present in the 1940s, appears more frequently after the large-scale decolonizations of the 1950s and 1960s, as with films like *Black Narcissus* (Powell and Pressburger, 1947), *Heat and Dust* (Ivory, 1983), *A Passage to India* (Lean, 1984), and the television series *The Jewel in the Crown* (Morahan and O'Brien, 1984), as well as films made outside Britain like *Bhowani Junction* (Cukor, 1956) and *The Rains Came* (Brown, 1939), remade as *The Rains of Ranchipur* (Negulesco, 1955). Imperial modernism gives primacy to the crisis of empire under dissolution, but it salvages the breakdown through a sympathetic enactment of Western trauma and by the unifying force of its aesthetic style.[46] Imperial modernist and, to a lesser extent, romance texts are artistically tormented by their colonial assumptions, whereas a realist imperial text barely acknowledges them. If ideological contradictions between the imperial defense of coercion and liberal celebrations of equality are suppressed in the realist mode and symbolically reconciled within romance, they are interrogated in modernist modes of imperialism.

Despite stylistic differences, all three modes are manifestations of an imperial rhetoric adapting to a more populist, democratic politics. In a circular way, the domestic expansion of Britain's political franchise had been aided by empire: recalling Hannah Arendt, imperialism politically emancipated and organized the bourgeois classes of Britain by drawing them into state politics to protect their economic interests in the colonies.[47] The evolution of modern state power paralleled the state's management of an ever-broadening mass of citizens and consumers. To offer only a few indexical instances from the late nineteenth century and the early twentieth: British reform bills in 1867 and 1884 increased suffrage, changing the nature of the British Commons; in 1851 visitors of all classes were invited to Britain's Great Exhibition, and in 1857 the South Kensington Museum opened its doors to the general public, including the working classes;[48] by the early 1900s, demands for better standards of living and equal opportunities dominated the nation's political agenda; and the acts of 1918 and 1928 extended women's franchise. The historical emergence of the masses created modern public (and concomitant private, domestic) spaces through the convergence of an expanding civil society and new technologies of vision, leisure, and consumption, which changed the realms of operation, the preoccupations, and consequently the nature of state disciplinary power. For the British State of the twentieth century, a specter of unpoliced masses and spaces merged the "nightmares of empire" with "the fears of democracy."[49]

The twentieth century marked the emergence of a neocolonial morality among old imperial states, abetted by international organizations such as the World Bank and the International Monetary Fund, which were formed as a consequence of the world wars and which allowed for novel modes of control over decolonizing nations by hiding the interests of Western (U.S. and West European) states within measures such as loans, debt structures, and international standards for product quality. All subsequent discourses of power have owed a formative debt to an international morality articulated during the early twentieth century that required relations between (and within) nations to be framed as developmental and consensual rather than exploitative and unilateral.[50] The aesthetics of late empire connote a poetics of imperial self-presentation dispersed over the fields of media, culture, and political rhetoric, shaping notions of power and identity *during and after* the end of formal colonialism. The modes of realism, romance, and modernism represent three recurrent styles of imperial self-representation in a decolonized, democratized world.

U.S. President George W. Bush's arguments for war against Iraq in 2003 recreated a naturalized, realist understanding of U.S. global rights, inflected with the romance of his nation's (or its neoconservative administration's) mission in the world. British Prime Minister Tony Blair's speech to the United States Congress in the same year portrayed the romantic hero's anguish over an imperial commission: "Britain knows, all predominant power seems for a time invincible, but in fact, it is transient. The question is, what do you leave behind? And what you *can* bequeath to this anxious world is the light of liberty."[51] American post-Vietnam films such as *The Deer Hunter* (Cimino, 1978), *Apocalypse Now* (Coppola, 1979), *Born on the Fourth of July* (Stone, 1989), *Platoon* (Stone, 1986), and *Full Metal Jacket* (Kubrik, 1987); Britain's postwar horror films like *The Quatermass Xperiment* (Guest, 1955); Australian "landscape" films like *Walkabout* (Roeg, 1971) and *Picnic at Hanging Rock* (Weir, 1975); and debates on racial reparation, all reprised a modernist crisis by interrogating imperial culpability.

Distinguishing a (realist) textual formation that maintains a fiction of ideological unity from (modernist) ones that explore empire's internal inconsistencies throws my reading out of step with influential poststructuralist analyses of colonial discourse, which are invested in the systemic instability of *all* formal (textual) and formational (epistemic) structures.[52] The fear of "historylessness: a 'culture' of theory that makes it impossible to give meaning to historical specificity" compels me to distinguish a theorist's deconstructive strategy—through which she finds points from which knowledge unravels to expose its foundations (or lack thereof) — from a text's propensity toward such unravelings.[53] Through a tripartite systematization of imperial film style, I undertake a cultural and historically immanent reading of form, rather than a formalist reading of culture. I aim to comprehend varied justifications that a nonegalitarian system articulated astride a break between preexisting colonial and nascent neocolonial power-relations. The analysis of form, in this instance, allows history to seep in by reviving the heterogeneity of imperial responses to decolonization.[54]

To comprehend the detailed workings of each mode, I pursue close readings of three British imperial films — one realist, one romance, one modernist — showing that each is an "omnibus" text, borrowing from multiple film genres even while constructing imperial relations through one primary aesthetic lens.[55] *Sanders of the River* utilizes classical realism as well as the naturalist-realist perspective of colonial and ethnographic cinema, but it deviates from the rules of realism to draw on the "attractions" of a Hollywood western, a musical, and a safari (chapter 4). *The Drum*, like *The Four Feathers*, is an adventure film that uses tropes from melodramas and westerns, though a play with stylistic excesses brings its romantic vision close to the aesthetic of modernism (chapter 5). *Black Narcissus* combines the fantasy genre with melodrama to operate predominantly within the modernist mode, but it may also be read as a corrupted romance narrative (chapter 6). Realist, romance, or modernist modes of imperial representation are "parceled out" among a variety of genres, each carrying a "genre memory" that performs specific political functions for its dominant aesthetic.[56]

The pre-eminence of the western, the documentary, the melodrama, and fantasy (or horror: fantasy's evil twin) in British empire cinema points to overlapping sympathies in their generic defenses of imperialism. A brief detour through Peter Brooks's statement on melodrama's fascination with the social subconscious helps explain the continuum between these genres, when each genre is understood for its labored redress of empire as a democratic form. Brooks notes, "At least from the moment that Diderot praised Richardson for carrying the torch into the cavern, there to discover 'the hideous Moor' within us, it has been evident that the uncovering and exploitation of the latent content of mind would bring melodramatic enactment."[57] In describing modernism's desire to reveal the unconscious, Brooks conveys little self-awareness about the features attributed to mind's internal darkness. The mind, the melodrama, and the "us" are complicitly white, European, and Christian when Brooks imagines a cavern-bound Moor as a figment of alterity. To paraphrase Brooks, at least from the moment that the "Moor within" became a product of fantasy and source of fear in Western literary texts and critical commentary, it has been evident that Anglo-European exploitations of melodramatic content would be premised on assumptions about their racial, religious, or national others.

Unlike the modernist melodrama described by Brooks, genres operating under the dictates of imperial realism manage variously to split the forces of Self-Other, colonizer-colonized, Christian-Moor, and in so doing control difference. Within realism, violent domination is the only way to democratize the colonized world, which is viewed through Manichean, bipolar divisions. When the generic structures of a documentary, a western, or an adventure tale operate within the realist modes of empire, they reify oppositional principles. When they function as imperial romances, on the other hand, they manage dualities within the more ambiguous realms of myths and symbols. In distinction to both realism and romance, modernist imperial fiction—the most melodramatic of the three modes—holds up a terrifying mirror to Europe, and the hideousness that was safer when attributed to a figure of alterity turns horrific when recognized within. Orientalism and racism lie in the deep structure of empire's modern melodramas, generating its internal, quiet moments of terror. The modernist optic on empire brings the colonizers and their mental landscape into harsh perspective, drawing attention to their fragmented and fallible subjectivities through style. This display of crisis betrays only the most elusive link to imperial politics, as the chaos of doubt replaces the rational boundaries of realist certitude.

As with most textual depictions of weakness, modernism's exhibition of imperial vulnerability is gendered, and women frequently bear the burden of representing (and absolving) an imperial nation's frailties. While male-centered western and adventure genres typically follow realist and romance structures, modernist imperial texts manifest themselves in female-centric melodramas, as in Black Narcissus and Bhowani Junction. Heterosexual white men in mixed-race homosocial frontiers depict realist visions of vigorous imperial triumph, while modernist imaginings of empire are narrated through white female protagonists undergoing physical or psychic tests in colonies before arriving at deeper, spiritual truths. Effeminized men of color are equally pliant substitutes in modernist narratives, as in the actor Sabu's American Indian character, Manoel, in The End of the River (Twist, 1947), or Robert Adams's African character, Kisenga, in Men of Two Worlds (Dickinson, 1946). Romantic pursuits of imperial missions are suspended somewhere in the middle, with both male and female protagonists undergoing measured self-exploration before providing salvation to the colony and to themselves.

Assessments of form offer crucial resistance to the banality of ideology-spotting and to the limitations of auteur-driven film criticism by being mindful of the pressures applied to social beliefs not only by directorial but also by the commercial, industrial, and aesthetic compulsions of cinema, while grasping cinema's role in the production of ideology. The categories of imperial realism, romance, and modernism allow an exploration of the filmic medium's specificity, because each mode draws on the cinematic apparatus's reconstitution of time, space, vision, and spectatorship in presenting a specific account of empire. Cinematic stances can be related to neo-imperial (British) or protonational (Indian) cultural vocabularies when a film's aesthetic is understood to mean a film's attitude toward a referent, readable through camera angles, mise-en-scène, color, editing, sound, or narrative structure. British empire films typically depict British protagonists working in and withdrawing from colonies, so the primary referents of such narratives are male or female imperial and colonial bodies facilitating imperial labor in a colonial place. Each aesthetic mode reconstitutes this constellation of referents—of gendered bodies, racialized labor, and politicized location—through representational devices such as narrative, image, and sound to produce a particular kind of knowledge about Britain at the end of empire. The three modes may be read, therefore, as epistemic reconstitutions of imperialism (productive of neo-imperial views) through cinema.

In commercially popular empire cinema, locations in India and Africa typically signify "empire."[58] Consequently, despite my book's overall emphasis on Britain in relation to India, I include an analysis of *Sanders of the River*, a popular British film set in the territory that is present day Nigeria. This inclusion is instructive to my interpretive framework: in the course of my research, I found that the realist mode of Britain's commercial films from the 1930s was reserved almost exclusively for Africa. Since realism is the mode most dependent on the suppression and reification of colonial hierarchies, the fact that it was repeatedly employed with reference to Africa rather than India carries historical significance. Excluding British commercial representations of Africa would be inexcusable in formulating an aesthetic framework for evaluating late British imperial cinema, because stylistic variations imposed on colonial place corresponded closely to political shifts within the imperium. Africa was subjected to a more stringent visual regime of containment at a time when India was close to independence and considered a bad precedent for Britain's African colonies. In British discussions of African cinema after 1947, India became an unnamable bad ambition with a potential to set off inexpedient aspirations toward nationhood in African colonies. Colin Beale, secretary of the Edinburgh House Bureau for Visual Aids, noted in 1948, "In the re-shaping of the world today the trend of recent events in the Empire is bound to set up aspirations and ambitions which may conflict with plans for African's [sic] ultimate good. How can the film be used to teach the African the need for those qualities of judgment and perseverance—to name two required—with which he can win the best for his people."[59] Though India, Africa, and in some cases the dominions (like Canada in The Great Barrier) functioned as imaginary territories for the production of neo-imperial discourses, there are internal differences in imperial attitudes toward the represented place. My analysis of Sanders highlights that film style is notable not only for how it visualizes imperialism but also for who it utilizes in its representation.[60]

British films with imperial themes increased in the 1930s. In India, however, British empire films were received unfavorably or were subject to severe excisions and withdrawn from exhibition for fear that they would provoke political unrest in a subcontinent that was in the grip of a nationalist movement. At the same time, repressive censorship did not permit the development of an identifiable genre of anticolonial Indian films. Seeking directly oppositional anticolonial Indian films as a contestatory discourse to Britain's empire cinema is a misguided endeavor, because in the face of political prohibitions against overtly antistate representations, Indian cinema's commentary on imperialism was frequently implicit. It was also dispersed across various units of film discourse such as film songs, film dialogues, and film sets.[61] More significant, as Aijaz Ahmad observes in relation to Urdu novels written between 1935 and 1947, subcontinental fiction conducted its nationalist anticolonialism "in the perspective of an even more comprehensive, multi-faceted critique of ourselves: our class structures, our familial ideologies, our management of bodies and sexualities, our idealisms, our silences."[62] In effect, unlike British fiction, subcontinental fiction was not interested in the "civilizational encounter" between Britain and India; it explored the historical moment as a confrontation with internal solidarities, privations, and alienations. "Anti-imperialism" is a weak analytic category through which to scrutinize colonial cinema, given its ineptness in conceptualizing this dynamic.

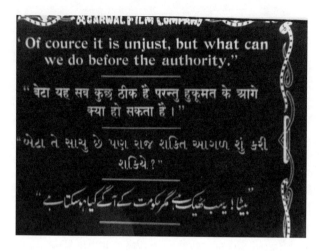

2. Anti-imperial sentiment was embedded in several aspects of cinema, as in these intertitles of *Ghulami nu Patan*. Courtesy NFAI.

Films like *Diler Jigar/Gallant Hearts* (silent, Pawar, 1931), *Ghulami nu Patan* (silent, Agarwal, 1931), *Amritmanthan* (Marathi/Hindi, Shantaram, 1934), *Amar Jyoti* (Hindi, Shantaram, 1936), *Pukar* (Urdu, Modi, 1939), *Sikandar* (Urdu, Modi, 1941) and *Manoos/Admi* (Marathi/Hindi, Shantaram, 1939) bear investigation not because they are correspondingly paradigmatic of anti-imperialism, but because they contain a configuration of trends identifiable in pre-independence Indian films (Chapter 7). If British empire films reimagined an imperial nation as a liberal democracy, smoothing out contradictions, Indian cinema defined a civil society in the absence of a sovereign nation-state. In direct contrast to British empire cinema's fantasy of retreat, Indian films invented an identity by the visual reclamation of a homeland. Symbolically transforming the colonial place into a national territory, Indian cinema produced *parallel* aesthetics of realism and modernism. The discussion of realism, romance, or modernism in Indian cinema from the colonial period serves as a pendant to the preceding analysis of British cinema's imperial modes, by revealing the particularity or contextually bounded nature of aesthetic terms, as each mode exemplifies Britain and India's varying responses to decolonization.

As with British empire films, Indian colonial cinema reveals the deeply gendered nature of a nation's imaginary. Where the colonial male is one of the disruptive and controlled subjects of British empire cinema, the colonial female is Indian cinema's subordinated subject, variously and unevenly managed or reworked in each film's representation of a new civil society. Femininity, deployed as a sign of national vulnerability in imperial texts, contrarily appears as a symbol of nationalist assertion in the colony. Cultural historians of India argue that traditionalism and reform occupied dialectically antagonistic positions in the production of nationalism in colonial India. A primary nexus for the contest between tradition and modernity was the female body, which served as ammunition for the neotraditionalists (who prescribed female behavior through reinterpreted scriptural doctrines to assert national identity) as well as the reformists (whose programs of female emancipation fit Western norms of liberated femininity and frequently served as justification for imperial dominance over a regressive society).[63]

In her analysis of late-colonial Hindi-language publications that were a key resource for neo-Hindu nationalists in prescribing normative social behavior and sexual propriety, Charu Gupta observes that "women emerged as a powerful means of brahmanical patriarchal attempts to hold power, consolidate social hierarchies and express caste exclusivities."[64] At the same time, she notes a rise in Hindi-language women's journals (Grihalakshmi, Stri Darpan, Prabha, Chand) that supported women's involvement in public activities, emerging alongside an increased awareness of women's rights and "new ideals of companionate and monogamous marriages."[65] Under nationalism, in this instance, two kinds of social reinvention incited each other: one wrought by communal, caste, and class norms of female behavior that used women to consolidate ideas of national identity and cultural purity; the other initiated by a politicization of women as the nation's modern citizenry.

Existing scholarship focuses on the conflict between colonial India's communal revivalism and modern reformism as well as their consonance in creating a new patriarchy under India's seemingly secular nationalism, wherein tradition and modernity were made consistent with the nationalist project through the (rhetorical, social, political, communal) subjugation of Indian women. To quote Partha Chatterjee's well-known argument, "The new patriarchy advocated by nationalism conferred upon women the honor of a new social responsibility, and by associating the task of female emancipation with the historical goal of sovereign nationhood, bound them to a new, yet entirely legitimate, subordination."[66] Arguably, however, Chatterjee's suggestion that colonial nationalism selectively adapted modernity while carving out a space for cultural sovereignty on the bodies of women overdetermines women's function in recuperating a patriarchal ideology, rather than thinking of them as stress points for an unstable compound.[67] Decolonization demanded an all-inclusive definition of political franchise, and even in their most nominal form such incorporations incited anxiety within India's new nationalist discourse, bringing the contradictions of modern Indian politics to the fore.

Films from the colonial era disturb rather than reassure prevailing (old or new) patriarchies, by presenting wide-ranging configurations of the female in relation to the new nation's familial, communal, and psychic life. Colonial films rarely appear seamless in their production of a new nationalism, neotraditionalism, or patriarchy, as they write different scripts for women as social subjects. In *Amar Jyoti*, *Azad* (Hindi, Acharya, 1940), *Chandidas*, *Kunku/Duniya na Mane* (Marathi/Hindi, Shantaram, 1937), *Pukar*, and *Sikandar*, female protagonists are portrayed as willing or unwitting agents who test a man and the laws of his community. In *Amritmanthan*, *Bandhan* (Hindi, Acharya, 1940), *Diler Jigar*, and *Neecha Nagar* (Hindi, Anand, 1946) fictional female characters have to prove themselves worthy of belonging to a future, utopian community with their men. Women move with men in the search for a better community in *Dharti ke Lal* (Hindi, Abbas, 1946) and *Janmabhoomi* (Hindi, Osten, 1936), and they lead men toward a better nation in *Brandychi Batli/Brandy ki Botal* (Marathi/Hindi, Vinayak, 1939), *Diamond Queen* (Hindi, Wadia, 1940), *Thyagabhoomi*, and *Hunterwali* (Hindi, Wadia, 1935). In these narrative variations the films imagine different futures for the nation in relation to its citizens, with women operating as a textual figuration of various unmanaged (political, communal, regional, caste) differences within the nation.

This claim appears to make "woman" into an übercategory of social analysis by subsuming all nationally subordinated communities under the sign of the female, which is not my intention. Insofar as women did not experience their lives irreducibly as a "woman" so much as, say, a middle-class Allahabadi Muslim woman or as a woman from a rural Tamil Thevar family, competing social, regional and religious affiliations extended themselves through gender identity. In this sense, women were in fact one of many constituencies that posed a problem for normative definitions of a secular and inclusive India, all of which constituencies *also* operated through the category of gender.[68] Films marked the female body with signs of caste, region, religion, profession—but coded this body as unmarked to signify pan-national universality and appeal—as a precondition to giving it cinematic form. Films thus called forth more than one kind of creative invention in integrating the female into a fictional social totality. Integral to heteronormative commercial cinema's creation of desire and insidiously part of all film narratives, women offer a heuristic means to comprehend a film's labored production of a secular, modern society in relation to its internal differences.

Immediately relevant to a discussion of internal difference is the plight of Indian Muslims from all regions of the colony. As prominent bearers of communal difference in prepartition India, Muslim men and women were sundered by a secularism that included them only on condition of assigning them minority status and a sectarianism that recognized their personhood only on condition of religious, cultural, and political separatism. Indian colonial cinema marks their presence and privations in many ways. Colonial Indian film music is unimaginable without composers like Rafique Ghaznavi, Kamaal Amrohi, Naushad, Ghulam Haider, Khursheed, Nurjehan, and Shamshad Begum. Colonial Indian film genres, texts, music, and scripts were shaped by Muslim artists, several of whom—like Ghaznavi, Haider, Nurjehan, Khurseed, along with the writer Saadat Hasan Manto—left for West Pakistan after partition at incalculable personal cost.[69] More profoundly, as Mukul Kesavan proposes, "Islamicate forms" constituted and gave shape to India's cinematic imagination.[70] Ghazals, Muslim socials, "Urdu, Awadh, and the tawaif have been instrumental in shaping Hindi cinema as a whole—not just some 'Muslim' component in it."[71]

If the colonial film form absorbed Islamic culture, it also internalized a deep apprehension about inassimilable internal heterogeneities that, on the political front, potently manifested itself in the conflict between Indian Hindus and Muslims. Similar to British imperial modernism's transmutation of an anxiety of decolonization into introspective and stylized intimations of disaster, Indian colonial films hint at the inadequacies of a secular imagination. An unnamed dread of a nation that may not cohere lurks behind colonial film texts. A rare film like Shejari/Padosi explicitly enunciates a fear of disunity. More often, films released around the time of independence, like P. L. Santoshi's Hum Ek Hain (1946), tutor the nation on national integration (which Shejari does as well). But all colonial films offer their particular genre-refracted representation of India's "social problems" (similar to those predicted by Chandidas and Churchill). Films that appear on surface to celebrate Indian nationalism remain haunted by the consequences of political sovereignty. They repeatedly give cinematic form to the afflictions of modern Indian society in order to suggest utopian resolutions; afflictions imagined as an excess of conservative traditionalism and reactionary religiosity or, on the contrary, as a surfeit of scandalous modernity.

With regard to the female figure in colonial cinema, realist "socials" that depict contemporary India—Chandidas, Janmabhoomi, Thyagabhoomi, Bandhan, Azad—aesthetically integrate women into what Aamir Mufti calls the "affective economy of nationalism."[72] Reminiscent of Chatterjee's argument, such tales of social reform imagine contemporary Indian social problems like casteism, rural underdevelopment, alcoholism, and the denudation of tradition and family values under corrupting Western modernity, and invariably subsume female emancipation within resolutions that affirm a new reformist and nationalist patriarchy. At the same time, historical romance films (like *Diler Jigar*, *Ghulami nu Patan*, *Pukar*, and *Sikandar*) and modernist myths (like *Amar Jyoti* and *Amritmanthan*) depict women who pose a challenge to India's emerging nationhood through aesthetic templates that oppose the realist mode of socials, always understanding realism in the revised terms of Indian cinema (chapter 7). Kwame Anthony Appiah argues that colonial nationalism produced the assertive and didactic mode of realism.[73] But as a political movement that sorted a heterogeneous population into internal majorities and subservient minorities to invent a national totality, colonial nationalism also produced the exploratory, interrogative, and traumatized mode of modernism by pointing to the potential impossibility of a unified "India." Expressions of such skepticism can be read in film form, agitated around the figure of the female in historical romances and modernist myths in particular.

As a cultural *form*, colonial cinema grappled with the possibility of a modern India through stories told as myths, as feudal precolonial histories, and as contemporary socials. The structure of their fiction was contingent on finding a place for decolonizing subjects within these inventions. And so the films repositioned the nation's internal subjects to imagine a community and assess the past with varying degrees of confidence about a new era in politics. As a commercial *commodity*, these articulated visions needed an audience. Similar to British empire cinema, Indian colonial films were in competition with other film imports within their domestic market. They drew on a range of artistic influences—Hollywood's popular film genres, Europe's art cinemas, Britain's novelistic and dramatic traditions, Indian classical and vernacular forms of visuality and performativity—to reconfigure cosmopolitan and local styles and present a formally hybrid cinematic vision of alternative sovereignty. The difficulties in nationalism's assimilationist project produced the narrative and visual obstacles of colonial films, which were either polemic and pedagogical in their nationalism or deeply prophetic of a nation's unattainable ideals.

Gayatri Spivak has demanded that efforts to historicize formalism make transparent their "ethico-political" agendas. Examining preeminent descriptions of postmodernism by Jameson, Lyotard, and Habermas, she argues that they assign the status of "cultural dominant" to limited, Eurocentric manifestations of late capitalism, which when extrapolated into the next new universal historical narrative effectively repress heterogenieties across place and continuities over time.[74] To be fair, Jameson is only too conscious of history's agenda; in his words "Only a genuine philosophy of history is capable of respecting the specificity and radical difference of the social and cultural past while disclosing the solidarity of its polemics and passions, its forms . . . with those of the present day."[75] But as Spivak deconstructs a critic's location during the act of interpretation, Jameson's formal ontologies to interpret social texts based on buried (unconscious) structures appear to invest too much authority in the scholarly interpreter, and by extension in the interpreter's Eurocentric epistemology. Though I assume a similar risk by making texts and contexts speak through my theoretical constructs (as does any writer), my effort is to link form and history in a manner that actively resists universalization as well as notions of complete temporal rupture. My attempt to localize the aesthetics of realism, romance, and modernism in cinema owes a debt to the larger project of "provincializing Europe," to borrow from Dipesh Chakrabarty.[76] My claim, quite simply, is that cinematic realism, romance, and modernism each provided a visual and thematic regimen for the political upheavals in Britain and India, in ways expressive of the contests within and pressures upon those two entities confronting a new identity and relationship, a new destiny.

part one ✳ **IMPERIAL GOVERNMENTALITY**

Viscount Sandon (Shrewsbury, Unionist) said that this [Films
Quota] Bill was necessary for social and domestic as well as for
Imperial reasons.
—*The Times*, 17 March 1927

It is no secret that the Government, and indeed practically the whole
of the country, recognizes in the Bill something which far outstrips
any ordinary trade legislation. Apart from the purely trade aspect,
there is the deeper question of Empire, of the Imperialistic Outlook.
—*The Bioscope*, 2 June 1927

The British [film] industry needs a larger market within which to
extend its scope. The British Empire is an obvious field, but it is
untilled. Distribution is largely controlled by American capital. . . .
The British industry has a legitimate and encouraging opportunity
to enlarge its field; but it is an opportunity which must be coura-
geously seized, and without delay.
—*The Film in National Life*

two * **ACTS OF TRANSITION**

The British Cinematograph Films Acts of 1927 and 1938

In 1927 Sir Philip Cunliffe-Lister, president of Britain's Board of Trade (BT),
supported the Cinematograph Films Bill, drawing both enthusiastic applause
and sharp criticism in the British House of Commons. Arguing against the
bill's proposed quota for British films in the United Kingdom, free-trader
Philip Snowden (Colne Valley, Labour; also Chancellor of the Exchequer, 1924
and 1929–1931) accused Cunliffe-Lister of being "simply a tool in the hands
of the Federation of British Industries," complaining that if the BT president
had his way, "he would impose a quota restriction on every trade in the country, and, for instance, compel every greengrocer to stock a certain proportion
of British fruit." [1] Within sight of an economic depression, the British State's
urgent consideration of a protectionist, nationalist economy was matched
by the issue's severe political divisiveness. British film, like British fruit, was
caught in a national debate over tariffs versus free trade.
　　Imperial conferences held in 1926 and 1932 made it obvious that the imperial question was a significant part of prevailing discussions about state
and industry.[2] Both conferences aimed at improving trade relations within
the empire, and by the 1932 Conference, held in Ottawa, the political climate

in Britain had shifted definitively in favor of protectionism. In the preceding year the Labour government led by Prime Minister Ramsay MacDonald had been replaced by a pro-tariff, coalitional "National Government," also under MacDonald. Reflecting this change, the Ottawa conference initiated a policy of imperial preferences by creating a zone of trade incentives restricted to the empire. Also known as "empire free trade," the policy notionally retained the sense of an open market while appeasing the protectionists.

The British State's first modest protection of its film production with the Cinematograph Films Act of 1927 (or the Quota Act) anticipated this relationship between nation and empire. The policy was carefully worded to offer special concessions to empire-made films entering the British market, in the hope that British films would receive similar favors from colonial and dominion governments. Perhaps a measure of its controversial nature, suggestions of imperial preference were hidden in the strategic ambiguities of policy language rather than declared as an explicit part of the act. Existing scholarly accounts of the Quota Act, referenced throughout this chapter, focus on the policy's domestic significance to the exclusion of its submerged imperial dimension, thus missing the centrality of empire to Britain's geopolitical position between the two world wars. Though British investments in colonial enterprises were increasingly unpopular because of their diminishing returns, the British State and its domestic industries persistently attempted to mobilize the empire to national advantage.[3] The manner of this mobilization expresses the impact of decolonization on the British State's and film industry's self-definition.

Arguably, the centrality of imperial markets to Britain's global primacy during the nineteenth century made it a field of investigation for British filmmakers and policy makers seeking bulwarks against Hollywood. But the Quota Act's timing is of interest. By 1927 British filmmakers well knew that the empire was neither a viable nor a coherent entity with regard to its receptivity to British films. The Federation of British Industries (FBI) noted that the United States had more theaters than the British Empire, and each theater had considerably greater seating capacity, with audiences of greater "comparative wealth" to occupy those seats.[4] The FBI also knew that harnessing empire markets would not put Britain's film industry on par with Hollywood's. Despite this foreknowledge, the organization cast Britain's national industry within a framework of imperial aspirations in its 1926 petition to BT President Cunliffe-Lister. Arguing that American films exhibited in the British Empire were "obscuring the prestige of the mother country, and

greatly injuring British trade," the FBI requested that the BT "move for legislation" in the empire "against the wholesale usurpation of British kinemas
by foreign films."[5]

An initial Economic Sub-Committee report to the Imperial Conference
of 1926 that set the Films Quota Bill in motion contains *discrete* evaluations
of the so-called empire market. The report does not, in other words, collapse distinctions between self-governing white-settler dominions like Australia and New Zealand (where British films entered free of duty), Canada
(where Britain received tax concessions as the "most favoured nation"), and
the Irish Free State (which paid preferential duty to Britain); self-governing
nonwhite-majority dominions like Southern Rhodesia (where British films
paid no duty); and nondominion, nonwhite territories like India (where British films paid the same tariff as other film imports).[6] Given the state's cogni-
zance of the empire's diverse cultural, racial, and linguistic affinities and tax
structures, the appearance of blanket terms like *inter-imperial* and *empire market* in discussions of the Quota Act created homogeneity where none existed.
Evidently, in the British film-quota debates, the term *empire* signaled less an
actual region than a desired one, regarding which the British State perceived a
proximity and a prerogative. The genealogy of the 1927 Quota Act as it moved
through the annals of British state departments highlights a dialectic between the imperial desire for an empire market and its frustration. The Quota
Act's imperial designs read not only as a narrative of failure (in that an empire film market couldn't be produced, so it couldn't be won) but also as a
narrative of fantasy.

Prioritizing a critical cultural analysis of state policy by focusing on the
language of the Quota Act, as opposed to that of the individual players, offers
tactical advantages. As a liberal parliamentary democracy, the British State
was more than the sum of its parts. Individuals and groups arguing for the
need to utilize Britain's imperial influence in expanding the scope of British
film distribution could not, and did not, transparently assert their will on the
state. Rather, in a Gramscian sense, the modern state machinery mediated its
civil society's competing demands to formalize and bureaucratize a political
and economic agenda for its national film industry. During the 1920s, for example, a few voluntary organizations (funded by shareholder capital and state
grants) encouraged the production of imperial-themed British films and promoted them within Britain and throughout the empire.[7] One such organization, the British Empire Film Institute (BEFI), started in 1925, had a distinguished "Grand Council" (including Sir Arthur Conan Doyle), and it enjoyed

the support of the king, the British prime minister, and "members of Parliament of all parties." Its goal was "to encourage the production and presentation of all British Films, that faithfully represent the achievements, ideas and ideals of the British Commonwealth." The organization gave awards to films with "British scenarios dealing with Imperial, Historical" subjects, in the hope of creating an "atmosphere" which would build "an intensified demand for the new pictures, pictures of Imperial Value, of our great Colonial achievements."[8]

The BEFI argued that imperial territories gave Britain an edge over the United States and that the distribution of British films in the empire was imperative in view of native susceptibilities to moving images. Thus the sentiments of its members conveyed a sense of Britain's importance ("Our past history is too precious an asset to the Anglo-Saxon race to permit it to be . . . belittled, by the presentation . . . of films produced on foreign shores," said the Rt. Hon. The Earl of Meath), national pride ("Our far flung dominions should enable us to discover climates, even more suitable for film production, than that of California," said the same), and anger ("I have long felt bitterly the obvious degradation that is fostered by the American Films. I cannot see why the trade-profits of such an injurious system should be allowed to render it permanent. . . . The evil is almost worse in Eastern countries, I hear, among other races, where the exhibition is a slander on civilization," said Sir Flinders Petrie). Though not a member of the institute, Sir Philip Cunliffe-Lister (formerly Sir Philip Lloyd-Graeme, created Viscount Swinton in 1935 and First Earl of Swinton in 1955) was like many of his fellow aristocrats in that he believed in the British Empire. Unlike them, however, he headed Britain's trade and manufacturing industries as the BT president (1922–1924, 1924–1929, 1931). By his initiative the Films Quota Bill was first proposed in Parliament. He also served as secretary to the state for the colonies (1931–1935), embodying the enduring weld between colonial affairs and national industry.

Cunliffe-Lister's political sympathies and peerage become significant insofar as they affect his official portfolio and allow him a part in the contest between lobby groups with competing interests in domestic and imperial protectionism. With the quota bill becoming an act, the effort to activate imperial distribution of British films was no longer the mission statement of one among several discrete organizations but was structurally constitutive of a national film policy. On the one hand, British film producers played to the imperial anxieties of Cunliffe-Lister and like-minded lords and parliamentarians to press for state assistance and to provide a secure market for British films at home and in the empire. On the other, the state gave bureaucratic form and juridical legitimacy to their arguments by approving the Quota Act. With the implementation of the act of 1927 and its amendment in 1938, one of a range of competing positions toward the British film industry solidified into regulatory state form. It defined the terms of engagement for subsequent domestic and colonial dissent against the British State and influenced each sector of the British film industry.

The embedded imperial assumptions that adhered in the policy, however, lie less in the act's stipulations and effects than in its premises: in the details of policy discourse—including the language of official lobbying as well as the popular discussions surrounding film policy and policy lexicon—resides the sociocultural context of anxieties and ambitions within which the act was concretized. The British State was hesitant to interfere directly in the legislative matters of its colonial and dominion governments, instead emphasizing diplomatic efforts and commercial trade initiatives to promote British films within the empire. The state's temporary acquiescence to mobilize its empire as a market for commercial British film producers through a combination of cooperation, diplomacy, and combativeness toward the dominions and colonies was distinctive to this period of negotiations. Operating through implicit and strategic trade terms was one of the few ways in which the British State, caught between assisting its domestic film industry and withdrawing from direct control over colonial and dominion governments, could assert its economic preferences. The actual elusiveness of empire film markets that accompanied the British State's prolific discussion of their potential exploitability altered the policy debates, making the debates emblematic of changing political relations during late empire. In effect, the language of the Quota Act expressed the prevailing power play between Britain and its empire.[9]

Imperializing Britain: British Film as "British Empire Film"

Before the Quota Act, the British government's involvement with films had pertained to taxation, censorship, and the regulation of theaters. Following the Quota Act of 1927, however, all films had to be registered as "British" or "Foreign" with the BT prior to their exhibition in Britain, and unregistered films were not allowed to be screened. Controversially, the act required film renters (distributors) to acquire and exhibitors to screen a prescribed number of British films (calculated by footage, as a percentage of all registered films).[10] The act further specified that the quota of British films was to increase on a sliding scale, beginning at 7.5 percent for the distributors and 5 percent for the exhibitors in 1927. By 1936, when the Act was to be reviewed, 20 percent of all films rented and exhibited within Britain were to be British.

The act stipulated guidelines by which the BT could identify a film as British.[11] Among other factors, a film could be registered as British if it was made by a British subject or a British company, if its studio scenes were shot in a studio in the British Empire (unless otherwise authorized by the BT), if the author of the original scenario for the film was a British subject, or if 75 percent of the wages were paid to British subjects or domiciles of the British Empire.[12] According to this act, then, films made anywhere within the empire could be categorized as "British," and by this definition films from British dominions and colonies were eligible for a quota in Britain.

This was the regulatory birth of the "British Empire film," a confusing, changeling term that appears in various documents to refer to films made with British or empire resources and, quite contrarily, to describe films originating from colonies and dominions. The imperial push for British cinema's preferential treatment within empire markets rested on the Quota Act's definitional ambiguity between "British" and "British Empire" film, which was claimed as the basis for a similar ingress of British films into imperial markets. Such ambiguities were not exclusive to the Quota Act but part of a general fuzziness between references to empire-*made* films and British films made with empire *resources* that is evident in other documents as well. To quote *The Bioscope*, a British film journal, 1927 was an "opportune" time "for the big boosting of every Empire-made film," because there was a rich "fund of literature and historical material from which to make our own—speaking Imperially—epics of colonisation, our own 'Birth of a Nation' and 'Covered Wagon.' "[13] In the article, "empire-made films" are completely equated with British "epics of colonization."

Such strategic vagueness surrounding the term "empire film" first appeared at the Imperial Conference of 1926. The Economic Sub-Committee report, titled "Exhibition within the Empire of British Films," noted "that the proportion of British films, that is, films produced within the Empire by British Companies employing British artists, to the total shown at Cinema Houses in the United Kingdom amounts to scarcely 5 per cent, and that the position throughout the Empire generally is as bad, and in some parts even worse."[14] The report offers suggestions for economic reforms to assist commercial British film production: "The principal proposal for Government

BOARD OF TRADE.
CINEMATOGRAPH FILMS ACT, 1927.

REGISTRATION FORM C.

Evidence of British Nature of Film entitled

application for the registration of which was made by

on the .... 19 ....

I/We declare that the following particulars set out in paragraphs 1 to 5 below relating to the film entitled..

are true to the best of my/our knowledge and belief.

Signature of the Maker(s) of the film..

Address..

Date..

1. The photographing was begun on..19........,

   and finished on........................, 19........

2.—(a) The scenes photographed in a place (whether within a building or not) where sets were erected for the purpose occupy........................feet of the film, and were photographed in the following places (give names and addresses of studios), and nowhere else :—

(b) The only scenes taken outside the British Empire were as follows (state the scenes and the number of feet of the film occupied by them) :—

* Strike out the words which do not apply.

3. The particulars given in paragraph 4 exclude payments made to one foreign producer / actor or actress.

3. The Quota Act of 1927 required an official definition of a "British" film. Courtesy B F I National Library.

action, apart from methods of taxation, and one that has been strongly urged by a number of bodies interested in the revival of British picture production, is the establishment of what is known as the 'quota' system, to be imposed on either the exhibitors or the renters or both."[15] The main body that "strongly urged" state involvement was the FBI, with whom the quota initiative began. Formed in 1916, the FBI was a powerful organization, dominated by the ship-building, iron, and steel industries, that represented the concerns of British trade and industry to the British state. The Economic Sub-Committee's report reflected a preliminary petition "To Revive [Film] Production," submitted by the FBI to Cunliffe-Lister in 1925. This petition for government intervention is an early document that conflates "British films" with "Empire films" in a manner advantageous to the British film industry.[16]

As the term *empire* (as symbolic phrase) threads through the quota de-bates, the Quota Act, and the act's 1938 amendment, it reveals the weave of empire's influence (as material reality) on shifting national policy. In propos-ing strategies by which the government could increase capital for the pro-duction of British films and provide an assisted market for their exhibition, the FBI's petition suggests Germany's quotas as a role model.[17] In addition, it recommends secure national funding for British films on "National" and "Empire subjects," such as films about the "nation's heroes, scientists, and prominent literary men and women," obviously conceiving of the empire as a domain of British protagonists and British industry. Throughout the docu-ment, the term "Imperial" refers to themes, facilities, and markets that ex-pand the domestic film product by exploiting "the marvellous and varied re-sources of the Empire."[18] Similar usage of the term was favored in 1926, when the FBI was joined by the Film Manufacturer's Committee and the Film Producer's Group, the latter representing sixteen British film companies, in-cluding British Instructional Films, British Screens Classics, Gainsborough Pictures, and Gaumont Company.[19] Immediately lobbying Cunliffe-Lister in their own interests, the FBI's Film Group noted that Britain's facilities and studios could produce "12.5 per cent of the films required by the Empire's kinemas," but for this the British companies "must know that they have a reasonably assured market."[20]

Here was a happy coincidence between the conservative elements of the state that worried about Hollywood's impact on the colonies, and the FBI and the British film producers' appeal that linked national pride to a robust trade of British films in the empire.[21] The free-trader Philip Snowden wasn't far wrong in thinking that the FBI had Cunliffe-Lister's ear, given the following carefully worded resolution passed at the 1926 conference through the BT's efforts: "The Imperial Conference, recognizing that it is of the greatest importance that a larger and increasing proportion of the films exhibited throughout the Empire should be of Empire production, commends the matter and the remedial measures proposed to the consideration of the Governments of various parts of the Empire."[22] The chief "remedial measure," of course, was the Films Quota Bill. The home (British) government assured colonial and dominion governments that such a bill would promote "Empire produced" films in Britain. Empire governments were commended to consider similar measures in their markets. In effect, during this imperial conference, underlying concern about the lack of British films in imperial markets translated into a manifest support of "Empire-production films" in Britain.

The Films Quota Bill in this manifestation was of a piece with other efforts demonstrating Britain's interest in imperial cooperation. The EMB, for example, was established in 1926 to revive imperial trade in various commodities, and "it sought to influence consumer choice, not by financial means—tariff barriers—but by propaganda."[23] Advertisements about Britain's reliance on empire products and corresponding information to the empire about Britain were intended to create an awareness of the empire as a live economic and social entity. In 1932 Sir Stephen Tallents, president of the EMB, noted in his pamphlet "The Projection of England," "If we are to play our part in the new world order, we need to master every means and every art by which we can communicate with other peoples. The need is especially urgent between ourselves and the other parts of the Empire. We are experimenting together in *a novel political organization*, in which are joined together peoples most widely separated from each other in space and character."[24] In the new multicolored and multiclassed order, wrote Tallents (eerily echoing Prime Minister Blair's speech defending the United Kingdom's support for the U.S. war on Iraq in 2003), "the English people must be seen for what it is—a great nation still anxious to serve the world and secure the world's peace."[25] In the same spirit, the British Broadcasting Corporation (BBC) initiated new foreign (Arabic) language broadcasts in 1938, to "make the life and thought of the British peoples more widely known abroad."[26] The 1948 conference "Film in Colonial Development" started new programs to train African filmmakers because, as the inaugural speaker noted, "We are recognizing today that Empire (if we continue to use that particular word) is not an opportunity of exploitation to our material advantage, but the occasion of service."[27] In an early index of this public-relations oriented developmental turn, proposals for a film quota in Britain emphasized benefits for the colonies and dominions and demonstrated acute self-consciousness about the term *empire*. At home, the bill was drafted with careful discussion of its phraseology.[28]

Proposals for the actual wording of the bill traveled back and forth between the BT and the Customs Office prior to the bill's introduction in the House of Commons. A Finance Act from 1922 that extended trade preferences to film negatives produced in the United Kingdom was used as a guideline.The first discussion of the Films Quota Bill pertained to the parameters of the commodity, and the quota was applied to film positives as well as negatives. The second discussion fixed the parameters of place. The Customs Office suggested, with an emphasis on its key terms, "It might be possible to substitute British Empire for United Kingdom. . . . (This is a concession to British *enterprise*: there is no condition that the picture must be *made* in the Empire)."[29] Though the final Quota Act did have a stipulation regarding the film's place of origin, these preparatory talks defended the substitution of "British Empire" for "United Kingdom" by appealing to "empire" as a form of *trade* rather than *territory*. The argument that Britain could benefit from an extension of privileges to its empire depended on treating empire less as a (static) point of production and more as a (mobile) space for British enterprise. Here the empire becomes not so much a place as a spatialization of British industry, which disaffiliates territories from their regional politics and economies only to assimilate them as a transnational space for British trade. The rhetoric, in fact, was not so much colonial as protoglobal.

Several contradictions strained at this formulation of empire. At one end, the interaction between a conceptually deterritorialized market and a would-be expansionist national enterprise pointed to nascent efforts at globalizing British film production. At the other end, this particular reascription of empire as space rather than place depended entirely on state power, to the exclusion of capital mobilization. Preliminary discussions of the quota bill were imperialist in their premise but transnational in their expectation. The state was straddling two divergent discourses. A distinguishing aspect of a global market as opposed to an imperial one is that while imperialism depends explicitly on political and territorial dominance, globalization functions through a more decentered apparatus.[30] Globalization produces insidious forms of domination that are difficult to localize, though privatization *requires* state acquiescence, and it may collude with state control. Partnerships between corporations in different nations or a dispersal of the sectors of one industry across national territories creates transnational circuits of operation and privilege. In Britain's case, Hollywood's transnational collaboration with British film exhibitors and distributors threatened the British State's sovereignty over its film industry. U.S. distribution centers in Britain's colonies and dominions also gave Hollywood a wider and more organized base of operation. To counter Hollywood's successful globalization, the British Films Quota Act participated in maneuvers through which the British State laboriously and with challenge attempted to recast imperial territories as a global market potentially available to British industry. Britain could not compete with the United States by transforming the emerging "commonwealth" into its global playground because in addition to Britain's weaker market forces, the empire was increasingly subject to competing foreign interests and comprised independent economic and political wills. Britain's command over the empire was precisely what was in contest, as colonies and dominions were caught up in defining a sovereign national place.

Parochializing Britain: "British Empire Film" as British Film

In 1927 the BT sent copies of the film bill to colonies and dominions like Australia, Canada, and India, where inquiry committees used the bill as leverage to initiate parallel moves.[31] Provincial legislatures in Canada proposed a screen quota for empire-produced films, with the British Columbia legislature taking the lead in 1929. The Cooper Organization, a pressure group representing the U.S. Hays Office, which was funded largely by U.S. distributors, thwarted this Canadian bill.[32] Meanwhile American studios looking to beat the British quota system found a loophole in the term "British Empire films." Since films produced in Canada counted as "British films" under the terms of the 1927 Quota Act, U.S. companies were lured into producing films in Canada and using them as quota films in the British market. Australia, on the other hand, passed quota legislations similar to the one in Britain, requiring the exhibition of a percentage of locally produced films. The British film industry began to fear that foreign distributors supplying to both dominion and British markets would distribute Australian films rather than British films, since they could technically fulfill the quota in both areas.[33]

Proposals to consider imperial preference within the Indian market did not fare well either. In 1927–1928 the Indian Cinematograph Committee (ICC) was constituted to consider issues such as censorship, the status of the Indian film industry, and possibilities for imperial preference. The ICC conducted an exhaustive investigation of the Indian film industry and produced four fascinating volumes of written and oral interviews (termed "evidence") from 353 interviewees (defined as "witnesses") who were primarily film producers, exhibitors, distributors, actors, and censors, along with newspaper editors and educationalists working in India.[34] With regard to the question of instituting some quota for British Empire films in India, a majority of the members of the Indian film industry interviewed by the ICC felt that the inclusion of British Empire films in the Quota Act (which was still a bill when the ICC conducted its interviews) would not lead to the entry of Indian films into Britain. Moreover, they asserted that business initiatives by British film producers were preferable to policy changes.

> No artificial aid is . . . needed to advance the British film in this country. We entirely endorse the remarks of the Australian Board of Censors in their report for 1925: "If fewer British films are imported into this country the reasons are generally well known. The prices have something to do with it. Whereas other countries have agencies here, British producers are scarcely represented at all." As in Australia, here also there is no accredited representative of the British film industry. When British Empire films can show the quality and finish and can be had for the same prices as other Western films, there will be no difficulty in those films finding such a market as is available in this country.[35]

Several witnesses considered proposals for trade reciprocity to be a smokescreen for British interest in the Indian market, as is evident in the ICC's extended exchange with an outspoken Indian film exhibitor, Rustom C. N. Barucha.

> MR. GREEN [British member, ICC]: Does not the Bill, as I have endeavoured to explain to you, give a better opportunity for Indian-made films to be exported to England?
>
> ANSWER [Mr. Barucha]: On paper it appears that by the mere passage of this Bill in England, the market will be thrown open for Indian films, but I am not sure if that would be beneficial to India in the long run. Theoretically it appears that Indian films will have an open door in England, but I am not sure that there will be any appreciable and genuine demand for them in England.
>
> . . . I will go a bit further and say this. Suppose India now definitely commits herself to the policy of participating in what is called the British

Empire scheme. For the present we are allowed to produce our own pictures to meet our own demands and needs. But I do not think they are really anxious to have Indian pictures in England. I dismiss that idea altogether from my mind at once. What is the guarantee, I ask, Sir, that the next step will not be the imposing of some condition which will prevent Indian pictures being manufactured in our own country, and the only result of this Bill will be that we will be compelled to have British pictures.

MR. GREEN: The Bill is not going to be applied to India.

COL. CRAWFORD [British member, ICC]: The point is, does the producer want an opportunity to sell his goods in the world market? Is it of any value to him?

ANSWER [Mr. Barucha]: The idea undoubtedly looks splendid . . . [but] I have grave doubts about it. You need not accept my statement alone. . . . This will be clear from other circumstances also. How many Indian-made articles, let alone Indian-made films, find a ready market in the Empire? I cannot sell a single Indian-made shoe in England.[36]

This exchange brings to light the insubstantial reach of the term "British Empire film" (and Barucha's enterprise in trying to sell shoes when films failed him). What did a British Empire film look like? Which films finally benefited from the Quota Act? If it referred to an Indian film as much as a British film, under what conditions would a British renter and exhibitor distribute or screen Indian films? In theory, for instance, all the Indian films discussed in this book, having been made within the empire, could have served as quota films in Britain. But in fact none of them were screened in England, so theory did not always translate into practice.

According to available records, some Indian films *were* in fact registered as British films and *were* beneficiaries of the British film quota. A 1930 issue of *Film Report*, a British trade journal of the Cinematograph Exhibitors Association, assessed five silent Indian films—*Durgesh Nandini*, *Madhuri*, *Anarkali*, *Krishna Kanta's Will*, and *The Tigress*—which were booked by British renters under the Quota Act.[37] The journal describes *Durgesh Nandini* as "an Indian production, played by natives. As a production, it is extremely crude. . . . The picture is for all practical purposes just a Renter's Quota."[38] *Madhuri* is estimated as "another of those films which, being made in India and interpreted by a native cast, rank as quota," and neither film is given release dates.[39]

Rental bookings clearly had little to do with screening the film or finding an audience. One of the loopholes in the 1927 act was that while British renters were legally obligated to acquire a percentage of British Empire films, they were not penalized if no one booked them for exhibition. So British renters used Indian films to fill their British Empire film quota, because they were longer and cheaper by the foot. Whereas American and British features measured approximately 5,000 to 7,000 feet in length, Indian features ranged between 10,000 and 14,000 feet, and were attractive to renters because a few inexpensive Indian films satisfied the letter of the renters quota law. The Indian exhibitor Barucha was accurate in his prediction that the passage of Britain's Quota Act would not lead to any significant increase in Britain's receptivity to Indian films and could not be claimed as valid grounds for a reciprocal quota in the colony. Based on the overwhelmingly negative response of witnesses, the ICC reported to the government of India that regulatory assistance for British films in India was unnecessary and unwelcome.

The British Empire film purported to serve the empire while acting on behalf of national interests. A nation with a history of imperial power could appear to represent cosmopolitan concerns even while its argument was at base parochial, by virtue of the fact that it could refer to overseas markets while protecting a domestic commodity. The cosmopolitanism promised by the empire acquired particular significance in relation to Britain's competition with Hollywood. A mundane example of this, which makes an oddly frequent appearance, is the dreary weather of the British Isles. The advantages of locating outdoor shoots for British films in the empire were brought up in both houses of the British parliament, as in this exchange from the House of Commons in 1927.

> MR. HARRIS: This country is handicapped by its climate. One of the reasons of the immense success of the American films is that they have many months of dry sunshine in which plays can be produced in the open air. . . .
> VISCONT SANDON: What about the rest of the Empire?
> MR. HARRIS: That is one of the ways we can get over the handicap.[40]

If the predominance of Hollywood films in the world film market since 1919 reinforced the idea that its narrative and visual content carried a type of universality against which competing cinemas had to mobilize a domestic allure, Britain's presumed proximity to its imperial territories appeared to be its opportunity for access to an exclusive base of appeal.[41] With little definitional negotiation, the empire represented the strengths of the British nation combined with the advantages of transnationalism, and it came to be said that "no single country can offer to cinematography so fruitful a field as the British Empire."[42] Thus, in discussing empire films the Quota Act traded on two meanings of the term *empire*: (subtly, sentimentally) as a national British possession and (explicitly, in the words of the British ICC member Colonel Crawford) as a "world market."

Not coincidentally, commercial British blockbusters with imperial themes that became popular in the 1930s invested a similarly dual significance in the concept of empire, as the work of two film producers, Alexander Korda and Michael Balcon, illustrates. Despite their difference of opinion over viable options for British filmmaking in the face of American screen domination, Korda and Balcon both produced imperialist epics. Balcon produced Ealing Studio's and Rank Organization's *Scott of the Antarctic* (Frend, 1948), and was behind such Gaumont-British films as *The Great Barrier*, *King Solomon's Mines*, and *Rhodes of Africa*.[43] These empire films were quality products that qualified for national quota. Korda—a Hungarian who became a naturalized British citizen and was, like Balcon, eventually knighted—had ties with United Artists and produced big-budget films with an eye toward British, imperial, and American markets. Unlike Korda, Balcon passionately believed that while British films could aim for profits from "the home and Empire markets," British national identity was best expressed through domestic themes. As the film historian Charles Barr observes, despite working successfully with MGM in the late thirties, Balcon was happy to leave his Hollywood collaborators for Ealing Studios where his prolific tenure as studio head was characterized by a successful mining of strongly local "English" themes, in films such as *Passport to Pimlico* (Cornelius, 1949) and *Whisky Galore!* (Mackendrick, 1949).[44] According to Balcon, "The British producer can make no greater mistake than to have the American market in mind when planning and costing a picture. Not in that way will the British film ever become representative of British culture."[45]

The same sentiment was expressed in the prescient 1932 British report *The Film in National Life*:

> a narrow and uninformed nationalism controlling at home a foreign competition with which abroad it is unable to compete, is sterile. Broadcasting, like photography, has done much to break down the barriers between nations; the film can do more than either. A self-conscious internation-

ism, however, would defeat its own ends. A film which has been designed to be international is rarely a work of art or good entertainment. . . . We look forward with confidence to the time when the film industry in Great Britain . . . is producing films which are an unequivocal expression of British life and thought, deriving character and inspiration from our national inheritance, and have an honoured international currency.[46]

Commercial films about the empire were the perfect answer to these concerns. The empire was part of British history, and it simultaneously possessed a territorial and visual scope to demonstrate the largesse of Britain's national theater of performance: picturesque, bare-chested Indian princes and fierce African chiefs could be part of Technicolor fables about British identity. With Korda's and Balcon's productions, empire films came to represent an avenue out of "uninformed nationalism" and "self-conscious internationalism" by being expansively national and unselfconsciously international. With their success in domestic and U.S. box offices, they also went a long way as ambassadors for Britain. In 1945 the 9th Earl De La Warr, president of the British Board of Education (later Postmaster General, 1951–1955), reportedly "urged that one of the most important factors in building up a closer understanding with the United States was to have greater understanding in America of what the British Empire — and that particularly referred to India — really meant."[47] Churchill had worried earlier that "the loss of India, however arising, would be final and fatal to us. It could not fail to be part of a process which would reduce us to the scale of a minor Power."[48] With Britain losing control over the empire as a marketplace, empire films captured it as a narrative and an image for international audiences, symbolically realizing a material fantasy of the Films Quota Act.

Unlike the fantasy, however, the dominions were not willing to be Britain's California. While the quota regulation and British empire films produced a form of imperial cosmopolitanism, colonial and dominion film industries drew frequent distinctions between British films and Indian, Australian, or Canadian films, localizing their arguments. Differentiating national or regional self-interest from British expressions of interest in an empire-quota scheme was a crucial step in the Indian film industry's assertion of nationalism. Rejecting the idea that an empire quota would promote trade reciprocity between Britain and India, Indian film personnel emphasized that its benefits were nearly exclusive to the British film producer.

Dissenting Nation: Defining British Film

That British film renters stockpiled Indian films to meet their British film quota clearly indicates that the British film industry was not a unified entity. The pro-quota lobby consisted of film producers (who enjoyed the sympathies of some Conservatives and Liberal Unionists), while British film exhibitors and renters were against protectionism (which found support among Labour representatives). The partisan nature of the quota proposal remained at the forefront of all domestic debates over it. In the House of Commons, Ramsay McDonald (prime minister of Britain's first and second Labour governments in 1924 and 1929–1931, and of the "national" government in 1931–1935) called the Film Quota Bill a "party Bill," because "it does not consider the full needs of exhibitors and producers and renters. . . . It has been prompted over almost Clause by Clause by one side engaged and interested in the controversy—the side of the producers, and not all of them, but one section of the producers."[49]

The industry's dissent legitimized state involvement. Ostensibly, the state crossed its boundary of regulatory restraint in relation to the British film industry on the grounds that the industry could not achieve consensus through its own devices. During the second reading of the films bill in the House of Commons in 1927, Cunliffe-Lister argued, "The effects of the constant exhibition of foreign films on the sentiment, habit, thought of the people is obvious. The picture shows the foreign flag, styles, standards, habits, advertisements, etc. . . . I submit that the need for the development of the British film, from a national point of view, is firmly established; and if it cannot be developed without Government intervention, then, I submit, the case for Government intervention is made out."[50] Interestingly, however divided the pro- and anti-quota lobbies were on the question of quotas, competing factions paid allegiance to the construct of a nation. In these debates, the nation acquired an external fixity and emerged as a sanctioning entity. On the pro-quota side, the FBI emphasized film as a commodity that had imperial, educational, cultural, and trade value.[51] In 1925 the organization had argued to the BT, "The film has enormous power in influencing the masses, and especially the growing population throughout the Empire. In the U.K. alone it is computed that 20,000,000 people visit the kinemas each week. That this powerful influence should be directed from foreign countries and convey the ideas and customs of those countries instead of those that are British is deplorable."[52] Two years later, the FBI's Film Group did not have to belabor its line of argument, which was already accepted by Cunliffe-Lister: American films endangered national culture and siphoned out precious capital; a guaranteed market for British films would attract capital to domestic production; this could be found in the domestic and empire markets, if the state protected them.

British renters and exhibitors, who would bear the brunt of the regulation, had a more difficult case to defend, because their position revealed the schisms within the film industry and undermined the idea of an ideologically coherent national industry. Nevertheless, they adopted two lines of attack against the quota. First, they represented the exhibition and distribution sectors as the crux of a national film industry. If the FBI emphasized reciprocity in empire trade, film exhibitors stressed the possibility of bilateral arrangements with Hollywood. In return for giving Hollywood greater access to the British market, they suggested, the United States might be willing to prioritize the import of British films.[53] Arguing for the significance of Britain in the world of film, the Cinematograph Exhibitor's Association (CEA) noted that "the British market has increased in relative importance for American pictures."[54] (In fact, by the 1940s Britain would become the most lucrative overseas market for Hollywood).[55] Given the dismal state of British production, exhibitors were the only ones qualified to sit at a negotiating table with the Americans. As Charles Lapworth, a spokesperson for the exhibitors, insisted, "It has got to be acknowledged, that for all practical purposes the British exhibitors are the British film trade."[56]

The anti-quota lobby also linked national pride to a commitment to free trade, arguing that quotas were antithetical to British thought. If perceived to be part of a state quota, all British films would be reduced to the status of also-rans. They would be treated as the penalty a British exhibitor paid to screen Hollywood films that were on the market through the logic of the market, unlike state-stipulated screenings of British films. "The British film would become the powder wrapped in foreign meat to make the dog swallow it, the medicine to deserve the jam. If Government officials had gone out of their way to discredit British films, they could not have hit upon a more ingenious device."[57] It would serve to "stultify the British Nation in the eyes of the Empire and to advertise its incompetence to the world."[58] A quota, in these terms, would compromise British national identity and British film quality.

These arguments went to the heart of the state's avowed economic philosophy of a "free," industry-driven marketplace, which had been Britain's

E.E. LYONS R. VICTOR DAVIS J.N. BLAKE SIR P. CUNLIFFE-LISTER E. HEWITSON G.F. MACDONALD W.J. STEPHENSON W.R. FULLER CAVAZZI-KING

THE QUOTA IS DEFINITE!
Sir Philip Cunliffe-Lister's Straight Talk
Record Attendance at Annual C.E.A. Dinner

The Rt. Hon. Sir Philip Cunliffe-Lister, President of the Board of Trade, was the guest of honour at the Annual Dinner of the Cinematograph Exhibitors' Association, held at the Hotel Victoria, Northumberland Avenue, London, on Tuesday evening last. There was a magnificent attendance of personalities both from within and without the trade. Among those present were Sir Harry Brittain, M.P., the Hon. H. P. Colebatch, C.M.G., Sir Robert Donald, Lieut.-Com. J. M. Kenworthy, M.P., T. J. O'Connor, M.P., Lord Danesfort, Lord Sandon, M.P., Sidney Bacon, Michael Balcon, Captain J. W. Barber, Ritson Bennell, S. J. Bernstein, W. N. and Mrs. Blake, J. Frank Brocklige, Lieut.-Colonel A. C. and Mrs. Bromhead, J. Cabourn, Chas. H. Champion, F. H. Cooper, A. Cunningham, Tom E. Davies, J. Davis, H. Victor Davis, Colonel Harry Day, M.P., A. and Mrs. Dent, L. D. Dickson, Councillor J. H. and Mrs. Devener, T. C. Elder, W. Evans, E. W. Fredman, W. R. and Mrs. Fuller, F. Fumagalli, James George, Norman Hart, A. B. King, Lloyd Langdon, Alfred and Mrs. Lever, E. E. and Mrs. Lyons, J. McBride, Neil McLean, M.P., F. W. Morrison, S. G. and Mrs. Newman, Thos. and Mrs. Ormiston, W. Fowler Pettie, Ralph J. Pugh, S. Rowson, A. George Smith, J. A. Thorpe, Alderman E. Trounson, J.P., H. T. Underwood and T. A. and Mrs. Welsh.

Letters and telegrams of regret were read from G. H. Blackburn, Sir Wm. Jury, Lord Burnham, Lord Ashfield, Sir Frank Dicksee, Sir Burton and Lady Chadwick, T. P. O'Connor and Lord Beaverbrook.

"The Future of British Films"

Sir Philip Cunliffe-Lister then rose to propose the coffly toast (excepting that of "The King") of the evening— "The Future of British Films." "I have long envied the salaries of film stars," he said, "but now I also envy their hours I. I am glad that the great industry which you represent recognises the importance of British films, which have an importance far outside one industry or group of industries. That is why the whole Empire is taking an interest in British films. I am glad you have acknowledged that this is a question which cannot be treated as a trade issue—it is something which affects the whole trade of the British Empire.

"How many people realise the importance of the film industry to the trade of the whole Empire. I have been told by every representative whose job it is to watch British trade interests or prestige what a factor the film is. Take trade alone. You

pay £1,500 for the front page of a daily newspaper in order to advertise. Just consider the effect on trade if day by day not a chance page, but something which the public pays to look at, is regarded by millions. The film leaves an indelible impression on the mind. I have evidence from all over the Empire and from foreign countries of what the film industry can do as a promoter of trade. In trade alone this great industry can influence millions of people.

Greatest Commercial Traveller

"The film is the greatest commercial traveller any industry can have. A film shown to millions of people conveys the ideas and character of those who produce it. More important, if we are to prosper, is the atmosphere created for Britain. The British outlook can easily be lost. Supposing the whole British Empire to-day depended on foreign literature, or a foreign Press, would you not say that it was an outrage on civilisation? Does British literature or the British Press speak to a wider public throughout the world than films? Does not this show how vital is the toast— 'The Future of British Films.' Those are considerations which draw your industry outside and above the ordinary commercial considerations. Far wider interests are involved in it. It is not a national question but a national pre-occupation.

The Imperial Conference

"The recent Imperial Conference,' which had no time to waste on unimportant business, devoted no small part of its time to British films, and it passed a resolution setting out the desirability of increased showing and exhibition of British films, and calling upon the Mother Country to give a lead. You don't find statesmen of every Dominion devoting time to unimportant subjects unless something else is involved in addition to trade.

"No Government faced with this resolution from the Imperial Conference could fail to respond to the call, and if we had many would have called us to account. Facing the problem in its true perspective there cannot be any two minds about the desirability of showing more British films throughout the Empire.

Certain That Need Was There

"The right action has been taken. I am not one of those who feel that a Government should plunge in. If matters can be solved without outside interference, so much the better. I have been criticised for being too slow, 'I was determined before acting to be certain that the need was there, and

that nothing but Government action would meet the case. If the trade had agreed as to action, the Government would have been well content to leave it alone. To do one justice you must admit that that opportunity was not taken advantage of. I cast no reflections when I say that trade efforts failed.

The Two Problems

"There are two problems—Blind-booking and the Quota. Both are dealt with in the Bill, in the preparation and drafting of which I owe a great deal to Mr. Ormiston's Committee. There are two principles that of putting some limit on the power of the industry outside this land of forcing films on exhibitors of this land, and that some system of Quota is inevitable. These will be threshed out in committee, and I welcome any proposals which will make it more effective. I say equally firmly, that I will reject any proposals which will make the measure nugatory.

"I invited representations of exhibitors, renters and producers to consult with me, and I said they could come unfettered and have free to oppose. I thank those exhibitors who spent hours with me devising the terms of the Bill. On my own initiative I added the clause relating to the Advisory Committee, so that when the Bill becomes law I shall have the best and most constructive advice of an expert committee.

Quota Points

"One word on the Quota. I don't think anyone has ever concealed the fact that the quota must form part of any proposals. I think it is fair and businesslike that the quota is placed upon the renter in the first instance, and later in time and lower in amount on the exhibitor. The renter's quota is always higher than that of the exhibitors, so that they are encouraged to collect the best and not the worst. I have made the quota lower than was advocated in some quarters. I did this because I was determined that there must be competition.

"I claim that all requisites have been met. The only criticism that could be made is that we cannot produce films in this country. I do not believe it. British films are no new venture. Before the war British film producers were pioneers. I ask any man who was an exhibitor in those days to say if he was not showing British films far in excess of the quota. But for the war there would have been no need of Bills.

"We have authors, producers, actors, technicians. Is it seriously said that British films cannot be produced? America herself rationale for participating in a fierce competition with other Western nations to acquire India and Africa. With industrialized nations turning to protectionism, Britain resisted abandoning economic liberalism more than any other state, as the policy had been a cornerstone of its global dominance.[59] So, facing the possibility of quotas, the CEA could legitimately argue that the state was delivering exhibitors "to certain loss by forcing inferior films upon them to bolster up an industry which lacks the enterprise necessary to defeat the foreign producer."[60] The bill would bring "loss and disaster" to one section of the trade and "easy profits" to another which had neither deserved it, nor shown its worth. This was possibly a "political conception of justice" but "not in accord with British traditions in this respect." "All the Exhibitors ask is that they should continue to enjoy the same freedom as other men of business, to invest money to what they consider the best advantage."[61]

The ethic of merit was harder to sustain when the United States benefited from the proceeds of the British film market and fractures in Britain's film industry showed in the state's departure from avowed proclamations of the neutrality of market economics. The FBI and the state hoped that a domestic quota would stave capital outflow and attract investment by causing American companies to set up production units in Britain, boosting film production and possibly enabling Anglo-American cooperation. As it happened, United Artists was the only large U.S. company to achieve anything like a reciprocal relationship with British film producers.[62] Warner-First National and Fox set up production units at Teddington and Wembley, respectively, to supply their quota. Other American companies contracted British producers, creating as many as 59 new companies in 1929.[63] A few of these companies grew to the stature of major production units, but many were short-lived and produced films of variable quality, referred to as "quota quickies." Thus when the act was reviewed in 1936, a recommendation to institute some quality control on the films was passed by requiring a minimum labor cost of £7,500 per film.[64]

Despite the damaging consequences of subordinating distribution and exhibition to film production, it is doubtful if British films would have survived without some form of protectionism. As the film historian Sarah Street points out, "Much maligned, quota quickies nevertheless provided work for British technicians and valuable experience for directors, and there is evidence that some were popular with regional audiences."[65] Simon Hartog notes that one of the unannounced objectives of the Quota Act of 1927 was "the creation of one or more British combines."[66] The inflow of capital into the production sector stirred up the ambitions of city investors and film-makers who had an eye on the international market, pushing the industry toward rationalization and reorganization. The two combines that emerged and dominated the 1930s were Gaumont British Picture Corporation (GBPC), formed by the merging of Gaumont and Gainsborough, and Associated British Picture Corporation (ABPC) resulting from a merger between British International Pictures (BIP) and Associated British Cinemas (ABC).[67] However, concerns about Britain being "still a Hollywood Colony" arose again in 1944, when the British film industry integrated into the duopoly of ABPC and Rank Organization, both with significant ties to Hollywood's major studios.[68]

Dissenting Empire: Amending British Film

In 1938 two events altered the Quota Act's slippage between "British" and "British Empire" film: first, the colonial and dominion film industries responded unfavorably to assumptions of reciprocity built into the phrase "British Empire film"; second, the FBI advised the BT to amend the Quota Act's terminology as a consequence of uncooperative empire film markets. In 1936, two years before the Quota Act came up for renewal, the BT submitted a report to Parliament reviewing the act. This document, also called the Moyne Committee Report, recommended that the protection of a revised Quota Act be extended to "British Empire" films, but exclude "Dominion and Indian" films from a renter's quota.[69] By defining these films as British in the initial act of 1927, "It was not unnaturally anticipated that in the course of time reciprocal treatment of this kind would be given to films made in Great Britain by other parts of the Empire where film quota legislation might be passed. . . . This hope has generally not been fulfilled."[70]

Dominion and Indian films, not a category in the previous act, now needed to be distinguished from the definition of what constituted British Empire films, for a few reasons. In Australia, New South Wales and Victoria instituted a local quota for Australian films within the region. In response to the BT's objection to New South Wales raising its distributors' quota in 1935, the New South Wales government pointed out that their quota was regional and did not affect the rest of Australia. However, as correspondence in 1937 from the BT to the Dominions Office (R. D. Fennelly to C. R. Price) indicates, local Australian quotas did affect the national film industry because New South Wales distributors dominated over Australian film distribution. At the same time, a BT study of Canada revealed that a "United States-controlled renting company operating in this country is making arrangements to meet its quota obligations here by producing at Vancouver the Wild West type of film which it previously produced in Hollywood."[71] Confidential correspondences name Central Films as the main production house in Vancouver, making low budget films for Columbia Pictures International (a subsidiary of Columbia Picture Corporation of America) purely to fill renters quota in Canada and Britain.[72] Though no films are mentioned, the standing committee reviewing the British Film Quota Act expressed the conviction that Canadian and Australian film industries were in a good position—economically, culturally, and linguistically after the introduction of sound—to produce films for a British audience and encroach on Britain's market.

Consequently, a memorandum (signed by "R.A.," possibly for R. A. Wiseman of the Dominions Office) notes, "The producers feel very strongly that legislation passed here [in Britain] to protect their industry, which is at the moment in a very depressed condition, should not be of such a character as to give to Empire films all the advantages of films made in Great Britain unless the particular part of the Empire from which they come is affording us something like reciprocity."[73] Based on these recommendations, the BT proposed the disqualification of the following films from a quota.

   (i)   of films of inferior quality produced in British Columbia on behalf of United States interests;

  (ii)   of films made by native producers in India which are quite unsuitable to the United Kingdom market; and

 (iii)   of films produced in Australia for the purposes of the local legislation which can also count here.[74]

Despite requests from various dominion governments (particularly New South Wales, Canada, Australia, and India) against the amendment, the new 1938 Quota Act changed its stipulation.[75] To qualify for a quota in Britain now, a film had to be shot in studios or represent the labor of subjects domiciled in the United Kingdom (the Isle of Man and the Channel Islands), and *not* in the British Empire.

In correspondence prior to the amendment, the imperial expectation of reciprocity, implicit in the 1927 act, was made explicit. The changes came full circle to foreground what the state always knew to be at the crux of a British film quota—"the definition of 'British' in the Films Bill."[76] The original definition of British Empire in the Quota Act was straightforward: "The expression 'British Empire' includes territories under His Majesty's protection and territories in respect of which a mandate on behalf of the League of Nations has been accepted by His Majesty."[77] But as internal governmental correspondence reveals, the state's detailed consideration of the multiple deployments of the terms British and empire were tactical in an environment in which domestic opinions were sharply divided over Britain's domestic as opposed to its imperial obligations. Nonspecific references to "British Empire films" conveyed the impression of catering to Britain as well as its empire without committing to a preferential treatment of any one area, appearing to be noncontroversial on the question of imperial preference, which inspired anything but consensus within the British nation. The motion to disqualify dominion and Indian films from British quota privileges, for example, was passed in the House of Commons but was not supported in the House of Lords, which remained invested in the possibility of empire preferences and an empire market.[78]

The Britain that was in competition with Hollywood was a shifting entity, casting about for a market within its nation and its empire. Between the world wars, British dominions, colonies, and India continued to carry some of their archaic significance of being national prerogatives of the imperial nation while also bearing an emerging sense of an international community. Certainly, imperial relations were not strictly transnational, in that they did not involve relations between sovereign nation-states. But with the 1926 Imperial Conference's proposal to replace "Empire" with "Commonwealth," the former became a slippery term. This was revealed in the film-quota debates, particularly when it was suggested that Dominion and Indian films should count as "stateless films." One of the proposals for amending the 1927 Quota Act was that dominion and Indian films should count neither as British nor as foreign films. In practical terms, designating empire films "stateless" meant that British renters and exhibitors could not use films produced in the empire to meet their domestic quota for British films. But neither would British renters and exhibitors have to provide British films to fulfill a quota against empire films, as they would with a foreign film. The "[Quota] legislation at the outset should be confined to films made in the British Isles, but the area could be enlarged by the ad hoc addition of other parts of the Empire as and when thought fit. . . . In the meantime, they would be 'stateless' films."[79]

By imagining Indian, Canadian, or Australian films as floating free of their national moorings and in hoping to rationalize them on an ad hoc basis, the British State attempted to produce and control empire trade in a new manner, one adaptive to shifting relational boundaries within the imperium. This was not entirely viable; the idea of stateless films was ultimately dropped because it "would be a very difficult task to decide whether a particular Dominion (or part of a Dominion seeing that in Australia and Canada, for instance, [the Quota] was a State and not a Federal Matter) had done enough to earn reciprocity."[80] In this crisis of representation and adjudication we see an occasion when the British State attempted and failed to differentially integrate the empire into one flexible national regulation, because each sector of each film industry within the empire asserted its regional and national particularity.

"Modernism takes on as one of its missions the production of new meanings for space and time in a world of ephemerality and fragmentation," argues David Harvey.[81] Read in relation to its larger cultural moment, the Quota Act was a modernist imperial British film policy because its fragile production of a commodity called the "British Empire film" betrayed the motility of its context. The policy's semantic reformulation caught the state's definition of its realms of power in an act of transition. Official redefinitions of the British film commodity, desired and unforeseen uses of regulatory terminology, and subsequent amendments serve as the very chronicle of political change.

While the reasons for encouraging preference for British
films into India are mainly *economic*, I would not omit from
consideration arguments deriving from the *political* effect
of good British films.
—British Economic and Overseas Department, 1934

Is it not the truth that a film which will affect the prestige
of the white races in this country is a film to which objection
can be taken on *moral* grounds in practically every case.
Why drag in the purely *political* side?
—H. Hamill, Bombay Board of Film Censors, 1927

three ✳ **EMPIRE AND EMBARRASSMENT**

Colonial Forms of Knowledge about Cinema

The history of British imperialism in India is a history of India's rendition into meticulously organized data. As the anthropologist Bernard Cohn
has shown, India's governance was conditional on the colony's comprehen-
sibility to its foreign administrators, who interpreted and represented the
colonial land, its people, and their practices through familiar matrices of
grammar, history, science, and law. In British India control was an effect
of instrumental and incidental knowledge-production.[1] However, principal
changes in the imperial state's self-definition in the 1930s produced corresponding reassessments of its administrative machinery. So if the tran-
scription of Indian legal traditions into text-based models of British case
law was an important investigative modality of the state, by late empire the
question of appropriate evaluative precedent was far from clear. A case from
1936 serves as a good example. That year, an Indian named Soumyendranath
Tagore used the word *imperialism* in a speech, which led members of the Indian
Intelligence Bureau and the legislative department to argue over precedents,
distinguishing between cases in which the word had been deemed seditious

(*Emperor v. B. T. Randive, editor,* Railwayman) as opposed to permissible (in speeches by Indian nationalist leaders that had not warranted arrest). Legislators determined that using the term *imperialism* to describe a "government as established by law in British India" was sedition. In a strong case, Tagore's defense lawyers argued that he "never mentioned Government" and "by Imperialism he meant Capitalism." [2]

This incident, though minor, suggests an imperial government that rigidly proclaimed its affiliation to legal process: the key question debated was "whether an attack on imperialism amounts to an attack on the Government." In its colonies, the British State supported perceptions of a dichotomy between government and trade by censuring accusations of state domination while tolerating public criticism of imperialist trade practices. The projected distance between the realms of politics and economics, between state power and the capitalist market, is central to understanding why an initiative that started in Britain as an exploration of potential empire film markets was always reconfigured as something else in the colony: moral concern for colonial viewers, state interest in India's industrial development, cultural reciprocity.

In the last decade, transnational economic alliances have created global classes of privilege and destitution, provoking scholarly pronouncements about the decline of the nation-state as a "vector of historical change." [3] Though this may be too premature a dismissal of state power, it addresses a distinct loss in the ability of states (and multistate coalitions) to utilize overt international force in the pursuit of economic self-interest *unless* accompanied by moral justification. Michael Hardt and Antonio Negri propose a similar argument regarding the use of morality in war, though I disagree with their periodization. A "just war," they suggest, was linked to ancient imperial orders, which was expunged under the age of modernity and nation-states to reemerge only within the present paradigm of transnational economies. [4] They base this argument on the premise of a complete historical rupture between the eras of colonialism and transnationalism. As with their larger thesis about the novel nature of power in what they see as today's limitless and spatially dispersed world market, they polemically challenge the possibility of rearticulated historical continuities.

For Britain, the bureaucratization of colonies through the state's assumption of control over diverse economic adventures in the mid-1800s occurred in tandem with (and necessitated) a suppression of the state's investment in imperialism's profit motives. Only when the British State formally proclaimed itself as the governing authority over disparate territories did it need to disaggregate the logic of administration from that of capital. Proclaimed evacuations of the state's economic interest in foreign territorial occupation endowed respectability to the state, sacralizing the ethics of control and intervention. By the Boer wars (1899–1902), a critical counterdiscourse attacking the rapacity of colonialism made the state's economic ambitions definitively embarrassing within the metropole.[5] The two world wars, subsequent decolonizations, the proliferation of nation-states, international courts of arbitration, and peace-keeping forces of the first half of the twentieth century further consolidated the idea that violent political intervention was defensible only when used as an ethical necessity.[6] In a long-standing history of calling empire by other names—enterprise, uncontainable masculine energy, progress, religious salvation, civilization, what-have-you—Britain's state-level disavowals of economic imperialism, which can be traced to the middle of the nineteenth century, added a distinctively contemporary and contemporarily moral flavor to previous mythifications.[7]

When film historians accept at face value the British State's use of prevalent moral and racial anxieties to authorize an investigation of the Indian film market, they overlook a host of submerged economic rationales that complicate the language of moral panic. In a psychoanalytic reading of British anxiety about racially inclusive public and on-screen spaces in India, Poonam Arora examines imperial responses to British and Hollywood melodramas that depicted multiracial images to a mixed-race crowd in Indian theaters.[8] More in the category of social history, Prem Chowdhry's extensive research provides insight into the censorship and reception of imperialist Hollywood and British films in India, to narrate their effects on race relations, colonial nationalism, and imperial ideology.[9] Indeed, British state files are rife with observations about the detrimental effects of Hollywood films on colonial audiences. The following statement, issued at the international parliamentary conference "Pernicious Influence of Pictures Shown on Oriental Peoples," which took place on 5 August 1932 in Ostend, Belgium, expressed a widely held opinion: "The simple native has a positive genius for picking up false impressions and is very deficient in the sense of proportion. By the unsophisticated Malay, Javanese or even Indian and Chinese, the scenes of crime and depravity which are thrown on the screens are accepted as faithful representations of the ordinary life of the white man in his own country."[10] As shockingly racist as this characterization of colonial viewership might sound to our ears, it was at the time more socially and morally legitimate for the conference's participating parliamentarians from Britain, France, Netherlands, and Japan to express concern about impressionable natives than to discuss colonial film markets in purely economic terms. While their worries may have been genuine, that anxiety nevertheless facilitated their (by then unspeakable) economic interest in the colonies.

Moral anxiety was a defensible ground for banding against American cinema's domination of European and Asian colonies. By isolating imperial racism in our historical reconstruction, we simplify the mechanics of racism and run the risk of neglecting financial interests that acquired common cause with alarmist discourses about lower classes and darker races. We also miss the embedded contradictions of cinema under imperialism. As Chowdhry describes in careful detail, Britain's empire cinema was offensive to Indians. At the same time, initiatives collectively referred to as "Empire film schemes" were promoted on the back of the British Films Quota Act and were premised on the belief that British filmmakers could produce commercial films that appealed to Indians. Britain's schismatic construction of India as a land of naïve natives (provoking England's racial fears) who were also canny consumers (promising an untapped market) coincided in its efforts to comprehend Indian cinema and its audiences.[11]

In 1927 key points of contact between the state and the Indian film industry clustered around a state-funded fact-finding mission. Concomitant to the quota proceedings in Britain, the ICC was conducting an official inquiry in India, with a proclaimed focus on "the question of as to whether the censorship was lax and particularly whether a certain class of films were being exhibited which were harmful to the prestige of the white people."[12] This made a compelling platform for rationalizing an investigation of the Indian film industry when economically motivated state inquiries were tactically impossible and rhetorically unmentionable in India's nationalist climate. However, challenges to the ICC—including dissent within the committee's inner ranks and its encounter with vocal members of the Indian film industry—created a series of fractures between and within the state and industry. If each disruption resulted in a reformulation of the state's agenda, with the government attempting to reauthorize its role on the grounds of morality, it also demonstrated a fragmenting imperial state.

Unlike Chowdhry, I am less inclined to perceive "the coherence of the explicit message of colonialism, imperialism and racism" in British film policy and attempts "to demolish the nationalist rhetoric of one India."[13] Mechanisms of differentiation were incessantly at work to undermine the binaries of imperial Britain and colonial India, producing an archive of information on colonial cinema that is not so much sealed in imperialist ideology as "co-authored" by Indians and demonstrative of imperial breakdown.[14] What was initiated with imperial intent—with the FBI prevailing on the British State to seek trade privileges within the empire—could not be pursued because of challenges from *within* a state-sponsored agency and from a colonial film industry developing *outside* the limits of state control.

Beyond the adaptiveness of imperial state discourse, then, I am interested in the historical conditions of its transformation in relation to cinema. In this period, the ICC meticulously interrogated the Indian film industry, but their interrogation was accompanied by lively, if disorderly, rumors about Britain's attempted takeover of the Indian film market. As a collective, this archive describes official (commissioned) and contingent (rumored) forms of knowledge about the British State and the Indian film industry, generated within the metropole and the colony. Each studied the other, gauged limits, and defended opposing and on occasion complicit interests in India's film market. Much about the Indian film industry was also remaindered in this cycle of official reports and unofficial rumors. The arbitrations, rumors, and reactions in the wake of the commission, the shifts in the interviewers' locutions, and their elisions capture the mediations of the moment.

Commissioned Colonial Knowledge

After the 1926 Imperial Conference's recommendation that all empire territories undertake "remedial measures" to "encourage the exhibition of Empire films," the government of India declared that it was "incumbent on India in common with other parts of the Empire to consider whether or not she should take any steps to give encouragement to the British Empire films."[15] Indian members of the legislature had raised questions regarding India's film industry in previous years, but it was not until the BT prioritized empire markets that the state felt the need to issue an official directive to collate information on Indian film production and film audiences.[16]

ICC'S FORMATION * The Indian Cinematograph Committee attracted controversy from its very inception. On 14 September 1927 the home member J. Crerar moved a resolution in the Indian Legislative Assembly recommending that the governor general of India appoint a committee "to examine and report on the system of censorship of cinematograph films in India and to consider whether it is desirable that any steps should be taken to encourage the exhibition of films produced within the British Empire generally and the production and exhibition of Indian films in particular." [17] This resolution generated several questions in the Indian legislature, "confined mainly to the question of British Empire films and the constitution of the Committee." [18]

The significance of such questions cannot be undermined, because they draw attention to two signature events influencing the political climate of the ICC interviews: the Government of India Act of 1919 (implemented in 1921) and the Simon Commission of 1927–28. With the Government of India Act, India's Central Legislative Council was made bicameral, which meant that it was divided into the Legislative Assembly and the Council of State, with more Indians represented in both bodies. Provincial councils were also expanded and the electoral franchise extended to approximately five-million educated, land-owning Indians. These circumscribed inclusions of an exclusive class of Indians into the colony's decision-making process for restricted areas of legislation (education, public health, agriculture) were reviewed by the controversial Simon Commission, whose inquiry of colonial India's constitutional reforms overlapped with the period of the ICC interviews. [19] Because it lacked Indian representatives, the Simon Commission's visit to India provoked widespread demonstrations, riots, black flags, and slogans of "Simon, go back." If Indian members of the film industry expressed suspicion about British trade initiatives in the empire, Indian members of legislature feared the creation of a state agency empowered to adjudicate for the Indian film industry on a unilateral basis, through yet another "all white" committee.

Home Secretary H. G. Haig's resolution in the Council of State on 15 September 1927 altered the proposed cinematograph committee's objectives, emphasizing that the question of empire preference was driven by cultural rather than trade concerns on the part of the state.

> I do not think the Imperial Conference really had mainly in view trade interests at all. I think they had mainly in view the cultural and social side, and certainly the Government of India have [sic] not any trade interests in view. Their interest in the matter, so far as they have any interest at all, is simply that the proportion of films showing Empire conditions, Empire manners, should be increased. But the Government of India have [sic] come to no conclusion on this matter. They have been asked to consider the problem, and they remit the problem for the consideration of a Committee with a non-official majority and themselves express no opinion. [20]

Each successive stage in the FBI-initiated inquiry into the possibility of a protected empire market for British films in India diluted the issue of protectionism and accentuated the question of censorship. The "non-official" majority committee promised by Haig implied that there would be some Indian representation on the committee. Despite Haig's disclaimers, members in India's Council of State again questioned "the implications of the reference to British Empire films."[21]

The committee's intentions proved to be a source of tension throughout the interview process, eliciting defensive statements from committee members and guarded responses from witnesses. Thus when the ICC's newly nominated Indian Chairman Dewan Bahadur T. Rangachariar made his inaugural speech, he repeated that the committee was only "incidentally" interested in the possibility of creating Indian quotas for empire films.[22] He assured an interviewee, "The whole origin of this committee is due to agitation that there was a certain amount of misrepresentation of Western life so serious as to lower the prestige of the Westerner in the East."[23] He explained, "When members examine you, you should not understand it in the light of a cross-examination in court. This is not our object here. We want enlightenment . . . so please do not misunderstand us because we are all here on a common public purpose."[24] These statements are in conflict with subsequent official (and unofficial) portrayals of the interviews, which connect British trade interest in India with the ICC's appointment.[25] Rather than suggesting the commission's duplicity, such contradictions must be understood as endemic to the form of the bipartisan inquiry committee and systemic to this conduit of late-colonial state power in India.

The committee nominated by the Government of India's Home Department on 6 October 1927 was bipartisan in that it was divided equally between British and Indian members. The committee chairmanship was bestowed to Rangachariar, an advocate at the Madras High Court. The other Indians were K. C. Neogy, who went on to chair India's first finance commission in 1951, and Sir Ebrahim Haroon Jaffer, a prominent Pune businessman and father of parliamentarian Ahmed Jaffer, who would later become Mohammed Ali Jinnah's close associate and an important member of the Muslim League. As members of British India's legislative-judicial system, Col. J. D. Crawford, A. M. Green, and J. Coatman were the Englishmen nominated to the committee. The British members, particularly Green and Crawford, raised questions about granting preference to British films more frequently than other members. In contrast, the chairman often sided with witnesses when they proved resistant to answering such questions.[26] Notwithstanding these differences between the ICC members, neither they nor their witnesses fell neatly in line with nationalist allegiances during the interview process. And so it was that Crawford led queries about encouraging films that met "the needs of India"; some Indian film importers supported American films rather than the Indian film industry; and British members of Bombay's Film Censor Board worried that Britain's concern over Indian censorship was a cover for British trade interests in India.[27] ICC members — both Indian and British — attempted to be impersonal and neutral as they sought "enlightenment" about Indian cinema, to quote Rangachariar, trusting the state machinery of rational dialogue within the committee's defined sphere of public interaction. The ICC's contradictions, failures, and successes were part of this liberal-imperial apparatus.

Significant aspects of this interview apparatus were its composition and its procedure. The ICC had both written and oral questions. While its written questions were fixed, the oral format allowed for open-ended discussion, which enabled witnesses to alter, circumvent, and subvert interrogations. To draw from the Bombay and Karachi data alone, the committee interviewed a total of sixty-four men (filmmakers, journalists, editors, educationalists) and nine women. Of the women, one was the popular Anglo-Indian actress Ruby Myers, whose screen name was Sulochana. The other women included (Indian) principals of girls schools, a (British) president of the YMCA, and a (British) representative of the Bombay Vigilance Society. In addition to those on the committee, then, witnesses were primarily men, those identified as respectable community members or those who could function as authoritative experts and specialists.[28] Mass Indian film viewers, the largest growing constituency of silent films in India, were excluded.

One of the important findings of the ICC was that though Indian films were low in supply, they were high in domestic demand. In a written statement to the ICC, Rao Sahib Chunilal Munim, a representative of the Bombay Cinema and Theater Trade Association (BCTTA) and an agent of Universal Picture Corporation, USA, claimed that one-third of the film audiences in India were educated and two-thirds were uneducated, and that the attendance of the "illiterate class" viewing Indian films was increasing. Based on box-office receipts of theaters screening Indian versus imported films, J. Stenson, supervisor for the Bombay Entertainment Duty Act, showed that Indian films were more profitable, though fewer in number, than imported

5. The actress Sulochana, seen here in a publicity still, was among those interviewed by the ICC. Courtesy USC Cinema-Television Library.

films. For instance, from 1 January to 30 June 1927, the difference in favor of Indian films was Rs. 41,519.[29]

The ICC's parameters point to the committee's intermediary position between the state and the film-viewing populace. The ICC's exclusive membership and careful selection of witnesses represented, in microcosm, the state's reproduction of its realm of power. The ICC was composed of public figures and private individuals who were to transmit the interests of a new industry to the state while also transforming the state's political authority into rational dialogue. The Government of India was entrusting experts to conduct a detailed study through individual interviews and to formulate an advisory report. The state was, as it were, expressing a desire to evaluate and manage cinema's unruly progress in a colonial space. If the ICC was an extension of the state's efforts to organize a new industry, it was also correspondingly a means through which the industry defined and asserted its will on the government. The colonial state permitted the mechanics of liberalism to critique state-power through its choice of a bipartisan body commissioned with a broad directive to conduct open interviews.

Liberalism here is deployed less as a political doctrine than as an "ethos of recurrent critique" of state rationality, wherein the state ensures the possibility of a public discussion and reflection on state machinery while also defining the parameters of such a critique. In a form of governance that sets limits on its own authority, institutions of the public sphere guarantee a measure of autonomy and self-determination by allowing individual and entrepreneurial liberties, freedom of expression, and democratic representation while also expecting citizens to internalize the mandate of the state.[30] As members of a new bourgeoisie, Indian representatives (and, to an extent, the witnesses) of the ICC functioned as free individuals. Consequently, the committee's membership, which included private Indian entrepreneurs like Jaffer, dismantled the colonial state's institutional exclusions by mimicking a liberal state's extended public sphere. But their participation permitted the committee to only partially approximate the operation of public bodies under liberalism. Under colonialism, as was to become obvious when the ICC submitted their report to the state, the committee's authority extended only insofar as it could confirm the state's preexisting intentions for the Indian film industry. The ICC's proceedings reveal the committee's mediate position in relation to the state when it simultaneously extended and contradicted the state apparatus.

PROCEDURE AND FINDINGS * The committee's interviews yielded copious material, as it collated in the four volumes of *Indian Cinematograph Committee 1927–1928: Evidence* information from oral and written evidence given by witnesses involved in different aspects of India's silent-film production in Bombay and Karachi (volume 1; hereafter, ICC *Evidence* 1); Lahore, Peshawar, Lucknow, and Calcutta (volume 2); Madras, Rangoon, Mandalay, Jamshedpur, Nagpur, Delhi, and Calcutta (volume 3).[31] The committee questionnaire contained forty-five queries, each with several subquestions. Questions were clustered under two categories: "Part 1: Film Industry in India," which covered questions about the profile of Indian audiences, their preference in films, schemes for taxation, and state involvement; and "Part 2: Social Aspects and Control," which dealt with the structure and status of censorship of "sex" and "crime" films in India, and the misrepresentation of India as well as the West in films seen by Indians. Part 1 included a subsection, "Films of the British Commonwealth," that interrogated India's willingness to concede privileges to films from the British Empire.

22. Should India participate in the policy outlined in the resolution of the Imperial Conference to give some measure of encouragement to British Empire films, and if so would such participation (a) assist the development of her own film industry, (b) assist in making herself better known and understood throughout the Empire and the world, and (c) improve the standard of Western films shown in India. Have you any suggestions as to the methods of putting such a policy into practice and the limitation if any?

23. (a) To what extent can cinema pictures be used for making known the conditions, resources and habits of the peoples, and the activities of the various Governments, of the British Commonwealth of Nations to each other? (b) What measures do you suggest for getting the various Governments to co-operate to this end?[32]

Note that the questions were quite open-ended: the ICC did not assume that the industry's interests were consonant with the state's directive to explore imperial cooperation, but it sought spaces of consonance. As only two of forty-five questions addressed British Empire films and because the ICC in general de-emphasized the question of imperial preference, critical readings of the interviews focus primarily on the committee's interest in the influence of Hollywood films in India and in Indian censorship.

B. D. Garga states, "The heart of the matter was the increasing popularity of the American film in British India. Church, State and prudery combined in an effort to check this influence in 'various parts of the Empire' . . . and if it backfired it was entirely due to Dewan Bahadur T. Rangachariar, a brilliant South Indian lawyer, chosen to head the Indian Cinematograph Committee in 1927."[33] Someswar Bhowmik ascribes less intentionality to the chairperson's interventions (although admitting that they were undoubtedly strategic) and points out that it was "no mere coincidence" that the 1926 Imperial Conference, "advocating Imperial Preference for Empire Films (only a euphemism for British films) within the British Empire," closely followed the British Films Quota Bill of 1927.[34] Bhowmik reiterates, however, that empire films were "subsidiary" to the committee's interest in the status of Indian film censorship.[35] Eric Barnouw and S. Krishnaswamy suggest in their classic study of Indian cinema, which still offers the best account of the ICC to date, that the committee "was entirely in the spirit of the times," because it was asked to report on the potential of "Empire films" in India. "The phrase 'Empire films' was elusive, but the committee was urged to consider it as including Indian as well as British films. There was a spirit of partnership about this."[36]

Negotiations regarding the concept of "Empire film" in British and Indian documents suggest that the question of empire quota was progressively muffled in the ICC interviews because of a shift in the political stakes of the issue. Adroitness about the question of empire preference on both sides of this encounter created a context within which protectionist schemes could be discussed only in wary, submerged, and finally negative terms. The interviews unfold the legitimization of certain concerns and the delegitimation of others, as witnesses presented flaws in the premise of empire film reciprocity to underscore Britain's limited understanding of Indian cultural tastes and conditions in different ways.

To begin with, ICC witnesses asked for clarifications. Proposals based on arguments of cultural reciprocity, cooperation, and moral uplift would require a definite legislation, and the details of such a legislation had not been forthcoming from Britain. So witnesses asked how an empire quota would be apportioned. How many Indian films, as opposed to African, Australian, Canadian, or British films, would be permitted into India as part of the scheme? The Bombay film-exhibitor Rustom C. N. Barucha favored reciprocal arrangements within the empire, but only with "a definite and unequivocal piece of legislation": "I am not accepting anybody's assurance. So that if there is a general agreement between the various parts of the Empire, and if we take Australian films, say 1 per cent, Australia should agree to take 1 per cent of Indian."[37] When Universal's representative in India, Rao Sahib Chunilal Munim, was asked for his opinion, he indicated that an empire quota would become grounds for the exclusive promotion of British films in India, without giving Indian films any distinct assistance in other empire markets. He was firmly "opposed to any question of Empire protection. I want no protection for British films as such."

Q: But supposing you want to get your Indian films a market abroad, how do you propose to do it?

A: How I want to adjust the position of India in the quota system?

Q: Supposing the rest of the Empire takes up the British Empire quota system, under that India has a right to take up the whole of it if the films merit it. You are definitely out to exclude British Empire pictures in India?

A: Yes, because I am apprehensive about the extent that Indian pictures will again be at a disadvantage.

Q: Therefore, if there is any British Empire system which is introduced in India, the whole of it should be allotted to the Indian producer?

A: Yes.

Q: There was one exhibitor who was rather frightened by this quota system, being concerned mainly with the exhibition of foreign films [in India]. Would it help you if you allotted or retained one theatre for the exhibition of foreign films only?

A: *Well, in that case — that is the crucial part of your question, though it comes last. . . .* [S]upposing you are going to attach some value to our friend's argument here that there will be some theaters in India, whether in Bombay or other parts of India, for whom it will not be a paying policy to have anything to do with Indian pictures . . . if they are going to be free from showing Indian pictures, they must not be tied-down to British pictures."[38]

As an agent of Universal, Munim had a vested interest in the promotion of U.S. films in India. But others less affected by the source of foreign films also resisted the restriction of imports to empire films. A. Soares, principal of Antonio De Souza High School, argued that quota protections were not merit-based and would curtail the import of quality films. An "American film would be penalised, not because it is a bad film, but because it is American. A premium would be set on an Empire film, not because it is good, but because it is Imperial. And what would happen if, because of tariff manipulations, worthless Empire films were dumped upon India?"[39] Barucha (whose answers always make good copy) worded his objection more strongly: "It is just possible that we might lose some of the magnificent American pictures, and then all that we will have will be the British-made pictures for breakfast, lunch and dinner. Till we are able to stand on our own legs, whether Empire, American, British or otherwise, I want to select my pictures for my own audience on merits."[40]

Like British exhibitors, Barucha makes an argument here for free-market competition, although the rhetoric of nationalism in the Indian context, as opposed to interwar Britain, was clearly aligned with entrepreneurial independence. This did not necessarily translate into cultivating nationalist

Indian producers and audiences, so it was distinct from the Gandhian Swadeshi movement, which emphasized the use of indigenous products to unseat the economic basis of British imperial policies. Arguments for the exhibitor's right of choice frequently highlighted the heterogeneous nature of colonial India's film industry; witnesses had different visions of the industry's future based on competing notions of the key audience demographic for Indian films. For importers like Munim and Ardeshir Bilimoria who worked in the silent-film era, catering to the Anglophone Indian viewer with Hollywood films appeared more financially viable than producing Indian films for mass Indian audiences.

Members of the BCTTA noted that India's educated and illiterate classes had varying preferences in film genres: "To the educated classes:- Indian Life, Topical Indian News, National Literature, History and Social Dramas"; "To the illiterate population:- Topical Indian News, History and Mythology, Folklore Romances."[41] Indian historicals and mythologicals drew the greatest crowds, and the films mentioned repeatedly include *Lanka Dahan* (Phalke, 1917), *The Light of Asia* (Osten, 1925), *Raja Harishchandra* (Phalke, 1913, remade in 1917), *Sacrifice* (Gandhi, 1927), *Savitri* (Mannini, 1923; an Italian film claimed as a co-production by India's Madan Theaters), *Sinhagad* (Painter, 1923), and *Sri Krishna Janma* (Phalke, 1918).[42] Attendance and film screenings varied based on the urban location of theaters. In Bombay educated Indians, Anglo-Indians, and Europeans frequented cinema halls in the Fort area that screened Western films. Indians of all classes and religions visited theaters in Girgaum, which was dominated by Indian films, and largely Hindu audiences fraternized theaters around Parel-Dadar, which also favored Indian films.[43]

Exhibitors argued that as educated Indians were close to Europeans in judgment and sensibilities, such audiences were *not* in danger of misinterpreting American films as representative reflections of all white people. Following a British Empire film scheme, if theaters like the Excelsior or Empire departed from exhibiting American films in favor of screening Indian pictures, they would incur heavy losses, noted N. N. Engineer, a representative of the BCTTA.[44] Munim pointed out that "the Empress tried a *Naladamayanti* film [based on a story from the Indian epic, *Mahabharatha*], and they got about [Rs]12,000. Then they tried to show the same film in the Excelsior, and they hardly got about Rs.50 a day."[45] Conversely, foreign films did not draw as many uneducated or the non–English-speaking Indian spectators, and enforcing an empire film quota on theaters in Girgaum or Parel-Dadar would inflict heavy losses on those exhibitors.[46] In sum, Indian exhibitors argued, the Indian "masses" supposedly in danger of being corrupted by American films were not very interested in them.

In a pattern of argument discernible in various interviews, witnesses noted that for uneducated Indian audiences, foreign films were indistinguishable from each other and less appealing, on the whole, than Indian films. Arguments about the ill-effects of American films on Indians assumed passive audiences, which witnesses challenged with portrayals of an active, discriminatory audience base, thus systematically reorienting concerns about morality toward the predilection of India viewers. Linking culture back to trade, witnesses also pointed out that protection for empire films in colonial India would not so much facilitate the flow of culture and cooperation within the empire as reinforce existing inequalities in film finance. There were three bases for this argument. First, an empire quota could not alleviate prevailing tariff disparities between imported film prints and raw film stock in India. Second, Indian films could not hope to get reciprocal treatment in the foreign markets because Indian filmmakers had restricted access to finances, technology, and training. And third, the Indian film industry had a promising domestic market and a unique familiarity with it, so that an empire market at this stage was neither practical nor desirable.

Several witnesses argued that if state intervention was to be encouraged at all, it should be to equalize tariff disparities between the import of exposed films (film prints ready for exhibition) as opposed to raw film stock (unexposed film that Indian filmmakers needed for their productions). Among others, I. K. Yajnik, editor of Hindustan and Praja Mitra (later a film scenarist and producer), noted that an Indian film was about ten times more expensive than an imported film because of unfair custom tariffs.[47] Ardeshir Irani, proprietor of Imperial Film Corporation, who in 1931 produced Alam Ara, India's first talkie, explained that exposed positives cost two annas per foot, which greatly undercut the cost of producing an Indian film after purchasing raw film stock at one anna per foot.[48] While foreign film prints were numerous and cheap, Indian films were more popular (Lanka Dahan and Krishna Janma had yielded several times their cost of production as profit to the producers) but scarce and expensive.[49]

Given the expense of raw film stock and Indian film production, Indian films were not sold but circulated at a percentage of box-office returns in urban areas and at a fixed hire in moffusils (small towns and villages).[50] This resulted in an undeveloped Indian–film-distribution sector because the producer dealt directly with exhibitors, and created a lag time before producers began work on their next film, given their increased dependence on box-office receipts. As Indian films couldn't compete with foreign films on an equal footing in the domestic market because of restrictive tariff rules and a lack of state support, state-sponsored discussions of Indian films for an empire market were meaningless.

Moreover, Indian film producers had little evidence that there was any demand for Indian films in England or the British Empire, though some filmmakers disagreed with this. In this regard the late 1920s and the late 1990s present an interesting counterpoint. In distinction to the period from 1947 to 1998, during which Indian cinema turned toward its domestic market, Indian producers considered the global market an attractive alternative in the colonial and transnational eras, given the government's lack of restrictions on the entry of foreign finance. In the 1920s, when U.S., British, and German producers showed an interest in India's domestic film market, Britain's empire quota proposals involved convincing Indian filmmakers of the possibility of an empire audience for Indian films. Like filmmakers today, colonial Indian filmmakers who wished to address a wider audience had to make high investments to plan for an international release, thus risking the possibility of having to alter content to appease a new market, possibly souring domestic audiences, and sustaining higher losses in case of a flop. The producer Himansu Rai, among the few who initiated international collaborations in the 1920s, commented on what it would take for Indian cinema to secure an international market: "There is no way unless one is prepared to risk very big sums of money and produce a picture as good as possible and then go to England with some ten thousand pounds, take a cinema house and begin showing there, even at a loss, and try to make the widest possible publicity."[51]

Few colonial Indian filmmakers were able or willing to do this. Speaking of the screenings of Sri Krishna Janma and Shahjahan in London, Ardeshir Irani commented, "But they were not at all liked by the people there."[52] Madan Theaters sent Nur Jahan and Druvacharita to England, but apparently they were returned.[53] As Barucha confirmed, the provision for British Empire films in the British bill would be a "dead letter" as far as India was concerned, because of the cultural specificity of Indian films.[54] Rustomji Dorabji, proprietor of Wellington, West End, and Venus Cinemas, noted that no other country could make films for the Indian market because they lacked the knowledge of the

Indian star system and of local themes.[55] Similarly, according to S. K. Naique, honorary general secretary of the Aryan Excelsior League, an organization that studied the moral and educational influences of the cinematograph industry, Indian films were popular in India despite the fact that they frequently fell short of the production standards of Western films because they were "better followed, understood and relished."[56] Narrating his memories several decades later, the film producer and director J. B. H. Wadia confirms this. He recalls seeing "Dadasaheb Phalke's memorable *Lanka Dahan* tagged to an American feature film in the old West End Cinema. . . . As a Westernised Parsee youngster I had a hearty laugh at the sight of a muscular Sita played by a male artiste" in Phalke's film, though "in the ensuing years I clean forgot the American film but have always retained the memory of *Lanka Dahan.*"[57]

Witnesses like N. D. Gandhi and P. S. Talayarkhan of Orient Pictures, who together produced the successful film *Sacrifice*, which was based on a Tagore play, felt that India as yet lacked the facilities and finances to compete internationally.[58] Others, like Soares, suggested that it was not so much a matter of technical facilities as cultural sympathies. Indian films would be "distinctive and unique," and Indian cinema's popularity could only be premised on the acceptance of those qualities.[59] So most witnesses believed that significant preparatory work was required before empire markets could become hospitable to Indian films.[60] This implied that a British Empire film scheme's foundational assumption of cultural reciprocity—based on the argument that India should open itself up to empire films as a way of getting Britain and its dominions to return the gesture—was nonsensical, given the lack of preexisting interest and understanding of India in other parts of the empire.

With such arguments, witnesses disarticulated the generic "Empire film" of the British film policy from the specific appeals of "Indian films." Whenever ICC questions linked the protection for empire films to increased cultural traffic within the empire, interviewees created a dialogic context within which such suggestions seemed tantamount to the sole promotion of British films in India. As R. Venkataram, assistant editor for the *Indian National Herald*, asserted, "Nationalist Indian opinion will not tolerate that kind of thing."[61] The primary defense of the Indian film industry against state incursion, however, was not based on patriotic grounds but on pragmatic and commercial ones. Audiences weren't created by dictating exhibitor quotas, argued Hague, Pathé's proprietor in India.[62] It was more a question of a film's theme and its appeal to audiences. In Munim's words, "There is no use in compulsion in these matters."[63]

ICC'S FINAL REPORT * In chapter 6 of the final version of the *Report of the Indian Cinematograph Committee 1927–1928* (hereafter, ICC Report), which was based on these interviews, the committee made a unanimous and persuasive case to oppose artificial aid for British films in India, because they stood a good chance of finding an audience, "provided that they are of fair or average quality and that the prices are reasonable."[64] (The ICC proposed that films of educational value, rather than entertainment films, could be exchanged between various territories of the empire by mutual agreement). A majority of the cinema-going public in India were Indian Hindus, Muslims, or Christians, unlike the settler colonies of Australia or Canada where a majority of the cinema viewers were of the same race as the British and shared similar social customs and habits. For Indian viewers, British and American films were equally foreign, and "if too much exhibition of American films in the country is a danger to the national interest, too much exhibition of other Western films is as much a danger."[65] Here the ICC was repeating a common perception among all witnesses: as H. Hamill, a member of the Bombay Board of Film Censors, commented, when it came to immoral films, the "danger will remain no matter who produces the film. Whether it is a British or an American company that produces, they will have to cater for people who want sensation."[66]

With India's economic conditions, the ICC argued, it "can afford but a poor market or outlet for Empire films," so "India stands to gain indeed if really her films can find an outlet to an equal extent to which Empire films can find an outlet here," but given existing circumstances, that was not likely.[67] Moreover, out of the 108 feature films produced in England between 1925 and 1927, India had imported as many as seventy-four films. Notwithstanding this fact, Hollywood films constituted 80 percent of India's film imports, while British films accounted for a meager 10 percent. As long as India was dependent on the United States for a majority of its imports while constituting no more than half of one percent of America's cinema revenue, Indian filmmakers could "ill afford to estrange" America by giving preference to empire films.[68]

Beyond being about imperial trade, the ICC Report pointed out that "imperial preference is a large and complicated question."

The question of Imperial Preference is so bound up with so many other political issues of a very vital and substantial character that on a small issue relating to the cinema industry, even if it were an aid to the Indian industry, a view which we do not hold, the question cannot be examined satisfactorily. The question is in fact bound up with issues political, racial, economic and the like. . . . It is the introduction of this question in the terms of reference to this Committee which has, in a great measure, induced the suspicions of the people of this country as to the motives of the Government in appointing it.[69]

In the final analysis witnesses not only rejected the impact of foreign films on Indian morality as adequate grounds for an empire quota but also proposed a special quota for Indian films in India. This altered the terms of discussion so radically that the committee's final report, reflecting its gathered evidence, recommended that Indian producers receive public financing for their films and that protectionist policies such as reservation of screens, theaters, or seats be extended exclusively to films produced locally.[70] "Even had we decided on an Empire quota for India, it is obvious that the whole of it would have been allotted to Indian films."[71]

This last suggestion was not unanimous. The final version of the ICC Report contains a minute of dissent, filed by the British members of the committee against a quota for Indian films and against financial support for Indian producers. The ICC's minute of dissent contradicts initial statements of the commission's goals, which in no uncertain terms include a directive to determine what kinds of "suitable Government action whether legislative or administrative may be an effective incentive and encouragement to private film production."[72] Confronted with demands for supporting Indian films, we find the British dissenters saying "God helps those that help themselves."[73] They argued against state support of "a luxury industry which without assistance has expanded rapidly and is earning good profits,"[74] remarking, "we object most strongly on principle to the suggestion that Government should give public money on easy terms or on any terms to an industry which by no stretch of the imagination can be regarded as a key industry."[75]

The ICC Report was celebrated as enlightened and forward-looking in Britain, but it contained too many undesirable recommendations to be put into practice.[76] Though the promotion of empire films within India was discussed in no more than one chapter of the report, the issue was given prominence in British reportage. The Times, an English newspaper, began an article on the report, "The British film maker will find little comfort in the recommendations of the Committee which has just reported on the cinema industry in India. Preferential treatment for British films is rejected. . . . [T]he fears of those who complain that Western films tend to bring Western civilization into contempt, and to demoralize the Indian public, are sharply dismissed as unfounded."[77] Perhaps this article, which finds the ICC suggestion to offer a quota for Indian films "rather startling," best expresses where British interests lay.

Studying the coeval origins of liberalism and imperialism in British political thought, Uday Mehta notes that "concealed behind the endorsement of [liberalism's] universal capacities are the specific cultural and psychological conditions that are woven in as preconditions for the actualization of these capacities."[78] With British Empire film schemes, the British Films Quota Bill utilized liberalism's language of political inclusion to get leverage within colonial film markets, leaving itself exposed to its own contradictions as the exclusionary basis of empire quota arguments came to the fore. With the ICC interviews, members of the Indian film industry dismantled quota proposals on the grounds of persistent structural inequities that eroded the premise of bilateral dialogue.

Contingent Colonial Knowledge

On 23 March 1928, Rai Bahadur J. P. Ganguly, undersecretary for the Government of India, wrote a letter to the secretary of the Government of Bombay demanding, in all seriousness, to know which Indian film production firms were British. Apparently, Britain's BT (Board of Trade) was anxious to receive information on Indian production companies, anticipating that Indian filmmakers would apply to register their films as British and claim quota eligibility under Britain's 1927 Film Quota Act. As the BT was responsible for registering all films, they required an immediate and complete report of Indian production firms. They requested a "body of information" to "enable the Board to come to a decision as to the registration of films submitted by firms in your territory, more particularly in cases where it is established that local [Indian] firms are truly British in character and sentiment."[79]

Quite apart from the notion that Indian firms could reflect a "truly British" character, India's undersecretary and the British BT were making some questionable assumptions.[80] They assumed that Indian production firms were traceable at a time when in fact the industry was disorganized, with some producers disappearing after a few films. They also assumed that the information to make "a determination in each case as to whether a film is British in the sense of the Bill" was quantifiable and that someone in India (in addition to the BT in Britain) had the wherewithal to preside over such decisions.

In India the task of gathering such information went to police commissioners (who were typically British and served as ex officio heads of regional film-censor boards), with the provision that "the owners of film companies were not told why the inquiries are being made." The police knew that secrecy would reduce both the amount of voluntary information given as well as the verifiability of information sources; acting on the advice of the police, the Government of India retracted their confidentiality clause and informed Indian production firms of the inquiry's purpose.

The police identified twenty-four firms producing silent films in India, including fourteen in Bombay and surrounding areas, four in Bengal, two temporary production houses in Madras, two in Punjab, and two in Delhi. The better-known firms were in or around Bombay, including Imperial Film in Grant Road, Kohinoor Film in Dadar, Maharashtra Film in Kolhapur, and Sharda Film in Tardeo. The police sent them questionnaires asking for such information as the firm's name, registration, owner's nationality, capital, types of films produced, and production capacity. The Indian response to the questionnaires was one of suspicion, skepticism, and apathy. Only six of twenty-four responded, with others claiming reluctance "as they do not expect to gain anything, it being considered by them most improbable that their films will ever be exhibited in England." Looking into this film industry, which was run on a more-or-less artisanal model, the police commissioners also found that "companies in the [Bombay] Presidency are reluctant to give any information . . . as they are afraid it would leak out to their rival companies." Without being an act of direct rebellion against the state, such obfuscation nevertheless hindered the state's efforts at systematizing information about the Indian film industry. Unlike the ICC investigators who fielded witnesses that actively deflected questions about an empire quota, police investigators encountered instead the absence of a public domain of citable information that could be collated and quantified. The fledgling Indian film industry blindsided the state because it was organized by another order of information, one based on a variable system of trust.

Rumors about the British film industry were among such informal intrusions into state power. Well before the ICC came to India, Indian rumor mills were abuzz with news of British schemes to dominate the Indian film market. There were two distinct waves of rumors—in 1925–1926 and in 1937–1938—preceding and following the passage of the British Film Quota Acts of 1927 and 1938. In 1926 news reached India that a million-pound British syndicate was under construction to promote British films in the empire. The Crown government had allegedly proposed the scheme to the Government of India and had taken contributions from the maharajas of Kashmir, Alwar, Patiala, Bikaner, Jaipur, and the Agha Khan.[81] The princely states may have been believed to have contributed to a British film syndicate, as most Indian princes were Crown loyalists and British protectorates. The British India government permitted them to maintain sovereignty over their kingdom, so their culpability in a purported British scheme to dominate Indian cinema must have seemed plausible. The syndicate was reputed to have undertaken the construction of Indian cinema halls in order to screen exclusively British pictures.

A year later, in January 1927, *The Bioscope*, a U.S. film journal, reported that Alexander Macdonald ("explorer, traveler, author") had registered a company called Seven Seas Production with capital of £10,000 to produce empire-themed films. In February of the same year *The Bioscope* ran an introductory announcement of a company called British International Film Distributors, which was to offer British films for distribution all over the empire, with the exception of Canada. *The Bioscope* also ran an article titled "Indian Circuit for British Group?" which contained an interview with J. J. Madan, managing director of Madan Theaters, the largest importer of foreign films in India. Madan was quoted as saying, "Some important British Financial Groups are anxious to obtain control of our chain of ninety-one cinemas in India, Burma and Ceylon."[82] None of this was substantiated, but the reports confirmed prevailing anxieties in the Indian film industry and vitiated the ICC initiative, as was clear in an exchange between the film exhibitor Barucha and A. M. Green, a British member of the ICC, wherein Barucha responded, in a convoluted manner, to a question about his opinion on a British Empire quota in India.

> MR. BARUCHA: On that point I would invite the attention of the Committee to the preliminary remarks which the Chairman of this Committee made on the opening day. In which he tried to make it clear that the present inquiry was an inquiry on its own merits and not a propaganda business. There are certain circumstances which as far as the [Indian film] trade is concerned it is very difficult to get away from. I am point-

ing out now a small circumstance which occurred some time in June or July last when we had in India a visit from a gentleman called Captain Malins who ostensibly was making a tour on a motor-bike throughout the world. The significance of his visit comes in this way, that he seemed to go a little out of his way when he got a resolution passed before the Calcutta Parliament to the effect that the American films were subversive of all morals and religion . . .

Q [A. M. GREEN]: He is in no way connected with this Committee?

A: After that came the announcement that a British Syndicate has been formed in England with a million pounds capital and an empire wide scheme. There was also at the same time the announcement that Sir Chimanlal Setalvad was placed at the head of the Syndicate's ramification in India. So all these three things put together there is some justification for the public to suppose that there is some scheme which will be put forward at the end of this enquiry with which the country, as a whole, may not be in agreement.

Q: I hope I shall be allowed to put my question to the witness, and after that he may be allowed to make his protest, if necessary. I can assure him that I had no intention or anything of that kind in my mind. I have not even yet developed my question. I do not see the relevancy of his remarks at all.

A: The relevancy of my remarks comes in this way . . .

CHAIRMAN: I cannot say that his remarks are altogether irrelevant.

A: Thank you, Sir. There is the public feeling and a large section of the trade is also saying the same thing; so that before the trade is committed to any attitude on the question of quota, it is only fair to the trade that they get a clear idea of what exactly is meant by the whole thing.[83]

In this interaction, the interviewer is put in the distinctly uncomfortable position of having to account for the Indian film industry's skepticism of the ICC's motivations, based on three preceding and seemingly unrelated events. In the course of his interview, Barucha returned repeatedly to these incidents, insisting that they were "the three material circumstances that cut at the root of the good will which an Inquiry Committee like this should carry in its wake."[84] Like other witnesses, Barucha circumvented the immediate questions to respond to the subtext.

Contrary to Barucha's fears, however, British efforts to promote commercial British films in the empire were unsuccessful, or dispersed and unstable at best. Ardeshir Bilimoria, director of Madan Theaters in Bombay, which had a veritable monopoly on the exhibition of imported films, felt that educated Indians would exhibit an affinity for British rather than American films, because when his theater screened British films like " 'The House of Temperley,' 'The Prisoner of Zenda,' 'Rupert of Hentzau' and 'England's Menace' . . . [t]hey were a great draw. But unfortunately this particular company [unnamed by the witness] ceased to exist as soon as the war came." [85] There is no evidence of a large-scale, organized distribution network for commercial British films in the empire, and no British distributors were posted in India in the 1920s. Regimental and club cinemas of the 1920s, which screened films exclusively for British military troops and club members, imported films directly from America, Germany, and England. B. D. Gupta, managing proprietor of some of these exclusive theaters, noted that in 1926 he had imported only one film from Britain because "British pictures which are really good are produced at an enormous cost and I cannot afford to purchase them at all." [86] American comedies and adventures starring Charlie Chaplin, Harold Lloyd, Jackie Coogan, and Douglas Fairbanks were both affordable and popular with expatriate British and local audiences.

After the arrival of talkies, local branches of Indian and U.S. distribution companies distributed British films. For instance, British and Dominion films were distributed by Madan Theatres, Gainsborough Pictures films were distributed by India's British Empire Film Corporation, and Korda's London Films productions were frequently distributed by local representatives of United Artists, USA, though Korda also used Indian companies such as New India Distributors. Several British films were also distributed in India through Gaumont and Pathé-India.[87] While the British State did not assist in the distribution of commercial films (distinct from shorts, documentaries, nonfeatures, and propaganda films), there is evidence that a few individuals and organizations attempted to systematize empire-wide schemes.

In 1926, prior to the Quota Act, the FBI sent an "offer" of "Co-operative Marketing" to the BOT, arguing that "the great American companies have elaborate distribution organizations in the Dominions," while British companies suffered through a lack of coordinated distribution.[88] The FBI offer proposed an organization to provide dominion exhibitors with British films and projected the company's set-up costs at £200,000.[89] In 1930 the secretary of state for the colonies appointed a Colonial Films Committee to examine, among other things, "the supply and exhibition of British films" in the empire. With the FBI's help, the committee set up a distribution company called the British United Film Producers (BUFP) with a provision of up to £1,000 from colonial governments, to distribute British films to the colonies "at reasonable trade rates."[90] None of these organizations added up to a million-pound syndicate, and there is little information about which films, if any, were distributed by these firms.[91] But such proposals, frequently no more than blueprints, do suggest that rumors of British interest in an empire market were not baseless. In Britain explorations into the possibility of organized distribution in the empire accompanied discussions of protective quota legislation.

Rumors have always held a special discursive status in colonial society, and in this case, anticolonial hearsay was a tangible and constant form of resistance to actual and potential colonial film schemes. Ranajit Guha points out in his foundational essay on Indian peasant insurgency that there is a "correspondence between the public discourse of rumor and . . . popular act[s] of insurrection."[92] Indian rumors about a British syndicate wishing to monopolize India's film industry were of a very different order than those that pushed a political rebellion to its crisis, but the similarity lies in their rhetoric of opposition against a foreign state, which had the power to legislate. Identifying rumor as a unique mode of utterance in the colonial context, Guha notes that rumors distinguish themselves from the "ideal site of official truth," by appearing to participate in a collectivist discourse.[93] (Additionally, rumors can be imbued with sanction when put in print, as with rumors of a British film scheme for India which, when repudiated by the ICC, became part of the construction of an official truth). Rumors are ambiguous, anonymous, and difficult to authenticate. They are transitive, reappearing in different versions at different times, bringing diffuse fears about socioeconomic inequities into the realm of discussion.

These aspects of rumors about Britain's empire scheme appear in the wake of BT's 1936 *Moyne Committee Report*, an assessment of the 1927 Quota Act that renewed interest in empire film markets in Britain. In 1937 the British paper *The Morning Post* reported that the British State was offering a subsidy to its film industry to set up "film studios and cinema theaters in India with a view to competing with Germany and America."[94] The Indian newspaper *The Times of India* printed these reports under the alarmist title "Threat to Indian Film Industry" (5 August 1937) and *The Statesman* announced a "British Proposal: Preparing Subsidy Scheme" (27 August 1937). Quoting these articles, the newly formed Indian Motion Picture Producers Association (IMPPA) wrote to the British BT (in 1937 and 1938) demanding verification or denial of the reports. The rumors gave popular resentment a point to rally around, giving voice to the Indian film industry's anxieties about imminent state policy. Members of the Indian Legislative Assembly raised angry questions about the alleged scheme in Parliament.[95]

A passionate pursuer of this issue was the nationalist politician S. Satyamurthi, a member of the Indian Legislative Assembly and later president of the Motion Picture Congress of India in 1937 and 1939.[96] Satyamurthi was active in India's Non-Cooperation Movement and frequently spoke out in Parliament against film censorship. He supported cinema as an object of study and as a nation-building force, and exercised great influence on Tamil film artists like K. B. Sunderambal and M. K. Thyagaraja Bhagavadhar. According to the film historian S. Theodore Baskaran, Bhagavadhar, a leading South Indian star and singer, gave up imported silks to wear homespun khadi at Satyamurthi's request.[97] The parliamentarian's response to the government's refusal to address the legitimacy of the empire-scheme rumors was one of sarcasm.

> MR. S. SATYAMURTHI: May I know the reason why the Government of India do not wish to write to the Secretary of State for India and find out if there is such a proposal? Can't they afford one *anna*?
>
> THE HONOURABLE SIR THOMAS STEWART: In the interest of economy.
>
> MR. K. SANTHANAM: May I know whether the British Government are protecting the film industry in England by a quota system?
>
> THE HONOURABLE SIR THOMAS STEWART: I submit that [the need for this question] does not arise.[98]

The British quota was a sensitive issue and became, in India, a referent of the state's benevolence toward Britain's national film industry, as well as its active indifference or ill-will toward Indian cinema. The state refused to remove high tariffs on raw film stock entering the colony, thus artificially suppressing the growth of indigenous film trade, and supporters of Indian industry were not averse to highlighting such discrepancies in state policy during empire-quota discussions. Though the state did not issue a denial at Satyamurthi's request, it did leave a paper trail of confidential discussions about the testy exchange over rumors of empire-subsidy schemes and empire syndicates.[99] Internal letters within Britain's Public and Judicial Department at the India Office questioned the appropriateness of Satyamurthi's question:

could the Government of India be questioned on potentially private syndicates?[100]

Officials in Britain admitted knowing of plans for syndicates but asserted that the government had "never been approached." The truth of this statement is difficult to verify: the FBI certainly approached the state in 1934 and 1938 to initiate imperial preference in films with India, but efforts of private syndicates are harder to trace.[101] R. Peel, secretary of the Public and Judicial Department, India Office, dismissed the rumors as "entirely a figment of the *Morning Post's* imagination," noting that reports of syndicates were received with "great hostility in the Indian press."[102] Nevertheless, news items of this nature persisted, and in 1938, *The Film Daily*, a U.S. trade publication, reported that two British producers—Capt. Norman Eric Franklin and Sir William Frederick O'Connor—had acquired £50,000 from a private syndicate in Britain to set up a production unit in India. Captain Franklin is reported to have said, "We expect to arrange for the rest of our financing in Hollywood during the next month."[103]

A significant difference between the first round of rumors in 1927 and their resurgence ten years later was that the Indian film industry had expanded and formalized in the meantime. It acquired stability with the emergence of sound technology and studios. It gained official presence with organizations like the IMPPA, registered under the Company's Act on 8 October 1938, joining the ranks of organizations like the Federation of Indian Chambers of Commerce and Industry (FICCI), which was formed in 1927 under the leadership of G. D. Birla and Sir Purshottamdas to represent Indian capital against the colonial government. The film industry had also gained access to public opinion through nationalist film journals like Bombay's *filmindia*, the Madras-based *Talk-A-Tone*, Calcutta's *Varieties Weekly*, the Gujarati-language *Chitrapat* and long-standing *Mouj Majah*, as well as the self-proclaimed "Biting, Fighting, Attacking Journal" *Sound* in the 1940s.[104]

By the late 1930s, the British State was already severely divided on the issue of intervening in India on behalf of British film trade, aware of the uproar that any structural, policy-based alteration to a colonial industry could produce. In 1937, for instance, Sir Ralph Glyn of the BT attempted to reintroduce a discussion of empire film quotas, writing to Rt. Hon. Oliver Stanley of the Board of Education, "Possibly, whilst the Film Bill is before Parliament and in most people's minds, you may be able to suggest something that would also have the approval of the India Office."[105] R. D. Fennelly of the BT pursued the possibility with members of the India Office (particularly R. Peel and A. Dib-

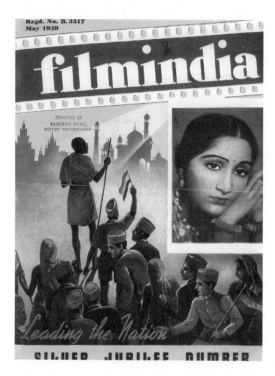

6. Indian film journals consolidated their position with appeals to nationalism. Courtesy NFAI.

din), who were restrained and discouraging in their response: "The American film no doubt predominates in India for the same reason as it predominates in this country, because it is in the main better and cheaper than the British film. Any attempt to subsidise the British film industry in India would be most unpopular and would probably do more harm than good. This seems clear from the fuss which arose from a statement made by the *Morning Post*, entirely on its own initiative, to the effect that H.M.G. [His Majesty's Government].were proposing to subsidise the setting up of British film studios in India."[106]

Official consensus in Britain moved toward the notion that FBI's interest in exploiting an Indian film market was best left to commercial initiatives. Britain's Department of Overseas Trade concurred that "any film shown [in India] which was known to have been subsidised would cause more political trouble in the country" than provocative British or Hollywood films.[107] Ironically, though the ICC interviews of 1927 were intended as a possible preamble to a British Empire film scheme in India, they instead marked the beginning of the state's demurral from involvement in India's film industry.

Limits of Colonial Knowledge

Several Indians who resisted the state's interference in Indian cinema nevertheless shared their colonial administrators' beliefs that film was a nonessential commodity and a symbol of degenerate technological modernity. If legislators like S. Satyamurthi were convinced of cinema's value, other officials could be heard expressing familiar doubts about the new habit of visiting movie theaters. To quote Gaya Prasad Singh, who represented the seat of "Muzaffarpur cum Champaran; non-Mohammadan," in the Legislative Assembly on 1 March 1933: "Just to be shut up in a dark room in the evening with all sorts and classes of people and sexes is not a very happy idea for me. (Laughter)."[108] Urban, educated Indians worried about the effect of cinema in "backward" areas, weighing the question in terms of the effects of undeniably good technologies (like the railways) against the influence of dubious ones (like cinema, motorcars, and firearms).[109]

Similarly, the nationalist possibilities of cinema influenced filmmakers in different ways. The director Dadasaheb Phalke claimed, "My films are *Swadeshi* in the sense that the capital, ownership, employees, and the stories are *Swadeshi*," while the producer-actor Himansu Rai spoke of cinema as an "International Art" that could only improve with foreign collaboration.[110] The key question "What is cinema?" was politically charged in a colonial context because it required a simultaneous response to India's status in relation to modernity and nationalism. Discussing and legislating for the Indian film industry—which was subject to colonial state policies while it drew from, and promoted the values of, India's emergent civil society—accentuated the complexities of the colony's new social formations. A motley mix of people joined the Indian film industry from divergent classes, castes, professions, and religions. Additionally, a diversity of political attitudes toward nationalism and a variety of backgrounds forming India's film industry produced a heterogeneous range of artistic ambitions for cinema. This factor eludes the government files of Britain and India.

Indeed, the archive's historical realities are delimited in the sense of being produced by official discourse in at least two obvious ways. First, the interviews recreate a contained public sphere of dialogue officially deemed rational and representative, replicating (rather than interrogating) the ideologies and subjectivities of interviewed personnel. Second, urban, rural, and moffusil constituencies of mass Indian cinema-goers are commented on and statistically calibrated rather than included in their own voices, because they cannot be accommodated among a body of experts. The fractures and fraternities between the imperial state, the ICC, the emerging entrepreneurial class of Indian filmmakers, and the commentators on the industry were revealed in the interviews.

Himansu Rai was someone the ICC interviewers could understand well. They shared his respectable educational and class background. At the time of his interview, Rai was flush with the success of *The Light of Asia* and had just completed co-producing *Shiraz* (silent, Osten, 1928) with Berlin's UFA (which had bought the film's distribution rights in Europe) and British Instructional (with rights to Britain). Co-productions were not the norm at the time, so ICC members were extremely interested in Rai's testimony. His films suggested the possibility of an international and perhaps imperial circuit for Indian cinema. Unfortunately, Rai informed the ICC, though the German company Emelka had distributed *The Light of Asia* in Europe, he had found no interested exhibitors in Britain. This appeared to confirm what Barucha, among other exhibitors and producers, had reported to the ICC: "If the answer really depended on the merits of the Indian picture, I would have said I expect my pictures to be popular in America or in England. But that is not the only factor operating in the world to-day. Racial prejudices have got to be overcome. There are some people who, if they come to India and see an Indian picture, are bound to like it; but as to getting it across to their own country and exhibiting it there, it is *infra dig*."[111] Surprisingly, Rai disagreed with this explanation despite his negative experience in Britain. He was convinced that Britain's indifferent treatment of his film was not because of Indian cinema's cultural non-exportability but because of his associate Niranjan Pal's poor business acumen.[112] Taking charge of failing business, Rai used his acquaintance with Sir Atul Chatterjee, the Indian high commissioner in London, to procure a screening of the film at Buckingham Palace to an audience of King George V and Queen Mary. This raised trade interest in the film.[113]

Rai was clearly an enterprising man. Colin Pal, the son of Rai's longtime collaborator Niranjan Pal, wrote about the time that Rai noticed a shot of a Delhi tram with a "Buy Dunlop Tyres" sign in a modern scene from *The Light of Asia*, then promptly took the film to Dunlop executives and acquired Rs. 10,000 for retaining the shot, which was just enough money to hire an Indian theater for screening the film. In addition to his initiative, however, Rai's social connections repeatedly assisted his career. His vision of film as an international art was facilitated by his access to international markets.

Born into a wealthy Bengali family, Rai studied law in London (where in 1924 he met Niranjan Pal, later the scriptwriter for several of his films). According to his own testimony, Rai spent close to fifteen years in Europe and visited studios in the United States, Germany, and Britain. His acquaintance with Indian Trade Commissioner Lindsay gave him access to appropriate distributors in British International for *Shiraz*. And when he turned his attention to making sound films for the Indian market in 1934 (after Germany shut down under the Nazi government), his studio, Bombay Talkies, had five prominent Indians on its board of governors, each of whom had been granted knighthood by the British Crown.

The ICC was more likely to select witnesses like Rai and speak to them at length, because they represented educated, English-speaking, knowledgeable specialists in the field. As an official body that approached the interviews as a form of administrative modernity, the ICC netted people who approximated to their idea of enlightened, modern individuals. The official interview apparatus built in certain social and political biases. For instance, to acquire a fair spread of the industry the ICC interviewed 239 Indians (157 Hindus, 38 Muslims, 25 Parsis, 16 Burmese, 2 Sikhs, 1 Christian), 114 Europeans, Americans, and Anglo-Indians, with a total of 35 women.[114] The ICC's attempt to be communally representative replicated the colonial (and later the nation) state's practice of identity-based divisions, apportioning each group a representative ratio that was presumably in accord with its perceived significance. (Numerical strength was also a factor, in the sense that India's Hindu majority received greater representation, but that does not explain the nominal presence of women on the committee.) Communal, national, and gender divisions simultaneously politicized those indexes of identity by transforming them into a primary template through which individuals participated in the state system, and attenuated cultural or class-based interconnections between individuals. Ideological *differences* such as those between Parsi men (like exhibitor Rustomji Dorabji and producer Homi Wadia) or between Hindus (like Rai and the director Baburao Painter), as well as cultural *affinities* across nationalities (between the Indian Rai and the British A. M. Green) are suppressed by the ICC's numerically driven communal-national paradigm for selecting a sample of representative witnesses.

Baburao Painter, another popular contemporary filmmaker, came from a very different social background than Rai. Born into a family of painters and craftsmen (hence the moniker), Painter's life exemplified the coexistence of artisanal and modern modes of production in Indian silent cinema.

Painter drew on personnel and resources established by pre-existing modes of indigenous entertainment and economy while experimenting with cinematic techniques such as the use of filters, fades, indoor lighting techniques, and shade gradations within black-and-white film.[115] Indian aristocrats who commissioned him to paint their portraits funded his initial film work and lent him clothes, horses, and weapons. Making good use of his props, many of Painter's silent films were in the mythological and historical genre (like *Sairandhri*, 1920; *Sinhagad*; *Sati Padmini*, 1924; and *Bhakta Prahlad*, 1926).[116] Whereas both Rai's and Painter's film studios had a tremendous impact on their own and the next generation of Indian filmmakers (Ashok Kumar, Dilip Kumar, and Kishore Kumar started their careers in Rai's Bombay Talkies, the latter two after Rai's unexpected early death; V. Shantaram, Damle, and Fattelal began at Painter's Maharasthra Studios), the two diverged greatly in filmmaking practices.

As Rai told the ICC in 1928, "No production, say, steel or wood, or any other things can be undertaken unless there is a demand. In the same manner no pictures should be attempted in India unless we are assured that we are going to sell those pictures. . . . For this reason it is of the utmost importance that a demand should be created in the International market for the consumption of Indian pictures."[117] Rai's efforts to aim for an international audience with a self-consciously elite creative group, led by the German director Franz Osten, produced orientalist depictions of India in a style of filmmaking markedly different from Painter's. Prints of Painter's silent films *Sairandhri* and *Savkari Pash* (a.k.a. *Indian Shylock* [1925]) do not survive, but accounts of his use of social commentary, realism, and historical drama intimate his films' implicitly local audience. *Sairandhri*, celebrated by the nationalist leader Tilak, was based on the Marathi play *Keechakvadh*, which was banned by the British for its allegorical protest against Viceroy Curzon. *Savkari Pash* was a realist drama of the evils of the Indian feudal system.[118] In contrast, Rai's *The Light of Asia*, *Shiraz*, and *The Throw of Dice* (a.k.a. *Prapancha Pash* [Osten, 1929]) used spectacle, mystery, and romance to convince its international audience of the films' Eastern authenticity. Witness the opening titles of *Shiraz*: "*Shiraz* was produced entirely in India. No studio construction or artificial light has been used. The actors are all Indians."[119] With Painter's films there is more of a sense of a nation addressing itself rather than producing itself (visually, thematically) for a Western audience.

The question is not one of deciding which director's films best represented the nation as much as understanding *how* each realized an artistic vision within the industrial, political, and social constraints of colonial India. In surveying Indian cinema, the ICC was consolidating a selective sample of these visions as representative of the period. From all reports, Rai was devoted to raising the level of respectability of the Indian film world, and with Bombay Talkies he "was determined to recruit men and women from good families, graduation being the minimum qualification."[120] This was also his effort in earlier years, according to his ICC testimony to the chairman.

> Q. Are they [Rai's actresses] fairly respectable people?
> A. So far as I know all of them were respectable.
> Q. Did you have any difficulty in getting them to join?
> A. Very much.
> Q. I suppose the actors also were from a respectable class of people.
> A. Yes.[121]

As is well known, early Indian cinema had few female entrants. Traditional Hindu and Muslim families considered the profession disreputable, so early filmmakers followed the theatrical tradition of using men to play female parts. One of the most popular women of theater was a man, Bal Gandharva, whose female lead in Marathi plays like Sharada, Subhadra, and Ekach Pyala set fashion trends for gold-embroidered saris.[122] The illusion, however, was difficult to sustain under the cinematic medium's mimetic impulse. Women from the more progressive Anglo-Indian community entered the profession, rechristened and reinvented to portray icons of Hindu femininity on silent screens. Rai's heroine for his first feature, The Light of Asia, was played by a fourteen-year-old Anglo-Indian girl, Renee Smith, née Sita Devi (who was also interviewed by the ICC).

In contrast, Painter's actors and actresses for his first production, Sairandhari, were male wrestlers and female kalavantins, commercial musical artists (who were not included in the interviews). These actors came from professions affiliated with cinema's lowbrow roots. Kalavantins and courtesans were affected by the reduction of the princely purse under colonialism, as their aristocratic patronage was replaced by the vagaries of a commercial marketplace. Stigmatized as bazaari auraten (women of the marketplace) or as prostitutes of different ranks, modern-day courtesans found respectability in the film industry once the profession acquired social acceptance and glamour in the 1940s. (Courtesans-turned-actresses include Paro Davi and the star Nargis, daughter of Jaddan Bai.)[123] According to an account of Sairandhari, Painter's female lead Gulab Bai and her fellow cast member Anusaya Bai were ostracized from their kalavantin communities "because they had dared to apply make-up and act" for the film, a debasing gesture in 1921 even by the standards of their socially marginalized profession.[124] In the differences between Rai and Painter's social milieu of actors lies a broad range of conflicts navigated by colonial filmmakers trying to create an ideal cinematic lingua franca for India.

To assure a film's success, industry personnel had to define a hegemonic central space in literal and artistic terms, and the manner in which directors, actors, or legislators defined this space rehearsed their class and nationalist politics. With regard to space in the literal sense of a theater's arena, the ICC interviews included film importers who complained about Indian audiences, wishing to keep their viewers segregated by class and race. Rustomji Dorabji, who screened American films in his theaters (Wellington, West End, and Venus), complained to the ICC that when he screened the Phalke film *Lanka Dahan*, he had to disinfect his theaters to convince his regular audiences of its cleanliness, which confirmed his belief that "the modes of life of different people are different. The type of people who like Indian pictures—their way of living is quite different and generally they are people who chew beetle leaves and they make things very dirty."[125] Similar reservations attached themselves to India's linguistic variety. Several Indian film exhibitors told the ICC that cultural tastes and references were provincially specific in India, so a film from Bengal was as alien to a Bombay resident as a British film.[126] Compounding this was the practical problem of providing silent films with intertitles comprehensible to several linguistic constituencies. To some importers, a universal lexicon of film, visual or linguistic, appeared incompatible with India's multiplicity.

The importer Ardeshir Bilimoria, speaking to ICC member Sir Haroon Jaffer, suggested India's variety was more conducive to cacophony than to the development of a universally comprehensible cultural and literary script.

> Q. Can you suggest any method by which this language difficulty could be overcome?
> A. I myself cannot suggest anything unless there will be a universal language for India, and that is English.
> CHAIRMAN: Make everyone learn Hindi. Thank you, Mr. Bilimoria.[127]

The Anglophone exhibitor's and the nationalist chairman's variable solutions to mainstreaming the industry points to the fundamental issue at hand. Definitions of what constituted a (linguistic, and ostensibly aesthetic) normative film language differed radically based on individual social and political sympathies as shaped in relation to a colonial society. "It is within the power of our film industry to make Hindustani the 'lingua franca' for India and we shall make it so," proclaimed Chandulal J. Shah in the Indian Motion Picture Congress in 1939, and one can imagine how ominous that may have sounded to politicians, filmmakers, and film audiences under the Madras Presidency, which strongly protested the official imposition of Hindi in southern India in 1937.[128] I bracket the complicated question of aesthetics for the last chapter and conclude with two observations about colonial India's linguistic and social diversities, which posed challenges to the production of such normativity.

After 1947, Hindi-language cinema dominated the Indian market while only the exceptional regional-language filmmaker crossed over to national audiences. Early sound cinema of the 1930s had yet to acquire the entrenched practices of independent India's film industry, and the market's hegemonic division (between Bombay's nationally distributed Hindi films versus its regionally distributed vernacular-language films) was as yet inchoate. The common practice of making early sound films in more than one language prevailed in the 1930s, as filmmakers of several regions attempted to negotiate India's multiplicity at a linguistic level in efforts to create what the scholar Mukul Kesavan calls a "metropolitan, pan-Indian form" of cinema.[129] V. Shantaram pioneered this bilingual trend by producing *Ayodhyecha Raja* in Marathi and *Ayodhya ka Raja* in Hindi in 1932.

In its linguistic and aesthetic experimentation at a time when the potential of a broadly multifaceted, multilingual national industry appeared to be a live possibility, the late-colonial period echoed some more recent trends in Indian cinema. Since the late 1990s, a fragmentation of Indian film audiences under the influx of foreign corporate capital, increasing multiplexes, neoliberal state policies, and competitive cable-television channels has created two equal and opposite pulls on Indian filmmakers who desire a national audience. In addition to the conventional wisdom that films must be star-studded and ideologically safe Hindi-language musical melodramas in order to reassure distributors and earn significant national profits, an increasing number of Indian filmmakers are drawn to producing lower-budget "crossover" films for niche audiences or to producing the same big-budget film in two national languages. As a result, in addition to the expected Hindi film fare with a bankable star cast like *Baghban* (Chopra, 2003) and *Veer-Zaara* (Chopra, 2004) are films with new themes and faces, as in Bhatt-family productions like *Mur-*

der (Hindi, Basu, 2004) and Jism (Hindi, Saxena, 2003), or in English language and bilingual films like Mango Souffle (English, Dattani, 2002), Everybody Says I'm Fine! (English, Rahul Bose, 2001), Ayutha Yeruthu/ Yuva (Tamil/Hindi, Ratnam, 2004), and Mumbai Express with Kamalahasan (Tamil/English, Rao, 2005). This phenomenon is further complicated by the emergence of diaspora and Indian filmmakers producing films for international and South Asian diaspora audiences: like Mira Nair's and Deepa Mehta's films; American Chai (Mehta, 2001); American Desi (Pandya, 2001); and Mitr—My Friend, (Revathy, 2001), all primarily in English.[130] The ideological unity of a nation and its affective address in cinema, always a tenuous construction, has proven volatile when under formation and restructuration in both the colonial and the global eras.

The foundational crisis of Indian nationalism stemmed from its efforts to manufacture universals out of diverse linguistic, class, caste, regional, and religious communities that were minoritized and subordinated as a precondition to participating in the national collective. In a society defined by the "problem" of collectivities, Indian directors and producers confronted with a new medium that depended on a mass audience defined the ideal Indian film form and film-viewing experience in variable and contradictory ways. Beyond the ICC testimonies of witnesses like Dorabji and Bilimoria, who saw no clear means of homogenizing a film's address without segmenting audiences or excluding sections of it, is the film producer J. B. H. Wadia's vision of commercial cinema. Wadia recounts, in later years, his appreciation of the boisterous and diverse mass Indian audiences of silent films. He evidently saw Hollywood films from the cheap seats, though it meant that the "ones who had a smattering of the [English] language would read aloud and translate [titles] in a Babel of their respective vernaculars for the benefit of those who did not know the common language of the British Empire."[131] Wadia recalls lying prostrate on the front benches to hold seats for his friends, shouting at screen villains and heroes, and looking at V.I.P. seats where "the door keeper would enter pompously as if he was a super star coming on the stage from the wings holding a silver pigani (spray) of rose water." Not surprisingly, Wadia's popular early productions were front-bench, crowd-pleasing, stunt-action films and fantasies like Toofan Mail (1932) and Lal-e-Yaman (1933).

Each film-industry member constructed an idiom of Indian cinema that responded to his or her definition of Indian cinema's key consumer base, and their answers to the ICC reflected this. Beyond evaluating the witnesses' personal politics, discussions of the ICC must keep an eye toward how the committee was institutionally predisposed to sorting cinema's representative constituencies. As products of a colonial society, the committee's members and its witnesses navigated between indebtedness to imperial modernity and an investment in a national industry. Their definitions of cinema immediately expressed their own varying positions in an intermediary space of (cultural, political) subordination to the colonizers while pioneering a (cultural, political) form.[132] The unquestioned use of English for the ICC's exchanges suggests the committee's institutionally mediate position; so does its strict adherence to individuals who were deemed film "specialists," and its loyalty to institutions considered socially relevant or elevating (such as school principals, heads of local YMCAs, or members of societies monitoring public morality) to the exclusion of less socially established or reputable industry participants. In an absence of the ICC's interest in the opinions of India's growing mass film audience, their perceptions remain inaccessible to analysis, but interrogating the boundaries of the ICC's investigative parameters and of their witnesses' evaluative ones underscores the intersecting colonial and national forces shaping the interviews.

*

In 1933, six years after the ICC interviews, a lengthy debate ensued in the Indian Legislative Assembly over one of the committee's suggestions. An Indian assembly member proposed a resolution demanding that the British India government remove import duties on raw film stock entering India.[133] One of the people speaking in favor of the removal of the tariff on film stock was K. C. Neogy, who had served on the ICC board. He refers to the ICC in the following manner.

> I have heard uncharitable critics of Government say that the reason why the enthusiasm of Government in regard to this [ICC] inquiry had oozed out was to be found in the recommendations of the Committee itself. These uncharitable critics say, for instance, that one of the objects of the appointment of this Committee was to get a kind of preference for the British film producer in the Indian market. . . . To their surprise, continue these uncharitable critics, the Government found that this Committee, composed as it was of an equal number of Englishmen and Indians, had positively refused to make any recommendations of that character. On the other hand, they made a series of unanimous recommendations for the development of and encouragement of the Indian industry. *I quite admit*

that most of the recommendations would involve a financial outlay on the part of the Government, but there are certain recommendations which would require not so much financial assistance."[134]

Neogy uses the rhetorical trope of "uncharitable critics" in interesting ways. Perhaps I am one of those uncharitable souls today, in that I foreground the ICC's origin in British trade initiatives. But Neogy uses the device to stage a series of criticisms against the government as well, for its neglect of the ICC's mildest recommendations. As he notes, the commission's suggestion to remove taxation of raw film stock would neither have required financial outlay nor would it have counted as state protectionism. Compared to the positive state support extended to British films with the Quota Acts, the imperial state was actively hurting Indian cinema with its tariff policy.[135] The Indian Department of Industries and Labor, represented by Sir Frank Noyce, put a damper on the motion to remove raw film tax in India once again, by arguing that the state could not be compensated for its loss of income from the tax cut. As with the ICC interviews, nothing was achieved for the Indian film industry, and the state maintained its status quo. But the process called into account inconsistencies in British state policy regarding film in the empire.

A historiography that includes markets that didn't materialize, films that were not distributed, and bills that were not passed reveals conflicts that existed as disruptive preambles to regulatory initiatives. Among such conflicts lie shadowy histories of resistance to the state. In the British State's numerous standing committees, inquiry commissions, roundtable conferences, and acts through which it governed India, the consignment of the ICC's final report to some dusty filing system might well be a testimony of its success; in a contrary sense, it is the report's function as a failed preface to any regulation that makes it an ideal locus for studying how and why imperial ideology collapsed, adapted, and re-presented itself in different forms when under attack. However subtly, the Indian film industry, itself under definition, played a role in reshaping the British State's agenda, particularly when it was uncooperative in furthering state policy initiatives.

In 1937 when the FBI and the BT expressed renewed interest over the possibility of mobilizing an empire film market, the India Office flatly discouraged them. To quote A. Dibdin of the Economic and Overseas Department, direct state involvement in the Indian film industry was impossible because "nowadays . . . any question of tariff adjustment tends to become a matter of bargaining in which each side expects to receive an equivalent of some kind from the other." [136] The colonial film industry's new expectation of real reciprocity put paid to further negotiations. Noting that Britain produced commercial films for home rather than Indian consumption, the India Office suggests that British producers should first establish themselves in Britain and "first seek to penetrate the American market" before attempting to enter the colony.[137] Interestingly, British empire films that transformed India and Africa into picturesque themes for commercial blockbusters did precisely that: they won America.

part two ✳ **IMPERIAL REDEMPTION**

Philosophically, then, the kind of language, thought, and vision that I have been calling Orientalism very generally is a form of *radical realism*.

—Edward Said, *Orientalism*

"I am Sandi who gives you the Law."

—British Commissioner Sanders to African tribes, *Sanders of the River* (1935)

It was only that a certain inventive legerdemain was required to permit the empire to appear attractive in national drag.

—Benedict Anderson, *Imagined Communities*

four ✳ REALISM AND EMPIRE

Defining imperial realism in film entails clearing a path through a profusion of descriptions about cinema's encounter with reality. Christopher Williams observes that "the first major realist function film has fulfilled consists of the ability to provide various kinds of documents, i.e., accounts of things outside itself," and that the "second area of form which is important in a discussion of realism is the area of narrative." The author goes on to negate this division between documentary realism and narrative realism, noting that while such distinctions "have some virtue on the descriptive level, I doubt whether their opposition as theoretical concepts is helpful in thinking about film. Their meanings overlap too much; and there is also too strong a sense in which no film is realistic or naturalistic."[1] Though no theorist of realism denies cinema's inalienably technical apparatus, contrary to Williams's suggestion we may shift the emphasis away from cinema's excessive artifice and examine instead the processes by which film struggles to "enframe" an abounding world to produce meaning. Photography and cinema's "excess of mimesis over meaning," to use Tom Gunning's evocative phrase, makes the techniques through which film bends reality to its representational purposes revelatory of the ambitions underlying its style (and hence, of its politics).[2]

Artifice is certainly part of naturalism (wherein form refers to an external world and operates with a documentary sense of truth) as well as classical or high realism (wherein form invisibly follows the internal rules of a narrative), but abandoning their differences ignores the *manner* and *end* to which each form makes objects from the world submit to re-presentation.

At least since film theory took a linguistic turn in the 1970s, classical realism in cinema has been discussed as a historical product as well as a cultural symptom.[3] Most frequently analyzed with reference to the nineteenth-century realist novel and classical Hollywood cinema, this form of realism is defined as a hierarchy of discourses structured to be most completely readable or comprehensible from the point of view of an "ideal," textually-produced spectator-position. According to this definition, realism's textual functions parallel and reinforce bourgeois capitalism's institutional functions, of which they are a part. In Althusserian terms, individuals are "interpellated" as social subjects under capitalism because its injunctions are not represented as dictatorial impositions but reproduced as obvious, common-sensical, and true.[4] The spectator/reader is sutured into a realist text much as a social subject is constituted by capitalist, patriarchal structures—invisibly and through an internalized prioritization of the socially hegemonic perspective. With this critique of classical realism's ideological operation, 1970s film theory sought unconscious and conscious contradictions within realist texts. Film criticism looked for moments of subversion, of textual unraveling, of hegemony's displeasure in realist texts, and found its critical gestures mirrored in modernist, avant-garde cinema.[5]

At variance with this analysis of realism as ideological construct, but with similar aspirations to define radical ways of seeing and interpreting the world, earlier definitions of realism by theorists such as André Bazin, Siegfried Kracauer, Georg Lukács, and John Grierson sought to articulate an ideal form of artistic expression: ideal, that is, to an emancipatory agenda and/or to a medium like film. They explored cinema's photographic potential for indexicality to probe ontological links between image and reality at the instant of recording. Alternatively, their questions revolved around cinema's ability to reveal material connections between individuals and their social totalities, against modernism's preoccupation with the subjective state of alienated beings. Instead of focusing on realism's rupture, as in the case of later psychoanalytic and poststructuralist film theorists, Lukács connected literary realism with a liberatory promise by arguing that genuinely realist art functioned to de-reify reality. For Lukács, realism penetrated appearances to "reproduce the overall process (or else a part of it linked either explicitly or implicitly to the overall process) by disclosing its actual and essential driving forces."[6] According to him, the primary function of realism was to reveal the truly dialectical nature of social reality, hardened in art forms that presented objects or human relations as "a finished product." To qualify as realist, art had to show the world "as a moment in a process . . . in constant vital interaction with its preconditions and consequences, as the living result of the (class) human relations between those people."[7]

By Lukács's definition, imperial realism would be the very antithesis of realism in that it dehistoricizes colonial relations, making the ideology of one race, nation, and class stand in for a totality. Classical definitions of realism point to art's promise to disturb the bounds of ideology, to humanize, and to bring the audience into astonishing proximities with the world and its social relations. Contemporary theories of realism suggest cinema's possible subservience to a political ideology. Combining both insights, prototypical empire films of the 1930s such as Sanders of the River or Rhodes of Africa can be read as texts that deploy realist techniques at the behest of imperialism, betraying cinema's potential to create startling encounters with unexplored realities or with undisguised social truths.

In imperial cinema the realist mode traditionally functions through documentary realism as well as narrative realism. Frequently, cinematic representations of imperialism presume to present colonial subjects naturalistically, as is well illustrated in the abundant use of documentary footage from the colonies, incorporated with a minimum of motivation within the narrative sequences in Sanders of the River and Elephant Boy. The naturalist mode of realism contributes to a defense of "enlightened" imperialism, portraying colonial subjects in a state of savagery or infancy and in need of assistance. (Interestingly, the scenes that were censored from Sanders before it was screened in India included twelve feet of "close-ups of dancing semi-nude negro girls" from reel 4, which were edited out by the Bombay Board of Film Censors in India; the anthropological justification of the scene that made it permissible for white audiences did not apply to a nonwhite viewership. Other scenes deleted for the Indian screenings included black-on-white violence and white men calling each other "bloody swine.")[8] The British themselves are represented through another mode of realism, one that was closer to classical Hollywood realism, with carefully constructed sets and continuity editing normalizing their social and racial hierarchies. Certainly, documentation of colonial dances and animals are also presented as if unmediated by technology or power, so no scene in a realist film is exempt from a deliberate erasure of artifice. But it is important to distinguish conventions of naturalism and of narrative realism in the first instance, to highlight how they vary in technique and purpose while sharing the operative paradox of cinematic realism's necessary reliance on artifice.[9]

In addition to the naturalism reserved for colonial subjects and the classical realism for the colonizers, *encounters* between colonized subjects and the ruling race occur within a mode of narrative realism that reproduces spatial divisions between colonizer and colonized as obvious.[10] According to historians of silent cinema, this "referential heterogeneity" created by a combination of naturalism and realism is potentially a product of different modes of address and spectatorial positions—derived from actualities, newsreels, political cartoons, and narrative fiction—that competed with each other in articulations of early film form. Kristen Whissel explores the relationship between early cinema and U.S. imperialism in Edwin S. Porter's The "Teddy" Bears (1907) arguing, for instance, that "while the disjunction between outdoor and indoor space marks this film as pre-classical, its ability to codify these differences (and thereby make disjunctive space into narrative space) is symptomatic of the film's historical position on the threshold between the cinema's preclassical and classical modes of representation."[11] By these terms, *Sanders* is an anachronism in 1935, for though its narrative codifies the differences between outdoor (documentary and process) shots as well as indoor (studio) shots, it retains a stylistic disjunction between them.[12]

During the film's production, the two kinds of realism came into direct competition when the producer Alexander Korda disagreed with his brother, the director Zoltan Korda, over the making of *Sanders*, and with the filmmaker Robert Flaherty over *Elephant Boy*. Alexander Korda wanted to make narrative and melodramatic imperial sagas, while Zoltan Korda and Flaherty supported the documentary form. In the case of each film, Zoltan and Flaherty shot on location before the material was partially incorporated into a narrative with back projections and studio sets at Denham Studios, so that each film's final version contained discordant styles that combined location shots with studio photography and artificial effects.[13] As a film, *Sanders* is not always artistically coherent, but its dissonance affirms the "radical realism" of a variegated realist text that posits—at every turn, but in different ways—a transparency between representation and meaning. The consequences of such a style for imperialist ideology's adaptation to a more liberal era of politics can be unearthed by following *Sanders*'s multistranded realist mode through its treatment of colonial bodies, colonial place, imperial work, and the very act of narration.

Imperial Narration

Sanders of the River is about District Commissioner Sanders (Leslie Banks) and his administration of the lower Isisi tribes, who are tyrannized by King Mofalaba (Tony Wane) during his regular raids for slaves and women. In keeping the peace of the land, Sanders is assisted by the British officers Tibbets (Robert Cochran) and Hamilton (Richard Grey) as well as his native ally Bosambo (Paul Robeson), chief of the Ochori. At the film's conclusion, Sanders has effected a "regime change" in the Isisi by eliminating Mofalaba and nominating Bosambo as the new king. The film begins with a set of intertitles over a fluttering Union Jack, as Robeson's famous "canoe song" extolling the virtues of Sanders plays on the soundtrack.[14]

> Sandi the strong, Sandi the wise;
> Righter of wrong, Hater of lies.
> Laughed as he fought, worked as he played;
> As he has taught, let it be made.

> [Intertitle 1] Sailors, soldiers and merchant-adventurers were the pioneers who laid the foundation of the British Empire. To-day their work is carried on by the Civil Servants—Keepers of the King's peace.
> [dissolve]
> [Intertitle 2] AFRICA.
> Tens of millions of natives under British rule, each tribe with its own chieftain, governed and protected by a handful of white men whose everyday work is an unsung saga of courage and efficiency.
> [Intertitle 3 fades in]
> One of them was Commissioner Sanders.

As the titles fade to black, a spinning globe fades in and stops at Nigeria. This dissolves to a wall map of the "District of Commissioner Sanders," followed by a final dissolve to a zoom out from the nameplate on Sanders's door as the man himself appears, pipe in mouth.

Intertitles, maps, and globes are used abundantly in imperial films to mark fictional representations as facts and locate them in a geographical space and historical time. Jean-Louis Comolli argues that fiction that presents itself as history uses two orders of meaning: the order of belief (the viewer must believe that the fiction is real) and of knowledge (but they know that they are watching reconstructions). In historical fiction there is more to believe against, as there is more to de-negate, a "body too much" of referential information that impedes our faith in the fiction.[15] Arguing against this, Mimi White notes that the body of "historical" reference that is supposedly anterior to the fictional text may be used self-reflexively by the text and the audience. The viewer is called on to evaluate the text using this information (an "extra body of reference" rather than a "body too much"), as historical films establish their validity by engaging viewers with referential material preceding and surrounding fiction.[16]

Sanders, like all imperial fiction, incorporates realist indices to periods and places, and the film's fragments of reality—maps, location shots, footage of indigenous peoples, excerpts of Kroo, Ochori, and Yoruba tribal songs recorded on site and advertised as authentic—exist to endow the same order of legitimacy to the fiction. So the film opens with a song that borrows its rhythms from a Nigerian boat song but transforms the lyrics into a paean to the fictional Sanders, implying that a native lore has sprung up around the protagonist. By re-scripting an African boat song into a song about Sanders and making it a recurrent thematic sound, Sanders gets an emotional authenticity and the film appears to merely recreate an environment rather than propagate a worldview. Colonization is portrayed as acceptable to people who incorporate validations of empire in quotidian expressions of their daily life, such as their music, speeches, and wedding rituals. Intertitles labor to this effect in Michael Balcon's *Rhodes of Africa* as well, when they state that Rhodes was honored by the Matabele, "the very people he had conquered," with their royal salute, "Bayete!"

The opening titles in *Sanders* similarly legitimate the hero, although he is not a pioneer-adventurer but a bureaucrat, typically not an ideal candidate for thrills. But the excitement of the place (AFRICA in capital letters) and the scale of the work undertaken (an "unsung saga" of "a handful of white men") outweigh the bureaucrat's potential dullness (the "everyday work" of "one of them" civil servants). Not long before *Sanders* was made, Winston Churchill had celebrated civil service in India as a superior form of impassive selflessness.

Our responsibility in India has grown up over the last 150 years. It is a responsibility for giving the best possible chance for peaceful existence and

7. A Nigerian boat song is sung in honor of Sanders on the Lower Isisi River. Courtesy USC Cinema-Television Library.

progress to about three hundred and fifty millions of helpless primitive people who are separated by an almost measureless gulf from the ideas and institutions of the Western world. We now look after them by means of British Officials on fixed salaries who have no axe to grind, who make no profit out of their duties, who are incorruptible, who are impartial between races, creeds and classes, and who are directed by a central Government which in its turn is controlled by the British Parliament based on twenty-nine million electors.[17]

Everything Sanders says in the first scene confirms his neutral performance of duty at the behest of British taxpayers.

Work is a significant aspect of all imperial films because imperial rule legitimates itself by making certain claims for the significance of the colonizer's work. Consequently the first sequence establishes Sanders's matter-of-fact attitude toward his task. When junior officer Tibbets looks wistfully out of the window, dreaming of future decorations for bravery, Sanders says in clipped tones, "Stop thinking of that Victoria Cross of yours. What you're in for is tramping through swamps and jungles. The only decoration you get:

mosquito bites." In consonance with the intertitles, Sanders neither seeks nor expects any recognition: his is an "unsung saga." But recognition is nevertheless conferred on him by the film's eponymous title, its characters, mise-en-scène, camera angles, and nondiegetic text.

Following cinematic convention, the nondiegetic text occupies an omniscient and controlling position in relation to the film's visuals, directing attention to key events and invoking scenes that visuals display faithfully. Scenes of harvest, fecund banana trees, and happy Africans accompany intertitles that report

> Five years of harvest, peace, and plenty. Under Sanders' just rule the People of the River enjoy their primitive paradise.

The relationship between titles and images replicates the relationship between Sanders and the cinematic world, in that the titles could almost be his internal thoughts, so seamlessly do they overlap and affirm the film's reality.[18] Sanders's subjective vision permeates the film's form, and his vision mediates our access to all versions of this reality.

In other words, in addition to being the film's central protagonist, Sanders is the central consciousness that serves as the touchstone for the film's internal coherence and veracity. "Realism offers itself as transparent," says Catherine Belsey, and Sanders presents a mise-en-abime of transparency. Sanders takes imperialism to be a self-evident good, which mimics the film's presumption of imperial benefits, which in turn mimics Sanders's perspective, ad infinitum. The other characters (English and African) exist to validate this hermetically sealed echo chamber of reality that surrounds Sanders; consequently their relationship to fiction is one of incomplete knowledge. In such a narrative, there is room for narrative suspense only when one is at the same level of awareness as the characters who have no agency beyond anticipating Sanders's actions. When Sanders departs for the Government House to get married, leaving a new Commissioner Ferguson (Martin Walker) in charge of the residency, the collapsing order in his wake reflects the audience's lack of certainty about what will ensue in the narrative.

Sanders's absence effects an immediate crisis, with the arrival of two ill-intentioned men who spread rumors: "Sandi is dead. There is no law any more." They distribute "Gin and Firearms," and an emboldened Mofalaba kills Ferguson on the assurance that Sanders is dead. Sanders rushes back, but when asked for his command he retorts, "I don't know." Subsequently, there are no more titles. The film builds its climax by withholding the protagonists' plan of intervention, which, in accord with the concomitant omniscience of Sanders and the intertitles, demands the suspension of all nondiegetic communication with the audience. The film's evisceration of narrative agency for everyone but Sanders contributes to the construction of a mythic status for his character. Unlike empire films in the romance mode, this film doesn't defend imperialism as the manifest destiny of a race or a class. Unlike an imperial modernist text, it does not offer a stylized meditation on the irrevocable struggles of those who inherit that destiny. The certitude of *Sanders* is conveyed by a textual attitude wherein every aspect of the film form creates, overtly and invisibly, a world according to Sanders. Consistent with this, the film's protagonist is a figure who never questions the value of his colonial mission.

Imperial Work/Imperial Identity

Unlike protagonists in romance and modernist imperial fictions, heroes in the realist modes are not altered by their colonial place of work. They are typically white men who have a certainty of purpose, demonstrate no self-reflexivity about their mission, and encounter an alien land to change it rather than be changed themselves. They are self-assured and "unperturbably English, unaffected by the atmosphere, customs or climate of the alien lands."[19] To maintain this integrity of imperial character, the film's shots are designed with clear spatial divisions subordinating the African to the white man. In the first sequence of *Sanders*, we witness two settings. The first is Sanders's living room. This area, with couches, windows, and alcohol, is spatially unified; the camera and the characters have great mobility within the room. British officers (and Sanders's African servant, Abibu, who stands respectfully at the margins of the frame) inhabit this space, which is safe for easy movement and an exchange of whiskey. The second setting is Sanders's office, where Sanders meets Bosambo. The office is spatially divided in a way that the living room is not. The shot is split into screen left and screen right, with Sanders and Hamilton seated on one side of the table and Tibbets lounging behind them. Bosambo walks into the room and stands facing them across the table, framed by various maps of Africa. The camera loses its mobility, providing only two positions other than the establishing shot, namely, the British point of view and the African point of view. In imperial realism, "the colonial world is a world cut in two."[20] Any form of social interaction outside the formal palaver is taboo. Deviations from spatial division occur either during mo-

8. Imperial realism's regime of visual segregation makes Sanders invulnerable. Courtesy USC Cinema-Television Library.

ments of conflict or during formal ceremonies, which bring their own relational hierarchies.[21]

The filmic apparatus endows the character of Sanders with a position of privileged isolation from his surroundings. Despite his references to the rigors of life in Africa, his work is portrayed as mental rather than physical. He plans, gives orders, thinks, and smokes his pipe. When his men shoot at Mofalaba's settlement, he remains off-screen so that he always appears in command, visibly and invisibly controlling the natives who work, fight, gather fruit, dance, and follow orders. Narratively speaking, there are only three exceptions to Sanders's apparent inviolability: his fever, the fragility of peace at the residency when Sanders is replaced by his colleague Ferguson, and the competing visual presence of Bosambo.

At a key point in the film, Sanders commands junior officer Tibbets to keep his steamboat "Zaire" in midstream, as he feels his body succumbing to malaria. Retreating from the natives and his fellow officers for his moment of weakness, Sanders is nevertheless exposed to the audience in his sweat-drenched delirium. Embedded in these depictions of the imperial body's response to a colonial place are varying shades of a defense for the empire's place in the British nation. This is particularly true given the extent to which the represented imperial body is an allegory for Britain, especially at a time when colonial officers were upheld as ambassadors of the nation. In an effort to streamline colonial administration, late-imperial state policy decreed that colonial officials could only be selected from certain classes of British society. The film historian Jeffrey Richards argues that the hero Sanders epitomizes all the criteria used in selecting colonial administrators from 1910 to 1948, noting that English public schools were considered the ideal model for colonial administrators and that testimonial letters for prospective candidates commented on their "agreeable" manner, "well-balanced mind," and their ability to maintain "the best traditions of English government over subject races." [22] Unlike his counterparts in imperial fiction, Sanders is never homesick or submerged in danger. Yet his confident exterior only serves to emphasize that "something can always happen in this part of the world," as Sanders warns ominously when a colleague does not return from an expedition.

In imperial films defenses of empire range from the notion that officers pursue their missions *despite* lurking dangers (as in *Sanders*) to the idea that *only* treacherous colonial frontiers can provide appropriately epic terrains for testing true courage and heroism (as in *The Drum* or *The Four Feathers*). The mosquito bites and fevers that assail Sanders proclaim the possibility of danger, but they are dangers easily contained and resolved. In apparent opposition to the imperial-realist hero's invulnerability to the colonial place, Ferguson, the film's one serious casualty, meets death at the hands of Mofalaba's men. As Sanders's replacement, Ferguson pays with his life for not being Sanders. He is at a loss when Mofalaba's men start rioting and has the misfortune of being surrounded by British officers who make unhelpful remarks such as "Sanders' life's work destroyed in a week!" "You must be quick and strong now like a father with his misguided children. Like Mr. Sanders would. Or else much, much blood will flow very soon."

In a desperate bid to regain control Ferguson visits Mofalaba but dies at his hands. Before he dies, he threatens the African king with images of an avenging Sanders: "I tell you he will come, and wherever you may hide, he will smell you out and throw your body to the fishes." The episode points to a generic tendency in imperial films to convey that for some district commissioners (or military officers, as in *The Drum*, or female missionaries, as in *Black Narcissus*) to succeed, others must be sacrificed. A death typically conveys either the enormity of the challenge that colonizers face and handle unperturbed, or the moral triumph (rather than the physical actualization) of imperial values. With Ferguson's death, *Sanders* makes the more straightforward claim that Commissioner Sanders plays a difficult role in maintaining the peace of Africa. Clearly addressing contemporary concerns about the expense of imperial expansion, the film portrays Sanders as a supporter of peace. Subduing Tibbets, who wants to break Mofalaba's neck, Sanders cautions that the "British taxpayer won't be delighted" with war, because "it'd cost him a thousand pounds." Within this context, Ferguson's death gives Sanders a motive to expend taxpayer money on war and empire.

The justification of violence is central to abstracting imperialism as a defensible practice, and in imperial cinema the British are portrayed as a peace-loving people who use violence as a last resort. (In *Sanders* Mofalaba says derisively, "It is easy to lie to the English. They want peace. If you say you want peace they will believe you." In *The Drum*, a native ally rhapsodizes, "England has offered us friendship. If England is our friend, we shall have peace.") Sanders, for instance, does not mount an attack on Mofalaba until the old king relentlessly provokes him by enslaving women, distributing guns and alcohol to witless natives, killing Ferguson, and kidnapping Bosambo and his wife, Lilongo (Nina Mae McKinney). This, anyone would agree, justifies violent retribution.[23] Ferguson dies to demonstrate that Sanders is judicious in his use of force, strengthening the imperial-realist narrative's derivation of legitimacy from its central protagonist, whose actions within the plot consolidate the metanarrative justification of empire.

To argue that nothing in the film interrupts its defense of imperialism does not do justice to Paul Robeson as Bosambo. Audiences at the time were familiar with Robeson's status as a respected African American actor who, in his own words, was "100 per cent in agreement with the Communist Party position on self-determination for the colonies and for the Negro people in America."[24] Given his history of political activism, Robeson came under a lot of criticism for his part as Bosambo, and his exchange about *Sanders of the River* with close friend and fellow activist Benjamin J. Davis Jr. makes a compelling testimonial of his dismay at the film.[25] By Robeson's account, he agreed to act in the film because he believed it would show Africa's rich culture. "Robeson dressed in a leopard skin along with half a dozen other guys from Africa, all looking more or less the same, seemed to me to prove something about my race that I thought worth proving."[26] In fact, the film rarely allows Robeson to be seen with the film's Africans except when they are

9. As Bosambo, Paul Robeson hoped to reconnect African Americans with Africa. Courtesy USC Cinema-Television Library.

reduced to back-projections. Robeson later spoke of the film as a lesson in how a film's editing could completely alter what actors perceived to be its intent. He walked out of the film's premiere screening in London, subsequently denouncing the film in public and reputedly attempting to buy its rights to prevent distribution.[27]

Within the film's logic as well, Robeson's overwhelming screen presence and his delivery frequently gives the impression that his character's behavior toward Sanders is a strategic device to achieve his own ambitions. His dialogue, too, seems at times to affirm this: "I lie to anybody when I think it is good for me"; "Every time I have seen the beautiful face of your great King [of England], my heart has filled with joy"; "I'm a Christian for Lord Sandi, but for you [Lilongo, his wife] I shall be of the true [Muslim] faith." Though Bosambo's function within the film dilutes Robeson's potential, Bosambo's possible double-speak and his unique status in relation to Sanders become apparent the instant his character first appears on screen. Bosambo stands in a loincloth, falsely claiming to be the chief of the Ochori tribe. Sanders looks at him unwaveringly: "Is that not a lie, man?" Bosambo admits, "It is a lie, Lord." "It IS a lie, man," confirms Sanders, demonstrating superhuman control over others. Sanders walks to his files and pulls out one on Bosambo. A close-up of the file shows Robeson's photograph along with the text "Liberian negro, convicted for habitual petty larceny. Escaped from St. Thome prison." The file entry on Bosambo points to the use of diegetic text within this film. In opposition to the intertitles, which are declarative "truths" endorsing Sanders's view of imperial relations, the diegetic text of the film offers secret information that is either about Sanders (tom-toms drumming messages of Sanders's rumored death in the jungle) or available only to Sanders (Morse code, files). Sanders either gives definition to that which constitutes the film's reality, or forms the center of reference for every event, person, and object within the film.

The files reveal that "Sandi," the legend known to his African "children," and "Sanders," the man known to his colleagues, maintains his mythic stature with technologies of military and bureaucratic surveillance.[28] The secret that keeps him in control of the area is the panopticon of the British Empire, with its privileged access to the colony and its secret codes. However, technology requires mystification to maintain its authoritative position, and European rationalism, with its classifications and method, presents itself as supernatural to the natives, who believe that Sanders has "ears as long as an elephant, eyes on the top of [his] head and in [his] back and where other men sit." British officers appear equally amazed by Sanders's vast knowledge.[29] Only Bosambo skirts the edges of his omniscience, as their first meeting reveals.

> SANDERS: Didn't you know that no man can be Chief in the River territories without my permission?
> BOSAMBO: I knew, Lord. But I also knew that YOU also knew that I MADE myself chief of the Ochori.
> SANDERS: And you knew that I knew because of my magic?
> BOSAMBO: Lord, I knew that you knew by your spies, who are everywhere, who are called the eyes of your Lordship.

The myth of superhuman omniscience is revealed as a network of administrative data-gathering, and here we have a moment of acquiescence between two men regarding the levels of implicit and explicit knowledge necessary to maintain the precarious balance of imperial power. Despite great disparities of position and power in the sequence (Sanders sits fully clothed, while Bosambo stands half-naked, lit by bright lights during Sanders's scrutiny), both men appear to understand the operation of authority more than any other white or black man in the film. Such moments, however, are fleeting in a film that never carries Bosambo's position in relation to imperial authority beyond the mildest flirtations with insubordination. He is quickly transformed into an emasculated figure who needs Sanders to rescue him from Mofalaba. Nevertheless, he is also the sole figure who constitutes the permissible outer limits of interrogating imperial authority within the reality of this fiction.

The native who completely defies imperial authority is, of course, the evil Mofalaba. He appears to have no grandiose visions of absolute power, other than following the custom of raiding for slaves and cutting down those who stand in his way (unlike Ghul Khan in The Drum, who wants an Islamic Empire). Significantly, Bosambo throws the fatal spear at Mofalaba when Sanders and his army come to the rescue. This death of the bad native at the hands of the good one (the corresponding image in Black Narcissus is the good colonizer killing her evil counterpart) reveals a close doubling of the two figures. Together, Bosambo and Mofalaba encompass a range of imperial perceptions regarding the colonized. To an extent, this is Said's point about orientalism with Bhabha's emendation. Though both theorists agree that an evocation of the oriental is crucial to the West's self-definition, for Said orientalism is a self-referential system that constitutes the non-Western as a unified entity, for which "it is frequently enough to use the simple copula is," as in the formulation: the orient is sensual and the West is rational.[30] Against this, Bhabha argues that "for Said, the copula [is] seems to be the point at which western rationalism preserves the boundaries of sense for itself," but such "signifiers of stability" ignore the various contradictory roles played by non-Western subjects in Western discourse.[31] Consequently, the orient is better designated through signifiers of instability which show the "ambivalence" of Western-dominant discourse toward an East constructed as simultaneously despotic, childlike, sensual, menacing, and so on.[32]

In Sanders depictions of a friendly Bosambo and a malicious Mofalaba are structurally necessary to the portrayal of Sanders, but in contrast to other modes of imperial representation, imperial realism maintains strict boundaries between enemies and allies. Bosambo does not find in himself a dark echo of Mofalaba; Mofalaba is never charming or enticing. The categories of "enemy" and "ally" remain unproblematized. To particularize Bhabha's analysis, though non-Western subjects play contradictory roles in colonial discourses, certain discourses are founded on the suppression of ambivalence and occupy a position of apparent anachronism in (and after) the twen-

10. Mofalaba, the slave-raiding African chief. Courtesy USC Cinema-Television Library.

tieth century, because they deny the historical troubling of colonial, racial, gendered, and class-based binaries. Imperial realism builds an amnesiac world, channeling its horror of an anticolonial populace that chants "the last shall be first and the first last" through imagining easily isolatable native enemies amid a sea of native allies.[33] The native subject who is similar-to-me-but-not-me (manifested in the threatening figure of Ghul Khan in the romance narrative *The Drum*, and in the uncanny moments of the modernist film *Black Narcissus*) is erased from the realist mode, in which categories of good and evil are clearly segregated, and distinguishing between them never provokes the central narrative or moral crisis.

The Manichean nature of realism need not prevent us from reading against the grain of a realist text. Following Sanders's return to his residency, he calls for a palaver with his African allies to reprimand his "black children" for their unruly behavior. In defense of his tribe's action Chief Koolaboo says, "My young men heard that your Lordship was dead, and their hearts were filled with a great joy." Sanders replies, "Well, now they know that I'm alive." Koolaboo admits, "Yes Lord, and their hearts are filled with sorrow." The episode seems to reveal that the basis of Sanders's rule is, above all, terror, and the Africans' obedience to him is motivated purely by their interest in survival rather than by their recognition of the British administration's greater good. This is a pleasurable reading, but recognizably perverse because the repeated trope of natives as children who need to be ruled with a firm hand attenuates any insistence that the film depicts Sanders as a terrorizing force on Africans.[34] As with the justification of violence against Mofalaba, the episode of lawlessness only vindicates Sanders's aggression. The film's resolution depicting a transfer of power from Sanders to Bosambo thus represents an empire founded on constructive cooperation rather than force. The portrayal of empire as an arena of cooperation invalidates accusations against British imperialism with nationalist aplomb.

During the transfer of power, Sanders sits and Bosambo stands facing him, the light behind him fanned out in rays, as though heralding him as the new king.

SANDERS: Bosambo, you are king of the river. Your new people like you. I hope when I come back in ten moons they will still like you.

BOSAMBO: Lord Sandi, I have learnt the secret of government from your Lordship.

SANDERS: You have?

BOSAMBO: It is this. A king ought not to be feared but loved by his people.

SANDERS: That is the secret of the British, Bosambo.

Sanders—who insists on an official marriage registration between Bosambo and Lilongo, so that Bosambo will forsake polygamy, and permits the old king all his customs except slavery, because "slavery I will not have, King Mofalaba"—fulfils his work as an agent of modernization. In opposition to Mofalaba's reign of terror, which is an end unto itself, Britain's enforcement of law through violent retribution is represented as a necessary prelude to democracy and self-governance.

Sanders of the River, *The Drum*, and *Black Narcissus* all end with the departure of the English from a colony after having restabilized narrative and political order. In *Sanders*, though, the abdication of power is not final, and Sanders promises to return in ten moons to assess his nominated ruler's progress. Because the text does not provide a strong antagonistic principle against imperial hierarchy (with hierarchy here referring to both the social ordering of races and the narrative ordering of events), there is no strong sense that imperial presence will be unwelcome, as in imperial romance, or unnecessary, as in imperial modernism. The fantasy of a repeated return to colonial authority is incorporated into the figure of the colonial ally, who is adult enough to understand the secret of governance but child enough to repeatedly err. We hear similar conceptualizations of African audiences, who are described as (eternally teachable) imperfect subjects and (eternally insatiable) ideal consumers. "Most white people go to the cinema to be entertained. Africans would come in their thousands to be instructed and would be entertained as a side issue. The African has so much to learn that this could continue almost *ad infinitum*." [35] The *Sanders* version of Africa redeems imperialism in the literal sense of Britain "making good" on its promise to tutor the "less-developed" African, who might need an indefinite number of lessons. And so the film keeps open the fantasy of a supervisory British State.

Multiple Realisms

Imperial cinema's arguments about colonization's pedagogical and modernizing value for colonial subjects worked in parallel ways with domestic support of developmental programs for the British underclass. The political push toward a protectionist, enlightened state amid contentious departures from the individualist, laissez-faire market system envisioned new welfare policies in the colonial and domestic arena. This progressive impulse was equally motivated by an intent to tame socialist uprisings of the workers and the poor by making less-enfranchised constituencies a more visible and active part of national life. In cinema, if the Quota Act was one aspect of a benevolent state adopting measured protectionism toward commercial films, the state's cultivation of noncommercial, educational films aimed primarily at the British middle classes was another. The pioneering work of John Grierson, supported by Stephen Tallents (in his capacity as secretary of the EMB and later as public-relations officer of the General Post Office) is well known in this context. [36] Using the word *documentary* for the first time to describe Robert Flaherty's *Moana* (1926), Grierson saw in the new representational form a unique way of bringing the faces, routines, and lives of Britain's working classes and colonial subjects to the British bourgeoisie. [37] Grierson's leadership at the film units of the EMB (1927–1933) and the GPO (1933–1937) aimed to define a cinema that raised its viewers' consciousness by exposing them humanistically to the neglected faces of industrial Britain.

The EMB and GPO film units' experiments with film form gave documentaries an enduring vocabulary, comprised of a voice-over, music, lyrical vista shots interwoven with select individual lives, and (under Alberto

Cavalcanti's control of the GPO film unit in 1937) direct-address interviews. Though *Sanders* is a commercial film, it may be usefully evaluated against the British documentary film movement of the 1930s for a few reasons. First, both the documentary and the commercial empire film depicted Britain's national and/or colonial "others." EMB and GPO documentaries aimed to educate British audiences about British workers, colonial lands, dominion markets, and diverse topographies by means of a cinema that was experimental, socially committed, as well as paternalistic. Given the overlap in target markets and depicted themes, one may legitimately ask if (and how) the familiar combination of social responsibility and paternalism in state- and privately sponsored documentaries about the colonial subjects and British working classes intersected or varied from commercial imperial cinema.[38] Second, more than any other commercial films, the groundbreaking documentaries of the EMB and GPO film units exploited the visual medium's ability to reveal diverse locations, lifestyles, and customs as much as its ability to tell a story. *Elephant Boy* and *Sanders* shared the stylistic idiom of combining actuality footage with narrative realism. Such coincidences in film language are not entirely surprising given the occasional duplications in film personnel; for example, Korda's *Elephant Boy* was partially shot by Robert Flaherty, who also shot *Industrial Britain* (1933) for the EMB and *Man of Aran* (1934) for Michael Balcon.[39]

On closer scrutiny, it is the dissimilarities between the documentaries and the empire film that better clarify their distinct cultural functions. Martin Stollery convincingly demonstrates the documentary film movement's location and assimilation into the tradition of European art-film discourse of the 1920s and 1930s, which points to differences in the sites of exhibition and reception of documentaries as opposed to commercial films. Documentary films were primarily screened at nontheatrical locations such as London's Imperial Institute, circulated among film societies in Britain and film festivals in Europe, or lent out by the Empire Film Library to educational institutions.[40] Stollery's analysis, along with that of Ian Aitkin and Sarah Street, effectively situates the documentary movement's aesthetic alongside British and European modernist cinemas, evident not only in their more specialized travel circuits but also in the documentary filmmakers' self-conscious emphasis on personal vision, artistic style, and references to other film movements (particularly the Soviet montage school).[41] In addition to differing from empire cinema in their deliberate distancing from the commercial film form and exhibition sites, British documentary films expressed a liberal politics despite institutional limitations on their narratives and images. In corporate-sponsored colonial films such as *Cargo from Jamaica* (Basil Wright, 1933) and *Song of Ceylon* (Basil Wright, 1934), Stollery argues, anticolonial and prosocialist commentary is necessarily hidden to evade detection. The films' critique of the state lurks in strategically placed voice-overs and in the juxtaposition of images of low-paid, plentiful native labor against absent British work forces clearly displaced by mechanization, thus presenting a camouflaged critical commentary that is picked up in journal discussions of the 1930s.[42]

Though the aforementioned films portray Jamaica and Ceylon as Britain's exotic, less-developed periphery, the colonies are treated as spiritually rejuvenating counterpoints to civilization in a manner that affiliates their presentational mode to imperial romances. Romances endow greater complexity to the colonized place than realist narratives, as they acknowledge a physical and psychic dependence between the imperial metropolis and the colony. This is also borne out in films of the documentary movement that deal with white working classes in ways visually parallel to the colonial documentaries, such as *Coalface* (Cavalcanti, 1935), *Drifters* (Grierson, 1929), *Housing Problems* (Anstey, 1935), and *Industrial Britain*; these films differ from each other in terms of structure, poetics, pacing, and sound, but share with colonial documentaries an interest in making unknown lives visible to middle-class audiences through a lyricism of images and an emphasis on human nobility. Korda's imperial films, in contrast, are for-profit ventures that incorporate a variety of sentimental appeals and cinematic seductions—like stars, songs, staged battles, and ethnographic footage—to attract mass viewership.

Audiences attending Korda's imperial films did not merely see a film. They were given an evening of entertainment filled with pageantry, music, costume, and "authentic" documentary footage of unfamiliar places. This "thrilling" aspect of filming within the empire was underscored in interviews with the director Zoltan Korda and the production manager G. E. T. Grossmith. Narrating their experience of recording African songs and dances, Grossmith emphasized the novelty of "never-before seen or heard" movements and sounds: "A thousand savage warriors in huge ostrich feather hats, buffalo shields, and spears were told by the interpreter that the great white man, Mr. Zoltan Korda, wanted to hear their national songs. It was no good explaining we were a film unit, that would have conveyed nothing at all. . . . The thousand men formed themselves into a battle square and commenced to sing and dance for ten solid days and ten nights. They never stopped!"[43]

Zoltan Korda added, "We had the Acholi [tribe] do some dances for us, but we were warned that we must be wary. These natives take their dancing seriously. We talk about dancing marathons. Every dance with the Acholi is a marathon. And ever so often one of them would dance himself into a frenzy when he felt he must kill whosoever was nearest to him. . . . We were compelled to arrest and lock up an average of about six 'actors' every day."[44] Though also dabbling in the shock effects of exposing bourgeois England to the lives of the English poor, the documentarists aimed to use film to ennoble and humanize domestic and colonial labor.[45] In contrast, the documentary footage in *Sanders* spectacularizes and sensationalizes Africans, and the film's surrounding publicity makes them incorrigible curiosities. As noted in "Interesting Facts about *Sanders of the River*," "The 20,000 African negroes who take part in this picture received most of their wages in the form of cartons of cigarettes."[46]

In their analysis of the documentary movement, Katherine Dodd and Philip Dodd argue that for Grierson and other documentary filmmakers, films were as much about including the workers within the nation's self-image as they were about instructing the nation on the lives of its invisible majority. The documentarists portrayed the working classes as heroes rather than victims, whose bodies provided a reinvented image of the nation. "The documentarists' obsession with working-class masculinity should be seen as one of the ways that a new, alternative version of manly Englishness could be first imagined and then stabilized. The films themselves make clear that not only should virile, heterosexual, working-class masculinity be welcomed into the nation, but that such a masculinity might serve to incarnate it."[47] The Dodds present the revival of masculinity through working white or native bodies as a necessary cure for the ailing aristocratic male body, which was proving an inadequate symbol for post-imperial Britain.

In fact, both imperial and documentary films can be understood as responses to a crisis in national identity demonstrable in representations of masculine heroism, with the difference that commercial imperial cinema's use of naturalism to resolve the underlying crisis in (national, masculine) identity varied from the G PO and E M B films' deployment of images to do the same. Unlike the documentaries, *Sanders* rigorously avoids depicting white protagonists through the naturalism reserved for Africa and Africans, while also prioritizing narrative realism over documentary footage in the film as a whole. The narrative segments provide, in Colin MacCabe's phrase, "the realm of truth" against which all other images are verified.[48] Considering both empire films and documentaries as the collective output of a nation, the repeated depiction of working-class white men through a documentary gaze that never falls on white aristocrats speaks of a prevalent politics of form.

Documentary realism is used several times in *Sanders*. To mention the first few longest instances, the rumors about Sanders's death are followed by a montage of stampeding animals, feeding vultures, dancing men, burning huts, and running warriors. A three-minute segment of a dance ensues after a title informs us,

> The fighting regiments—made bold by the news of Sanders' death—whip themselves to frenzy by the fearsome Lion dance.

Belying premature celebrations, Sanders soon returns on his plane. His flight to the residency is conveyed through another documentary sequence, involving shots of the aircraft, birds in flight, splashing hippos, running ostriches, stampeding bison, and giraffes. These are primarily long aerial safari shots in which the camera is airborne, mobile, and occasionally subjective. Within the formal logic of *Sanders*, creating visual continuity or contact spaces between the two races within a documentary format carries the danger of stripping the English of their narrative power. However, while the aviation sequence is a rare occasion on which Sanders and his jet appear in the same frame as "documentary Africa," the distance in species and space contain any possible threat to the imperial body.

Stollery notes similarities between the aerial sequence in *Sanders* and Paul Rotha's imperial aviation documentaries (a similarity noted by Rotha himself, according to Stollery), although aviation documentaries used voice-overs, while *Sanders* shows a silent spectacle of a triumphant metal emblem of Western modernity swooping over Africa's wilderness.[49] These sequences are embedded into a narrative that utilizes Sanders as its referential center, but their duration and distinct mode of presentation give them a feel of independent segments within the film. The startling difference between the film's documentary mode and its narrative realism gives pause, at least in terms of its disruption of the film's flow and its shift in spectatorial engagement. In an admittedly structuralist definition of political art according to an "ultraleft fantasy," Colin MacCabe, among others, argues that to be progressive, art should be able to break the "imaginary" relation between spectator and text, disrupting the unity of sign and referent to bring to light the obscured rules through which a realist text orders its discourse.[50] With regard to the two realisms in *Sanders*, we may well ask if the documentary attractions produce intentional or unintended artistic and ideological interruptions of the narrative segments. Do the blatant specularizations of tribal Africans or wild safari animals shock the audience out of the representational network of the narrative, exposing its mechanisms?

Clearly, such discussions are incomplete without considering historical viewers and their relationship to a film's discursive organization.[51] To current viewers, *Sanders* is immediately visible as a racist film. While modern audiences do not need an interrupted narrative to be conscious of this film's politics, as intervening social struggles against discriminatory images have granted most of us such awareness, the historical viewer was not politically naïve either. The most compelling example is the controversy surrounding Paul Robeson's role in *Sanders of the River*, a role that was criticized by several political activists in the United States, including, as mentioned previously, Robeson himself. Moreover, another British film, Gainsborough's *Old Bones of the River* (Varnel, 1938), directly lampooned *Sanders* and provided a satirical antidote to the film. Subverting an imperial trope, the opening intertitles of *Old Bones* are placed in a parodic rather than indexical relationship to the film's ensuing visuals.

> Darkest Africa—where in primeval surroundings amidst crocodile infested waters, a handful of Englishmen rule half a million natives— teaching the black man to play the white man.

In this irreverent variation, titles generically deployed as unmediated statements of truth are called out as conventions supporting an ideology. *Sanders* and *Old Bones* (and their respective political attitudes) function as historical interlocutors of each other, so that the proclamation of imperial values in *Sanders* can be understood as an absolution of empire in a context in which there was dissent against it.

At the time, many objected on artistic grounds to Korda's ham-fisted combination of anthropological film and fictional narrative, without exploring its impact on the film's ideology. In a review of Korda's *Elephant Boy*, John Grierson conveyed his perplexity at the film's style: "I merely note the alien strangeness of its juxtaposition [of Flaherty and Korda's filming] in this film. With its synthetic spectacle of studio, camp scenes and West End voices it brings the film at every turn to an artificial, different plane. . . . The film drives on under the lash of the synthesis."[52] Michael Powell, who shot most of *Black Narcissus* in a studio, was uncomplimentary about Korda's decision to divide the film shoot between Denham studios and Africa rather than present a unified artistic vision.[53] More recently, the film historian Jeffrey Richards wrote, "The resulting film reveals the split approach, with the documentary footage sometimes uneasily woven into the narrative, filmed in the main at Denham Studios with imported Cardiff dockers as extra natives."[54]

In fact, Korda brings narrative and documentary together in a manner that allows neither form of realism to politically or aesthetically invigorate, displace, or question the other. Unless we want to be formulaic about progressive art, we cannot posit that the mere fact of an interruption through a collage of other attractions breaks the identificatory processes of narrative. "A mere tableau structure is insufficient to reflect social contradictions or break the complacency of our (spectatorial) position. . . . [T]he scenes may not necessarily become dominant over the reality expressed in narrative."[55] The documentary sequences in *Sanders* leave the spectator in the same position of authority in relation to the images as do the narrative segments, and, to paraphrase Lyotard, both modes "preserve our consciousness from doubt" by stabilizing the meaning of the referent to enable easy affirmations of white, male, and British superiority.[56]

But to be persistent in this line of inquiry, we may still ask if such a reading overvalues the ideological aspect of realism, abdicating an understanding of the differences between the two realisms in experiential terms. Can a fragmented realism allow images to establish a novel "intimacy" with the spectator, to use Rachel Moore's term? In Moore's theorization of film as modern magic, she points to numerous occasions when films depict the "primitive's" "first contact" with technology in a manner that allows modernity to rehearse its own wonderment with itself. In films like *Nanook of the North* (Flaherty, 1922), Moore argues, "Through the contrivance of primitives' eyes we see the marvel of technology's recent past, and through the technology of the camera itself we enjoy the fine nuances of primitive gesture. Technology makes the primitive primitive and, at the same time, the primitive makes technology magical."[57] Moore calls attention to the Epsteinian *photogenie* of cinema, its "ability to touch you with no hands, elate you, shock you," which are suppressed by psychoanalytic, cognitive, or cultural readings of film.[58] To this end, she beckons us to early film theory's "primitivist impulse," defined in part as a discernibly modern and Eurocentric fascination with the figure of the primitive, and with the cinematic medium's potential for animism.

Bringing Moore's reconsideration of early documentary realism as a modernist project to *Sanders*, we may ask if, in their experiential dimensions, Korda's documentary segments permit a new way of interrogating the film's content. A brief comparison between *Sanders* and a contemporary commercial fiction film that incorporates narrative and documentary footage helps emphasize the historically inflected nature of this cinematic experience. It contextualizes the use of realism and naturalism as dual aesthetic environments through which colonial images were delivered to the spectator within proximate contexts and periods of production.

The British director Thornton Freeland's *Jericho* (1937; released in the United States as *Dark Sands*) tells the story of an African American man who escapes to North Africa and becomes a sheik. As Jericho Jackson, Paul Robeson reprises his role from *The Emperor Jones* (Murphey, 1933). Jericho is part of a company of all-black troops being shipped to France at the end of World War I. When Germans torpedo their ship, Jericho fights to save black soldiers who are treated like cargo and left to die by the racist white officers controlling the vessel. In the ensuing scuffle Jericho accidentally kills a white man. His race makes this an unpardonable crime, so when a friendly white soldier named Captain Mack allows him a moment's respite from incarceration, Jericho gives his friend the slip and flees as a stowaway on a ship bound to North Africa. In the sequence that most memorably captures the aesthetic play between documentary and narrative, Captain Mack, having been disgraced by accusations of helping Jericho, is on a relentless quest for revenge. One despondent day, Mack enters a movie theater to distract himself. The theater is screening an ethnographic film of a North African tribe going on its annual journey for salt. This brief film-within-a-film contains all the familiar tropes of its type: the authoritative voice-over, shots of abject but noble Africans, their objectification by a seemingly impersonal camera. The spectator (along with Captain Mack) experiences the shock of seeing Jericho, who had hitherto been part of the primary film's narrative segments, represented as a North African sheik subjected to documentary techniques reserved for the representation of Africans.

Freeland, clearly borrowing from the visual tropes of contemporary 1930s documentaries, exploits cinema's ability to alter the filmed subject and affect the film's spectator by destabilizing the relationship between viewer and the represented object. Korda's vision for cinema in *Sanders*, on the other hand, uses varied visual styles to suppress the possibility of such discovery, pleasure, interrogation, or shock. In a broader sense, the film deprives documentary of its own poetics (as elaborated by Michael Renov), by making those sequences perpetually subservient to an ideological vision regulated by the narrative sequences.[59] To refer back to Rachel Moore's analysis, her theory of cinema rests on a conceptualization of the medium as part of modernity's dizzying encounters and transformations. She writes about cinema's promise of a contact between estranged worlds — of the modern man meeting (and creating) the savage; of the savage meeting (and enabling) the modern; of cinema's magical mutability meeting modern fragmentation — as best captured in the writings of early film theorists. This promise of cinematic modernity as a radically transformative encounter is *denied* in *Sanders*, unlike in *Jericho*, which uses realism in modernist ways to retain that possibility. Imperial fiction's romance and modernist modes have a propensity to utilize color, sound, and image to stay alive to the mythic, abstract, and poetic aspects of cinema while conveying their worldview. The consequences of this visual pleasure for a film's politics can be seen in *The Drum* and *Black Narcissus*.

The depiction of Bosambo and Lilongo, the two African allies of Commissioner Sanders who are played by recognizable African American stars, present a third dimension of representation in *Sanders*, which lies somewhere between the visual idioms of narrative and documentary. Bosambo and Lilongo are characterized by shots that fit neither into narrative realism nor documentary naturalism. Two shots stand out in particular. The first occurs when Bosambo sings about Sanders against a back-projection of boats on the Isisi River. He is filmed in a studio, but his background visuals are provided by the projection of actual documentary footage. In the second image, Lilongo repeats a dance performed by African tribes; while she is supposed to be one of them and mimics their actions, she is filmed on a studio set, and her image is spliced to follow the dance outside.

Within the film, as well as extra-cinematically, Robeson and MacKinney are not equivalent to white British actors, black British extras, or to anonymous members of African tribes. In the film they play Anglophone Nigerians who show their proximity to the British by forsaking polygamy and offering their loyalty to the Crown. They are also the only romantic male-female duo in an otherwise masculine imperial adventure; they have the longest speaking parts among actors playing Africans; and they are the only characters that sing. Pro-filmically, they are the film's only African American actors. They both create a new and desired market for the movie and add to its salability with their musical numbers. Reflecting their in-between status, which straddles the narrative authority of the whites and the objectified specularization of Africans, these two figures are reproduced through hybrid shots that combine documentary and narrative fiction. They are in African costume but do not blend with an Africa that is depicted either in documentary form or through constructed sets, projections, and sleight of editing. Nor do they assimilate with their fellow white protagonists, because shot compositions enforce a visual racial segregation. The film's most experimental hybrid shots center on these two figures and are produced to relay and reinforce the relational and social hierarchies of the film's narrative sequences.

What gives *Sanders*'s techniques a kind of imperialist "radical realism" akin to Said's definition of orientalism is the film's ideological organization of images at multiple levels. There is no contact between real and "studio" Africans, no tribal dancers with speaking parts, no black British or African American actors in the documentary sequences, and no nudity in the narrative segments. Realism and naturalism coexist in the film, moving in a "lash of synthesis" without touching each other. They are unified by an ideology that depends on a prohibition of contact between the two forms in order to prevent a destabilization of the film's assumptions and to stall disorientations of our politico-visual experience. And so most profoundly, imperial realism refuses contact with its own historical moment, when divisions between colonizer and colonized were under attack. Colonial administration is accepted as the only route to democracy for a black nation, and the contradictions of that position are either suppressed or evaded.

(I take Romanticism to be the genesis of the modern, of the
sensibility within which we are still living) in that modern
art has typically felt itself to be constructed on, and over, the
void, postulating meanings and symbolic systems which have
no central justification because they are backed by no theol-
ogy and no universally accepted code.
—Peter Brooks, *The Melodramatic Imagination*

Some people are born free, they can do what they like without
concern for consequences. But you were not born free Harry,
and nor was I. We were born into a tradition, a code which
we must obey even if we do not believe. And we must obey it,
because the pride and happiness of everyone surrounding us
depends upon our obedience.
—Ethne Burroughs, *The Four Feathers* (1939)

five * ROMANCE AND EMPIRE

Imperial romance films of the 1930s are Scheherazadian tales told in the
face of an abyss, creating grand narratives of legitimation for an empire and
its sustaining vision while confronted with imminent dissolution. Northrop
Frye has argued that just as the Bible may be considered the (Judeo-Christian)
epic of the creator, romance is a "secular scripture" or the epic of the creature.[1] Without accepting Frye's universalizing conclusion of romance as "the
structural core of all fiction,"[2] we can still perceive its operation in late-
imperial films that sacralize Britain by endowing significance to the very
thing that was under threat of becoming ordinary, a mere nation among other
nations.[3]

Imperial romances spin out secular equivalents of a theological universe.
Men are driven to establish control over foreign lands in obedience to an unidentified higher command that is vaguely a composite of nation, lineage,
honor, duty, and justice. Their enemies are not just plotting Afghans, violent African chiefs, or petty Indian rulers, but the abstract forces of sadism,
greed, corruption, cowardice, perversion, and disorder. The colonized and
their lands represent the white romantic protagonist's "underworld," ma-
terializing to test the (typically masculine) hero or to assist him in the real-

ization of his destiny. If colonial forces arrayed against the British Empire are suppressed by imperial realism, romance transforms them into myth.

A myth's fantastic elements and history's documentary solemnity appear to have little in common, but there is a refracted similitude. Freudian theorist Michel de Certeau situates historical writing in the context of Europe's encounter with the New World. No longer a mere chronicle of kings and invasions, the invention of historical writing depended on a secular notion of linear, forward-moving time and on scientific methods of description that identified the present as a causal product of a series of preceding events. Following de Certeau, this mode of narration facilitated (and was in turn validated by) Europe's assimilation of the New World as its primitive past. Historical writing, as part of the larger project of European enlightenment, demanded a differentiation between those who appeared to be progressing in time (the Self) from those who seemed to be stuck in it (the Other). Europe's modern historical consciousness was founded on a sense of transcendence and control: over the past, the irrational, the unknown, the newfound lands, the primitives, death, and all things placed outside the pale of knowledge and reason.[4] In this argument, then, history is a mythic rewriting of Europe as the technologically advanced, enlightened, masculine present, and of the New World as Europe's untamed, feminized, living past.

History's potentially mythifying impulses alert us *against* making easy distinctions between the registers of myth and history and present an argument *for* connecting myth to modern modes of description. Roland Barthes, on a more quotidian level, further expands the notion of myth by arguing at length that "the mythical is present everywhere *sentences are turned, stories told* (in all sense of the two expressions): from inner speech to conversation, from newspaper article to political sermon, from novel . . . to advertising image."[5] What makes British imperial romances fascinating in the context of this discussion is that they strain to combine popular representations of empire (myth as the *doxa* behind everyday practices of modern life, as elaborated by Barthes) while anointing those narratives with a sense of a sacred, higher cause (myth as the foundational story of a race or nation, as described by de Certeau) and endowing them with the referential weight of past events (myth as history reinterpreted).

Alexander Korda's film *The Drum*, for instance, looks like a Penny Dreadful and tells the romantic tale of a frontier adventure while making geographical and thematic references to British wars fought in Afghanistan during 1838 and 1878–1879. Similarly, *The Four Feathers* recalls the Crimean War

(1854–1856) and British campaigns in the Sudan under General Gordon and General Kitchener (1884–1885, 1896–1898) respectively. In this chapter as previously, I elaborate on imperial romance by using a paradigmatic film form to discuss its attitude toward the colonized and colonizing bodies, the colonial place, and the act of narration, beginning with the film's representational devices or the narrative and visual acts through which it transforms history into myth.

Imperial Description and Colonial Place

The Drum depicts a fictional place called Tokot, bordering British India's frontier province of Afghanistan. A swift summary of events relating to the two Afghan wars will situate the film's myth in relation to the territory's historical significance. Afghanistan was a notoriously difficult terrain for the British government (an observation repeated in reports on the U.S. war in the same region in 2002). In 1820 the East India Company entered into a peace treaty with the ruling Muslim emirs of Sind, India, because they feared a Russian invasion through the Khyber Pass in Afghanistan and the Sind further south.[6] During this period, Dost Mohammed, the new ruler (or khan) of Afghanistan, ousted the previously Anglo-friendly Shah Shuja. Making the customary move of gaining politico-economic control over a territory by participating in domestic conflict, Sir William Macnaghten of the East India Company offered military assistance to Shah Shuja and marched a British Indian army of occupation to the area. The cost of maintaining a British residency and an army in the mountainous regions consumed surplus income generated from Indian and Afghan treasuries, and a combination of the expense and the onslaught of an Afghan winter destroyed Macnaghten's armies. Dost Mohammed returned to his throne after a British war that had expended twenty-thousand lives and over fifteen-million pounds sterling. To recover the cost, the British invaded the fertile peasant community in the Sind, in contravention to their treaty, and posted Charles Napier as Sind's first British governor.

The second Afghan war was equally ill conceived. During Dost Mohammed's reign, the British followed a "butcher and bolt" policy to intimidate the independent Pathan tribes of the region. After Dost Mohammed's death, directions from the Tory home government under Benjamin Disraeli led to increased British presence in Afghanistan. By 1878, under British India's Viceroy Lytton, a British army occupied Kabul and Kandahar and Major Louis Cavagnari, the British political resident of Kabul, dominated puppet-king

11. Tokot's "verile and magnificent spectacle" in *The Drum*. Courtesy USC Cinema-Television Library.

Yakub Khan. On 12 September 1879, the Pathans assassinated Cavagnari and his army in their residency, resulting in a massive retaliation by the British army. Atrocities committed during this rampage and the expenses of a war that was longer and more wasteful than predicted resulted in the replacement of Lytton by Lord Ripon, the end of Disraeli's government, and a cessation of Britain's adventurist policy in the northwest provinces.[7]

So the frontier province of Afghanistan served as a good metaphor for the Raj's vulnerabilities. In *The Drum* that contentious territory becomes a symbol of the threats to the British Empire and of imperial valor in the face of danger.[8] Though set in its contemporary period of 1938, *The Drum*'s plot evokes both prior Afghan wars. The film's British protagonist, Captain Carruthers (Roger Livesey), proposes to set up a protectorate in Tokot to prevent gun-running and insurgencies, planned by kingdoms extending from China to Afghanistan, against British India. Like the historical Louis Cavagnari, Carruthers establishes a residency in Tokot, promising peace in return for a subsidy for the region's ruler and his son, Prince Azim (Sabu). As soon as Carruthers leaves Tokot to get married, violence reigns in the new protectorate (much as in *Sanders*). Ghul Khan (Raymond Massey), the ruling Khan's brother, loathes the British and dreams of reviving a pan-Islamic empire. He murders his brother and attempts to kill his nephew, Prince Azim, who flees to Peshawar with his faithful servant Wafadar (Roy Emerton). Fratricidal Ghul then requests that Carruthers return to Tokot and deceitfully endorses the old treaty while setting a trap to slaughter the British regiment on the last day of Moharram. Though young Prince Azim, British ally Muhammad Khan (Amid Taftazani), and loyal servant Zarullah (Lawrence Bascomb) put themselves in danger's way to warn Carruthers, eventually it is the British governor's army from Peshawar that intercedes to save the day, restoring Tokot's British residency and Prince Azim's crown.

In addition to the film's plot, which incorporates details from both Afghan wars, Captain Carruthers makes an explicit reference to historical events during his second trip to Tokot.

> CARRUTHERS: Do you remember Sir Louis Cavagnari? He was British resident in Kabul.
>
> MAJOR: Yes, when was that?
>
> CARRUTHERS: About sixty years ago.
>
> MAJOR: A bit before my time! He was massacred with all his escorts, wasn't he?
>
> CARRUTHERS: He walked into a trap with his eyes open. And so did Gordon.
>
> MAJOR: Yes, but he got out of a good many tight corners before he was cut down in Khartoum.
>
> CARRUTHERS: Exactly, and as a result of that, Kitchener conquered Sudan and we've had peace there for two generations. A not unusual preliminary to our establishing law and order is the murder of one of our representatives.

Whereas *Sanders* makes references to the real by using footage and recordings from Nigeria at some unspecified time of British occupation, *The Drum* and *The Four Feathers* are particular in their historical periodization. Like *The Four Feathers*, which inserts its narrative into Kitchener's campaign in Sudan and attributes the campaign's victory in no small part to the film's fictional protagonist, *The Drum* identifies Carruthers as a successor to the historical Cavagnari and Gordon. Here fiction is legitimated by its emplotment within historical memory, not by an embeddedness in documentary footage. The retrospective projection of Carruthers as one in a line of residents creates a tradition of British colonial presence linked to king and empire, though exclusive privileges of trading and governance in India belonged to the commercial East India Company until the late 1800s. In the film's account, Carruthers is merely channeling his predecessors who sacrificed themselves for the greater cause of peace and legality. Actual historical facts and figures intervene to locate the fiction, while fiction inflates each fact into an abstraction. Abetting the rhetorical inflations of dialogue are the film's camera angles, color, and music, which raise each cinematic image to the level of a spectacle that interrupts our relationship with the referential real. If *Sanders* encouraged an illusion of transparency between image and world, *The Drum* excites our vision by exaggerating reality.

Brightly hued illustrations reminiscent of British pulp fiction from the 1800s frame *The Drum*'s opening credits, recalling military adventure tales printed in the popular magazine *Boy's Own Paper*. An acknowledgement to the Indian ruler the mehtar of Chitral for his permission to film in the territory is followed by visual sequences that identify the film as a Kiplingesque narrative about the "Great Game" of empire, involving espionage and fraternal military societies. Accompanied by music swelling to the tune of "Rule Britannia" and dramatic drumming, the familiar spinning globe stops at an area marked as the Northwest Frontier, between India and Afghanistan, then dissolves as long pans take us to a "Tribal Territory" where snipers with machine guns shoot at Indian soldiers of the British army. The scene cuts to (a much older) Sanders talking to His Excellency the British Governor of India.[9] The men discuss Carruthers, who suspects an infiltration of ammunition into the Northwest of India. On cue, the scene cuts to Carruthers in disguise as a native, speaking a kind of artificial, antiquated English that connotes native-speak in imperial films. Presumably proving his Eastern credentials, Carruthers begs for food, curses, heckles, and passes unnoticed among the Pathans who inhabit the area. Under cover, he is slipped a piece of bread with an encrypted message about gun trading. Throughout the sequence, chaotic street sounds mix with the claps and chorus of male Pathan singers.

The then new technology of Technicolor photography redefines and enhances the colonial location. Most of the exterior shots of *The Drum* were filmed in Wales, with some footage from Chitral. In reality, Chitral was under significant government surveillance. Several British government files from the late 1920s and early 1930s indicate that the British were extremely suspicious of the possibility of colonial resistance in Chitral.[10] Though there does not appear to be conclusive evidence, the British India government was informed of anonymous letters in Gurmukhi (the Sikh script) to His Highness the Mehtar, "urging him to murder all the British in Chitral." [11] The government issued secret warnings to the mehtar, asking him to "not meddle in Afghan affairs." [12] The files were confidential at the time, but such concerns must have been widely known, as they found their way into a commercial narrative set in the same location. Rather than exploiting the film's immediate proximity to Chitral, Korda's film exploits cinematic artifice by replicating the location in studio sets (designed by Vincent Korda, Alexander and Zoltan's brother) shot in color (by George Perinal).

Against the norm of black-and-white film, early Technicolor technology brought a new dimension of signification that was exploited by animated shorts, musicals, and historical films, all of which delved into the realm of fantasy.[13] In *The Drum* color has the effect of overlaying a sense of exoticism, otherworldliness, and adventure to the narrative, as appreciated by several film critics of the time. According to the British journal *The New Statesman and Nation*, *The Drum* was "the first film to make one really grateful for colour." [14] A "real money-spinner," it was, in the words of the British *Film Weekly*, "a virile and magnificent spectacle, an outstanding achievement." [15] The American *Motion Picture Herald* hailed it as a "spectacle melodrama." [16] On its re-release in 1944 it was again celebrated for its photography "in brilliant Technicolor, fashioned in circumstances that pay exciting, breathtaking tribute to British rule in India." [17] *The Cinema* called it an "army melodrama" providing "popular entertainment for all classes." The film was said to have "colorful material developed on spectacular lines with glorious mountain scenery, artistic interiors, teeming bazaars, barrack squares, panorama of marching men, parades and martial music, culminating in a thrilling massacre sequence." [18]

Prior to *The Drum*'s release as well, film critics commented on the aptness of Technicolor technology for films with colonial themes. A 1937 essay that discussed the subject of "Filming Eastern Subjects in Colour" commented, "The two-dimensional monochromatic cinema is unsuitable to subjects of an Eastern character. The 'gorgeousness' of the East, the popular idea of lavish splendour with which the average Western mind associates, say, India, is an association indissolubly bound up with colour. . . . With the evolution of a successful and practical colour system, however, a very different case presents itself. Something of the 'unreality' of the East is then available for the Westerner." [19]

Orientalism finds luxurious scope in Technicolor. The journal quoted above imagines an India that resists monochromes, revealing something of the "average Western mind" that links the place with unreal splendor. Color translates the colonial place in a manner commensurate with its marvelousness, preserving the fantastic aspect of India for a Western audience. Yet *as a translation*, Technicolor "produces strategies of containment" by fixing the colonial place within a familiar referential network of fantasy, domesticating India and rendering it legible.[20] The drama of articulation at play here, wherein color becomes the perfect medium that can both allude to and contain India's excess, presents itself in every dimension of *The Drum*.

The double hermeneutic of a surplus (of beauty, thrills, threat, and danger) and its containment is visible at the level of visual, aural, and narrative representation. Myths about British heroism cannot be constructed without voicing every anxiety about its dissipation. To transform the site of colonization into a fantastic theater of primeval conflict between good and evil, the film exaggerates the East beyond proportion. Dramatic sounds cue the presence of colonial locations and persons, amplifying their visual strangeness with an equally distinctive aurality: Ghul Khan's murmurs of an Islamic takeover intrude into the sounds of a British band; drumbeats emanate from a richly hued Tokot; gunshots herald Prince Azim on horseback. Sarah Street notes that sounds in *The Drum* are "used to signify the conflicting narrative themes which are to follow: native culture vs. British identity; Indian use of military technology vs. British policing of the Raj."[21] In addition to underscoring the oppositions, sounds enhance the threat of violence swamping the British: most memorably, when Ghul Khan's men fling Zarullah's chopped head through the resident's window, interrupting Mrs. Marjorie Carruthers (Valerie Hobson) at her piano singing "A Penny for Your Thoughts." In the visual and aural conflicts between Christianity and Britain versus Islam and India, the latter begin to inch closer, suffusing British sounds and spaces, dwarfing them with danger.

Yet even as the colony acquires an overwhelming presence, its threat is delivered to viewers in well-worn forms. To this end, imperial romance films repeat key tropes from earlier traditions of literary romanticism. Saree Makdisi, Rajani Sudan, and others have carefully shown the interconnections between British imperialism, nationalism, and the literary romanticism of the 1700s and 1800s.[22] There was a historical concomitance between the emergence of a romantic imagination and Britain's modernization through its ever-expanding imperial realm of industry, which fed the need to create inviolable, mythic, internal dominions (as in the works of Wordsworth, Blake, Byron, Shelley, and Austen). In fact, imperial romantic adventure films also

12. White protagonists besieged by black bodies in the Khalifa's prison in *The Four Feathers*. Courtesy USC Cinema-Television Library.

bear a resemblance to Gothic romance novels of the eighteenth century, such as Horace Walpole's *The Castle of Otranto*, M. G. Lewis's *The Monk*, and Mary Shelley's *Frankenstein*. Consider the following structure of the Gothic narrative as identified by Northrop Frye and Peter Brooks, famously repeated in Germany's 1930s expressionist films and in J. R. R. Tolkien's *The Hobbit* and *The Lord of the Rings* series from 1937, 1954, and 1955.[23] The Gothic narrative begins with a decline in the protagonists' status. This may be a descent into a world of darkness, cruelty and labyrinthine plots, or a break in a protagonist's consciousness. The descent induces a change of identity (or a double identity with only the demonic double involved in the descent), and devices for escaping from this world often involve a sacrifice, magical helpers, and talismanic objects that restore memory and rightful status. The descent and ascent are polarized, and resolutions typically entail a strongly expressive and affective articulation of occult and antagonistic forces.

In imperial romances like *The Drum* and *The Four Feathers* protagonists enter a chaotic colonial realm. They are assisted by people of lesser rank (subordinates, native allies) or guided by talismans (the drumbeat in *The Drum*; the Senghali mark and the shaming feathers in *The Four Feathers*) during their submergence in danger or false consciousness. The colonial land and its people expand to fill the antinomies of the Western protagonists while also providing them fortuitous assistance in fulfilling imperial destinies. Thus, the expressive devices of imperial romances—such as their use of color, music, and mise-en-scène; their concatenation of dramatic action; their use of characters as symbols—send mixed cues. The form's hyperarticulation of opposing forces through exaggerated signifiers of the colonial place and powerful antagonistic people make imperial romances a fulfillment of the empire's reactionary fears about the colony. At the same time, such dangers allow romantic heroes to prove their allegiance to higher codes of nation and empire, elevating colonial history into a form of reassuring myth. The imperial romance's ambiguity lies in the protagonist's submergence in a period of difficulty, when both equal and opposing forces confront each other. In these times of crisis, a melodramatic "desire to express all," to act out all anxieties associated with the dissolution of empire surfaces, giving romances a potentially problematic relationship to the dominantly imperialist ideology of their narrative.[24] Just as film melodramas serve an "ideological *function* in working through certain contradictions to the surface and re-presenting them in an aesthetic form," imperial romances call out all elements that threaten empire before affecting artistic reconciliations.[25]

White male protagonists of imperial romances appear to be governed by the logic of melodrama when they articulate their anguish at colonial expeditions. But a fiction's *terrain* of action remains as important as its narrative mechanisms. Weighing the family and domestic space against a Western frontier or an urban jungle that are coded masculine, Laura Mulvey points out that whereas "the Western and the gangster film celebrate the ups and downs endured by men of action, the melodramas of Douglas Sirk, like the tragedies of Euripides, probing pent-up emotion, bitterness and disillusion well known to women, act as a corrective [to the overvaluation of men in patriarchy]."[26] Korda's imperial romances overvalue men to the point of physically evacuating "female protagonists and women's concerns" from their topography.[27] (Set in a warring province of Afghanistan, *The Drum* has no more than one British female who serves as a foil to the masculine narrative.) In this respect, imperial romances appear to share greater genre affinities with the Hollywood western.

In making and unmaking these genre analogies, I call less for transposing theories (of the melodrama, the western, and the empire film) and contexts (of Hollywood and Britain) than for comprehending national, racial, and patriarchal representations that deploy key qualities of melodramas and westerns simultaneously. British imperial films resolutely disassociate the work of empire from the new British bourgeoisie, using the aristocracy as their class-surrogate to "deal generously with [white] male fantasy" of the wild, wild east.[28] At the same time, the aristocrats are vicarious figures for imagining imperial collapse. British empire films of the 1930s and 1940s include dark visions of thwarted, suffering, hysterical, sacrificial, and almost effeminized white, masculine bodies. The social significance of such masculine melodramas to British society in the 1930s is illuminated by existing theorizations of Hollywood and British "women's films" of the 1940s and 1950s, because the foreign frontier of colonial place functions ideologically and symbolically for the white male in much the same way as does the domestic sphere of family for the white female. The colony for the empire film's male, like home for a melodrama's female, represents an inhospitable terrain of denied desires, as well as a possible location for resuscitating self-worth to compensate for a lack of social and material power. The colonial place is accentuated as a symbolic playground for the Englishman's passion, temptation, choice, victimization, transgression, and triumph during a period of declining political control.

Film theorists have noted abundant affinities in the mythmaking function of British imperial cinema and the Hollywood western.[29] First, British India's northwest frontier province of Afghanistan or the camps and forts of British residencies in Africa are much like the imagined territories of the American West, because in these locations a wide cast of characters come into contact with each other, and their racial types, vocations, lifestyles, and values create symbolic conflicts resolved within the narrative. Second, both westerns and imperial films typically celebrate a racist and nationalist version of history. Social prejudice against ethnic white immigrants during the late 1800s made the American Northeast considerably less amenable to racially inflected nationalist mythmaking when compared to the Southwest.[30] Like the American West, colonial territories offered spectacular and dangerous locations for the portrayal of British heroism during late empire. Ella Shohat and Robert Stam contrast Hollywood westerns to U.S. films about the American Revolution to show commercial cinema's disproportionate representation of America's western expansion.[31] They note the genre's propensity for a "condensed spatiotemporality," by which they mean the genre's obsessive return to specific historical events, which raises those events to iconic status and transmutes them into historical trauma.[32] In this aspect as well, British empire narratives overlap with Hollywood westerns.

The American western is convincingly argued to possess an ambiguity in replaying threats to the film's protagonist, and as metonym, to its nation. Critics note instabilities at the heart of the western, as a genre that defines national identity through explorations of its outer limits.[33] This structure of instability points to a historical link between the film genres of the western and the melodrama. Arguably, the generic forms of literary melodramas emerged in relation to the Anglo-European world's long passage from community-based feudalism to modern, capitalist, market-based individualism. As aesthetic expressions of America and Europe's internal redefinition during the expansion of capitalism, melodramas and westerns display narrative tropes of the eighteenth-century Gothic novel, which itself harks back to an early period of revolutionary social change after the collapse of church and state following the French Revolution.[34] In twentieth-century Hollywood productions, both bourgeois forms once again offer an artistic matrix to rehearse new crises of social reorganization in America. As film critics note, in Hollywood westerns (most obviously in films like Rio Bravo, Hawks, 1959; The Professionals, Brooks, 1966; and The Wild Bunch, Peckinpah, 1969), the contradictory valuation of mercenary figures negotiates capitalism's rationalization of economic practices.[35] In Hollywood's melodramas (like Stella Dallas, Vidor, 1937; All that Heaven Allows, Sirk, 1955; and Written on the Wind, Sirk, 1956), familial and sexual conflicts serve as a receptor and descriptor of the desires, fantasies, and fears unleashed by a restructuring domestic sphere.[36]

This characterization of the two genres greatly simplifies them, but it allows two broad hypotheses: first, that film westerns and melodramas are critical aesthetic terrains for comprehending cultural and social change; and second, that these terrains are gendered by the societies from which they emerge, typically, through the western's underlying prioritization of a public display of action and a masculine textual address, as opposed to melodrama's preoccupation with private spheres of family, psyche, and emotion and use of feminine spectatorial address. Sexual difference is central to the narrative and visual economy of British imperial romances whose mechanisms of social signification overlap with these two divergently gendered genres. The cultural function of imperial romances can be clarified by the apparent conflict produced by its combination of two distinct textual and generic appeals.

In this sense, I am not repeating Rick Altman's important observations about the intrinsically contaminated nature of all film genres or the strategic genre-mixing of studios (to produce a "Western melodrama" or "Western comedy") but pointing to shared mechanisms of social signification across the western and the melodrama that come together, in revealing ways, in an imperial romance.[37] In other words, at question is not how an empire film borrows from westerns and melodramas, but how a certain mode of imperial cinema uses the generic qualities of a melodrama and a western to mimic the romance of loss, submergence, endangerment, and victory, rehearsing a centrally modernist response to the shock of denuded sacrality. This is partly my investment in calling the form "imperial romance": it retains a sensitivity to shared ideational substructures in cultural narratives and aesthetic forms from periods of radical social transition, but also permits historical specificity.

Masculinity and femininity are cognate mechanisms in the assertion of racial and national identities.[38] The melodrama of The Drum or The Four Feathers, which justifies the British Empire by erasing women and representing homosocial interactions between men who fight, endure, and sacrifice for each other, is a product of the same imperial patriarchy that exploits the melodramatic potential of female sacrificial figures to probe the collapse of colonial structures in Black Narcissus. In one sense, the women's physical erasure from masculine romances appears to reinforce an imperial patriarchy. At the same time, though, the resulting all-male sexual address of imperial romance creates a strong sense of impossibility or fatality that clings to the personal relationships laboring to redeem empire.

Witness the first twenty minutes of The Drum. The film offers a barrage of scenes demonstrating alliances between Afghan and British men, here including a Scottish regiment of working-class, white subalterns. As the film's entire cast of cross-race, cross-class "allies" are introduced, they reiterate the value of friendship in a manner that does not engage with the debate of freedom versus foreign rule, but displaces it onto a drama of personal loyalties. The final referent for their alliances, the British Raj, has a conspicuous absence of rational arguments in its favor. The vacuum is filled by the emotionalism of male friendships. As with most bourgeois fictional forms, the political manifests itself at the level of personal relationships in imperial novels and films, so that the colonial acceptance or rejection of British characters enact fantasies of reconciliation between Britain's imperial past and the postcolony's national future.

Modernist imperial fictions do not permit such reconciliations. E. M. Forster's A Passage to India ends with a thwarted relationship between two men, the Indian Muslim Aziz and the Englishman Fielding. Aziz says to Fielding, " 'We shall drive every blasted Englishman into the sea, and then'—he

13. A coalition of allies in *The Drum*. Courtesy USC Cinema-Television Library.

rode against him furiously—'and then,' he concluded half kissing him, 'you and I shall be friends.' 'Why can't we be friends now?' said the other, holding him affectionately. 'It's what I want. It's what you want.' But the horses didn't want it—they swerved apart; the earth didn't want it, sending up rocks through which riders must pass single-file." [39] The recalcitrance of the colonial place against all attempts at relational reconciliations between two races, most vivid in the modernist mode, is present in a different shape and form within the imperial romance. Initially, the negation of relationships that is so insistent in imperial modernism (the horses don't want it, the earth doesn't want it) seems absent in an imperial romance. But as the film unfolds, indications of the impossibility of (relational/political) reconciliations bring the romance close to modernist narratives. These interruptions come explicitly from powerful and vocal anti-imperial antagonists (like Ghul Khan) and, more subtly, from the powerlessness of native allies (like Azim).

Stylistic indications that intimacies between Azim and Holder, or Azim and Carruthers (like Aziz and Fielding in Forster's novel) lack a future begin to associate imperialism with a yearning, an essentially unquenchable desire for a rapprochement between colonizer and colonized. Films like *The Drum* or *The Four Feathers* gesture toward relationships which lie at the limits of

the unthinkable, such as the intensely personal and potentially erotic interactions between men, and the voyeuristic display of Sabu (a young male
Indian actor) for the film's presumptively white male audience. Implicit prohibitions against and transgressions of such portrayals offer a new optic on
the power play between colonizer and colonized. Voluntary alliances between
(colonizing and colonized) men in imperial romances create homosocial and
homoerotic relations as an alternative bond against the threat of colonial
revolution. The potential of such alliances both to validate and to threaten the
identity of a heterosexual, white, and aristocratic England propels the ambiguous erotics of romance.[40] And the ambiguities of such relational negotiations can be linked to contemporary strains and shifts in Britain's politics,
particularly to its need for a broad coalitional base of colonial and working-
class allies, its desire for strong, redemptive images of white masculinity, and
its acknowledgement of national vulnerability.

Imperial and Colonial Identity

Imperial realism's constructed coincidence between the film's central character and its hierarchy of meanings, as in the consonance in *Sanders* between
the protagonist's subjectivity and the film's intertitles, comes untethered in
the romance of empire. Imperial romances enhance the *fantasy* of spectatorial identification—always a fantasy in that there is no guarantee of its
exact approximation with textual mechanisms—because the visually seductive, extranarrative dimensions of shots dilute the "I" of the fictional protagonist and of the filmic narrator. As an absolute overlap between the protagonist's subjectivity and the film's diegesis weakens, characters accrue a
symbolic and structural significance within a crosscurrent of other elements
in the film. Consequently, though the romantic protagonist is symbolically
central to the imperial narrative, unlike realist texts he is only a node within
the film's network of meanings rather than its central structuring principle.
To invoke Elsaesser's remark about melodrama, romances "have a mythmaking function, insofar as their significance lies in the structure and articulation of the action, not in any psychologically motivated correspondence with
individualised experience."[41]

   In *The Drum* the protagonist's story serves less as a focus than as a frame for
the film's multiple characters. The hero's significance is further complicated
by the star status of the film's actors, particularly Sabu.[42] In a trade journal in
1938 *The Drum* is advertised as "Sabu in Technicolor," and he is said to "play

14. From a mahout to an international child star: Sabu in the publicity for *Jungle Book*.
Courtesy USC Cinema-Television Library.

the lead."[43] The Indian actor Sabu's own rags-to-riches life reads like a fantasy tale: the orphaned son of a *mahout* (elephant caretaker) in the service of
the maharaja of Mysore, he went on to become an international child star.
Flaherty's and Korda's film crew discovered Sabu while shooting for a film
that was to become *The Elephant Boy*. In *The Drum* Sabu (a.k.a. Sabu Dastigir
and Selar Sheik Sabu) plays the role of native ally Prince Azim.[44] After achiev-
ing renown for his role in *The Elephant Boy*, Sabu worked with Korda on *The
Drum*, *The Thief of Baghdad* (1940), and *The Jungle Book* (1942) with similar success. He eventually migrated to Hollywood and fought on behalf of the allied
powers in World War II, also becoming something of a gay icon in the United
States. When the British journal *Kinematograph Weekly* described *The Drum*, it
listed Sabu, Raymond Massey, and Valerie Hobson as the film's stars, with
Roger Livesey getting a mention in the journal only after the film's reissue in
1944, subsequent to Livesey's fame with Powell's and Pressburger's *The Life
and Death of Colonel Blimp* (1943).[45] (A recent online source notes that A. E. W.
Mason wrote *The Drum* specifically for Korda, as a vehicle for Sabu after his
success in *The Elephant Boy*.)[46]

Livesey's lesser-star status at the time of *The Drum*'s release coincides with his cinematic character's greater susceptibility to the colonial place and its people. Carruthers is influenced and externally altered by the foreign territory and inhabitants. The land impinges on his body and psyche. Romantic protagonists adopt disguises at great risk to their selves, unlike Sanders, who barely stops smoking his pipe to deal with Nigerian unrest. The romance hero's visual subservience and narrative vulnerability is enhanced by a nostalgic sense of home that permeates the film, a sensibility accentuated by England's distance from the frontier colony. Typically represented by the Englishwoman but also by the English garden, manor, piano, and port, the ideals of domestic peace and stability are both a comforting dream and an endangered vision, threatened by the frontier.

Arguing that the story of exile lies at the heart European civilization, John Durham Peters traces a thematic link from biblical narratives to literary and philosophical romanticism. Quoting Novalis, a German romanticist, Peters notes that the two sides of romanticism are homesickness and being at home everywhere, a perpetual nomadism and exile characterized by a yearning for all that is ideal and perfect, symbolized by the home, the nation, the absent element.[47] In imperial romances, colonial travel reproduces a conservative relationship to one's nation, romanticizing it as a beacon of beatific virtues. *The Drum*'s use of sound further enhances oppositions between the frontier's danger and the comfort of upper-class British domesticity, indicating the place's hostile intrusion into the idea of a British home. The film's treatment of Ghul Khan provides one of the most interesting expressions of colonial intrusions into the British residency, in no small part because of Raymond Massey's performance. He steals every scene he is in and states facts that official Britain must refute. When Carruthers returns to Tokot with a large military escort, for instance, Ghul storms into the British residency on horseback to say, "Are these troops your escort, Your Highness. Or are they an army of occupation?" Ghul Khan's eloquent verbosity far surpasses other men, though the film and film journals of the time equate eloquence with Eastern treachery. Britain's *Picturegoer Weekly* approvingly notes that Mohammed Khan, a Muslim ally with an English education in *The Drum*, has dispensed with "Oriental preamble."[48]

The film presents Ghul Khan as too suave for the wholesome British, but the result is that he frequently overshadows others with his charm. Observe the following scene, which takes place in the British residency of Tokot. The English appear huddled, making the best of being at Ghul Khan's mercy. *The Drum* perfectly captures the isolation of the British in a location like Afghanistan. While scenes of the office and the ballroom at the Governor's headquarters in Peshawar are expansive, the English look cramped and beleaguered at their Tokot Residency. Into such a setting, Ghul Khan enters with complete self-assurance, flaunts his difference, singles out Marjorie, and flatters her to immoderation.

> GHUL KHAN (bowing): In our country we have many orchards . . . the most lovely of all is now in the British regiment.
> MARJORIE CARRUTHERS: What a lovely speech. Why can't you say things like that, Major?
> MAJOR: Oh . . . well . . . I never could, you know . . .
> GHUL KHAN: The western world, madame, refuses to learn our scant virtues, the chief of which is the grateful admiration of beauty.

Ghul, the antithesis of the silent native, is a composite of many enemies of the British Empire and of British imperial narratives. He is an educated native who uses his education to muddle the "inside/outside" categories of imperialism by demonstrating great ease in English social situations even while undermining them.[49] As a character, he is Hitlerian in his ambitions, making him an immediately recognizable figure in 1938. He tells his priests, "Victories are not gained by an ignorant rabble led by a fanatic *mullah*. They are won by an army marching to one man's order, fighting to one man's plan." Whereas the mullah gazes into a bowl of clear water to prophesy the future, Ghul turns to strategic planning and military cartography. But for all his propagation of rationalist methods, he is also openly an Islamic traditionalist.

Two sequences highlight the multiple terrors that Ghul's particular combination of traditionalism and conversance with modernity holds for the British residents. British ally Mohammed Khan and Carruthers plan a clandestine meeting in which Mohammed Khan hopes to tell Carruthers about Ghul's conspiracy to slaughter him and his troops. Ghul intercepts these plans, kidnaps Mohammed Khan, and takes his place at the secret rendezvous. To everyone's alarm, he returns with Carruthers to the British residency. The people at the residency are flocked around a fireplace.

> GHUL KHAN (walking in): What a peaceful scene. An English island in our alien snows. The fire and the whiskey.
> MARJORIE CARRUTHERS: A whiskey and soda?
> GHUL KHAN: I wonder if Mohammed Khan would have had one. Still, why

15. Ghul Khan plans to revive a pan-Islamic empire in *The Drum*. Courtesy USC Cinema-Television Library.

not? With his English education and sympathies. Our religion forbids it, but that wouldn't disturb Mohammed Khan. That is, if he were in good health.

The second sequence, striking a similarly sinister tone, occurs when Ghul plans to ambush Carruthers. Carruthers is seated at Ghul's palace on the last day of Moharram, and they watch a woman dance.

GHUL KHAN: Why is it that when I was in London and Paris, the ballroom dancing always impressed me as something unspeakably vulgar and barbaric.

CARRUTHERS: Perhaps because Your Highness feels that women should never dance *with* men.

GHUL KHAN: Only *for* men.

CARRUTHERS: You think if they dance together, the man loses a great deal of his dignity.

GHUL KHAN: And the woman something of her chastity.

CARRUTHERS: We believe in the equality of rights.

GHUL KHAN: Equality of rights? Have you ever heard of a lamb persuading the tiger to live in peace with him, and respect this equality of rights? Has the musket equal rights with the machine gun?

Ghul Khan comments on the British as if *they* were the exotic ones. Clearly, in overruling gender equality, Ghul represents the conservative boor. Women, only recently acknowledged as an electorate in Britain, were a safe community for the film to present as an example of British egalitarianism. Nevertheless, Ghul's secondary argument that only those in equivalent positions of power can determine equal rights carries a historical resonance. In the late 1930s, during World War II, Indian nationalists opposed both fascism and imperialism, and consented to support the British only if guaranteed democracy and independence in their homeland. In a film riddled with social hierarchies and spatial polarizations, Ghul's statements sound suspiciously like an Indian nationalist's refusal to discuss imperial Britain's talk of partnership when one side continued to define the terms.

Placed in a context in which it stands for the regressive, conservative position, a legitimate comment about inequality is thus invalidated—a strategy that is not unusual in imperial texts. In *The Four Feathers*, for instance, the film's protagonist Harry Faversham (John Clements) hands in his resignation to the North Surrey Regiment on the eve of the regiment's departure to Khartoum, where they are to assist Kitchener in his fight against the Khalifa. Faversham is disgusted at "the futility of this idiotic Egyptian adventure. The madness of it all. The ghastly waste of time that we can never have again." He goes on to raise economic and moral objections against the invasion: "I believe in our happiness. I believe in the work to be done here to save an estate that's near to ruin. To save all those people who've been neglected by my family because they preferred glory in India, glory in Africa, glory in China." Here Faversham sounds exactly like those who had criticized imperialism in Britain for over two decades. Listen to J. A. Hobson's economic argument against imperialism: "A nation may either, following the example of Denmark or Switzerland, put brains into agriculture, develop a finely varied system of public education . . . or it may, like Great Britain, neglect its agriculture, allowing its lands to go out of cultivation and its population to grow up in towns, fall behind other nations in its methods of education . . . in order that it may squander its pecuniary and military resources in forcing bad markets and finding speculative fields of investment in distant corners of the earth, adding millions of square miles and of unassimilable population to the area of the Empire." [50]

Faversham touches a nerve in Britain's domestic debates about empire, but two factors negate his arguments. Faversham later confesses that he was deluded in placing his duty to home above his duty to "a crowd of African peasants." His criticism of the war was merely a cover for cowardice, and it is this awful truth that he must atone for in the remainder of the film. The film's timing also nullifies his position. Whatever the fictional referent, in 1938 all arguments for and against war were in large part aimed at Britain's policies toward Nazi Germany. Until 1938, Neville Chamberlain's government followed a policy of appeasement with Hitler, and there was great indecision about the value of direct aggression. The Drum would have been released just when the tide was turning in favor of war, when pacifism appeared to be a coward's route. Grafting this context onto empire gives imperialism the weight of moral righteousness; Ghul is repeatedly presented as regressive in order to recuperate progressiveness for the empire. The Drum justifies British distrust of educated Muslims, of Indian political reformists who sought to invent indigenous forms of secular modernity, and of Hitlerian authoritarianism by combining caricatures of all these categories in Ghul Khan. Similarly, The Four Feathers vilifies anti-imperialism by making Harry Faversham's internal weakness, his doubt and fear of war, the film's key antagonistic element.

At the same time, Harry Faversham and Ghul Khan are their narrative's central acknowledgments of difference. As a character, Ghul marks the presence of insurmountable difference in Britain's empire. If he says more in defense of self-determination than Mofalaba ever did, Prince Azim—like Bosambo in Sanders but more poignantly—remains mutely involved in situations that reveal his secondary status. Early in the film, Azim attempts to show off his stature by staging an elaborate charade, ordering his own men to shoot at Carruthers and the British troops so that he may save them. Carruthers, like Sanders, sees through Azim's game instantly. In a conversation that is the moral equivalent of Sanders's reprimand to Bosambo ("Is that not a lie, man?"), Carruthers makes Azim promise that he will not indulge in such wasteful make-believe and will always tell the truth.[51] Much later, when Azim gets wind of Ghul Khan's conspiracy to kill Carruthers, the dethroned prince rushes to inform the British forces at Peshawar. In a farcical set of scenes that serve no immediate plot-related function other than to emphasize the rungs of a diplomatic ladder and the exaggerated ceremony at each rung, Azim undergoes repeated frustration as he attempts to warn the British governor of Ghul Khan's plan, only to find that no one in the British army believes him.

As Azim meets a British army sergeant stationed in Peshawar, then the colonel, and finally the governor, the contrast between the little half-naked boy and the formally dressed officers gets more exaggerated. These sets of scenes are "excessive" within the film's narrative, as they stand out in their iterations (each officer of each tier behaves the same way and says the same thing). The film legitimizes the governor's misgivings by making the native emissary so young, but the governor's reluctance is based on a mistrust of Azim's intentions and a belief that he could not be selfless or truthful. Such elements, including the attempt at humor with each repetition, mark the narrative's difficulty in accepting the native informant's credibility without compromising its fundamental position of mistrust against native characters. Indians in this film may be narratively and visually significant, but they are finally impotent. Despite Azim's closeness to Carruthers at the interpersonal level, he must acknowledge that the British officials "did not believe me."

An imperial romance's mythmaking confronts narrative impasses because the dramatic conflict of the film is markedly between two contradictory principles governing the British nation—its imperialism and its liberalism. The empire's enemies and allies (here, Ghul Khan and Prince Azim) are focal points of a symbolic nexus through which oppositions between the promised inclusions and actual exclusions of empire are represented and imperfectly reconciled. Most often the narrative relevance of these imagined characters is limited to the role they play in accommodating conflicting ideologies. Thus, Ghul Khan's death removes an inconvenient reminder that imperialism *cannot* coexist with assertions of complete colonial independence, and Azim's reinstatement affirms that empire and colonial nationhood can coexist *only* when colonial subjects accept their role as recipients of imperial charity. That Carruthers believes Azim in a way that the British governor and his staff cannot, however, signals discrepancies within the imperial system. We are briefly aware that cooperation between Carruthers and Azim does not extend beyond them, because Azim's word carries no weight with the British State. Azim's impotence identifies a problem in the reconciliation of empire with reciprocity, when their fundamentally fallacious equation is not evenly sustainable by an imperial text.

Erotics of Imperial Romance

Sabu's eroticization by the camera adds another crosscurrent of signification to his character Azim's imperial function. Ella Shohat points out that homoeroticism "can simultaneously permeate homophobic colonialist texts," partially as a byproduct of the erasure of women that permits intimate all-male relationships.[52] At this tantalizing point, Shohat shifts her attention away from the possible pressure such homoerotic deviations might place on a colonial film's politics, focusing instead on colonial cinema's fulfillment of heterosexual fantasies. She argues that in a film like The Sheik (Famous Players-Lasky, 1921), the dark male body represents the white masculine id, giving the white male license to see his repressed passions and desires expressed in exotic locations. Examining the same film and figure, Miriam Hansen provides a different reading of desire. She notes that Rudolph Valentino is simultaneously responsive to female fantasies (given that his fan discourse was marked by female desire and sexual difference) and to traditional patriarchy (because Valentino, as the object of desire, fulfils fantasies of female subjugation and abuse). Hansen argues for a more complicated notion of spectatorial identification in cases where women are aligned with the desiring look and desired men are endowed a liminal sexuality. In this instance, Valentino controls and dominates the virginal female, but he is also feminized and dominated by the film's vamp figure, and his excessive, self-destructive romanticism weakens his heterosexual, masculinist coding.[53] As Hansen shows, the spectatorial sadomasochistic rituals unleashed in films set in "other" lands reveal not dominant sexual binaries of men desiring women or women desiring men, but a more ambiguous "deep blue sea of polymorphous perversity."[54]

The male worlds of The Drum and The Four Feathers offer few opportunities for a "straight" coupling between the desiring look and the object of desire, so that the brown male body is eroticized (in The Drum) and the white male body victimized (in The Four Feathers) without any corresponding revaluation of a female gaze. While such a predominantly masculine address in the film does not preclude complex spectatorial involvements, it does make the erotics of male imagery conditional on an adoption of the feminine as part of masculine role-play alongside a marginalization of the real female. Following the all-male textual/sexual politics of imperial films, Sabu's beautified dark body as Azim in The Drum and Captain Carruthers, Harry Faversham, and John Durrance's vulnerable or tortured white bodies in The Four Feathers make interesting studies in contrast.

In The Drum's imagery feminine desire does not solely actuate Sabu's glamorization. Narratively and visually, the Scottish drummer boy Bill Holder (Desmond Tester) provides the softer complement to Azim's story.[55] Over the course of the army's residency in Tokot, Holder and Azim become close

16. The friendship of a prince and a drummer-boy in *The Drum*. Courtesy USC Cinema-Television Library.

friends despite their differences in race and social position. Holder composes a drumbeat for Azim that the young prince uses as his secret code, and Azim wants to *be* Holder, a drummer boy in the Scottish regiment. But they trade tunes more easily than roles, because a brown prince cannot pass for a white drummer boy.

If, following Judith Butler's argument, gendered (*and* racialized) bodies have "no ontological status apart from various acts which constitute their realities"—an observation that is undeniably true of celluloid bodies—then the circumscriptions of Azim's corporeal reality can be sketched in the following ways.[56] His body *can* be fetishized in a British film that keeps him shirtless for half its playing time; it *cannot* become an anonymous white body, because it has less racial transferability than a Carruthers or Faversham who can "go native" at will; and it *can* get physically proximate to a working-class white body. The raced and classed valuation of each body permits them circumscribed ambits of social interaction and defines their visual potentialities. Sabu is legitimated as an object of voyeurism because his exoticism is easily commodified and feminized within an imperial film's image regime. Thus the most memorable glamour shot in this film is reserved not for Mrs.

Carruthers but for Azim, as he sits atop a wall under the moonlight with Holder. The intercut shots show Azim aglow in Holder's admiration ("You're a blinkin' marvel Azim!"; and at an earlier point: "Anything that's mine's yours."). The sequence is composed of medium and close-up shots in a film in which the woman is typically depicted via medium and long shots, giving greater intimacy to the Sabu-Holder relationship and a higher erotic charge to Sabu's image.

While the feminization of the native male body within an orientalist visual economy is commonplace, I place it among several maneuvers that collapse the distance between colonizer and colonized to grasp the film's tentative redefinition of imperial relationships. As Corey K. Creekmur and Alexander Doty propose, ostensibly mainstream texts flirt with queerness, creating complex encounters between such texts and their readers and temporary interruptions to dominant, heterosexist ideologies.[57] I want to hold on here to both dynamics: the unusual proximity the film permits between two male bodies, and its persistently discriminatory visual treatment of the brown as opposed to the white male, which reinvests the image in dominant ideology.

Prem Chowdhry discusses the uproar in India over the film's obsessive focus on Sabu's dark skin, which was considered incongruous and not "authentic" in someone playing a member of the fair Pathan race.[58] In addition to marking his difference from the other characters, the film exploits Sabu's skin as beautiful. Like the female body, Sabu's body is attractive because filmic devices endow greater spectatorial investment in the image. He is softly lit, backlit, alternatively overdressed or semi-naked, frequently glistening. (It is hard to resist noting that in *Black Narcissus*, Sabu's character pleads earnestly with the nuns, "You don't need to count me as a man!") John Justin, Sabu's co-star from *The Thief of Baghdad*, remarked that the actor had a "wonderful smile, most beautiful body," something a male star could say only about a young male colleague of color without putting his own heterosexual masculinity in jeopardy.[59] To use the language of psychoanalysis, in Sabu's films and in the extracinematic universe supporting his filmic persona, the dark figure's difference is disavowed by fetishizing or overvaluing his beauty. Simultaneously, phobic recognitions of difference are transferred onto the finally eliminated body of Ghul Khan in the film. In visual terms, Sabu's feminization maintains him in a position of subjugation while admitting an erotic susceptibility of the camera and audience to his image. Thus historically, a commercialized pull of fascination with the native's image is concomitant with admissions of imperial vulnerability to subject lands and peoples.

Mechanisms of voyeurism acknowledge the viewer's obsessive desire for the object. In a consonant operation, imperial fear manifests itself in forms as spectacular as imperial desire, only this time touched by a masochistic rather than voyeuristic visual pleasure. At his lowest point, Carruthers is shot in the arm and faces the prospect of Ghul Khan locking him in a wooden cage and parading him "through all the mountain states so that the people may know how the English are to be feared."[60] The moment of humiliation brings to a climax all that Carruthers has endured through the film: physical threat, verbal violence, and psychological pressure. His possible public humiliation hints at a debasement that finds fulsome visualization in The Four Feathers.[61] In a tight-knit group of male friends who belong to the North Surrey Regiment of the British Army, Harry Faversham and John Durrance (Ralph Richardson) are both in love with Ethne Burroughs, who reciprocates Faversham's attentions. When the regiment is called on to help Kitchener's campaign in Sudan, Faversham succumbs to an old fear of combat that has gnawed at him since he was a child, fears made worse by his father, who speaks constantly of the Faversham reputation for bravery in battle. Upon his resignation from his regiment, Faversham receives four white feathers from his three friends and Ethne, as a mocking symbol of his cowardice. To redeem himself, Faversham goes to Khartoum as a native Senghali, the lowest of low Arabs, whose tongues were sliced by the Kalipha in punishment for their revolt against him.

Faversham voluntarily submits to being branded with a hot iron on his forehead in imitation of the Senghali mark. Enduring great agony and humiliation, he anonymously helps his friends who remain unaware of his presence. In his guise as a mute and marked Arab, Faversham also saves Durrance, now blind because of overexposure to the desert sun. The star-crossed romantic triangle continues in Britain when Ethne is about to wed a blind Durrance despite her love for Faversham, whom she believes to be dead. However, Faversham returns after playing a crucial part in Kitchener's capture of the Kalipha's fort, and Durrance silently leaves the country on the pretence that his incurable blindness can find treatment in Europe, making a noble sacrifice so that Ethne and Faversham may be reunited.

The sobriety and forbearance that Durrance and Faversham demonstrate in their interpersonal relationships is belied by the hysteria and trauma manifested by their bodies in the desert and under the Kalipha's incarceration.[62] Interestingly, sequences depicting white male suffering were excised from the version of the film screened in India, indicating a political awareness of the extent to which such sequences were also open to voyeuristic viewing. ("In reels 8, 11, and 12, in prison scenes and also elsewhere, curtail drastically all parts showing white prisoners being dragged, jeered, whipped, kicked, fed and herded like cattle. Part of the scene showing a white native spitting in a trough containing food before allowing white prisoners to eat from it should be omitted entirely [107 and a half feet].")[63] Recalling Mikhail Bakhtin's distinctions between the Medieval "grotesque" and the Renaissance body, the realist body of Sanders is closest to the isolated, complete physical entity of a Renaissance hero. Sanders's fever and mosquito bites are neither spectacularly nor voyeuristically demonstrative of the body's (potentially regenerative) degradations, as are Faversham's scar and darkened skin or Durrance's blind dementia.[64]

Connecting the male bodies in The Drum and The Four Feathers are their positions in a play between the stylized depiction of a breakdown of institutional orders (of empire, nation, and family) on the one hand, and the narratively expedited force of predestination on the other. To elaborate, familial heterosexual bonds are diminished in both films so that the drama is not one of vertical ties to the past and the nation, but of lateral connections to one's male compatriots in a time of colonial crisis. In however limited a way, The Drum's portrayal of intimacy between a prince and a drummer boy humanizes the relationship between an infantilized native and a marginal white subaltern. For a brief moment, past structures appear to offer little sustenance, the ties of tradition appear loosened, and relational inventions appear possible. In The Four Feathers Faversham liberates himself from the burdensome pressure of his family tradition and name after the death of his father by voluntarily seeking to protect his male friends. In The Drum an orphaned Azim risks everything to help Carruthers and befriends the low-ranking, stray, subaltern Holder, who in turn teaches him his signature drumbeat. Similarly, Carruthers is married to the frontier rather than his wife, deriving his identity more from his fellow military officers than from his family.

However, these apparently voluntary acts of friendship only vindicate that which the institutions of nationality, empire, family, and class prefigure. The Four Feathers ends in England with a reinstatement of Faversham as a man worthy of his family name, with Ethne by his side. The Drum, which presented cross-class and interracial alliances between Holder, Azim, and Carruthers, concludes as they return to their respective places in the social hierarchy. Fraternal relationships that may have held a potential to displace the class- and race-bound divisions of empire are exposed as exceptional and finite in scope: they are primarily permissible in frontier zones, they are most intense in times of danger, and they facilitate a return to heterosexual, hierarchical, imperial normalcy.

Consolidating this romantic reinforcement of empire is the fact that the frontier, which inflicts the greatest degradation on the imperial male while also bringing him closer to his fellow men and native races, is rigorously contained by the fortuitous intervention of British bugles and troops. Physical suffering in colonies brings to surface suppressed truths: Faversham's fear of colonial excursions, Durrance's love for Ethne. They corporeally acknowledge psychic realities, manifesting unconscious expressions of distress in a way that is finally restorative of an imperial social status quo. The scar allows Faversham to redeem his masculinity and compensate for his initial emasculating wish to stay at home with the women. Durrance's blindness, almost an oedipal punishment for desiring beyond his reach, gives him a pretext for a noble sacrifice that reinstates the original, aristocratic couple to the narrative/social center.

With his act of sacrifice, Durrance comes closest to embodying the essence of melodrama. In his suffering, we witness the romance form's proximity to modernist imperial narratives, as the style introduces colonial forces that displace the visual and aural centrality of imperial protagonists and take a heavy toll on their bodies. The crucial difference is that the stylized performance of trauma alters the very mode of narration in modernism. Consequently, the modes of textual pleasure of a romance and modernist imperial film vary. In The Drum or The Four Feathers pleasure is embedded in seeing triumphant (colonizing and native) men who retrieve a valorous masculinity and assert their ascendancy after physical and psychic alterations. In modernism, the pleasure is in the sacrifice and the suffering.[65] This is partially a difference of degree: in the dialectics of an articulation of crisis and its finally conservative resolution, the latter is a stronger force in imperial romances. But the difference is also one of a gendered narration of history. In embracing the trauma of colonial withdrawal, imperial modernism more closely approximates the melodramatic mode because the crisis infuses and redefines aesthetic form. Not only are women more likely protagonists of imperial modernist films, but introspective, subjective, nonsingular, and perennially skeptical perspectives, coded as feminine and rigorously marginalized within realist and romance texts, become the defining template of modernist films, even when they are peopled by men. Destabilizing interrogations of the imperial perspective provide imperial modernism's very "sense of textualization."[66]

Men in imperial romances lack the rational, matter-of-fact conviction of a Sanders, a Rhodes, or a Clive who claims to know what is best for everyone. The argument of a romance, made more strongly by the visual, aural, and plot dynamics of a film than by psychologically motivated realist characters, is one of sentimentalism. Within this representative framework, women are typically circumscribed by a conservative imperialist ideology as they are assimilated into British domesticity and erased from colonial male fraternities. Only men, in limited ways, are permitted striations of significance in their symbolic role, because they are both the means through which imperial values are tested and the agents through whom empire is salvaged. In his often quoted statement of romantic nationalism, Ernest Renan said, "To forget and—I will venture to say—to get one's history wrong, are essential factors in the making of a nation; and thus the advance of historical studies is often a danger to nationality."[67] Postcolonial tabulations of colonial history threatened British nationalism, which responded by making empire generative of "a soul, a spiritual principle" of fraternal codes.[68] Romantic characters that risk everything to live by a creed seek the infinite within the infinitesimal.[69] They believe they are part of a *deus ex machina* and fall subservient to its roiling.

Prem Chowdhry's account of the Indian Muslim protests against The Drum points to the fact that such reassuring myths of empire were beleaguered. Resistance to The Drum came from within Britain as well. At the time of the film's release, some British scribes wrote about the film with great sarcasm, attacking its racist ideology and its clichéd use of generic imperial tropes. In the following film criticism published in England in 1939, the authors see no difference between The Drum and the sort of jingoistic fiction that characterized the previous century. "In this story of the North-West Frontier, every gesture, every gag, might have been lifted intact out of the Boy's Own Weekly of 1888. . . . The officers discuss the situation in great seriousness around a wall map. The problem is acute. Tokot is four days' march from where they are, will they be in time to suppress the revolt? (What about the Air Force? Sh! This is 1888.) . . . In keeping with the current conception of human rights in 1888, there is sadism, cynicism, and a contempt for human dignity packed tight into the picture. . . . [T]he officers bark at non-commissioned officers, and both grades talk to natives as if they were dogs."[70]

Despite its anachronisms, the fiction of The Drum works not by denying its present but by transforming social history into something cosmic. To take Prince Azim's example again, he is as much of a romantic figure as Carruthers after he is orphaned and isolated. Faced with the British governor's lack of confidence in him, Azim gallops up the mountains to warn Carruthers with his signature drumbeat; he can do no more than rely on private codes of communicating danger. Carruthers is similarly helpless, as he must walk into a trap with his eyes open and await reinforcements. In *The Drum* plans go awry despite overwhelming good-will between British commissioners and Indian allies, and they are resolved by the work of anonymous agents of the imperial state, like the governor's troops and an unnamed British spy. Oppositional elements are expunged and the fantasy of a pliable colony restored not by individual characters as much as by the narrative, generic, mythic, and statist powers beyond them. Aesthetic elements of predestination—powerful as a negative impulse in the melodrama of imperial modernism where a resistant India or Africa work their hostile will on imperial agents—present themselves as a reparatory and politically conservative force in imperial romance. This gives the form aspects of a "heroic modernism," in that an appeal to eternal myths saves the work of art from confronting a "formless universe of contingency."[71]

[The modernists] were involved in an effort of memory that
made the very lack of transparency of the past a conscious
form of concern.
—Richard Terdiman, *Present Past*

Africa as a metaphysical battlefield devoid of all recognizable humanity, into which the wandering European enters
at his own peril. Can nobody see the preposterous and perverse arrogance in thus reducing Africa to the role of props
for the break-up of one petty European mind? But that is
not even the point. The real question is the dehumanization
of Africa and Africans which this age-long attitude has
fostered and continues to foster in the world.
—Chinua Achebe, *Hopes and Impediments*

six * MODERNISM AND EMPIRE

European literature, art, and cinemas have experienced various internally
contentious modernisms, but to focus briefly on their overlaps I pilfer from
Eugene Lunn. Lunn identifies four significant directions in modernism's aesthetics and politics. First, he notes modernism's attention to form, and its
refusal to consider art as transparent or representative but as possessing a
density of its own; this formalism was used to different ends, as much to
express subjective perceptions (in impressionism and expressionism) as to
emphasize the potential of human labor (in constructivism or Bauhaus architecture).[1] Second, modernist art explored temporal and spatial simultaneity
and juxtaposition via techniques like montage (with the cubists), the over-
lay of mythical narratives to reveal their recurrence in the quotidian (as in
the writing of James Joyce), or experiments with psychological time (as with
Marcel Proust or Virginia Woolf). Third, modernism was a response to the
decline of religious and scientific certainties of the nineteenth century, embodied in the collapse of grand narratives of linear progression and attacks
on the notion of objective truths. Finally, modernism investigated relative
realities, enigmas, paradoxes, and ambiguities (as in the work of Franz Kafka

and Samuel Beckett), depicting a crisis in individuality, making character a playground for sensations rather than a unifying motif.[2]

Despite the explicitly "high culture" and high modernist bias of this definition, Lunn's systemization offers a preliminary approach to Fredric Jameson's and Edward Said's arguments linking European aesthetic modernisms to decolonization, a key event in the crisis of Western identity and modes of representation.[3] Beyond the impact of tribal and primitivist motifs on modernist art, colonialism and its collapse may be read as a constitutive, subterranean impulse of European modernism.[4] Alongside the rise of fascism and the two world wars, decolonization provoked European modernism's agitation around existing presumptions of wholeness, wherein progress, teleological history, state rationality, and the representability of reality were interrogated as fictions or illusions. The impossibility of experiencing moral horror at the genocide of the European Jewry without meditating on Europe's colonial rampage rang out in the words of the black-diaspora intellectual and surrealist Aimé Césaire, who saw the world wars as an exposure of the culpable "Christian bourgeois of the twentieth century" harboring "a Hitler inside": "What he cannot forgive Hitler for is not *the crime* in itself, *the crime against man*, it is not *the humiliation of man as such*, it is the crime against the white man . . . and the fact that he applied to Europe colonialist procedures which until then had been reserved exclusively for the Arabs of Algeria, the 'coolies' of India, and the 'niggers' of Africa."[5] Concentrated within the anxieties of European modernism, exacerbated by accusations of vocal and violent colonial subjects, was the shock of self-awareness, the fear of history, the confusion over one's capabilities, and the use of a disintegrating political present to confront a suddenly opaque past.

British imperial modernism exemplifies this self-reflexivity about the colonial experience, using form to interrogate the shock, horror, and loss attendant on the nation's break with its imperial legacy. Michael Powell's and Emeric Pressburger's film *Black Narcissus*, based on a novel by Rumer Godden, appears at first glance to have little connection with the book because of its disconcerting modernist aesthetic that calls everything into question. Its unstable quality resides in an element identified by the novelist, albeit disapprovingly: she did not like the film because "Powell saw the book as a fairy tale, while for me it was utterly true. . . . There was not an atom of truth in the film."[6] As a fairy tale, the film's gorgeously seductive colors and unreal landscape convey an ambiguity lacking in the novel, allowing it an interiority that is missing in the book.

In *Black Narcissus* five white female missionaries travel to Mopu, a fictional village in the Himalayas, where they open a school, chapel, and dispensary for Mopu's inhabitants. The place arouses several dormant desires and memories in the sisters, who slowly plunge into despair and insanity. Though some responses to this film have focused on its psychosexual dynamics, the film's constructions of imperialism and sexuality are too deeply embedded in each other to be divided up neatly.[7] In their evaluation of imperial narratives, Ella Shohat and Robert Stam refer to *Black Narcissus* as a film that "rings curious variations" on the theme of the Western woman who is subordinated to the Western man but remains dominant over nonwestern peoples. According to the authors, the nuns are "privileged filters and centers of consciousness" as the narrative is focalized through them, even though the Englishman Mr. Dean (David Farrar) embodies "textual norms" to the extent that narrational authority is relayed through his prediction of the nuns' failure at Mopu.[8] I accept this evaluation of *Black Narcissus* as fitting uncomfortably within the colonial canon but disagree with the centrality it ascribes to the nuns or the Englishman. *Black Narcissus* allows us to make larger claims about the nature of British imperial narratives during decolonization when we locate it in the context of other commercial films with imperial themes, or consider it in relation to the potentially anti-imperial political and literary concerns of its time.

Understanding *Black Narcissus* as an imperial film allows us the insight that place is always an important part of the imperial narrative. An incident from the film serves as a good conceit for this. While requesting a transfer out of Mopu, Sister Philippa (Flora Robson) says to Sister Clodagh (Deborah Kerr), "I think there are only two ways of living in this place. Either one must live like Mr. Dean or . . . or like the Holy Man. Either ignore it or give yourself up to it." To this, Sister Clodagh replies, "Neither will do for us." Narratives that utilize colonies as an imaginary landscape onto which they map national affirmations, desires and fears have similar choices. To maintain their integrity they must ignore the place, because narrative coherence is predicated on the continuation of the colonial territory as an unproblematic backdrop. To acknowledge the place as an entity is to disrupt the narrative and to accept that no presumptions or projections are possible. The place would have to constitute the central crisis in representation; it would have to become the consuming preoccupation of the narrative.

Black Narcissus—and arguably all imperial fiction in the modernist mode—demonstrates a collapse of available imperial narratives in that neither of these options are entirely available to the mode. The colonial place and people are not (cannot be) ignored, and yet they are not (cannot be) entirely embraced. Instead, the place is made central enough to impede the assumptions projected onto it. Simultaneously, a narcissistic preoccupation with the British experience is recuperated by vilifying the place or/and by aesthetically stylizing the narrative's collapse and rearticulated coherence. Discernible in literary texts such as Joseph Conrad's *Heart of Darkness* (1899) and *Lord Jim* (1900), or in E. M. Forster's *A Passage to India* (1924) prior to its emergence in cinematic texts, this modernist mode participates in a larger cultural production of neo-imperial narratives. Imperial cinema's modernist moments represent a cusp between the sensibilities of colonial and postcolonial discourses of empire.

Imperial Description and Colonial Place

Like other films that construct their fiction around an imperial encounter, *Black Narcissus* begins with an excess of written text and visual images that identifies its "alien" place. But, as with everything else in this film, familiar motifs are spun in unexpected directions. In *Sanders of the River* intertitles that name the time and place of their fiction make claims about the actuality of representation. Their relationship to the images is one of control, as the intertitles deliver to British audiences an alien land that is imagined as categorizable. In the romance mode, as in *The Drum*, place is linked more explicitly to traditions of representation connoting fantasy and adventure, destabilizing the assumption of realism. Like realism, intertitles function to make the "otherness" of the place unthreatening, but audiences are engaged simultaneously in a hermeneutic of excitement promoted by the novelty of Technicolor and sweeping panoramic shots.

In both the realist and the romance modes, sequences identifying alien territories by such elements as maps or spinning globes function to mark and manage the difference of the colonial location. The opening sequence of *Black Narcissus* alters this relationship between written text and image, calling into question the level of trust we place upon the information provided to us about the represented place and its people. Our first introduction to Mopu (very different from introductions to Tokot in *The Drum* or to Sanders's residency in *Sanders*) is filtered through three people, all of whom are less than objective about the place and the nuns' mission. As viewers, our experience

17. Sister Clodagh accepts her mission. Courtesy USC Cinema-Television Library.

of the place is mediated by our knowledge of the emotional investments of the characters describing or imagining Mopu.

First, we behold Mopu as an illustration seen by Reverend Mother Dorothea (Nancy Roberts) as she wearily pores over her book at a convent in Calcutta. She summons Sister Clodagh, and as the sister stands across the table from the Reverend Mother we get a familiar image of hierarchy within an (often military, but here religious) order. The shot–reverse shot exchange that occurs as Sister Clodagh is entrusted with a mission to Mopu is also characteristic of imperial films, in which, typically, an assignment is given to an officer who is then bound by duty and honor to perform it. The potentially hubristic qualities of the sister's ideals are established early, marked by the camera's careful attention to Sister Clodagh's reactions and to the Reverend Mother's concern. Within other modes of imperial representation, hubris is *not* marked, because it constitutes, in many ways, the preferred viewing position. But part of the function of *Black Narcissus*'s narrative is to teach humility and to reveal the flawed romanticism of believing in a mission of salvation.

There is, however, an indulgence of this romanticism, vindicated in a measured way by the film's resolution as will be discussed further.

The second and longer visual sequence introducing the place accompanies Mr. Dean's inhospitable letter to the sisters. Mr. Dean is a cynical Englishman working as an agent to the old Indian general who owns the lands of Mopu. As Sister Clodagh reads Mr. Dean's letter (to a voice-over narration in Mr. Dean's voice), the shot dissolves from the letter to Mopu itself. This first experience of the land is initiated by Sister Clodagh's imagination, based on Mr. Dean's descriptions. Her barely contained sense of pride at her mission and Mr. Dean's indifference to it mingle in a representation of Mopu that holds some room for doubt because of our potentially unreliable narrators. Our experience is irregularly mediated through the subjective and internally disparate collective consciousness of Mr. Dean, the Reverend Mother, and Sister Clodagh. The distance between the viewer and the place, created by our sense of the three characters imagining Mopu and our knowledge of their relationships to the place and the mission, debilitates the containment of Mopu within any singular perspective. These narrative and cinematic techniques mark the film as a presenter of fragmented realities, breaking significantly from the strenuously singular presentations of place within other modes of imperial imagination.

This impression is enhanced by the manner in which the narrative is sequenced. Sister Clodagh begins reading the letter, rendered in Mr. Dean's voice. The letter dissolves to Mopu, and after a description of Angu Ayah, the voice-over falls silent. Angu Ayah is the caretaker of the palace who talks to birds and hears the winds summon her in the voices of women that once inhabited the palace's harem. Appropriately, this figure who bridges Mopu's past with its present and quite literally inhabits the past (or is inhabited by the ghosts of the past) also becomes our vehicle for transition through time and space, from the convent in Calcutta to the palace in Mopu.

We are now confronted with Mopu in the present tense. In Mopu, we witness an exchange between Angu Ayah, Mr. Dean, and the general (simultaneous, in terms of time, to the exchange between the two nuns in Calcutta) as the arrival of the missionaries inspires humor and irritability. We witness the general's strangely enlightened despotism and his plans to feed the nuns sausages because "Europeans eat sausages wherever they go." We hear Mr. Dean's impatience at the general for offering the natives a dispensary when "they don't mind having ringworms" and listen to Angu Ayah complain that nuns "won't be any fun."

18. Mopu is created from stylized sets and miniature models. Courtesy USC Cinema-Television Library.

As we dissolve back to the photographs of Mopu scattered on the Reverend Mother's table in Calcutta, we bring an awareness that Mopu's cast of characters are antithetical to the sisters in disposition, motivation, and just about everything else. We also have an uncomfortable feeling that the sketches and illustrations on the Reverend Mother's table don't begin to capture the spirit of the place. There is a sense that while we began the journey into Mopu through Sister Clodagh's vision and Mr. Dean's supercilious account, we have received a signal of the disparity between the actual place and its imaginings. The illustrations on the Reverend Mother's table make Mopu seem grand, while our vision of it has combined the indefinably large (the history of the place making itself felt through Angu Ayah, the fluttering curtains, the sensuality, the whispering spirit voices) with the ignominiously trivial (the peevish exchanges between the general, Mr. Dean, and Angu Ayah). Our encounter with the place is mediated by a combination of accounts given by the film's central characters and by incomplete glimpses provided by an anonymous entity (the camera, the narrative), leaving a presentiment that something about the place is not quite enclosed within the characters'

descriptions. Shots of the Mopu palace, of the Ayah (maid) who squawks unnaturally at her birds, combined with sounds of dead women and howling
winds caught in empty hallways are all conveyed by the long shots of a camera working not at the behest of any one character's account but of its own
volition. We are provided, then, with an early intimation of the primacy of
the place and of its independence of will.

Several reviewers did not appreciate the film's diminution of characters
through the stylized depiction of the place (entirely constructed on sets), and
though it received Hollywood's Academy Awards for Color Cinematography
and Set Decoration in 1948, the film's critical reception was mixed. A few critics agreed that "Black Narcissus was a disappointment, redeemed only in parts
by its acting and its photography," an adaptation that "misses the mark."[9]
The film was panned for its "atmosphere" and "shadowy values." "Here is
a subject so tied up with profundities and intangibles that the best of filmmakers might well be cautious grappling with it."[10] When the film was released in the United States, The New York Times Film Review called the film a
"coldly tinged intellectual morality drama."[11] Britain's Kinematograph Weekly
advised that the film be booked for "better class halls" because, though the
film was "sincere and artistic," it was "singularly lacking in warmth, power,
purpose and lustre."[12] Critics predicted that popular audiences would "experience some difficulty in knowing what it was about."[13] Surface readings
of the film interpreted the story as a literal depiction of helpless and degenerate nuns, which provoked the ire of the Catholic National Legion of Decency
in the United States. The legion raised objections to the film as an "affront
to religion and religious life," causing some American release prints to be
censored. In particular, the film's flashback sequences, which depicted Sister
Clodagh's love affair in Ireland, were cut.[14]

Observations about the film's "intangibles" and their connection to colonialism came more easily to critics writing in the 1980s. In 1986 a review
in London's Time Out magazine observed, "It's not fanciful to see the film
as Michael Powell and Emeric Pressburger's comment on the British withdrawal from India," and The Listener noted, "in Black Narcissus everything is in
retreat."[15] The Village Voice from the same year said, "Like A Passage to India and
Heat and Dust, like The Jewel in the Crown and even Sir Richard Gandhi's award
winning Attenborough! but far more openly, Black Narcissus is a film about the
British. Next: India by the Indians."[16]

These later reviews were subsequent to a Powell-Pressburger revival in the
United States effected by the efforts of filmmakers like Francis Ford Cop-

pola and Martin Scorsese. Director Michael Powell had often received an uncertain reception in Britain and *Peeping Tom* (Powell, 1960), a film that gives photographic voyeurism a new meaning, confirmed the feeling that he was a "dangerous and unsound" filmmaker.[17] By the 1980s, however, his style of filmmaking—excessive, passionate, bizarre, and horrific—seemed contemporary in its insanities. According to Ian Christie, *Black Narcissus* was unusual "for a British film from the emotionally frozen 40s," but it "seems as if Powell and Pressburger survived the slings and barbs of contemporary critics to find their ideal audience in the 80s."[18] *The Listener*'s review from 1986 also argues that the film is "a complex crossroads where colour, race, sex, tradition, and female Blimpishness collide," in an "amazingly contemporary film."[19] Another issue of the same magazine remarks that the film is unusual for its time because it showed that Powell and Pressburger felt "the war required not a grim buckling down in national effort but a more unfettered exercise of the imagination."[20]

Apparently, while popular films like *Sanders of the River* and *The Drum* were experienced as anachronistic by the radical and progressive journals in their own time, *Black Narcissus* felt too modern and outrageous, too close to styles and concerns found in "high-class" forms of art such as the novel. Rather than posit some films as too advanced and others too outdated for a nation's political sympathies, I'd argue that collectively they demonstrate the range of a cultural text's possible relations to its history and context, particularly in a period of historical transition. While a focus on one or the other imperial film narrows our reading of dominant ideology, its variegated modes indicate internal fissures in empire fiction and connections across art forms, revealing more complex relationships between popular culture and prevalent aesthetic as well as political dispositions.

Nothing in the idealistic narratives about imperialism (such as the novels of Kipling, A. E. W. Mason, or Edgar Wallace, adapted in several empire films) provided for a conclusion of withdrawal and defeat. In the face of an eventuality greater than any acknowledged cause, a resolution in excess of avowed events, the modernist imperial mode responded with melodrama and irony. In both melodrama and irony, there is a disproportion between the signifier and the signified.[21] Melodrama, as Peter Brooks points out, postulates a signified in excess of the signifier, "which in turn produces an excessive signifier, making large and insubstantial claims on meaning."[22] E. M. Forster's Marabar Caves, Joseph Conrad's Congo River, Rumer Godden's Mopu are all places where things happen far in excess of explicable causes. The incommensurabilities between word, intention, and their meanings or consequences are attributed to a place that provokes the incomprehensible excess. The moral impact of these places on the imperial travelers is similar to the echoes in the Marabar Caves in *A Passage to India*, echoes that are "entirely devoid of distinction" but that still possess the ability to "undermine" a visiting European's "hold on life." [23] In modernist imperial narratives, white visitors to colonial lands may try to live by their principles, but irrespective of their intent they can exercise little control over a devaluation of themselves.

Irony, on the other hand, is opposed to melodrama in that its impact comes from understatement, from deflating the signifier and signified to respond to an inflated reality. [24] Mr. Dean, living some legacy of a Sanders gone horribly wrong, embodies this response in *Black Narcissus*. When asked which birds he shoots for the feathers on his hat, he says, "I don't shoot birds. When you've shot everything, it palls, doesn't it?" At Sister Clodagh's exasperation with the Holy Man's presence on chapel grounds (grounds that had belonged to the man before he became an ascetic), Dean remarks casually, "What would Christ have done?" The very title of the film is ironic, with its reference to an exoticized and bejeweled Indian prince's perfume that turns out to have been purchased from the thrifty Army and Navy store in London.

Thomas Elsaesser argues that irony is embedded in melodrama as an expression of differential levels of awareness. Irony signals a discrepancy between a circumstance and a response, particularly when protagonists either underplay the intensity of their emotions or desperately struggle against a fate that they are incapable of entirely comprehending. Elsaesser develops the latter aspect in relation to Hollywood's family melodramas, memorably calling their protagonists "pocket size tragic heroes and heroines" caught in a "tragedy that doesn't quite come off: either because the characters think of themselves too self-consciously as tragic or because the predicament is too evidently fabricated at the level of plot and dramaturgy." [25] In both instances, the irony gives spectators a special position of privilege: either by their knowledge of a protagonists' dramatic self-restraint or by a superior awareness of the protagonists' tragicomic inadequacy. The use of irony in *Black Narcissus*, repeatedly evoked in the context of the sisters' incomprehension of Mopu and its people, initially gives Mr. Dean and the spectators a smug satisfaction of knowing more than the nuns. The privileged spectatorial position of ironic distance from its protagonists indicates that, like Mr. Dean, the viewer may be privy to the mission's innate limitations and the place's inscrutable power.

Nevertheless, irony is not the film's sole or lingering flavor. It would be more appropriate to say that melodrama and irony tussle with each other in this film, with melodrama heightening every aspect of the protagonists' emotions and irony undercutting them. When the nuns are at a high pitch of anxiety, running in search of the escaped Sister Ruth ("It's Sister Ruth. . . . She's gone mad!"), Angu Ayah produces the very parody of their scream, and Joseph, the nuns' little helper, points out that the commotion "would be a very little thing" to the meditating Indian Holy Man. The combination—of the suppressed or exploding high drama of the nuns' emotions, always plagued by a character or a perspective that will not take them seriously enough—brings a dimension of internal duality lacking in other modes of imperialist fiction. The film's oscillation between irony and melodrama is symptomatic of its refusal to give us, the audience, a clear emotional cue for reading the text's imperial content. Herein lies its invitation to the uncanny in our encounter with the film.

In explicating the sublime in modernism, Jean-François Lyotard notes that the modern is "the art which devotes its 'little technical expertise' (son 'petit technique'), as Diderot used to say, to present the fact that the unpresentable exists."[26] Just as the uncanny in fiction may be evoked by a sensation of eerie familiarity with an alien object that escapes complete description, the sublime in literature is experienced as a sentiment (or presentiment) of a truth exceeding reality, of words that inadequately capture concepts. Both hint at something beyond the level of representation, something discomfiting to the present fiction. When irony and melodrama operate together in Black Narcissus to narrate an encounter between five female missionaries and a resistant land, they map out shadowy reasons for the disparity between the idealism of the nuns' intentions and the horrors of their visit. The evils visited on the encounter between the nuns and Mopu are found to originate not wholly in the nuns and not wholly in the natives. The mission fails because there is something indefinable in the place, conveyed through a sense of the uncanny that alters the possibilities of what the nuns can do, what they can be, and what they can expect to do or be.

Thus the encounter between the missionaries and the place may be understood through the related themes of imperial work and imperial identity, found in all three modes of the imperial imaginary during decolonization. For Sanders, work is a duty to his king for which he expects no greater reward than mosquito bites; the place, being benign, vulnerable, and responsive to Sanders, merely facilitates the accomplishment of his disinterested commitment to imperial labor. For Carruthers, in *The Drum*, work is "my India, the frontier," with all its danger and thrill. The place is a fabulous landscape with its vast mountains and unending possibilities of snipers and smuggling routes, impelling protagonists to deeds of daring. In *Black Narcissus* the place radically alters the nun's identities by overturning their existing expectations about themselves, their pasts, their role in an alien land, and their mission among its people. The film reveals another face of imperial work and identity.

Imperial Identity/Imperial Work

British expansion occurred through mercantilism, militarism, and mission-ary activity, the last of which was considered the most humanitarian of the empire's projects. Such distinctions make little sense, especially in light of the fact that early religious conversions were no less zealous than imperial trade and irremediably mixed up with imperial politics.[27] As J. A. Hobson, the earliest European to analyze imperialism as a politico-economic system, asked, "How much Christianity and civilization balance how much industry and trade?"[28] Significantly, in narrative fiction, if military officers and bu-reaucrats in a pliant colony emphasized the validity of imperial enterprise, female missionary nuns in a resistant land enacted imperial vulnerability. Im-perial modernist novels and films such as *A Passage to India*, *Bhowani Junction*, and *The Rains of Ranchipur* use feminine collapse and hysteria as a central trope, with the women serving as overused symbols of a nation's fallibility and confusion. In gendering the subject positions of authority and vulnerability, such narratives not only replicate imperialism's inherent patriarchy but also attempt to exculpate a discriminatory politico-economic system by drama-tizing the empire's retreat through representations of well-intentioned and fundamentally compassionate women.[29] Representing white women who re-spond to hostile and foreign lands with brave resignation fosters sympathy, and sympathy for the characters expands to create sympathy for their context and cause.

Three things stand out prominently about the sisters' work in *Black Nar-cissus*. Their order is voluntary in that it requires annual vows of renewal; it is defined not as a contemplative order but as one devoted to work; and work serves as a mode of self-realization and worship. In addition to providing a plot device for Sister Ruth's break with the order at the end of the film, the voluntary nature of the order emphasizes that the performance of duty is a matter of choice, conviction, and courage. This idea of voluntary service is filled with the melodramatic romance of a higher purpose, where the freedom to choose results in a daily affirmation of the order. Renan called the nation "a daily plebiscite," imagining a nation (much like this imagining of a religious order or of an empire) as a community of people who affirm a unified "spiritual principle" of their own free will. In this event, Sister Clodagh's Irish roots take on additional significance, since the novel and the film fantasize her willing subservience to British missionary work in India. Her faith, all the more meaningful for coming from someone who belongs to a region and religion subordinated by England, affirms a national British unity for the colonial mission.

As with the men in imperial films, work is the sisters' mode of self-actualization. In *Heart of Darkness* Marlow says, "I don't like work—no man does—but I like what is in work—the chance to find yourself. Your own reality—for yourself—not for others."[30] The concomitant of this is that in the absence of work, the sisters lose their identity: without colonial subjects, there is no need for imperial agents.[31] Typically, narratives validate imperial work by demonstrating its importance for the colonies. In *Black Narcissus*, however, the old general bribes the natives with money to attend the free school and dispensary opened by the nuns. The people of Mopu have to be coaxed into providing the sisters with minds to educate, bodies to heal, and souls to save, in order to legitimate the mission's presence in Mopu. The potential irrelevance of the sisters' work is emphasized with great irony throughout the film, particularly when the sisters' lessons comprise of teaching five-year-olds in Mopu how to spell "canon, warship, bayonet, dagger, gun," and of instructing the Indian prince to conjugate French verbs.[32]

Though the film provocatively questions the convent's value for Mopu, it is the place that is finally held responsible for obstructing work as a faith-affirming activity. Repeatedly, Mopu is perceived as a distraction, a temptation. Whereas in *Sanders* the Isisi River is neither seductive nor gets the better of the officer, in *Heart of Darkness* Marlow finds he cannot resist the hypnotic pull of the Congo River: "The snake had charmed me." Mopu is no exception, and there are several ways in which work in this Himalayan abode becomes more an occasion for excess than for self-denial, a source of extreme pleasure rather than purification.

Sister Philippa's experience with her garden offers a particularly poignant example, not only because the garden holds a wealth of cultural and moral associations within the biblical tradition but also because of Sister Philippa's own exacting, monastic standards for herself. The garden, in addition to

19. Dean and Sister Clodagh meet the Holy Man, the original owner of Mopu. Courtesy USC Cinema-Television Library.

being a postlapsarian location of tempted virtue and knowledge, is a significant symbol in imperial cinema. To temporarily empty the symbol of its potential ambiguity, within imperial films the garden functions as a symbol of the colony (as an unkempt wilderness) or as a code for civilization (as a tended field). Similar to the ambiguities of Hollywood westerns (see chapter 5), we see how modernist imperial films offer complicated constructions of a colonial territory that will no longer fit into the latter half of a civilized/savage binary. The categories that the nuns wish to impose on the land simply do not hold, as brilliantly shown in the scene in which the half-naked, silent Holy Man is declared to be "General Sir Krishna Rai, KCBO, KCSI, KCMG, several foreign decorations, too," a man conversant in English and several European languages, as well as the original owner of Mopu's lands.

Similarly, the place in *Black Narcissus* functions not only as an element that threatens "civilization"; it is also an entity that destabilizes travelers' identities by revealing *them* to be the outsiders. A dramatic exchange between Sister Clodagh and Sister Philippa regarding the garden is only one of sev-

eral episodes that are of interest in this context. Their conversation occurs
when Sister Clodagh discovers that Sister Philippa has planted fragile, exotic
flowers instead of hardy, useful vegetables in the convent's garden. When
reprimanded, the usually stoic Sister Philippa breaks down and requests a
transfer; although a transfer would be a mark against her, she feels she de-
serves to be punished for getting too engrossed in her work and in the place.

> SISTER PHILIPPA: I was becoming too fond of the place. I was too wrapped
> up in my work, I . . . thought too much about it. I'd forgotten.
> SISTER CLODAGH: Forgotten what?
> SISTER PHILIPPA: What I am. I was losing the spirit of the order.

Sister Philippa exemplifies a crisis of identity and a breakdown of its coherence, problematizing the relationship between the imperial agent and her
colonial work.[33] In this sense, the convent's garden serves as a metonym for
the interrelated functions of place, work, and imperial identity. The sisters
realize that if they are to keep "the spirit of the order," the place cannot make
a difference to them. Rather, their work must change the place.

To this end, the sisters practice their own forms of regimenting time and
space. Sister Philippa sets about planting potatoes. Sister Ruth (Kathleen
Byron) rings the bell on the cliffside chapel to mark the hours and to call for
prayer. Sister Clodagh takes down sensuous pictures from the palace walls
and changes the name of the "House of Women" to the "House of St. Faith."
But the obdurate sensuality of the place will not die.[34] When suppressed in the
architecture, it flowers in the form of the silent Kanchi (Jean Simmons) and
in the overwhelming attraction between her and the young general (Sabu). It
overcomes Sister Philippa, forcing her against her will to transform a well-
regimented garden into a pleasure-paradise. The spirit of the place mocks
them through Mr. Dean's vaudeville song: "No, I won't be a nun. No, I cannot be a nun. For I am so fond of Pleasure!! I cannot be a nun." The battle
between the irrepressible sensuality of the place and the regimentation and
restraint of the nun's work propels the narrative and its dramatic images. In
the chapel, as the sisters sing their Christmas carols, this sensuality explodes
in Kanchi's simmering looks (shot lingeringly by the camera) and in Sister
Clodagh's memories (bursting through in luminous flashbacks). Thus, the
mute place does not merely resist change: it makes its will legible through
imperial minds and bodies, as it revives the sisters' memories and erupts in
the form of spots and boils on their skin, inciting insomnia and headaches.[35]

In *Heart of Darkness*, before Marlow heads for the Congo River, a doctor ex-

20. Mopu makes Sister Philippa see too far and remember forgotten things. Courtesy USC Cinema-Television Library.

21. Sister Clodagh's mind strays from her prayers in Chapel. Courtesy USC Cinema-Television Library.

amines him. He measures Marlow's head with great enthusiasm and takes down careful notes, remarking, "It would be interesting for science to watch the mental changes of individuals on the spot."[36] In Africa, Marlow feels himself "becoming scientifically interesting."[37] Similarly, in *Black Narcissus* the place (rather than Mr. Dean) circumscribes the nuns' efforts by catalyzing their preordained failure. "It's the wind," says Sister Clodagh, explaining her weakness in Mopu. "It's the altitude." "It's the place with its strange atmosphere and new people." "There must be something in the water," complains Sister Briony, though Mr. Dean informs them that the problem with Mopu's water is its purity. The place seeps into Sister Philippa's daily routine in the form of a clarity that disallows the necessary amnesia required for discipline and obedience to the order. She thinks too much, sees too much, and questions everything, including the value of her work. When she uses her work to push away "distractions," the calluses on her hands from excessive gardening become another way in which the place claims her body. Most vividly, Mopu possesses and consumes Sister Ruth. The place ingests her and spits her out, a different person. If Sister Clodagh's present blurs into her past, Sister Ruth literally *becomes* her past. Her body enacts the most violent return of the repressed, where all denied history and passions explode onto the surface, transforming her very being.

Sister Ruth's degeneration into scarlet passions and cadaverous bestiality by the end of the film is not unique to her alone; to a large degree, all the nuns are implicated in Sister Ruth's insanity. The usual climatic spectacle of imperial films in which horse-backed British officers charge against native forces of evil instead manifests itself in *Black Narcissus* in the taut lines drawn between Sister Ruth in her red dress and lipstick and Sister Clodagh in her flowing white wimple, holding her bible, caught in a battle of wills as a melting candle marks time between them. Dramatically visualized as a split self in this scene, Sister Ruth is arguably a distended reflection of all the weaknesses and deviances that the nuns, particularly Sister Clodagh, experience in their encounter with Mopu. So if Sister Philippa was misled by the pleasures of her garden and Sister Honey by her compassion for children, Sister Ruth takes an unholy delight in ringing the chapel bell while looking down its murderous precipice. If the young general reminds Sister Clodagh of her past love for Con and an unacknowledged attraction manifests itself between her and Mr. Dean, Sister Ruth is consumed by her desire for Mr. Dean and by her need to become her past self.

Sister Ruth is first introduced by her absence at the table in the Calcutta convent. In this sequence, which occurs early in the film, the Reverend Mother and Sister Clodagh are selecting nuns for the mission at Mopu. From an area that looks down onto the cross-shaped dinner table, Mother Dorothea describes to Sister Clodagh the strengths of each of the nuns whom she selects. The sequence is theatrical, as the nuns—unknowingly but still on cue—do something to affirm the Reverend Mother's characterization of them. Sister Briony is selected for her strength (she picks up a large jug of water), Sister Honey for her popularity (she tells a joke and giggles), and Sister Philippa for her talent with gardens (she examines an apple). Sister Ruth is the only one who is recommended for the mission because she is "a problem"; appropriately, Sister Ruth is missing from the table. Her absence and her definition by negation—she is not there, the nun's vocation may not be her vocation—makes her character the vortex that absorbs the weaknesses of each of the sisters.

In *Heart of Darkness* Marlow says about Kurtz, "The wilderness had found him out early, and taken on him a terrible vengeance for the fantastic invasion. I think it whispered to him things about himself which he did not

know. . . . It echoed loudly within him because he was hollow at the core." [38]
Sister Ruth is the most susceptible to the place because she is, from the beginning, most devoid of any attribute or use. While Sister Clodagh is proud,
Sister Briony strong, Sister Honey popular, and Sister Philippa a gardener,
Sister Ruth is merely missing. Four of the five sisters respond to the wilderness, but only one becomes possessed by it. Only one steps over the edge.
As Marlow says of Kurtz, "He had stepped over the edge, while I had been
permitted to draw back my hesitating foot. Perhaps all the wisdom, and all
truth, and all sincerity, are just compressed into that inappreciable moment
of time in which we step over the threshold of the invisible." [39]

Imperial Redemption

Mere hesitation at the edge of their psyches' precipices is insufficient to ab-
solve the other sisters. The resolution of the film is significant for the way in
which the narrative is divested of its high emotionalism and the mission's
respectability salvaged after such a severe collapse. The cathartic release of
the film's high emotionalism is followed by a quieter cognition of the nuns'
suffering. The explicit demonstration of the nuns' despair allows for a recuperation of their dignity.

Violence is part of the resolution of all imperial films, as it combines a
cinematic spectacle and a narrative catharsis that restore equilibrium to the
story. As narrative flow is predicated on repeated reconstitutions of coherence, the violence is a climactic escalation of oppositions running through
the films. In realist films like *Sanders* signifiers of the colonizers and the
colonized do not occupy the same frame without a drastic regimentation
along racial categories. *The Drum* flirts with dissolving rigid boundaries but
abounds in confrontational visual arrangements that suffuse the white protagonists with danger. In *Black Narcissus* both the imperial encounter and the
climax are of a different nature. The film's divided frames are most dramatic
when they are "internal," that is, when they dramatize conflicts *between* or
within the nuns and pit signifiers of the colonizers against other signifiers
of colonizers (the lipstick-versus-bible sequence, Sister Clodagh's and Sister
Philippa's struggles against their memories).[40] Here, the agents of empire
internalize elements that are typically assigned to "bad" natives, or that are
expelled through a violence that does not require self-investigation. An in-
ternalization of conflict increases the horror of violence, as it comes from
the realm of the familiar, the self. Bhabha's analysis of the ambivalence of

22. Difficult internal struggles as Sister Philippa creates a garden of flowers rather than hearty vegetables. Courtesy USC Cinema-Television Library.

the colonial encounter is perhaps most applicable to the modernist imperial mode, where the colonial other becomes a "tethered shadow" of the Western self by becoming a part of her being.[41]

The power of the "uncanny" in Black Narcissus resides in the fact that its narrative crisis is not provoked by a battle between self and other (as in imperial realism) or self and an other who resembles the self (as in imperial romance). The terror derives from the fact that the protagonists, the sisters of St. Faith, cannot separate themselves from the alien elements of the place that eventually appear in the shape of Sister Ruth.[42] The film's crisis is instigated by a journey to an unknown land, but the resulting violence is performed through the psyches and bodies of imperial agents. The death sequence at the cliff, shot entirely without dialogue, testifies to this internalized confrontation, as does the fact that "Mopu" is pure artifice, a fantasy set.

Michael Powell and Brian Easdale, who was responsible for the music and sound score, rehearsed the actors with stopwatches for the death scene, "trimming or elongating movements so that the edited scene would exactly fit the written score."[43] As the film critic Harry Sheehan notes, the climax is a choreographed sequence that is cut and set to music, so that "emotion" takes "precedence over plot mechanics."[44] Sister Clodagh is ringing the chapel bell by the cliff at 6:00 AM, as her lips move in silent prayer. To a crescendo of music, Sister Ruth arrives out of the shadows and her desperate eyes fill the screen. She looks neither alive nor human as she moves stealthily toward the Sister Superior she hates. At this moment, the evil of the place is finally localized onto everything Sister Ruth represents. In her intent to kill a woman in prayer and in her macabre visual transformation, she finally passes beyond the reach of humanity.

This sequence of Black Narcissus is presented as a melodramatic tableau. In The Melodramatic Imagination Peter Brooks argues that melodrama is "motivated by a totally coherent ambition to stage a drama of articulation," where the conflict of moral sentiments is made explicit through the attitudes, signs, gestures, and expressions of the characters.[45] In the chapel-bell sequence, the movements of the two sisters, their radical opposition in appearance and desire, their twirl around the bell's rope, which sends the attacker hurtling down the cliff to her death, and Sister Clodagh's expression of extreme horror on which the camera freezes, all constitute a concentrated eruption of emotions—threat, danger, revenge, sin, fear, horror—that have run steadily under the film's text, ending with the triumph of the innocent. The musical score confers "additional legibility" on this otherwise silent tableau of emotions.[46]

Silence has a privileged place within this "drama of articulation."[47] Not surprisingly, the natives are the most mute of all. They are commented upon and evaluated (as in Mr. Dean's letter). When people like the young general do speak, they misspeak (he wants to study "physics with the Physical Sister"). Kanchi doesn't say a word in the entire film, preoccupied as she is with her sexual obsessions and her beauty. But Black Narcissus silences the non-whites while allowing them to be articulate signs of that which destabilizes the nuns. The "subalterns" that cannot speak in the Spivakian formulation are reproduced once again within dehumanizing Eurocentric categories (in that they are not allowed their perspective, their interiorities), but their very existence distresses and "distracts" the nuns. The native's lack of access to the symbolic realm is guaranteed within this imperial text, but their silence is imagined as threatening inscrutability.

Rumer Godden's novel describes the young general, played by Sabu in the film, as being "outside everything they [the nuns] had considered real; he was the impossible made possible."[48] In other words, Godden, the writer of stories about the British Empire, imagines all that might be unthinkable or unreal and creates an Indian character who gives expression to it. This is similar to the argument in the British journal that proposed that color film made "something of the 'unreality' of the East . . . available for the Westerner." [49] The operation of muteness in Black Narcissus is much like the operation of color in The Four Feathers and The Drum: it makes the East fantastic while guaranteeing access to that fantasy. In their silent combat, Sister Ruth and Sister Clodagh manifest the ineffable forces that have silently confronted each other in this narrative. The place, its people, the wind, the palace, the mountains, the gardens, all of which have been imagined as inscrutable and all of which have emerged in glimpses in the sisters' distractions, desires, sicknesses, and memories appear full-blown in the irrevocable transformation of Sister Ruth. With the final representation of Sister Ruth as a murderous and crazed animal, the imagined horrors of the place are made completely legible through her body and intentions.

Melodrama achieves a more complete form in imperial modernism, and its complexity lies "in the amount of dust the story raises along the road, a cloud of over-determined irreconcilables which put up a resistance to being neatly settled in the last five minutes." [50] A vagueness, due in particular to the unarticulated and undefined reasons for the sisters' defeat and retreat, contributes to the sense of unease at the conclusion. The destabilizing element in this film lies in its sublime manifestation of discomfort with the colonial encounter. In Black Narcissus, the antagonistic element is neither an evil native nor an avaricious European but the demon place that ultimately splits the romantic heroine in (minimally) two parts. The parallels between Sister Clodagh and Sister Ruth permeate the film's imagery, not just in their physical resemblance to each other but also in the striking sequences of Sister Clodagh's flashback to Ireland: her memory of running to meet Con, who is represented as an elusive whistle in the dark, portrays her love as full of the same coiled excitement, anxiety, and finally the same futility as Ruth's desire for Dean. The incredible sequence in which Dean rejects Ruth, in which he suddenly becomes the predator and she the prey, begins Ruth's complete transition to monster. Following a dramatic fade to purple, Ruth loses consciousness chanting Sister Clodagh's name, and Black Narcissus begins to explore fully its potential for horror.

By concluding the film not with Ruth's death but with Clodagh's redemption, the film retains, to paraphrase Achebe, a fulsome fascination with the restorative powers of colonial trauma for the colonizers, as exemplified by Sister Clodagh's role in the film. As an Irish woman in a British order, her

23. Sister Ruth lurks, transformed by her obsessions, her lipstick, and her red dress. Courtesy USC Cinema-Television Library.

memories of Ireland—shown in breathtaking images of translucent shimmering water and in the deep, rich colors of her grandmother's footstool and jewelry—make her sensibility the perfect conduit of the nuns' experience of marginality and denaturalizing alienation in a strange land.[51] The film's aesthetic modernism that thematizes this aspect of alienation could lead us to radical realizations of the "cultural imperialism *within* Europe that accompanies its domination over the rest of the world."[52] But the film abandons a critical presentism for an emotional look ahead and a look back. As Sister Clodagh therapeutically anticipates future missions, her status as émigré within England and Mopu becomes a way of romanticizing her commitment to her faith. And the nostalgic tone of Dean and Clodagh's last exchange leaves us with the distracting ache of their parting.

Sister Ruth's accidental death in the physical struggle between her and Sister Clodagh appeases the place and breaks its hold on the nuns. With this, two deaths are balanced at the end of the film—that of a native infant (which causes the people of Mopu to isolate the sisters) and that of Sister Ruth (after which the people of Mopu are reconciled with the chapel). In giving up one body for the one taken and in assimilating it into a strange land (at Sister Clodagh's request, Mr. Dean is to look after Sister Ruth's grave), the imperial

24. Sister Clodagh remembers trying on her grandmother's emerald necklace in Ireland. Courtesy USC Cinema-Television Library.

mission fantasizes its own conclusion. Sister Ruth's death is its ultimate exorcism. It allows for a catharsis of the evils of the imperial encounter, but is still insufficient to recuperate imperialism's redemptive ideal. This redemption occurs through the character and the experiences of Sister Clodagh.

Sister Clodagh goes through dramatic and positive changes by the end of the film. She can smile when Mr. Dean affectionately calls her "a stiff-necked, obstinate creature." She can share a sense of companionship with Mr. Dean, whom she was quick to judge on their first encounter. Like Sister Philippa with her garden, she desires a demotion as the just consequence of her failure at St. Faith. Her pride is no longer invisible to her but a weakness that she has had to confront at Mopu and a failing that she treats with ironic self-deprecation. Sister Clodagh's encounter with the inexplicable in Mopu has wrenched from her a more honest and noble response to her realities and her past.[53] For the first time in the film, painful memories that resurfaced in Mopu no longer haunt her, but make her a better person. Like Harry Faversham of *The Four Feathers* as he leaves for Khartoum, Sister Clodagh embarks on a life of self-abnegation full of difficult but instructive memories, rather than a life of denial filled with intrusive memories. The experience also lends her clarity and an ability to speak of her past. In her last exchange with Mr. Dean, the film represents the wisdom and maturity gained by this romantic heroine. Her loss, and the film's excessive style of narrating the story of her loss, is the fragile recovery of moral victory for the sister. Significantly, the nuns retreat not to go home but to continue their mission elsewhere.

In a finally, if tentatively, imperialist film, the collapse of its worldview is averted by a visibly modernist preoccupation with the Western self and by the film's redemptive thematics. As Sister Clodagh looks up to see Mopu fading into a mist, the place appears symbolic of the disappearance of several expectations that she brought to the mission. The clouds and the height of Mopu make it an unattainable ideal, but Sister Clodagh emerges as all the more admirable for her attempt to succeed. Mopu's disappearance also seals the place from inflicting any further harm on the sisters. No blame can be assigned to the sisters any more. In *Heart of Darkness* Marlow remarks on the degenerate Mr. Kurtz's last, defeated words, "The horror! the horror!" by saying: "Much better his cry, much better. It was an affirmation, a moral victory paid for by innumerable defeats, by abominable terrors, by abominable satisfaction." [54] The naming of horrors takes courage within this narrative as well, and Sister Clodagh gains a shaken but undefeated will to continue her work. Faced with its contradictions in the era of anticolonial nationalism, British imperialism forgives its own past; as imperial modernism suggests in multiple ways, you cannot accuse those who have suffered deeply, and you can accuse them even less if they are able to face their sins.

These heroines turn out to be more than pocket-book tragediennes. They are physically and psychically battered, but they acquire humility and a redoubled faith that absolves them of their inadequacies. An abstract and pure commitment to an ideal emerges as being more valuable than the realization of it. Such abstraction is convenient in a novel written close to India's decolonization and filmed in the year of India's independence. Talking to Michael Powell in 1990, a writer noted that "what grants them [the nuns] stature in Powell's eyes is that when they finally do come away, regardless of the humiliation undergone there, it is with a canter rather than a slink." [55] The actual loss of a territory is insignificant, these texts appear to say, when lost land and power can be symbolically recuperated as an eternal, moral victory. Here is Marlow speaking of Jim after his death in *Lord Jim*, "He passes away under a cloud, inscrutable at heart, forgotten, unforgiven, and excessively romantic. Not in the wildest days of his boyish visions could he have seen the alluring shape of such extraordinary success! For it may well be that in the short moment of his last proud unflinching glance, he had beheld the face of that opportunity which, like an Eastern bride, had come veiled to his side."[56] Sister Ruth has to die so that Sister Clodagh may be revived. In the frozen moment of Sister Clodagh's terror at the death of the crazed nun lies her "rebirth" into faith and her own illusory moral victory. As this victory can only be won through a thorough experience of defeat, imperial modernism explores the nadir of colonial encounters in a manner unlike other modes. But its admission of culpability does not explore a politics of self-critique, as it remains caught in an inward-looking cycle of guilt and absolution.

The argument that literature in the modern period invests art with a redemptive potential is prominently associated with the work of Leo Bersani. While my argument has been directed at a specific narrative and aesthetic form of imperial cinema, the similarity lies in an emphasis on art's aspiration toward a morality that allows aesthetics to function as "a corrective of life."[57] That British imperial films of the 1930s rehabilitate empire for an era of decolonization becomes clear from the range and function of empire cinema's imaginative modes. The coherence of the imperial self, presumed in the romantic and realist texts, is broken in the modernist narrative. Within the former modes, the unified imperial self is either sustained by memories of home or unthreatened by the alien place. In *The Drum* nostalgia for home gives the men something to fight for. *The Four Feathers* is driven by memories that are didactic. Amnesia becomes a necessary part of serving in the colonies in *Sanders*, and *Black Narcissus* is close to *Sanders* in this emphasis, with the critical difference that forgetfulness is impossible because the imperial bodies are in a radically different relationship to the colonial place. The place has entered the characters at a subconscious, subcutaneous level.[58] The significance of the breakdown of the imperial entity in *Black Narcissus* is that it foregrounds an aspect shared by all these representations of empire, namely, that the amnesia of the realist hero, the sustaining memories of the romantic hero, and the traumatic memories of the modernist hero are elements of narratives generated by a larger cultural loss. This is the loss of a transparent relationship of a nation to its past.[59]

Imperialism occupied an uneasy place in the future of the British nation, rendering the identity of an imperial protagonist problematic. Constructing heroic narratives of imperial nationalism presumed certain responses to contemporary criticisms *against* empire: it presumed to disavow the reality of anticolonial nationalisms (prominent in *Sanders*), to expel them in a mythologized confrontation (as in *The Drum*), or to give aesthetic expression to the breakdown of the imperial protagonist, allowing the film form to be guided by an awareness of this collapse (in *Black Narcissus*). The loss of a comfortable continuity with the nation's past was coupled with the necessity to comprehend that loss, as evidenced by the literary, cinematic, popular, and canonized narratives in the twentieth century that circled around the problem of empire in the longer history of the British nation. These must be understood as signs of a culture that produced absolving fictions of its nation's history in order to adapt to and incorporate political change.

part three   *   **COLONIAL AUTONOMY**

Sust banane vali filmen koyi aur hongi, meri *Diamond Queen*
nahin! (Other films may make you lethargic, but never my
Diamond Queen!)
— "Fearless" Nadia, *Diamond Queen* songbook, 1941

Whatever the academic theories of profit, not labour, not
capital, not skill, alone or in concert, can make profits for
an Industry, if there is no National Government to help it.
In this struggle of yours, therefore, you have a handicap,
for India has no National Government of her own. And
therefore, whether you wish it or not, the place of this
Industry will always be with those who are struggling to
achieve such Government for this country.
— Chandulal J. Shah, addressing the First Indian Motion
Picture Congress, 1939

seven ✳ HISTORICAL ROMANCES AND MODERNIST
MYTHS IN INDIAN CINEMA

Three linked factors may be disaggregated as formative influences on Indian
film aesthetics in the late-colonial era: their allusive commentary on the
nationalist project and on British imperialism through visualizations of a
new civil society; their origins in pre-cinematic as well as modern Indian
art forms; and their function in giving Indian films a competitive edge over
Hollywood and other film imports by borrowing and localizing their attractions. The task of teasing out and rethreading these aspects of colonial
cinema is made simpler by the foundational work of literary and film scholars
of Indian silent and early sound film. Consequently, a brief review of recent
theories of Indian cinema opens this chapter, directed by a focus on film art.
Such a summary prevents a construction of comparative frameworks premised on an implicit universalization of European or Hollywood aesthetic pre-
dilections. It also serves as a reminder that descriptions of "Indian" themes
and styles cannot be hypostasized, because asserting a cultural identity was
crucial to the industry's survival as a trade, which was artificially impeded
by its government and domestically dominated by film imports until the
late 1930s.

Just as British empire cinema reflected the circumstances of Hollywood domination and imperial destabilization, Indian films thematized a country's struggle for nationhood while attempting to gain a foothold in a colonially constrained and competitive domestic market. The construction of Indian sensibilities and visualities betrayed this cosmopolitan awareness of other market forces and films, and additionally created what the film historian Ashish Rajadhyaksha has called a "modern industrial idiom of neo-traditionalism."[1]

Aesthetic Terms as Terms of Comparison

Theorists of Indian cinema have challenged and extended the concept of realism as derived from Euro-American film theory in two related ways: through a study of the absence, resistance, or more properly the uneven incorporation of "Renaissance" constructions of perspective in pre-cinematic Indian cultural production; and by analyzing the function of realism and melodrama in the creation of a national consensus in postcolonial India. Rajadhyaksha developed the first approach in relation to Dadasaheb Phalke's films, and scholars writing for the *Journal of Arts and Ideas* in the late 1980s and early 1990s extended the analysis.[2] Rajadhyaksha notes that traditional Indian visual forms such as *pat* paintings, which depicted stories through images on a flat surface that would be lit and scanned serially by a mobile viewer, were premised on a "frontal encounter between a usually flat—often deliberately flattened—planar image and an audience gaze." Commercial market (bazaar) art and still photography introduced perspectival codes of figuration aimed at creating an ideal viewer position, to present a deceptive sense of three-dimensional reality. Early silent Indian cinema is constituted by a tension between these two forms of viewing, with a dimension of narrative temporality added to the flat *pat* aesthetic, thus combining the latter's emphasis on a "collective public gaze" with the former's mobilization of a perpendicular axis of perspective.[3]

Films like *Shri Krishna Janma* and *Kaliya Mardan* (Phalke, 1919) offer ideal examples of this dynamic combination of frontally direct address and contiguous spaces. In *Shri Krishna Janma* the audience is performed *to*, as Lord Krishna faces us while his devotees (identified by caste as the Brahmin, the Kshatriya, the Vaishyabhakta, and the Shudra) crowd around him and offer their prayers sequentially. Such a staged, frontal composition may be linked to descriptions of the look mobilized by a dominant mode of Indian cinema "governed by a pre-modern institutionalized structure of spectation embodied in the tradition of *darsana*."[4] The concept of darsana (seeing the temple deity; also used reverentially or sarcastically for more secular sightings, such as seeing a special friend or a friend rarely seen) carries explicitly Hindu connotations, making the term problematic as a generic model of South Asian visuality. Sandria B. Freitag expands Indian visual traditions beyond the darsanic to include the gaze mobilized in a courtly *durbar* (the ceremonial space where Mughal rulers met their subjects) and by live performances of the precolonial era.[5] Underlying all three notions of visuality is an element different from the voyeurism that sutures a viewer to the text as defined by Hollywood film theorists. Here there is more of a sense of interaction across distance, of iconity to the image, and of an explicitly (rather than invisibly) hierarchical structuring of the image that intrudes into film's mimetic capabilities.

Sumita Chakravarty explores an epistemology of non-mimesis in Indian art, particularly in classical Sanskrit theater's "*rasasutra* (theory of aesthetic enjoyment) of depersonalized emotions."[6] Borrowing from literary scholar Meenakshi Mukherjee, she argues that mimetic art was imported into India with Victorian novels and only partially assimilated into the indigenous novel of the nineteenth century, which subsequently exercised some influence on Indian film narratives. Following these definitions, we may conclude that realism is not an aesthetic intrinsically related to Indian pre-cinematic and early cinematic traditions, and that it was never entirely incorporated into the dominant form of Indian literature or commercial Indian cinema.

Situating these theories of Indian film form in relation to definitions of narrative or classical realism creates a revealing category crisis. If classical realism is a technique produced by subsuming cinema's spatiotemporal articulations under the dictates of narrative, then the Indian film form's affinity to nonrealism appears to be perpetually modernist, particularly (and paradoxically) when constituted by traditional Indian modes of visuality.[7] To clarify the confusion, we need to distinguish between nonrealism, realism, and modernism as aesthetic descriptors, and to introduce into our discussion the concept of modernity as a historical category.

Too diffuse and complex to allow a swift definition, modernity may be inadequately characterized as the secularization of religious, dynastic, and monarchic notions of time, space, polity, and community, initiated by scientific and technological revolutions since the 1700s. The filmic medium has been considered emblematic of late modernity because, like the railways, the X-ray, or the telephone, it utilizes technology and industry to alter the experience of time, space, vision, and sound. Arguably, premodern as well as nonrealist forms of visuality pre-existed modern *encounters* between non-realist, realist and modernist visual tropes in Indian cinema. In such descriptions, however, modernity becomes an inescapable condition of the nineteenth and twentieth centuries, and we may pause to consider if India's (or Europe's, for that matter) immersion in modernity during or after colonialism was ever all that complete.[8] More to the point, we need to ask what modernity meant to India. What was the degree to which it was embedded in colonial practices? What was the extent to which it acted as a transporter of Western imperialism? What was the manner in which the national category of "India" was defined in conjunction, opposition, or resistance to this modernity?

In answering such questions, theorists writing about the political modernity of the postcolonial state have enabled a historical inflection of and internal differentiation in the study of realism in the Indian context. I bracket modernism for the time being, as it has not been a central focus of critical attention in relation to colonial cinema. The reasons for this neglect and a case for revisiting modernism are explored further. For now, cinematic modernism, like cinematic realism, may be understood as a response to historical modernity. Specifically, modernism may be characterized as a range of aesthetic symptoms manifesting both the euphoria of change and "an anxiety of contamination" produced by the decolonization, democratization, commercialization, and massification of culture, society, and politics.[9]

Chakravarty views realism as a "stabilizing discourse" that attempts to control the unnerving changes of industrialization, urbanization, and the spread of consumerism in the modern Indian nation-state.[10] For Chakravarty, realism is primarily associated with the middle-class project of cultural consensus building. Consequently, she reads realist cinema's *failure* at the commercial box office—demonstrated through the poor popular reception of critically acclaimed Hindi films like *Dharti Ke Lal* (Abbas, 1946), *Neecha Nagar* (Anand, 1946), and *Do Bigha Zamin* (Roy, 1953)—as an index of middle-class alienation from the masses.[11] She carries this idea forward to the realism of "new or parallel" cinema of the 1960s and 1970s, such as *Ankur* (Benegal, 1973), *Garam Hawa* (Sathyu, 1973), and *Manthan* (Benegal, 1976), to note that such films lacked "a vital communication with or articulation of a larger national experience."[12]

Chakravarty's utilization of Indian films funded by state as well as private sources incorporating neorealist as well as classical-realist and experi-

mental styles to develop a broad theory of realism creates conceptual difficulties. The didacticism, regionalism, and naturalism of films funded by the
state-run Film Finance Corporation (visible in most films of the new-cinema
movement of the 1970s) are dissimilar in form and motivation from the self-
consciously experimental, progressive productions of the 1940s (like *Dharti
Ke Lal* and *Neecha Nagar* of the Indian Peoples' Theater Association, an anti-
imperial, anti-Fascist collective). For such differentiations and for a theorization of popular Hindi cinema in relation to state-funded developmentalist
realism, Madhava Prasad's analysis offers greater assistance. Prasad redraws
the map of realism by periodizing the dominant Indian film form in relation
to shifts in the postcolonial nation-state, discerning two forms of realism
involved in producing the modern citizen and creating a social contract post-
1947. The first is a "nationalist realism," wherein realism inheres in the promise to represent reality *as it is*, as in the work of Satyajit Ray or in Shyam Benegal's films in the 1970s. The spectator's gaze, Prasad argues, borrowing from
Neil Larson, coincides with the frame (in that the film appears as one with
reality), because there is an "*absence* of any obvious rationalizing authority at
the level of narrative." [13] This invisible mediating presence that transmutes
the representation of a specific, "regional" object into something apparently
national is similar to the construct of a citizen who is "neither singular" nor
"collective" but both simultaneously. [14]

The second form of realism toward which popular Hindi cinema aspires is
closer to Hollywood realism, or what Prasad calls realism as a "sign of bourgeois hegemony." [15] The conditioning imperative for this form comes from
a prioritization of "the features of a rationally-ordered society," where the
central unit of the narrative is an individual progressing with credible motivations and goals to ratify the rule of law of his or her own free will. This
narrative realism operates by "anchoring the spectator's gaze in a relation of
identification with a central character, and thus the citizen as the individual
embodiment of the legal order is called into being." [16]

Isaac Julien and Kobena Mercer offer similar descriptions of realism's statist functions in their descriptions of black British cinema's efforts to disrupt
realism. In their words, "Representational democracy, like the classic realist
text, is premised on an implicitly mimetic theory of representation as correspondence with the 'real': notionally, the political character of the state is
assumed to 'correspond' to the aspiration of the masses in society" which
may be represented by a film's central character *or* its form. [17] Amir Mufti
sees a structuring secular national consciousness present in influential late-

colonial Indian narratives like Mulk Raj Anand's *Untouchable* (1935), Nehru's *The Discovery of India* (1946), and Premchand's *Godan* (1936), which construct the representative national individual as the object or ideal addressee of their narratives. "For the Nehruvian, 'progressive' aesthetics that emerged in the 1930s under the influence of the Popular Front conceptions of the artwork and society, telling the truth of society in fiction — 'realism' — amounted to narrating the emergence of this consciousness — the abstract and secular citizen subject — as the highest form of consciousness possible in a colonial society."[18]

Though secular, nationalist consciousness may be produced through realism, Indian film theorists argue that a realism that resists interruptions to its diegesis and subordinates spectacle to narrative was never entirely digested by the Indian film form, given its predilection to melodrama, to an aesthetic of frontality, to tableau constructions and non-mimetic impulses. Prasad defines Indian cinema's dominant melodramatic form as a "feudal family romance," which heterogeneously assimilates a national consensus manufactured by India's ruling coalition of feudal/colonial and bourgeois/postcolonial élites.[19] The plots of these romances derive their melodrama from nonrealist twists ranging from switches in social rank, dispossessed children of aristocrats, oaths to secrecy, and people in disguise. These characteristics share an affinity with tropes of the Gothic narrative mentioned by Northrop Frye and Peter Brooks. Whereas Frye aims to identify transcendental structures rather than contextually specific ones and Brooks treats melodrama as a modern response to the desacralization of society, Prasad wishes to retain the pre-modern, pre-capitalist allegiances of India's emerging modern romance form. In structural terms, the romance is a manifestation of the contests and alliances between the emergent bourgeoisie and pre-capitalist overlords, as heterogeneous forms of capital combine to create a postcolonial national culture.[20] In ideological terms, the romance subsumes modern concessions to individualism within hierarchical and feudal depictions of family and morality.[21]

In sum, Indian film aesthetics have been theorized in terms of pre-modern forms of visuality resisting or cohabiting with perspectival visuality as well as classical realism under postcolonial modernity. The association of modernity with the rise of a native bourgeoisie, largely inheritors of social institutions established by the imperial élite, transcribes the struggle between pre-modern and modern visual or narrative regimes into a contest between tradition and modernity, anti-realism and realism, feudalism and capitalism, though not in neatly overlapping or perfectly chronological ways. Romance, providing the dominant (and dominantly melodramatic) structure for Indian films, is itself read as a site of contestation between precolonial (feudal) versus postcolonial (bourgeois) organizations of state power. Prominently, several theorists connect realism with the project of nation-building, particularly in the postcolonies. Quoting Fredric Jameson, Gyanendra Pandey, and Aijaz Ahmed, who identify the centrality of realism in writing the "biography of the emerging nation-state," Rajadhyaksha argues that the principle of scientific rationalism in the economic program of nationalist reconstruction found its "aesthetic counterpart" in realism.[22] Anthony Appiah makes a similar observation about the first generation of novelists from the colonies (like Chinua Achebe), whose novels provided "realist legitimations of nationalism: they authorize a 'return to traditions' while at the same time recognizing the demands of a Weberian rationalised modernity."[23] Realism here is theorized as the dominant form within which traditionalism finds (an albeit difficult and tenuous) reconciliation with modernity in an early phase of the postcolonial state, which is assertive in its defiance of imperialism and dedicated to the activation of a national, rational identity and subjectivity.

Modernism as an aesthetic mode (distinct from the historical experience of political, economic, and social modernity) is less privileged in discussions of colonial Indian cinema, with the notable exceptions of Geeta Kapur's and Ravi Vasudevan's readings of the "modern" in Indian art and film, also assessed in relation to the project of nationhood.[24] Answering the question "When was modernism in Indian/Third World art?" Kapur argues that the potential "formalistic impasses" of late modernism—such as its "sheer opticality," preference for "epiphany to materiality," and its "hypostasis of the new"—were impeded in postcolonial nations, which were constituted by deep investments in defining a collective history and national identity. She suggests that perhaps Indian art was truly modern only in the postmodern era of the 1990s, when the nation began to integrate drastically with the world economy through liberalization. Indian artists were "shocked out of the narrative of identity" to confront "the new without flying into a defense of tradition," coping with "cultural atomization without resorting to the mythology of an indigenous community."[25] However, Kapur notes, modernist tendencies of Indian art were not so much thwarted or deferred by the compulsions of national identity as perpetually fraught by that disjuncture, rendering modernism a "vexed site" in postcolonial art.[26]

Far from being a unifying domain of meaning and signification, national identity was itself a vexing construct. The theorization of realism as a cognate of nationalism sensitizes us to the production of a normative consciousness during the period of nationalist legitimation in colonial and postcolonial cinemas. It simultaneously desensitizes us to aesthetics as an indicator of the perceptual, experiential, and ideological disparities that were politicized, but never reconciled, by efforts to create a unified national entity. The study of colonial Indian films allows us to question the theoretical entrenchment of realism and nationhood as the privileged modes of modernity in colonial and postcolonial contexts, because challenges to postcolonial identity and feared inadequacies of nationhood were writ small in colonial cinema's aesthetic modernisms.

Divided Nation and Diachronic Forms

A social organism of strangers unified by their simultaneous existence in time and by their shared sense of events is popularly Benedict Anderson's notion of the nation as an "imagined community," consolidated through print capitalism. According to Anderson, realism provides an "analogue for the idea of a nation" by offering "a complex gloss upon the word 'meanwhile,' " as its narrative weaves together a profusion of occurrences into a simultaneity of comparable events.[27] At the same time it may be argued that such an expanding modern vision produced an inability to reconcile everything within the narrative compulsions of shared significance, when the shock of an elsewhere or the press of the other crowded in on the experience of the here and the now.

Though realism eventually emerged as the preferred mode of consolidating national identity in decolonizing territories, the fight for nationhood entailed an entire range of contradictory experiences that resisted unification, or that succumbed with difficulty to a collective agenda. Partha Chatterjee addresses this problematic in terms of the production of Indian nationalism in relation to the nation's fragments. Chatterjee describes anticolonial nationalism's crisis in imagining the colony as a national community (defined by collective tradition and a distinctive identity) governed by a modern state (derived from Western administrative forms), arguing that separating a material from a spiritual sphere, an inner from an outer domain, provided both a palliative to the crisis and a means of producing a hegemonic nationalism. Indian nationalism normalized itself by accepting Western superiority in the outer, material spheres of science, technology, and statecraft while asserting sovereignty over the inner spheres of domesticity, family, caste, and religion, expanding its sphere of influence through this demarcated and selective adaptation to modernity.[28] The female body, in this analysis, was one of the inner domains on which anticolonial nationalism carved out its realm of sovereignty to stabilize and unify itself.

It is certainly possible to argue that representations of gender and domesticity in colonial films often functioned to invest an inviolable traditionalism in Indian femininity. The figure of the female was frequently used to criticize degenerate modernization and to distinguish Indian customs from the immodesty of Western social norms. However, I think we do Chatterjee's insight a disservice if we place a constraint on the analytic of gender and doom women to the realm of tradition without interrogating the mechanisms of, or the resistance to, such assimilations.[29] As a collective, colonial films display a *variety* of stylistic efforts that both inscribe and destabilize a neotraditional nationalist ideology through representations of women.

To elaborate on film style in relation to the female figure, I take brief recourse to Aamir Mufti's astute reading of Saadat Hasan Manto's short stories. Mufti observes that Manto overturns three canonical forms of Indian nationalism, namely, the novel format, the realist narrative, and the symbolic sanctification of the nation as the allegorical all-embracing mother. Through short stories in which female prostitutes are central characters, Manto deploys ironic and defamiliarizing techniques to open up "the familial semiotic of nationalism to interrogation." [30] Mufti compellingly presents Manto's departures from realism and his deviations from celebrated literary and figural forms as an exposure of nationalism's inauthentic promise of universalism, a promise that Urdu literary formations could not extend unproblematically in the prepartition era.[31] Without leaping to the conclusion that any departure from realism automatically connotes a critical examination of nationalist ideology, I merely wish to underscore Mufti's interpretive strategy at this point. As a way of historicizing aesthetics in relation to politics, he deconstructs a literary canon to thematize dissonance within nationalism.

This opens up an additional perspective for the analysis of Indian film aesthetics. As Chakravarty points out, a film text's realism may mark its proximity to an economic class, evidenced by the Indian intelligentsia's celebration of Satyajit Ray's films of the 1950s and 1960s. The same so-called realist films may be assimilated within a modernist discourse of Third World "auteur cinema" in an international context. Additionally, the dominantly

realist text could possess more than one aesthetic mode. Historical oppositions to the production of a uniform vision may produce hybrid styles operating in tandem. Such a dynamic has certainly been noted in post-independence
Indian films. Arguing that myth demands a different order of belief and a
different psychic investment than realism, film scholars perceive a historical
break in the integration of realism with myth after India's independence. In
a complex analysis of the varying investments of narrative realism in mythic
material, Kapur notes that "in an earlier phase of nationalist consciousness
there was an ebullience of self-discovery through mythic archetype, folk and
popular forms," whereas after independence "the travail of the middle class
[was] worked out in psycho-social terms."[32] With the end of colonialism,
realism, as a discourse of rationalized modernity, replaced a previous "hermeneutic of affirmation" with a middle-class "hermeneutic of suspicion"
toward myth and traditionalism.[33]

Uncertainties regarding tradition were not the exclusive province of post-
independence Indian films, though the ebullience of nationalism in colonial India conspired to mask the presence of stylistic and tropic instabilities.
Films of the 1930s struck more than one note in conceptualizing tradition,
cultural identity, and nationalism through an aesthetic hybridity that was
historically specific to a period of enfeebled imperial rule, volatile nationalism, and a competitive film market. The representation of gender, and more
broadly the representation of difference, accentuated these instabilities. Articulations of a modern civil society demanded new roles for the nation's
problematic subjects. Varying aesthetic modes tugged toward opposing resolutions, pointed to different futures, and unsettled a straightforward trium-
phalism in the discourse of the emerging nation-state, as filmmakers invented a range of narrative- and image-types for including subaltern subjects
into a modern India.

The figure of the Indian female exposes the pitfalls of colonial nationalism and its uneasy relationship with tradition as well as modernity. Miriam
Hansen argues in connection with silent Shanghai films that while "female
figures may well be the privileged fetish of male/modernist projection and
stereotyping, they are also the sites of greatest ambivalence and mobility."[34]
She quotes the more "differentiated typology" of female figures offered by
Yingjin Zhang to propose that female protagonists "exceed or resist" allegorical labels, to embody the contradictions of the "New Woman" who "oscil-
late[s] among different types and incompatible identities."[35] Chatterjee's
focus on the "new patriarchy" and the "powers of hegemonic national-

ism to take in its stride a whole range of dissenting voices" suppresses the disturbance around the figure of this new woman.[36] Colonial cinema, predominantly reformist, patriarchal, and working within colonial bourgeois realist modes nevertheless shows glimpses of "creative, and plural development of social identities" that threatened the emergent dominant nationalist ideology.[37]

British empire cinema responded with at least three predominant aesthetic resolutions to the question, "Why do we retreat?" Despite the absence of an identifiable anti-imperial genre of Indian cinema during the colonial period, the dominant genres of historicals, mythologicals, and socials offered a diverse range of answers to their interrogatives: "Under what conditions will we get self-governance?" and "In what form or style may we imagine it?" Indian films in the historical genre depicted imaginary pasts, while mythologicals incorporated stories from Indian epics and *puranas*, or constructed fables to narrate allegorical tales about Indian society. Indian socials used contemporary settings to unfold melodramatic narratives about family and community.[38] Historicals and mythologicals were eventually superseded (though by no means erased) by reformist socials, which adapted elements of classical realism to a melodramatic template by the 1940s.

The aesthetics of realism, romance, and modernism cannot be neatly divided across these film genres, though arguably historicals and mythologicals offered fewer avenues for realism because of their investment in fantasy, pictorialism, ornate sets, theatrical dialogues, and allegory. Nevertheless in all genres, realist, romance, and modernist aesthetics intermesh to convey different attitudes toward colonial cinema's central referents: India's past, its future, and its modern constituents. Indian colonial cinema transposed visions of a future egalitarian civil society on its feudal past, though reclaiming a precolonial past for the nation demanded the difficult reconfiguration of India's internal subalterns as modern citizens. In the modernisms of Indian cinema's historicals and myths of the 1930s are cues to what stood in the way of a quest for ideological coherence and homogenization under the sign of the nation.

Historical Romances

In addition to monitoring sexual content, film censors of the 1930s excised material depicting political insurrection and civic disruption in Indian films. Almost in direct defiance, Indian historicals repeatedly enacted a crisis of au-

thority in governance. Historicals were different from socials in their place-
ment of a film's dramatic action in antiquity; they literally erased the presence of foreign colonizers by transposing visions of a future nation onto a
fantasized past. The political function of historicals was only thinly veiled
from the Government of India, which was quick to censor even the most
concealed nationalist message. In a lucid statement about historical literary
fiction, the Indian Legislative Department noted with regard to a case before the Allahbad High Court, "The mere fact that [a] book is in the form
of a history does not by any means make improper the conclusion that the
book is written with the intention of bringing into hatred and contempt the
present system of government. History is not written in water-tight compart-
ments and the reader of history is accustomed to look for continuity." Of
higher profile was the case of nationalist leader Bal Gangadhar Tilak, who
published a historical analysis of the battle between Shivaji and Afzal Khan
in his Marathi language journal, *Kesari*. Reacting to the *Kesari* article, members of the legislature asked how they might know "whether [Tilak's] intention was simply to publish a historical discussion" or "to stir up under that
guise hatred against the Government?"[39] The state gauged sedition based
on assessments of intent; novels and films were of interest to the state for
their submerged meanings and for their intentional as well as unintentional
effects. On the latter grounds, the film *Sikandar* was originally approved by
the Bombay Censor Board and subsequently uncertified (that is, the board
revoked its certificate in order to prohibit its exhibition) in cantonment theaters. The film depicts Alexander (Sikandar) the Great's invasion of India and
his confrontation with King Porus who, as the story goes, remained righteous in defeat. The film was censored because of its depiction of Sikandar's
mutinous troops and for its nationalistic pride in Porus.[40]

More than socials, which tended to be explicitly reformist tales addressed
to contemporary India, historicals and mythologicals possessed the allusive nature of a parable. The abstraction of evil in such films allowed them
great mobility in social criticism, as the wicked were used to symbolize both
imperial authoritarianism as well as regressive Indian customs. *Diler Jigar*
(a.k.a. *Gallant Hearts*) and *Ghulami nu Patan* are two surviving silents made by
the Agarwal Film Company in 1931 that tell stories of corrupt kings and in-
trepid swashbucklers, replete with fights, romantic love scenes, and chases.
Rajadhyaksha calls *Diler Jigar* a "freewheeling adaptation of the historical"
that brings together "Fairbank's *Mark of Zorro* (1920) emphasis on action and
decor, with the balletic Nautanki [Indian folk dance-drama] idiom, notably

25. Kalsen lashing his whip at the poor in *Diler Jigar*. Courtesy N FAI.

in the picturizing of the plentiful sword fights."[41] Though shots in both films are frequently framed as tableaus, they cinematically condense and expand time, and bring audiences to shocking proximities and vertiginous distances from the staged action. The films perfectly demonstrate Indian silent cinema's grasp of the medium's modernity put to the service of indigenous visual and narrative idioms.

In the first few shots *Diler Jigar* introduces the film's moral polarities: King Bholanath, "a benign King, the idol of the people," versus his plotting brother, Kalsen. (Intertitles for silent films were typically in English, Hindi, Urdu and a regional language, which in this case was Gujarati). King Bholanath, the "friend of the needy and the poor," is soon killed at Kalsen's command by his man Kritant. Time moves quickly in a series of suggestive dissolves from Kritant poisoning the king's drink, to a shot of the king's crown on a tray, to a shot showing the crown on Kalsen's head. Evil usurps power with a visual and narrative ease. This is economical: Kalsen's machinations, which convert his cupidity toward the crown into manifest reality, are conveyed through efficient dissolves. It is also melodramatic: the narrative is immediately identifiable as a world horribly out of balance, a perverted order.

Ghulami nu Patan has a similar structure and begins with the following intertitles.

> About the year 1818 in the reign of Rana Bhimsingh—the Emperor of Mar-
> war there was a system of slavery called "Gola." For peasants who couldn't
> pay the land tax, their women would be outraged, especially by Lord of
> Karangarth, Kumar Umedhsingh, and his lieutenants.

The first shot of the film moves from a close up of a wine pitcher to a
drunken king abusing women, followed by shots of male peasants attached
to a plough. The faces of the peasants remain insignificant; instead, close ups
of their twitching, bleeding backs, marked by lashes, convey their dehumanization as they are speared and whipped while tilling the land. The familiar
colonial predicament of famine and poverty caused by fixed imperial taxation and a lack of government assistance are transformed here into an almost
abstract image of subjection to authoritarianism.

Representations of absolute power and abject powerlessness bring to the
structure of historical films an element that A. K. Ramanujan identifies in
oral Indian folktales about women. Ramanujan notes that tales with male
protagonists and secondary female characters end in marriage "for they
speak of the emancipation of the hero from the parental yoke and the setting
up of a new family, as he comes into his own." In woman-centered oral folktales, however, the woman is already married or married early "and then the
woman's troubles begin."[42] In such stories, the woman's heroism lies in her
suffering and her righteous behavior, which restores value to her corrupted
domestic ideal. Hers is less a physical quest than a story of forbearance, devotion, and faith despite a betrayed ideal—a story of moral virtues that eventually restabilize her disrupted home life. (This is also apparent in the classical stories of Savitri and Shakuntala from the Hindu epic, the *Mahabharatha*).
Rather than essentializing these into male and female narratives, I would argue that the observation of structural repetitions in women-centered folk
tales provides the insight that female social subjugation receives formal acknowledgment in oral tales. A woman's exploitation and limited options for
deliverance are marked in folk narratives through suffering that commences
near the story's opening and through a depiction of her reliance on moral
virtue rather than willful action to reverse a wretched fate.

Diler Jigar and *Ghulami nu Patan* are commercial quest narratives about
strong men who reclaim a lost kingdom and gain a consort through their
brave deeds. More viscerally, however, these films also follow the rhythms
of woman-centered folktales, given their narrative's depictions of complete
abjection in a corrupted "home" and demands for moral strength. The two

forms of romance—of dispossession, travel, and a violent physical quest on the one hand, and of unfulfilled ideals, interiority, and a spiritual quest on the other—indicate two different categories of social positioning, frequently gendered as male and female. Their coexistence in historicals of the 1930s and their embodiment in both male and female characters implicitly appeals to both the revolutionary and pacifist factions of the nationalist movement, conveying that physical revolt is incomplete without inner strength in the attempt to regain one's domestic realm. The male character in *Neecha Nagar* maintains, "Qurbani ka sabak aurat hi sikha sakti hai" [the lesson of sacrifice can only be taught by a woman], but he must nevertheless learn this lesson to achieve his goals. Physical strength is presented as incomplete without patience and resilience during the nationalist struggle, and the socially gendered aspects of these qualities are necessarily androgynized to transform men and women into a national community. Substructures of (presumptively women-centric) melodramatic folktales are indistinguishable from (presumptively male-centric) action or quest narratives in a context where both appeals are used to redeem a people without physical or moral authority in their own home, by proving them worthy *in every way* of its reclamation. Like the Gandhian *satyagraha* (the struggle for truth), the pursuit of righteousness becomes the path of resistance for those deprived of constitutional means of justice. Forbearance here represents the tool of the materially weak and morally strong.

Indian historicals were structured as romances to tell stories of a colony's victimization and unrealized power by staking physical *and* moral claims on the homeland. Demonstrations of physical as well as spiritual strength are central to the progress of the historical film's narrative and to its specularization. On the surface, such colonial romances appear to share the rhythms of *imperial* romances when conceptualized in the broadest terms of abjection and eventual triumph. However, imperial fiction's drama of retreat (rather than reclamation) is founded on the physical evacuation of the female, who remains identified with an absent domestic space, retained in the narrative primarily through a spectral feminization of the colonial male. The colonial historical romance's inclusion of male and female subjects and its weakened gender-specificity in attributing (physical and moral, public and private) demonstrations of heroism pulls the narrative in new directions.[43] Historically motivated hybrid demands on narrative structures of address to the nation *alter* the possibilities for the portrayal of female characters.

In *Diler Jigar*, for instance, the murdered King Bholanath's son, Hameer,

26. Saranga comes to town with her fellow acrobats in *Diler Jigar*. Courtesy NFAI.

grows up in anonymity as an acrobat, unaware of his aristocratic roots. Unknowingly, he returns to his kingdom with his beloved Saranga and her brother Balbheem to perform street-entertainment acts. Hameer is a variation on the character of Azim, the dethroned prince from Britain's historical romance *The Drum*, living out his narrative fate in an Indian film that has erased the figure of a British ally and sketched in the figure of an Indian woman. The group's encounters with royalty occasion stunts and humor, as the brave trio scale walls, dance with swords, and are bewildered by royal clothes. A misunderstanding arises between Saranga and Hameer, when he spies her briefly dazzled by royal wealth and weakening to King Kalsen's lascivious advances. After this event, the two follow divergent paths in fighting the king. Hameer opposes the king openly, aroused by rallying calls that carry thinly veiled anti-imperial messages such as, "Stir yourself . . . at least to wreak vengeance upon this tyrant, who has ruined all your life and happiness" and "Friends, how long will you bear the tyranny of this king?"[44] Saranga, rejected by Hameer, turns into a masked avenger who protects Hameer and helps the oppressed. Saranga's silent fidelity and pursuit of a righteous battle are accompanied by physical heroics, which lead to her eventual reconciliation with Hameer. On the one hand, her veil of secrecy (in comparison to Hameer's direct confrontation of the king) dramatizes the predicament of

Indian women as symbols of inviolable national identity; this is the inter-pretation Rajadhyaksha prefers in his reading of the film.[45] On the other hand, Saranga's very entry into the public sphere of combat draws attention to Indian nationalism's impossibility without an inclusive and participatory politics.

In both silent historical films, women are portrayed as essential in facili-tating the downfall of evil regimes. In *Ghulami nu Patan* two of the most visu-ally memorable sequences involve talismanic objects used by women. Kamal-bala, the object of the dastardly King Umedhsingh's unwanted attentions, stands framed by a doorway in a picturesque medium shot with her father, followed by a flashback sequence that shows them helping a man who gives Kamalbala a ring, with the promise to help them in an hour of need. Her later use of the ring to remind the mysterious man of his word draws a powerful ally (Kartar Singh, the Lord of Amargarth and later her suitor) into the fray of the battle. The second visual sequence involves King Umedhsingh's wife, who betrays her husband by unlocking a prison door to help innocent captives. The scene takes on a symbolic function because of its extremely close shot of a gigantic lock that covers a third of the frame, with a key turned by the hand of this mysterious woman otherwise insignificant to the plot. Symbols in this instance endow the first woman's words and the second's deeds with a transformative power. Female figures rehearse a conflict between loyalty to a misguided authority figure (a king, a husband) and loyalty to a higher cause (justice, emancipation), altering the fate of the narrative by their choice of the latter. Such choices confront minor as well as major female characters.

Historical romances present an opportunity for equivocation around con-flicting principles, with each character intensifying the level of symbolic con-flict. Exaggeratedly dramatic speech influenced by Parsi and Shakespearean theater, multiple plots, heightened use of character for symbolism, reduced character development, and an episodic structure defeat the historical film's realism. Sohrab Modi's Minerva Movietone productions such as *Pukar* and *Sikandar* (which may also be considered early Muslim socials) contain dia-logues that acquire greater weight than the characters, altering the film's gender politics. *Pukar*, for instance, is about the conflict between mercy and justice, and the clash of personal and political duty. Sangram Singh (Sohrab Modi), a loyal servant of Emperor Jehangir (Chandramohan), hunts down his fugitive son and brings him before the royal court because, as a crimi-nal, his son is legal property ("kanoon ki amaanat"). Once Sangram Singh imprisons his son as a loyal subject of his king, he pleads for royal mercy

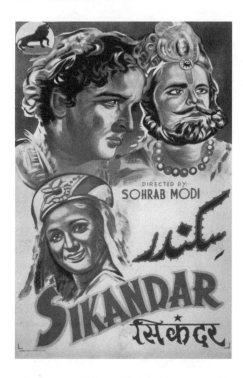

27. Film poster for *Sikandar*.
Courtesy NFAI.

as a devoted father. Jehangir is torn as well, as a man who would like to be merciful to his faithful servant's son and as an emperor who must mete out impartial justice. The film's central crisis is staged around Jehangir's wife, Mumtaz Mahal (Naseem Banu). The empress, aiming at a bird, accidentally kills a washerman. Before they discover this fatality, Jehangir and Mumtaz Mahal engage in an intense debate in which the empress role-plays the emperor and scoffs at his incomplete justice, which sentences to death a man who has taken another's life, without the ability to return life to the former. Jehangir initially argues against mercy but must eventually revise his position. The emperor finds a malleable and merciful justice preferable to blind law once he personally realizes the devastating import of a death sentence. In the process, Mumtaz Mahal has the opportunity to instruct her husband on principled action when she willingly accepts punishment, refusing to destabilize the basis of his authority or let him abandon justice for love. As a collective, these films give women the power of mind, morals, and physical action.[46]

Female displays of physical prowess in films like *Diler Jigar* also demonstrate Indian cinema's absorption of the appeals of Hollywood stunt and action films. By the end of the 1920s there was evidence of a growing audience base for Indian films, particularly among the lower classes. In 1928 the *Report of the Indian Cinematograph Committee* noted that "The [Hollywood] 'serial' . . . has lost its former popularity (with literate and semi-literate classes) and has been largely supplanted by the Indian film."[47] Homi Wadia's Wadia Movietone productions of *Hunterwali* (Hindi, 1935), *Diamond Queen* (Hindi, 1940), and *Bombaiwali* (Hindi, 1941), which popularized the physically powerful, masked, and "Fearless" Nadia with her whip and her faithful gang of rebels, drew directly from the Hollywood stunt film's palate of appeals. The producer J. B. H. Wadia later commented on the influence of " 'manly' heroines like Maria Walcampe and Pearle White" on him, in films where "Pearl White's prowess was a match for Francis Ford, William Farnum and Herbert Rawlinson. Ruth Roland and Helen Gibson were not far behind them in stunt-pulling and acrobatics."[48]

Beyond remodeling the Hollywood stunt film, Indian romances that featured the masked female vigilante confounded a parallel effort in North India to "purify" images of the Indian female. Charu Gupta discusses the Hindu nationalist efforts to "cleanse" Hindi literature and poetry of the influence of *sringar rasa*, which had been its dominant mode for over 300 years. Known as the "Riti Kal" of vernacular Hindi poetry and literature dating back to the late sixteenth century, this literature built on an earlier Sanskritic convention of combining sringar rasa with devotional poetry, as in Jayadeva's *Gita Govinda*. Riti Kal poetry played on the ambiguities between obsessive spiritual and sensual yearnings of the protagonist for their lover and (or) the divine. Erotic and detailed descriptions of the female body were a central trope of this poetry, which by the early twentieth century was decried as corrupting. As Gupta notes, during the modern "Dwivedi period" of Hindi literature, a powerful faction of nationalists reinvented India's past as heroic, austere, and masculine. Scholars like Bharatendu Harishchandra celebrated the *vir rasa* of literature, which was written in praise of the bravery of Rajput and Maratha warriors. Such literary nationalists also aimed to cleanse Hindi of the influence of Urdu, Persian, and Arabic in order to establish its Sanskritic linguistic purity.[49]

Happily, during this period of literary nationalism, cinema as a commercial mass medium depended on appealing to the largest possible audience base and invented an extremely contaminated language. As Mukul Kesavan argues, an Urdu-inflected Hindi thrived in Indian cinema because it was the more popular and prevalent linguistic form of colonial North India.[50] Addi-

28. An active woman from *Diamond Queen*. Courtesy NFAI.

tionally, in including the essential box-office ingredients of specular pleasures, dialogic flourishes, visual celebrations of the female form, and romantic love, cinema absorbed the excised sringar rasa and reinvented it for a
modern medium. Combining scopophilic delights, spectacles of bravery and
romance, comedy, and Hollywood-style antics to produce a visual language
that cannot be easily catalogued with other nationalist myths about militant
men and women (like the deified Rani of Jhansi), the historical romance incorporates Hindu nationalism's demonized trope of sringar rasa alongside
its valorized vir rasa. If cinema commodified the female form as never before,
its beautiful screen female with her sassy dialogues and whip appeared as an
abomination to those who preferred to keep their gendered rasas separate.

While it may be argued that Fearless Nadia's outré acrobatics were acceptable to Indian audiences because of Nadia's foreign origins (she was Australian), historicals stretched the Indian female figure to do more than physical
gymnastics. Pronouncedly, historical films depicted conflicts between forms
of governance; the potential corruptibility of *all* authority in these narratives
prioritized abstract principles (such as justice, righteousness, mercy) above
any king, father, or husband, thus presenting women with a range of commitments that superseded their duty as wives, mothers, daughters, and loyal
subjects. In *Sikandar*, for instance, self-respect and loyalty to country are more

29. The historical film mixes vir and sringar rasas with an ornate set and a picturesque Prithviraj in *Sikandar*. Courtesy N FAI.

important than familial duty. The film is well known in the annals of Indian film history for using the Indian King Porus's (Sohrab Modi) battle against the invading forces of Sikandar (Prithviraj Kapoor) as an analogy for India's struggle for independence. One of the sisters of a petty ruler opposes her brother in his wish to side with Sikandar's forces to win an internecine battle against Porus (an event reminiscent of the in-fighting that made the region pliable to the East India company's political ambitions). In this narrative, the woman's obedience to an abstract higher authority disrupts her assimilation within an existing familial structure, while it consolidates her allegiance to a future, utopian state.

This crisis of loyalty speaks to the absence of a national government at the center, which attenuates the cultural narrative's investment in a singular definition of authority. Prevarications around questions of governance offer resistance to techniques of classical realism. As argued by film theorists, one of the preconditions for classical realism is an *invisible* validation of a given social structure as the most rational one, with a unified protagonist embodying the ideal citizen and the narrative structure validating the dominant legal order. Narrative crises and dialogic situations surrounding the definition of proper conduct and authority interrupt such invisibility. Formally, in post-

30. Westernized Sridharan is an abusive husband in *Thyagabhoomi*. Courtesy N F A I.

independence–era films, family and state are closely allied with each other and the nation-state acts as the pervasive agent in a relay of authority that begins with the family.[51] In colonial films, however, the ideological relay between family, nation, and state is inhibited, given the actual absence of an *Indian* nation-state. In fact, the relay is under construction within the purview of fantasy and willed compulsion. As Chandulal Shah said in his address to the First Indian Motion Picture Congress, "Whether you wish it or not, the place of this Industry will always be with those who are struggling to achieve such Government for this country." Colonial cinema's realization of an ideal future society is contingent on an Antigone-like rejection of (the potentially authoritarian, unreliable, or corrupt) contemporary state/community.[52] The colonial historical most closely fulfils a people's romance with the notion of a future Indian nation, imagined as a predestined tryst with one's unrealized but innate, antique potential for righteous self-governance.

The historical romance's staged crises around the notion of governance acknowledges competing claims upon the ideal citizen/subject, whose choices bring them into conflict with their present community or governing family.[53] Within a patriarchal tradition where the woman is held as the generative center of her domestic sphere and frequently considered symbolically

31. Finally finding his conscience with the help of his wife, Sridharan becomes a nationalist in *Thyagabhoomi*. Courtesy NFAI.

indistinguishable from it, such admissions of conflicting interests are poten-tially transgressive. The Indian nationalist movement's appeal for women's increased involvement in public and political life registers its presence vividly in the Fearless Nadia films, which show images of physically strong women outside their homes, exercising, participating in public forums, or actively fighting the villains. In subtler ways, similar redefinitions of the woman's so-cial role manifest themselves in historical and mythological films that permit female characters to make choices *not* solely determined by their domestic loyalties.

Certainly colonial representations of women also recuperate a neotradi-tional patriarchy. In melodramatic socials as varied as *Gunsundari* (Shah, 1934) and *Thyagabhoomi*, for instance, misguided and Westernized husbands force their wives out of home, only to be humbled by the woman's chastity and indestructible traditionalism. In both cases, the narratives deify the female figure and represent her as the ideal woman of a future nation-state. His-toricals, however, have a weakened investment in the consequences of the woman's choices for herself. Primarily, her choice is either a pretext for rhe-torical pronouncements about individual or political ideals, or an alibi for spectacles of the new woman in action in public spaces, or in dialogic situa-tions. As Nadia says in *Diamond Queen*, "Hind ko azaad hona hai to Hind ki aurat ko bhi azaad hona hoga" [If India is to be independent, then so must her women]. The gap between secular nationalism's demand to emancipate women and religious nationalism's need to secure women from modernization, typically closed by the machinations of a new patriarchy, remains relatively open in colonial historicals.

Modernist Myths

If modernism, as Andreas Huyssen argues, is "a response to the long march of the commodity through culture," then colonial modernism was constituted partially as a response to the fear that national commodities would march to the tune of imperial technologies of production, vision, and power.[54] Modernism's ambivalence toward its own origins in the massification of culture was exacerbated in a colonial context, wherein the colony's national bourgeoisie were caught between two potential antagonists: the Western imperial state that controlled the terms of commercialization, and the subaltern mass consumer who betokened a debasement of the arts. Ascriptions to aestheticist notions of art's autonomy from the market and, contrarily, a faith in cinema's ability to democratize culture were both constitutive factors of Indian colonial cinema's modernism. Mythological films drew their impetus from both responses.

The director V. Shantaram's film *Amar Jyoti* can be understood as modernist myth in this sense: it illustrates that the mythic narrative navigates complex demands on colonial cinema to be modern yet Indian, commercial yet artistic, by aestheticizing a mass commodity. To do so, the film incorporates allusions to Indian myths alongside references to local forms of popular entertainment and stylized quotations from European art cinema, infusing idioms of accessible entertainment with a more elevated discourse. Like historicals, myths explore the realm of fantasy and legend that seems apparently removed from India's present. *Amar Jyoti* superimposes a mythic adventure upon the ostensibly "lower" genres of a stunt film to tell the story of the pirate queen Saudamini (Durga Khote).[55]

Saudamini is in rebellion against patriarchy, and by the film's conclusion she succeeds in symbolically passing on her eternal torch (*amar jyoti*) of revolt to the film's central romantic couple. Much of the film operates at the level of allegory, initiated by its abstract opening shot of flames floating and lighting each other. Their connotation of a spreading revolution is undercut in the first few sequences, which depict Saudamini and her men violently burning

32. Queen Saudamini scorns men and is seen here brutalizing Durjaya in *Amar Jyoti*. Courtesy NFAI.

a ship that belongs to Princess Nandini (Shanta Apte). Saudamini frees the ship's slaves and incites them to fight for freedom. This opening sequence sets up two central points of conflict: the dangerous closeness between *inquilaab* (enabling revolution) and *khudgarzi, badla,* and *zulm* (destructive selfishness, revenge, and atrocity), and the moral, social, and filial price one should be willing to pay for independence (*azaadi*).

Azaadi is a polyvalent signifier in the film, and characters use it while talking about the freeing of slaves from their masters, the liberation of women from men, and the struggle against social recidivism. In its time, the word necessarily connoted India's freedom from colonial rule, so that all the struggles portrayed in the film become associated with the new nation's agenda. As an aside, Indian film texts display as much of a bravura performance around the term *independence* (which translates into *azaadi* in Urdu and *swatantrata* in Hindi), as British regulatory documents demonstrate with the term *empire*. The songbook of the popular Hindi romance film *Bandhan*, for instance, opens with the following lines. "Swantantrata par manushya jaan de deta hai. Lekin ek aisa 'bandhan' hai jispar pranimatra janma bhar ki azaadi haste haste nyojhaavar kar deta hai . . . vah hai prem ka bandhan!" [Independence is something man will die for. But there is one "bond" for which humans abandon a lifetime of freedom with a laugh . . . the bond of love!].[56]

Colonial Indian films inserted references to independence on all possible occasions.

With its slippage around the term *azaadi*, *Amar Jyoti* equates political freedom with women's independence from patriarchy, but the fluidity of the comparison raises formal problems. The film cannot, with any consistency, develop its romantic subplot while maintaining its central protagonist's rigid adherence to a woman's independence from men. Accordingly, Saudamini's dedication to sexual, social, and political freedom is given a psychological motivation, closely related to her gender identity. Saudamini, it is revealed, was once desirous of being an *adarsh nari* and an *adarsh mata* (an ideal woman and an ideal mother) until the reigning *rani* (queen) separated her from her son. Saudamini's enmity with the rani is not developed in much detail, but it suggests that her rhetoric of independence is tainted by a personal desire for vengeance. Her message of sexual and social liberation, though not invalidated by this embitterment, is made fallible by it. Equally, however, the film may be read as an imaginary trajectory through which authoritarian hierarchies (of a patriarchal and imperial state) as well as rigidly individualistic philosophies (of the pirate queen) are purged in favor of an egalitarian and humane future, actualized by the film's final male-female dyad of Nandini and Sudhir. The couple brings compassion and romance to the life of an outlaw while holding forth the promise that future generations will inherit a radical politics.

The film's plot follows its two central female characters, Saudamini and Nandini. Saudamini captures Princess Nandini to aggrieve the rani (Nandini's mother), and convinces Nandini to join the battle for her sex (referred to as *jati*, or caste, as in *auratjat*, or the caste of womanhood). Nandini's union with Saudamini's cause, depicted in a sequence in which the two women embrace each other in solidarity, brings together various charged dialogues running through the film about gender inequities that make slaves even of queens.[57] But Nandini's decision to join Saudamini poses an immediate obstacle to her love for the shepherd Sudhir, who in an ironic plot twist is revealed to be Saudamini's long lost son. Now Saudamini's maternal love becomes a central issue in the film's romantic plot, because she must choose between her brand of separatist feminism and her son's happiness. Her beliefs appear to weaken in the face of her maternal instincts.

In reading the extracinematic public image of the actress Durga Khote (who plays Saudamini), Neepa Majumdar argues that Khote's educated, upper-caste, and overtly reformist social commitments permeate her screen persona and explain her progressive screen roles. Majumdar further proposes that the recuperation of an idealized notion of Indian motherhood subverts *Amar Jyoti*'s potentially radical message, by revealing "Saudamini's renunciation of 'womanly' qualities, such as romantic love, motherhood, and domesticity, to be an unnatural distortion of her true feelings."[58] Arguably, however, the film's stylized mise-en-scène, its theatrical dialogues, and the demonstrable influence of expressionist and baroque techniques on its visual imagery exceed the psychologically rendered realist, narrative containment of characters, suggesting significant artistic disturbance around the figure of a liberated woman.

The film's resolution does not dull its structuring conflict between a woman's desire for freedom versus her urges for romantic love (between Nandini and Sudhir) or maternal love (of Saudamini for Sudhir), both of which sentiments irredeemably embed these independent women into gendered social functions. Through the registers of visual and verbal excesses, the film offers what Miriam Hansen in a comparable context has called "a sensory-reflexive horizon for the contradictory experience of modernity," particularly in regard to its implications for women.[59] Too nebulous to be an outright critique of traditional constructions of femininity and maternity, the film's hybrid visual and performative style nevertheless presents multiple and mutually incompatible perspectives on womanhood.

Discussing early Shanghai cinema, Hansen proposes that it "represents a distinct brand of vernacular modernism, one that evolved in a complex relation to American—and other foreign—models while drawing on and transforming Chinese traditions in theater, literature, graphic and print culture, both modernist and popular."[60] Actress Durga Khote's persona and performance in *Amar Jyoti*, and director Shantaram's work during the 1930s navigated similar straits between the popular and avant-garde cultures in India, affecting their approach to cinema and their rendition of gender roles.

In talking about her relationship to films, Khote makes the incredible pronouncement that in the early days of cinema, "not many saw films for the reason that viewing films spoils the eye-sight."[61] The actress claims to have seen "only one movie and that was Maharashtra film company's *Karna*" on the urging of classical singer Bal Gandharva, because there was "no place for glamour and show business" in this "devotional film."[62] Her avowed resistance to the medium does not prevent her from celebrating the fact that V. Damle and S. Fattelal (who formed Prabhat Studios with Shantaram in 1929) took photographs of film rehearsals and gave her, in her words, an "ocular demonstration of the do's and don'ts for an artiste."[63] So while the actress emphasizes cinema's visual ability to reinterpret the dramatic crafts, she also stresses cinema's association with the arts and its possible uses for social uplift by contrasting the enduring relevance of Karna's moral message to the ephemera of films in general.

One may impute that the actress is mitigating the medium's potential disreputability, which derives from its status as a commercial and modern profession rather than an élite avocation. Her response also starkly reveals cinema's threat to the traditional separation between art and the public sphere, and its ability to create a new constellation of social relations by drawing members of different classes, castes, and genders into a shared work space and viewing site.[64] As noted by Majumdar, Khote did not fit the typical profile of a film actress, given her elevated caste and educational status. In fact, her response personifies the social anxieties provoked by the medium as commodified culture. In Amar Jyoti Khote essays her role to reflect this ambivalence toward the medium. On the one hand, Khote's deviations from the popular Sangeet Natak images of femininity dominant in Indian filmmaking may be read as her resistance to the medium's massification.[65] But the actress's high-minded interpretation of Saudamini as an uncompromising figure who makes public declamations of female power differs from her more classically realist renditions of the character's maternal love. Because other primary characters are unaware of Saudamini's maternal anguish, the camera registers her dilemmas in secret complicity with the audience, exploiting the medium's ability to convey an "ocular" intimacy between actor and viewer through close attention to detail.

Khote's shifting performance as Saudamini—which ranges from registering emotions with minute facial expressions to preaching female independence in declamatory style—communicate her sense of cinema as a private, individualized mode of mediated address as well as a theatrical form aimed at vast audiences and infused with a higher purpose. Shantaram's dramatic and visual rendition of Saudamini through different stylistic modes bespeaks a similarly complex attitude toward cinema's modernity. The costume-drama aspect of the film pulls toward cinema's mass-audience base drawn from popular theater, even as its deliberate references to international art cinema establishes the film's high cultural status. Shantaram's film integrates these dual impulses.

Shantaram Rajaram Vankudre trained under Baburao Painter. Unlike Khote, the director was a cinephile who drew on local as well as Hollywood and European modes of representation in *Amar Jyoti* and *Amritmanthan*.[66] In these films, the style of acting Shantaram learned at Gandharva Natak Mandali is combined with sequences of naturalistic acting; ornate backdrops reminiscent of the fantasies staged on Parsi theater coexist with spare expressionist sets and lighting; and symbolic abstractions exploit cinema's ability to visually manipulate the image in clear variation from the seamless editing of the film's narrative sequences. (According to his son, Shantaram was the first Indian filmmaker to use a telephoto lens, in *Amritmanthan*.)[67] The director takes myths as a representational form familiar to Indian film audiences but endows them with an aestheticism by manipulating the camera, creating experimental impressionistic and subjective shots, and incorporating techniques from European art films critically acclaimed in India. The function of such stylistic hybridity may be best explained through a contrasting example.

Examining the uses of myth in Prabhat Studios films on Hindu saints, Geeta Kapur argues that the pictorial conventions of *Sant Tukaram* (Damle and Fattelal, 1936) "give its imagery an iconic aspect, taking iconic to mean an image into which symbolic meanings converge and in which moreover they achieve stasis."[68] Through a series of deft connections, Kapur links the iconicity endowed by the film to the figure of Tukaram (played with great success by Vishnupant Pagnis) with the frontal and idealized compositional conventions of pre-Mughal and Mughal miniatures, Raja Ravi Verma's paintings, and Phalke's mythological films. Though "religious iconicity is mediated to secular effect in the filmic process" in *Sant Tukaram*, what remains constant in this relay of influence from Ravi Verma paintings to Damle and Fattelal films, according to Kapur, is an extension of iconic significance to the indexical sign in a manner culturally specific to colonial India.[69] The actor (or *patra* in Hindi; literally, "vessel") "is at once deity and man; he is a pair of signs—the iconic and indexical," understanding the two terms in the Piercian sense.[70] Thus as an index, the representation of Tukaram has a manifest connection to reality (like a thumbprint to a thumb, or the screen image of Tukaram to the actor Pagnis), and as an icon, the sign has symbolic meanings for a culture (as Tukaram's image emblematizes sainthood).

Shantaram's stylistic hybridity can now be summed up as follows. The transferable signification that Kapur posits between actor and the (indexical) image as well as (iconic) sign in *Sant Tukaram* cannot be extended to Shantaram's Prabhat Studios films. In *Amar Jyoti* and *Amritmanthan*, images and sequences become iconic through dense and allusive references to mythic texts. Their tangential commentary on the film breaks a potential stasis of meaning and disrupts the commutation of significance between referent, index, and icon. Shantaram's films convey a formalist opacity rather than a transfer of meaning between icon and image, suggesting that there was no single model for the use of myths in colonial film in this respect. For instance, *Amritmanthan* twice transports the audience into mythic sequences that depict the masculine Lord Vishnu transformed into the feminine seductress Mohini. As Mohini, Vishnu dupes the *asuras* (demons) into giving the *devas* (gods) the nectar of immortality. This mythic story about churning the ocean to yield *nectar* (literally "*amritmanthan*") is first triggered by the words of the evil priest Rajguru, and later by an ally to the good queen. Rajguru uses the myth to illustrate the necessarily arduous road to his victory, while the queen's ally beckons the myth to instruct the queen on the virtues of deception, because "kapati ke saath kapat karne mein koi paap nahin hai" [there is no sin in deceiving the deceivers]. The sequences are thus embedded in the narrative at the service of opposing characters, which effectively transforms the represented gods into polysemous icons whose meanings are mobilized equally by good and evil narrative forces. These weakened codes of meaning assignation in integrating mythic and realist sequences reveals the film's mobilization of diverse appeals, which are only *contingently* stabilized within the film's symbolic domain. The same may be said of the symbolism in *Amar Jyoti*. Under Shantaram's direction, Khote's Saudamini vociferously attacks society for the duration of the film and performs her protest in exaggerated terms. Cinematically, low-key lighting and iterative shots of waves crashing against rocks thematize the clash between Saudamini and patriarchy, giving the allegorically represented conflict enhanced visual gravity. Like the waves, Saudamini vows to never give up her fight against the rigidly rocklike dictates of an unjust society ("anyaayi samaj ke mazboot pathharon se"). On seeing her resolve, her male companion Shekhar remarks on the fearsome nature of the battle between the waves and the rocks, similarly speaking in metaphors ("kitni bhayanak jang chhidi hai dono mein!"). The cumulative visual and rhetorical accretion of the film's allegorical meaning prevents Saudamini's eventual departure from the life of piracy, and the film's narrative, from becoming a complete abandonment of her feminist rebellion.

Like the historicals discussed earlier, *Amar Jyoti* (similar to *Amritmanthan*) shows its characters deliberating over the best form of governance. Unlike realist films that inherit the nation's pedagogical function in their form, conflicts of political modernity are equivocated through declamatory dialogues. As Saudamini departs, Shekhar tells her that waves soften rocks. Symbolic shots of waves and rocks return, and disembodied lamps again light each other in an echo of the film's opening. Admittedly, the film's conclusion combines this metaphoric message of social change with a melodramatic appeal to the social icon of a sacrificial mother when Saudamini withdraws without revealing her maternal identity to her son, Sudhir. In this, Saudamini's narrative function appeases the social demand for a woman to identify with maternal emotions. But iterative spectacles that signify Saudamini's unassimilated retreat from society counteract the narrative's traditional valuation of sacrificial maternity.

In *Amritmanthan* and *Amar Jyoti* the uneven coexistence of the mythic/allegorical and narrative/realist sequences exposes the film's link to two distinct kinds of "cultural manifestations of mass-produced, mass-mediated, and mass-consumed modernity."[71] Mythic sequences counteract fears of cinema as a purely Western technology by mobilizing populism, and immortalizing a transient commercial medium by ascending to the level of eternal time and truths; narrative sequences endow the medium with a secular and bourgeois respectability. The film's narrativity flatters the viewer by expecting complicity and comprehension of a cinematic vocabulary shared with commercial Hollywood films and Indian socials. At the same time, however, my distinction between mythic and realist narrative sequences is at risk of creating a false dichotomy between two related manipulations of the cinematic medium. If myth and symbolism combat anxieties of the medium's ephemeral, consumable nature with a fantasy of timelessness, the realist narrative evades the same fear by hubristically imposing its own temporality. For this reason, they are best seen as a two-headed response to cinematic modernity.

Additionally, both mythic and narrative modes are connected because Shantaram anoints both kinds of sequences with stylized allusions to European films, staging an imaginary dialogue between his commercial film and the inaccessible circuit of international art cinema. Shantaram's film style occasionally displays a studied cosmopolitanism rather than an organic or unconscious modernism. To the extent that film aesthetics can function as an index of what was under negotiation during this historical period, Shantaram's varied address demonstrates not only his "vernacularization," as Hansen puts it, of cinematic modernity but also his studied deliberation over international film style. The distinction between colonial Indian cinema's "vernacular modernism" (as Indian filmmakers reconfigured cinema through local idioms of modernization) and a more modular modernism is essential to an exploration of Shantaram's conscious or *selective* use of expressionist techniques, embedded in his films almost as quotations.

Shantaram formed Prabhat Studios with Damle and Fattelal, leaving Prabhat in 1942 to create Rajkamal Kalamandir. In 1933, while visiting Germany to print *Sairandhri* in color, Shantaram had an opportunity to view several expressionist and *kammerspiel* films.[72] His subsequent films show an importation of European modernist techniques as his films creatively incorporate their styles. German expressionist techniques — chiaroscuro lighting and angular, distorted sets to convey psychic complexity — serve to mark *Amar Jyoti* and *Amritmanthan*'s artistic status within India, because they shield the films from criticisms aimed at popular Indian and Hollywood films of the 1930s.

Samik Bandyopadhyay summarizes comments from Indian film journals of the period, noting, "Both *Filmland* and *filmindia* in the thirties were fighting a lost battle against what they considered the 'Bombay brand picture with all action but no psychology.' . . . Prabhansu Gupta (*Filmland*, 31 January 1931) upheld Murnau, Stroheim, and Lubitsch as models, 'as sworn allies of emotional pictures . . . not panoramic and advocates of motion as the Yankee directors are,' and Niranjan Pal held up the 'technique' of German cinema, and 'art and life' of Russian cinema against the 'well made, sophisticated film plays to tickle our fancies — sugary, peppery, undress spectacles and so called sex-dramas' churned out by Hollywood."[73] Indian films that wished to identify with a more elevated form than the commercial Hollywood product self-consciously mobilized antithetical references to German and Soviet cinema.[74] Though Rajadhyaksha and Willemen note that Shantaram tried to break into the European market in the 1940s (his 1943 Hindi-language film *Shakuntala* was made with an eye toward export), in the 1930s he was embittered by the racism he encountered in Germany.[75] His trip abroad, invigorating to his sense of cinema's possibilities, was also one on which he suffered "the worst humiliation of his life."[76] His use of expressionist techniques was less a means of gaining the acceptance of international distributors and audiences than a self-conscious modernist rewriting of Indian cinema (visible later in Guru Dutt's films, particularly in the choreography of musical sequences).

The occasional modularity or importation of this modernism does not convey the style's foreignness to Indian cinema but rather the Indian film director's marked display of a cosmopolitan knowledge of the cinematic form. Techniques of European modernist films were utilized to specific ends within the colonial Indian context, revealing something of the style's significance to its application and something of the context's affinity to an imported style. In the next section, I examine specific textual occasions for such stylization to draw broad conclusions about its historical significance.

Multiple Modernisms

Amritmanthan tells the story of a mythical kingdom where the reformist King Krantiverma (Varde) opposes his powerful head priest, Rajguru (Chandramohan). Rajguru supports human and animal sacrifice (nar bali and pashu bali), and decides that the modern reformist king's obstructions to this form of worship must cease. With an otherworldly control over his people, Rajguru conducts a ritual to elect the king's killer in the presence of the fearsome idol of Goddess Chandika. Yashodharma (Kulkarni) is elected to murder the king, and for his dark deed, he dies by the sword of the king's guards. With the king murdered, Rajguru exercises authoritarian control over the kingdom and its princess, who is now crowned Queen Mohini (Nalini Tarkhad). Matters are eventually righted through the intervention of Madhavgupt (Suresh Babu), the orphaned son of ill-fated killer Yashodharma. Madhavgupt woos Queen Mohini and reveals to her the treachery of her head priest. Together, they regain her kingdom after Rajguru's death.

Admi, on the other hand, is a contemporary social and deals with the relationship between the prostitute Kesar (Shanta Hublikar) and the policeman Moti (Shahu Modak). Alleged by some to be loosely adapted from MGM's Waterloo Bridge (Whale, 1931), Admi depicts the social stigma against prostitutes that prevents Moti from marrying Kesar.[77] Kesar's humor, courage, and defiance in pursuing the relationship are sympathetically portrayed, but she is unable to escape her past and eventually murders her extortionist pimp. As she goes to prison, Kesar leaves a life-affirming message for the suicidal Moti, telling him not to give up the world for her love.

Despite genre differences between the two films, there is an overlap in artistic vision that I link not only to the director's predisposition but also to the realm of what appeared possible within the formative language of commercial cinema during the 1930s. Though Amritmanthan is a mythological film and Admi is a social, both incorporate expressionist and surreal techniques to construct a didactic message for the new nation by conveying an ineffable horror of religious and social recidivism. Admi combines a kammerspiel-film aesthetic in its lighting and settings with naturalistic acting and elements of narrative realism. Specifically, Moti and Kesar's encounters, Kesar's desire for a respectable life, Moti's desire for Kesar, and Kesar's discomfort at her own improbable fantasies of social acceptance are marked by asymmetrical visual compositions and chiaroscuro lighting. While the acting is always understated and reflects the psychological motivation of the characters, the mise-en-scène far exceeds the film's situational realism, as is immediately evident in the film's stylized opening sequence.

A man's and a woman's feet walk rapidly over a stony wilderness, and the film's credits stand out in relief on the rocks. (The setting prefigures the final scene where Moti runs after Kesar following her murder of the extortionist.) These shots are immediately mimicked in the first narrative sequence in which a canted camera follows feet walking through a gambling den, lit with high-contrast, low-key lighting. The men are revealed to be a raiding police force. Officer Moti's flashlight catches the prostitute Kesar in a perfect spotlight, framed as if in a tableau or a portrait shot. Despite his better judgment, he shields her with his uniform and lets her pass unnoticed by his fellow officers.

The film proceeds to depict a romance between the male agent of law and the female transgressor with a combination of psychological realism and stylization. Interestingly, despite its hybrid style, the film underscores a deeper binary between aesthetic artificiality and aesthetic authenticity by consistently presenting its own polymorphous style as best suited to the cinematic medium and to cinema's social function. Indeed, the film can be understood as a visual essay on the formal and social inefficacy of competing Indian film styles. The most explicit commentary on alternative directorial and studio styles occurs when Kesar and Moti stumble on a film shoot. This shoot replicates a famous song sequence ("Main ban ki chidiya") from Himansu Rai's then recent Bombay Talkies production *Acchut Kanya* (a.k.a. *The Untouchable Girl*) (Osten, 1936). The protagonists of *Admi* openly parody the shooting for its fakeness. In the film-within-the-film, the song of a *koel* (cuckoo bird) is revealed as the product of an elaborate orchestra, and we see that the lead actress wears a Western dress underneath her sari. In this lampooned version of *Acchut Kanya* the original film's popular romantic song is transformed into a song with inane, repetitious lyrics: "Premi prem nagar mein jaayen" [lovers go to love city]; "Premi prem ki bansi bajayen" [lovers play a love-flute]. Kesar and Moti watch the shooting and parody the song's syrupy words with their own mock lyrics about eating love's bread from love's stove smeared with some love chutney.

This was presumably an inside joke by Prabhat's classically trained composer Master Krishnarao (who "helped shaped Bal Gandharva's enormously influential populist versions of North Indian classical music") at the expense of Bombay Talkies' composer Saraswati Devi (originally Khursheed Manchershah Minocher-Homji) whose songs succeeded "because of their nursery rhyme simplicity."[78] Compared to Shantaram's socially didactic dialogues as well, Rai's dialogues had a digestible uncomplicatedness, apparently related to Rai and his associate Niranjan Pal's difficulty with the Hindi language. According to Colin Pal (Niranjan Pal's son), "Both Bengalis who understood precious little Hindi stipulated that no dialogue would be passed unless they could follow it. J. S. Kashyap [dialogue writer and lyricist] would literally tear his hair in trying to make his dialogue simple enough."[79] In addition to ridiculing Bombay Talkies for pandering to the public's taste for easy listening, Admi dismisses Acchut Kanya's treatment of love as unrealistic. The Rai-Osten film depicts a fatal romance between Pratap (Ashok Kumar) and Kasturi (Devika Rani), an untouchable woman, through narrative and visual strategies that are no less complex than Shantaram's. Since Acchut Kanya holds thematic and stylistic relevance to Admi's depiction of a prostitute who similarly faces social disenfranchisement and ostracism, Shantaram's parody can be read as a critique of other filmic treatments of social problems in contemporary India.

Himansu Rai, founder of the studio that produced Achhut Kanya, and his wife Devika Rani who plays the film's lead, both acquired work experience in the media industries of Germany and Britain. The foundations of Rai's film career were international: he started acting when he was in a theater group in London; his first film The Light of Asia (a.k.a. Prem Sanyas and Die Leuchte Asiens) was directed by the German Franz Osten and co-produced by Osten's brother, Peter Ostermayer.[80] This debut film opened in Berlin, Brussels, Budapest, Genoa, Venice, and Vienna in 1925. Rai's silent films Prapancha Pash (a.k.a. The Throw of Dice and Schicksalswürfel, 1928–1929) and Shiraz (a.k.a. Das Grabmal einer grossen Liebe, 1928) were pre-sold to UFA and British Instructional films. Karma (1933), Rai's first talkie, was made in English and exhibited to an international audience before the Hindi version was brought to India.[81] Though Rai established Bombay Talkies in 1934 to target the Indian market after the Nazi government overtook Germany's film-production facilities, the orientalism of previous Osten-Rai collaborations gave license to criticisms that their films had a foreign sensibility.

The rustic settings of Bombay Talkies films like Acchut Kanya, Janmabhoomi (1936), and Bandhan (1940) do betray a studio-based and "Anglicized fantasy of an Indian village," which could just as well be described as an urban Indian fantasy of an idyllic and undeveloped rural India.[82] In this sense, Bombay Talkies' films arguably fit into a kind of bourgeois realism that has been identified in post-independence Indian films. *Acchut Kanya* nevertheless shares an affinity with *Admi* in its integration of modernist stylization with realism and didacticism. Shantaram's reduction of *Acchut Kanya* to a placeholder for ineffective depictions of India's social problems becomes noteworthy in this context. Both *Admi* and *Acchut Kanya* criticize ossified social beliefs and reveal an awareness and engagement of international film styles, but *Admi* alone insists that its vision is more authentic. *Admi*'s elements of symbolism, fantasy, and expressionist sets and lighting are integrated into the film despite their stylistic variance from the film's realism, in order to pass judgment on competing "inauthentic" representations. In this sense, the film is a self-conscious attempt to define a style that is presented as socially responsible, aesthetically cosmopolitan, nationally appealing, and *truer* than other film styles.

Shanta Hublikar's famous song as Kesar reflects *Admi*'s self-aware articulation of a national address. Becoming a metonym of an Indian film reaching out to a mass national base, Kesar sings "Kis Liye Kal ki Baat" [Why Talk of Tomorrow] in six Indian languages to a clientele of Indian men from different regions. She entertains a Bengali, a Maharashtrian, a Punjabi, a Gujarati, a Tamilian, and a Muslim (of note, only the Muslim character is identified by religion rather than region), singing a verse adapted to their regional musical styles while wearing their characteristic headdresses. The intimate address of the singer who pokes gentle fun at her audience by imitating them and integrating their local inflections into her song meshes with the symbolism of a film seeking a national template for entertainment, smartly subsuming regional specificities under its own versatility.

As a counterpoint to this national fluency, Shantaram's use of expressionist techniques may be read as his attempt to engage a cosmopolitanism in addition to a regionalism, using a film language culturally coded as European to formulate a cinematic idiom that simultaneously marks itself as nationally authentic.[83] The combined forces of *Admi*'s claims to social authenticity and its modular expressionism are brought to bear on the film's content. In scrutinizing this film's style in relation to its depiction of Kesar in particular, I find that expressionist citations appear whenever the film thematically hints at the oppressiveness of a social order otherwise normalized through psychological and narrative realism.

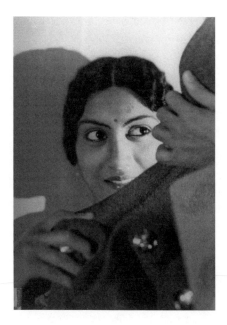

33. Low-key lighting marks
Kesar's transgressive desires
in *Admi*. Courtesy NFAI.

Kesar is a hooker with a heart of gold. But rather than being a martyr who is unquestioningly devoted to the male protagonist (the stock prostitute figure of several Indian films from *Devdas* [Hindi/Bengali, Barua, 1935] to *Muqaddar ka Sikandar* [Hindi, Mehra, 1978]), Kesar is a cynical, quick-witted, and sharp-tongued woman who challenges Moti to marry her. For most of the film, Moti is incapable of such courage and cannot act on his self-righteous desire to protect Kesar from her profession. While most of the visually remarkable sequences that utilize dramatic low-key lighting are in public arenas of disrepute (such as the gambling den and the prostitute's home), the more poignant ones take place in domestic settings. As Moti wakes up to his mother's song in the morning and faces his home's prayer area, for instance, he is cast in deep shadows. Without reading meaning as acontextually embedded in form, arguably the use of high contrasts and excessive shadows for otherwise innocuous occasions prefigures the disruption of domestic space, as when Kesar meets Moti's religious mother for the first time. It throws a lattice of unease and doubt on the film's depictions of normalcy in social and interpersonal relationships.

If in Sirkian melodramas color is almost a live entity showing the "inner violence" of characters, here lighting takes on an extranarrative function to show the inner violence of society.[84] The lighting and dialogue bring a dark presentiment of desires that lie in conflict with social expectations. They are used as cues that a prostitute cannot integrate into respectable society despite the fact that this society is composed of well-intentioned people like Moti, Moti's mother, his sister, and uncle. With its *stylization*, the film provides intimations of the enormity of the obstacles facing socially subversive desires and the hypocrisies underlying foundational social conventions like matrimony. With its *humanism*, on the other hand, the film articulates sympathy for this same society and its conventions, as dramatized by the other prominent couple in the film: not passionate star-crossed lovers but Moti's aged and affectionately squabbling neighbors, whom everyone treats as a model of compatibility. Through comic banter and realist depictions of domesticity, the film portrays a society of banal normalcy with sympathy. The stylization provides a counterpoint of tragic overtones, observing the cruelty of unwittingly exclusionary social normalcy.

At the film's conclusion, *Admi*'s strong central female character does not commit suicide (as happens in the MGM equivalent), but gives herself up to the police after murdering her pimp. Kesar's words, delivered to Moti by her young ward Manu, echo at the film's conclusion. "Behen ne kaha hai, prem ke liya duniha na chhodna" [Sister says, don't abandon this world for her love].[85] *Filmindia* editor Baburao Patel assessed MGM's *Waterloo Bridge* as "a romance pure and simple" that "makes light of hunger, poverty and unemployment" with "no social significance" in comparison to *Admi*, "perhaps the most vivid document of human emotions. Its bedrock is the regeneration of lost souls." Despite such celebrations of its social realism, *Admi*'s less-interrogated use of stylization indicates that we cannot read the film as purely edifying and reformist.[86] Unlike the film's realist segments, *Admi*'s expressionist sequences convey their meaning to the audience not by way of acting, dialogue, or narrative resolutions but through alterations to the mise-en-scène. These shots mark an explicit metatextual commentary by unconventional shot distances and a puncturing stillness of the realist narrative's flow to produce deliberately uncanny effects.

In *Admi* these effects are linked to the presence of the prostitute Kesar and to expressions of her transgressive desire. In *Amritmanthan* they accompany the dictatorial propagator of human and animal sacrifice, Rajguru. With a Langian Dr. *Mabusa*-like presence, Rajguru controls his people through an irrational mysticism that is cinematically conveyed by allusions to his powerful presence. His silently gesturing eyes fill the screen just before hideous acts of violence and betrayal; shapes of cowering people are reflected in those mag-

34. Rajguru looms large as a shadow in *Amritmanthan*. Courtesy NFAI.

nified shots of his eyes; his voice is heard from off-screen spaces; and we often sense him only as a looming shadow. These sequences are more frequent and flamboyant than in *Admi* but are similar in pictorial status as they stand out in relief against sequences internally marked as realist within the remainder of the film.[87]

Kesar and Rajguru are radically different characters: one is female, the other male; one is shunned thoughtlessly, the other obeyed blindly; one can find acceptance only under the condition of social reform, the other is resistant to social and religious change. But both are similar in provoking a social crisis. Their transgressions lie in wanting acceptance within communities that are either too conservative to transform (in Kesar's case) or too weak to resist traditional dogma (as with Rajguru). They are both powerful entities who demonstrate the severe shortcomings of Indian society and cannot be forgotten despite their narrative evacuation. If Kesar's words resonate at the end of *Admi*, Rajguru's death in *Amritmanthan* is unforgettably gruesome. Confronted with defeat by the reformist faction of society, Rajguru cuts off his own head, and his decapitated body places the head reverentially at the feet of Goddess Chandika. On seeing this horrible sight, the male lead Madhavgupt calls him "rivazon ka saccha ghulam" [a true slave to ritual].

Though representing directly opposing social modalities, Kesar and Rajguru are relentlessly committed to their beliefs. Their physical elimination from the plot is necessary because they raise uncomfortable questions about the society from which their stories emerge, a society that insists on the disreputability of a woman of the marketplace and the respectability of a God-man. Kesar and Rajguru also provoke the film's moments of extreme stylization. The characters are quite literally excessive in the sense that they are delivered to us through conventions that the discourse of contemporary Indian film criticism identified with international art cinema. Their stylization marks the unique textual status of specific themes by going beyond the realm of familiar visual tropes.

Shantaram's importation of a style that would have been coded as hyperaesthetic in its time was more than an auteur's affectation. It qualitatively endowed Kesar and Rajguru with a power extraneous to the narrative, because they represent elements inassimilable within their stories. In other words, the competing force fields of the resulting hybrid aesthetics in *Amritmanthan* and *Admi* point to a fundamental fault line in colonial Indian society. The crisis in both films is generated by the irreconcilables of a historical period in which India's nationalism depended simultaneously on a liberal discourse of social emancipation (as in the case of Kesar's ideals) and of traditionalism (represented negatively in Rajguru, but positively through the mother and the old couple in *Admi* and the reformist religion of the good king in *Amritmanthan*). Historically, neither anticolonial position could represent or produce unanimous political agitation against imperialism on its own terms. The tragic political failure to reconcile disparate nationalist demands are chronicled in the bloody partition of India and Pakistan, and in the continuing history of politically abetted communal, sectarian, and separatist movements in the region. Colonial films aiming for a national audience followed the commercial injunction to construct a compromise between nationalism's internal dissents because their success depended on appeasing (producing) diverse constituencies of film viewership. Films became figurations of the internal polarizations of India's nationalist discourse when they attempted to reach for multiple and potentially contradictory nationalist appeals to create a cinematic vision. Shantaram's colonial films begin to convey the explosive dialectics of an emerging India as soon as he combines the arguments of bourgeois liberalism with the sentimental and visual appeals of a populist culturalism, not only through his characters and themes but also in his modernist reworkings of the mythic and fable form. The films are so many artistic solutions to the problem of crafting a common set of values and visions not organically shared by a people who find that they have to share a nation-state.

The dominant form of bourgeois nationalism that defined itself in opposition to imperialism, best represented by the Indian National Congress Party, developed alongside regional-, caste-, and linguistically based nationalisms. A vivid example of this is the Self-Respect Movement and the Dravidian Movement in South India, which opposed Hindu Brahmanism and the emerging nation's northern Hindi hegemony while supporting Tamil regional and linguistic separatism, rationalism, and social justice for the backward classes. Characterizing this historical moment solely by its anticolonial nationalism and seeking the presence of that unifying mode within colonial films is a self-fulfilling exercise. The multiple self-determining agendas unleashed by a modern nationalism could not be solved within the framework of a nation-state, though nationalist discourses labored to produce this elusive, unifying address. Films from different linguistic regions of India that aspired to reach a national audience similarly confronted the problem of appealing to a people who did not ascribe to one national imaginary. Commercial films in the social genre (like Admi) found their solution in adopting the moralizing tone of social instruction. Myths and historicals (like Amritmanthan and Diler Jigar) appealed to the idea of a shared pre-modern past while distinguishing evil (feudally reactionary) lords from reformist (feudally enlightened) monarchs. In different ways, each genre provided a template for the uneven assimilation of modernity within the colony. Melodramatic socials were to become independent India's dominant cinematic form for manufacturing an imaginary civic society. But in the suppressed (unconscious and conscious, vernacular and modular) modernisms of colonial films lay a more troubled articulation of a national identity than we may have allowed for in our readings.

*

Nationalist struggles against colonialism and conflicts internal to nationalism were part of the Indian film industry's formative reality and part of the Indian filmmaker's environment. Consider two recollections from the 1930s. Anil Biswas, a composer who defined the first three decades of Indian film music and trained singers like Mukesh, Talat Mehmood, and Lata writes about his revolutionary years in Barisal, later part of east Pakistan. As a member of the revolutionary nationalist party in the early 1930s, Biswas expressed violent protest against imperial rule by making and throwing explosives. A friend speaks of going to jail with Biswas and singing anti-British Bengali songs that he had composed. After years of being imprisoned and struggling for subsistence wages, on his release, Biswas finally found work in the new industry of motion pictures.[88] He was already a familiar name to Indian filmgoers by 1943, when he composed music for Gyan Mukherjee's *Kismet*. His old political alliances resonate in the rousing nationalist chorus of the film's popular song, "Duur Hato Ay Duniyavallon, Hindustan Hamara Hai" (these alliterative lyrics embrace the essence of the "Quit India" anthem and can be somewhat inadequately translated as "Leave, Get Away, People of the World. India is Ours"). Silent- and early-sound-film producer J. B. H. Wadia did not share Biswas's revolutionary zeal, but he did support the Indian National Congress. His recollections of sitting in Kohinoor Studios trying to get a break in the film industry involve memories of heated debates on the comparative merits of British imperialists against other European colonizers.[89]

Imagining Wadia's casual conversations about imperialism in a film studio, which were probably preceded by other debates about comparative filmmaking techniques and the box-office performances of Hollywood and Indian films, makes one sense that distilling the nationalist agenda of a filmmaker's politics or a film's text barely captures this period. Anti-imperial nationalism was as ubiquitous as the daily newspaper; it defined, and was experienced through, the conditions of creating a commercially and nationally popular cinema. So, while it is possible to list instances when filmmakers took overtly anticolonial stances against the state (Shantaram, for instance, resigned as chief producer of the government's Film Advisory Board in 1942, following Gandhi's demand that the British quit India), such an enumeration does not convey the everyday struggle of turning a profit in a new industry or of inventing a viable popular cinema under colonial conditions. To grasp this aspect, I have discussed visual and narrative formations (of modernism and romance) in two prominent colonial film genres (the myth and the historical), because aesthetics and genre offer concrete ways to understand the multiple industrial agendas and complex political ambitions that shaped colonial films.

Colonial Indian cinema was a survivalist cinema. The unstable conditions of a new industry and the lack of state assistance meant that pioneering filmmakers like Phalke and Painter ended their lives in dire debt, and that aspiring filmmakers had to think of innovative ways to succeed. Films of the 1930s that aimed to define a domestically competitive Indian cinema, escape state censure, and address larger constituencies of Indian audiences were fascinatingly ambitious products serving many ends, as was reflected in their stylistic hybridity. To cultivate a cross-class domestic audience for Indian films, colonial filmmakers broadened their audience base by incorporating nationalist themes with appeals from Hollywood's popular spectacle-oriented stunt and action films. They also refunctioned aspects of Hollywood's classical realist and European art cinema appreciated by élite Indian theatergoers and Indian film critics. Under the stern censorship of a colonial state, allusive anti-state messages were embedded in mythic and historical narratives that simultaneously inscribed an Indian cultural identity on a medium tainted by its association with imperial modernity and commercialism. Formally, then, colonial films were flexible commodities that registered through their heterogeneity competing international influences, domestic political repressions, experimentations with film style, and the diversity of their consumer bases.

If colonial cinema encountered India's cultural modernity with experimentation and strategy, it confronted India's political modernity with anxiety and excitement. At a time when the nation did not have a sovereign state, films offered different fictional resolutions for imagining an individual's place in relation to their families, communities, and governing authorities in a future collective. Across colonial film genres, we find representations of individuals rebelling against corrupt authority (*Amar Jyoti, Amritmanthan, Wahan, Neecha Nagar*), envisioning a utopian future (*Wahan, Neecha Nagar, Janmabhoomi*), or impeded by their community's lack of foresight about such a future (*Admi, Kunku, Chandidas, Acchut Kanya, Bandhan*). Repeatedly, the energies of these narratives are consumed with problems posed by the community's traditionally disenfranchised subjects, because narrative and visual equilibrium is conditional on their communal integration. If, on the one hand, resistance to imperialism was contingent on political inclusiveness and a new visualization/narrativization of marginalized subjects, their very inclusion revealed the potential for internal factionalization within the new collective, its narrative, and its vision.

Colonial Indian cinema's varied stylistic imaginations of a new civil society reveal that threats of recidivism, internal decay, nativism, and communalism coexisted alongside an anticipation of a new nation. The Indian nation-state was as yet unrealized; it did not exert an official force to rationalize film form or to provoke systematic articulations of resistance. In the absence of the national entity in all but ideal terms, the competing demands on cinema—to envision a utopian state and a future society, to allusively protest imperialism, to outdo Hollywood, to create Indian audiences, to invent a modern form of art and entertainment, and, quite simply, to survive—appear in amazing clarity. The aesthetics of British empire cinema and colonial Indian cinema were a product of such heterogeneous pressures placed by decolonization on two film industries, their personnel, their strategies, and their imaginations, all of which may be too easily foreclosed if we solely attend to the unifying functions of their national cinemas.

NOTES

INTRODUCTION

1 Churchill, *India*, 126.
2 Nitin Bose's 1934 *Chandidas* was a remake of Debaki Bose's 1931 film of the same name. Nitin Bose was the cameraman for the original film.
3 Shohat and Stam, *Unthinking Eurocentrism*, 100.
4 Over the last few decades nation-states all over the world have confronted secessionist movements and supranational economic alliances, so it is not surprising that interrogating the embattled definition of a nation gained prominence within and outside academia. Key social and political texts read in various disciplines across the humanities have included Benedict Anderson's *Imagined Communities*, Ernest Gellner's *Nations and Nationalism*, Eric Hobsbawm's *Nations and Nationalism since 1780*, Miroslav Hroch's *Social Preconditions of National Revival in Europe*, and Anthony Smith's *Theories of Nationalism*. "National cinema" is now a normative category for structuring university courses in cinema studies, particularly for non-Hollywood cinemas. A few indexical examples show that the nation, though accepted as a legitimate category to organize analysis, is also always interrogated. Consider, for instance, the kinds of questions raised in *Edinburgh Magazine* 2 (1977), *Screen* 26, no. 1 (January–February 1985), Philip Schlesinger's "On National Identity," Stephen Crofts's "Reconceptualizing National Cinema/s," Susan Hay-

ward's *French National Cinema*, Andrew Higson's *Waving the Flag*, Mette Hjort's and Scott MacKenzie's *Cinema and Nation*, Sarah Street's *British National Cinema*, Tom O'Regan's *Australian National Cinema*, and Sumita Chakravarty's *National Identity in Indian Popular Cinema, 1947–1987*. Nevertheless, I argue that the category of the "nation" is inadequate as a grounding framework for an analysis of colonial and global forces defining British and Indian cinema at the end of empire in that it risks reifying the very entity that was produced and deployed by competing factions.

5 Foucault, *The Archaeology of Knowledge*, 26. Here he dismantles the a priori conceptual unity assumed for constructs like "science" and "literature."

6 Perry Anderson, "Modernity and Revolution."

7 The term *expression* evokes Fredric Jameson's notion of expressive causality. He proposes a theory of historical mediation in which distinct aspects of social life register similar contextual processes without necessarily transmitting identical messages or being directly connected to each other. Jameson's larger argument is that cultural texts rework the contradictions of real and *possible* social relations between individuals and dominant politico-economic relations, thus entailing a level of political fantasy. Both regulatory and aesthetic texts participate in the production of this political fantasy and are connected in that sense. Consult Jameson, *The Political Unconscious*, 17–102 and Colin MacCabe's preface to Jameson's *The Geopolitical Aesthetic*, x–xvi.

8 At the 1926 Imperial Conference, following an Inter-Imperial Committee Report by Arthur Balfour, dominions were defined as "autonomous communities within the British Empire, equal in status, in no way subordinate one to another in any aspect of their domestic or external affairs, though united by a common allegiance to the Crown, and freely associated as members of the British Commonwealth of Nations" (Eggar and Rajagopaul, *The Laws of India and Burma*, pt. 3, 1–2). India was recognized as "practically having an equal status with the Dominions" (Havighurst, *Britain in Transition*, 207).

9 Officially, Britain's Cabinet of Dominion Affairs was not renamed the Cabinet of Commonwealth Relations until 1947, when India and Pakistan became independent nations, but the term *commonwealth* had appeared earlier, in 1901, when Australia was granted dominion and commonwealth status.

10 "I do not believe in a Little England," said Joseph Chamberlain in 1903. Chamberlain, an influential British colonial secretary and liberal unionist, created enduring political controversy with his proposal that Britain should abandon free trade to pursue tariff reform and reciprocity within the empire. The imperial tariff was a political hot potato and led to Chamberlain's resignation from Balfour's unionist cabinet, which started a string of ministerial resignations protesting free trade orthodoxy. (Havighurst, *Britain in Transition*, 53; Judd, *Empire*, 187–200.)

11 Prior to World War I London had been the center for redistributing American films to other foreign markets for a number of reasons, including Britain's edge in shipping, its numerous theaters, and an absence of British tariffs on film imports.

Between 1915 and 1916 London lost its edge as the British State began regulating imports by imposing duty on American films, demanding licenses on all films exhibited, taxing luxury items to raise money for the war, and limiting currency outflow. Hollywood had the profit margins to withstand a restricted British market, and American studios whittled away British resistance through such practices as block booking (in which a set of films were booked into theaters as part of a package) and blind booking (which required unseen or unmade films contracted for production to be given a booking). (Chanan, "The Emergence of an Industry"; Low, Film Making in 1930's Britain; Richards, The Age of the Dream Palace; Thompson, Exporting Entertainment.)

12 For more on Film Europe consult Higson and Maltby, "Film Europe" and "Film America."

13 Chowdhry, Colonial India and the Making of Empire Cinema.

14 Kaviraj, "The Imaginary Institution of India," 10.

15 IOR, L/E/8/137, Federation of British Industries, "Memorandum: Films for Exhibition in India" (19 April 1934), 3.

16 In MacKenzie, Imperialism and Popular Culture, valuable essays demonstrate that Britain's investment in the empire did not diminish between the two World Wars. I agree, but emphasize Britain's necessary (material and symbolic) adjustments to reap the benefits of empire. In so doing, I deviate from the "dominant ideology" thesis of imperial power proposed by Constantine in the same anthology (192–231).

17 Typically, the terms "soft power" and "hard power" differentiate economic neo-imperialism from direct forms of political aggression and military control. For recent use in the context of U.S. power see Harvey, The New Imperialism.

18 Foucault, The Archaeology of Knowledge, 166–67.

19 The following sources offer a sampling of perspectives on Indian historiography: Bahl, "Situating and Rethinking Subaltern Studies for Writing Working-Class History"; Chandra et al., India's Struggle for Independence; Guha and Spivak, Selected Subaltern Studies; and Prakash, "Subaltern Studies as Postcolonial Criticism." Bipan Chandra and Vinay Bahl criticize the Subaltern Studies Collective on shared grounds. Bahl argues that the scholars create a new foundational category of the self-determining "subaltern" and in so doing retrieve the rational humanist subject they attempt to deconstruct. (Gayatri Spivak's introduction to the Selected Subaltern Studies anthology provides an excellent analysis of this question in the collective's early work). Both Bahl and Chandra argue that subaltern historians focus primarily on the differences between élite and subaltern groups and in so doing reify difference, simultaneously depriving the subaltern subject of instrumentality by equating subalternity with failed or partially manifested resistance. Both also find problematic the subalternist's use of colonial archives as primary sources, which risks turning the project into a discourse-analysis of élite historiography. My affinity with the work of the Subaltern Studies Collective should be

evident in this book, particularly in my analysis of the socioeconomic complexity and material significance of colonial discourses and archives, which are simplified by Bahl.

20 Manu Goswami addresses this lack with her historical theorization of the contradictory forces of nationhood and nativism in *Producing India*.

21 The colonized world has experienced an intersecting variety of imperial practices rather than one historical dynamic. Imperialism includes phases of informal colonization (prior to settlement or direct administration), formal colonization, and postcolonial underdevelopment. Africa, for instance, was subjected to slave trade long before it was subsumed under colonial administration by European settlements. For a discussion of imperial periodization consult Brewer, *Marxist Theories of Imperialism*; Bukharin, *Imperialism and World Economy*; Stoler and Cooper, *Tensions of Empire*; Lenin, *Imperialism*; and Nairn, *The Break-up of Britain*, particularly chapter 1, where he discusses the British state's constitutionalism, which evolved over several centuries. The revolutionary era of 1640–1688 laid conditions for the end of absolutism and feudalism while simultaneously initiating modern expansionism, making chronologies of empire messy and its modernity contradictory.

22 Stoler and Cooper, *Tensions of Empire*, 31. Also Benedict Anderson, *Imagined Communities*, 83–111; Cohn, *Colonialism and Its Forms of Knowledge*.

23 Harlow's and Carter's *Imperialism and Orientalism* provides an extended text of Thomas Babington Macaulay's "Minute on Indian Education," delivered on 2 February 1835 (56–62). For other scholarly analyses of the same see Anderson, 91; and Viswanathan, *Masks of Conquest*.

24 Hobsbawm, *The Age of Empire*; Hardt and Negri, *Empire*; Miyoshi, "A Borderless World?"; Morley, "EurAm, Modernity, Reason, and Alterity."

25 For details on the rise in cinema attendance in Britain during the 1930s consult Richards, *The Age of the Dream Palace*, 11–33.

26 Tallents, *The Projection of England*, 11–12, emphasis added.

27 *World Film News* 2, no. 8 (November 1937): 5, emphasis added.

28 Memorandum attached to an FBI letter to the government titled "Cooperative Marketing of British Empire Films: F.B.I. Offer to the Government" (10 November 1926), ref. no. 300/J/11, British Film Institute.

29 Said, *Culture and Imperialism*, 107.

30 For details consult Hobsbawm, *The Age of Empire*.

31 Hobson, *Imperialism*, xvii.

32 For the submergence of imperial discourse under moral justifications see chapter 3. Another shift in discourse has emerged as American "neo-cons" openly reclaim the language of imperialism, presenting it as a prioritization of U.S. national security and a protection of American interests.

33 Benedict Anderson, *Imagined Communities*; Arendt, *The Origins of Totalitarianism*; Prakash, "Who's Afraid of Postcoloniality?" The theorists proffer their analysis to different ends. Hannah Arendt argues that "in theory, there is an abyss between

nationalism and imperialism; in practice, it can and has been bridged by tribal nationalism and outright racism" (153). Gyan Prakash indicts Europe's political contradictions: "Europe had to endure the slaughter of millions in two world wars, undergo the terrible experience of colonial oppression coming home to the European soil with the ferocious rage of the return of the repressed . . . before it could reflect on the implications of the inner incompatibility of empire and nation" (193). And Anderson argues that contradictions between empire and nation radicalized the colonized elite (91).

34 I'm thinking of John Stuart Mill's "Considerations on Representative Government."

35 Kent, *British Imperial Strategy and the Origins of the Cold War, 1944–49*, 152.

36 As Kent shows, Ernst Bevin (foreign secretary to the postwar Labour government) and Bernard Montgomery (chief of the Imperial General Staff) worked toward a West European union to undertake colonial development. Such measures required long-term planning, while the costs of World War I demanded short-term colonial exploitation. In this sense, trade within the empire promised a stronger Britain while simultaneously serving as a reminder of Britain's dependency on foreign resources.

37 Grierson, "The Film and Primitive Peoples," 12.

one **FILM POLICY AND FILM AESTHETICS**

See Dana Polan's "Inexact Science" for an insightful analysis of Barthes's semiology.

1 This will be clear from the British journals quoted in chapters 2 and 3, and from the Indian journals in chapter 7. As an example of the latter see *filmindia* 4, no. 1 (May 1938).

2 *The Film in National Life*, 1.

3 *The Film in National Life*, 132.

4 Theorists of liberalism emphasize different social institutions as central to the state's political process. In Hegel's thesis the twin institutions of family and civil society actualize the universal principle of Reason, forming "the firm foundations not only of the state but also of the citizen's trust in it and sentiment towards it. [Family and civil society] are the pillars of public freedom since in them particular freedom is realized and rational" ("The Philosophy of Right," 73). Hegel also develops this thesis in *Reason in History*. For Mazzini, writing about "The Duties of Man," work, votes, and education are key institutions of the state. Within a Foucauldian framework, state rationality—no longer an expression of universal will but a function of the historical shift from a principle of sovereignty to governmentality—is dispersed over an entire population rather than located within a family unit. The state's authority derives from the management of this populace because "the finality of the government resides in the things it manages and in the

pursuit of the perfection and intensification of the processes which it directs; and the instruments of government instead of being laws, now come to be a range of multiform tactics" (Foucault, "Governmentality," 95).

5 This idea, developed as "biopower," is discussed in Foucault, *The History of Sexuality*; Donzelot, *The Policing of Families*; and Hardt and Negri, *Empire*. Recent film scholarship that broadens the scope of analyzing the state in relation to culture include Lewis and Miller, *Critical Cultural Policy Studies* and Street, *British Cinema in Documents*. Street offers key sources to investigate the British State's involvement with British cinema beyond censorship.

6 Cohn, *Colonialism and Its Forms of Knowledge*, 4. The imperial center used its colonies as a laboratory for modern economic, administrative, and educational systems, subsequently imported back into the empire's "metropolis," while internal and external colonies shaped themselves in engagement with the imperial nation-state. Particularly useful texts that present and extend this insight include Cohn, *An Anthropologist among the Historians*; Dirks, *Castes of Mind*; McClintock, *Imperial Leather*; Said, *Culture and Imperialism*; Stoler and Cooper, *Tensions of Empire*; Trumpener, *Bardic Nationalism*; Vishwanathan, *Masks of Conquest*.

7 Marx, "The British Rule in India," 94.

8 Though this perspective has not radically revised the study of colonial cinema, recent studies in globalization fruitfully reassess cultural production at the heart of empire from the perspective of its economic and territorial peripheries. Scholars of American popular culture demonstrate links between North America's regional, international, and domestic politics as the United States established a new paradigm of imperialism during and after the Cold War, and scholars of Asian and African diasporic and transnational culture destabilize the notion of a unitary hegemonic global center by recasting power relations in terms of alternative globalizations and multiple modernities. See, for example, Klein, *Cold War Orientalism*; Grewal and Kaplan, *Scattered Hegemonies*; Desai, *Beyond Bollywood*.

9 Chatterjee, *The Nation and Its Fragments*, 5.

10 To use the exceptions to prove the norm: John M. MacKenzie's anthology *Imperialism and Popular Culture* examines the "centripetal" effects of empire on British social history and popular psychology, but its containment within the field of empire studies has meant that it has not had an impact on fertile revisionist work on British national cinema in recent years, of which the essays in Justine Ashby's and Andrew Higson's *British Cinema, Past and Present* are a good example. This anthology begins with a thoughtful piece by Jeffrey Richards, a pioneering historian of 1930s cinema, who invites further reconceptualizations of the decade, an invitation that I accept in this book. Michael Walsh's essay in the same volume analyses Irish and British films on Northern Ireland in the 1980s, referring to challenges to British national identity since the 1960s. I believe there is a need to raise similar questions about the instabilities of the earlier era of decolonization. Regarding India, in an important anthology edited by Ravi S. Vasudevan, *Making Meaning in Indian*

Cinema, Stephen P. Hughes's essay focuses on colonial India. Another anthology, Rachel Dwyer's and Christopher Pinney's *Pleasure and the Nation*, includes four excellent essays on colonialism and culture. Someswar Bhowmick, Prem Chowdhry, and Gautam Kaul's books attend to colonialism and censorship, and S. Theodore Baskaran gives a vivid image of the Tamil film industry during the colonial era in *The Eye of the Serpent* and *The Message Bearers*, though the pre-independence period is only briefly discussed in the former text. Despite these important contributions, as well as pieces on the aesthetics of silent Indian cinema published in the *Journal of Arts and Ideas*, the pre-independence period of Indian cinema remains less represented in Indian film scholarship, partly because of archival difficulties and partly because the conceptual framework of national cinema forces scholarly efforts to begin with the formal arrival of nationhood.

11 Censorship in colonized India was not centralized under one board but housed in the provinces of Bombay, Madras and Calcutta, which were the chief ports of film import. The Commissioner of Police for the province was the *ex officio* chairman of each board, which meant that the Chairmen of Censor Boards were typically British. A combination of executives and non-official members made the board membership somewhat bi-partisan (including British and Indian members). Prior to 1922, a film banned in one province could run in another, but subsequent to a case over D. W. Griffith's *Orphans of the Storm* (banned in Bengal but screening in Punjab), it was decided that if one province banned a film, it had to send a copy of its order to other provinces. Certificates issued for a film by any one board were valid throughout the country though provinces could re-examine films, and banning films was relatively easy because certified films could be "uncertified" by the Central government at any point. For further discussion of film and press censorship, consult: Baskaran *The Message Bearers*; Barrier, *Banned*; Chowdhry, *Colonial India and the Making of Empire Cinema*; Kaul, *Cinema and the Indian Freedom Struggle*.

12 Thus British India was distinct from self-governing dominions (Australia, Canada, Newfoundland, New Zealand, South Africa, the Irish Free State), Crown colonies (Ashanti, Bahama Islands, Barbados, Bermuda, Ceylon, Cyprus, Falkland Islands, and others), protectorates (Basutoland, Bechuanaland, North Borneo, the Native States of India), and mandates from the League of Nations (Palestine, Iraq, Tanganyika, New Guinea, and others) (Eggar and Rajagopaul, *The Laws of India and Burma*, 1–14).

13 I use this theoretically overdetermined term, *autonomy*, with caution. In autonomist theories developed in the context of Italy in the late 1970s Antonio Negri and Mario Tronti inverted orthodox Marxism's emphasis on capital as the productive force that transforms the worker into "a particular mode of existence of capital," instead putting labor's struggle against capital at the center of their analytic. By emphasizing labor's insubordination of capital, the autonomists could redefine the history of class struggle as a process through which capital incessantly restructures itself to adapt to its antagonist: labor. Despite Hardt and Ne-

gri's objections to postcolonial theory, the field similarly reverses understandings of incipient global economic and political power by putting the colonized front and center in order to reevaluate the terms under which larger parts of the world were proletarianized and, in irregular ways, inducted into a world market. I use the term *autonomy* self-consciously, to evoke theories invested in starting their examination of power from the perspective of productive agents rather than regulating structures. See Lumley, *States of Emergency*; Negri, *Marx beyond Marx*; Lotringer and Marazzi, "Italy"; Hardt and Negri, *Empire*; Guha, "On Some Aspects of the Historiography of Colonial India" in *Selected Subaltern Studies*.

14 There were exceptions, as in 1940, when the state created a film advisory board to assist in the production of Indian documentaries in support of the World War II effort. But the industry also proved to be a safe haven from the state, when the same war led to an infusion of undeclared taxes or "black money" into the industry. Starting as an act of civil disobedience against the imperialist government's war, India's independence didn't alter the influx of disorganized and illegal capital into the film industry.

15 Shah, *Proceedings*, 157. The IMPC brought together representatives of "Indian producers, distributors, exhibitors, artistes, technicians, musicians, film journalists, authors, and film directors and authors" to "protect and advance the interests of the Indian Motion Picture Industry and allied industries, trades, arts and sciences" (2).

16 Baburao Patel, editorial, *filmindia* 2, no. 9 (January 1937): 4. Patel also claimed that United Artists, MGM, Warner Brothers, Columbia, Paramount, 20th Century Fox, and others backed Collins's journal.

17 Ibid.

18 Koch, *Franz Osten's Indian Silent Films*, 16.

19 In 1927 the *Report of the Indian Cinematograph Committee 1927–1928* acknowledged that "the supply of Indian films is not equal to the demand" (NFAI, *Report of the Indian Cinematograph Committee 1927–1928*, 20; app. L, 226). See also Chowdhry, *Colonial India and the Making of Empire Cinema*, 15; Rajadhyaksha and Willemen, *Encyclopaedia of Indian Cinema*, 30.

20 In "From Monopoly to Commodity" Brian Shoesmith challenges the orthodoxy of the 1930s as a studio era, arguing instead that the decade is better explained "in terms of a struggle between competing forms of capitalism in a volatile and changing market place" (68).

21 For a discussion of the competing interests in the colonial film market in relation to which Indian cinema stabilized itself see Jaikumar, "Hollywood and the Multiple Constituencies of Colonial India."

22 Barnouw and Krishnaswamy, *Indian Film*, 69.

23 So the cultural autonomy described here may be understood more as a "semi-autonomy (in the Althusserian sense)," which is to say that "the independence and self-sufficient internal coherence of the object or field in question" should

be understood "dialectically to be relative to some greater totality (in relation to which alone it makes sense to assert that it is autonomous in the first place)" (Jameson, *Signatures of the Visible*, 201).

24 Barnouw and Krishnaswamy, *Indian Film*, 135–91. Consult as well B. V. Jadhav, "Indian Film Industry: Government Inaction X-rayed," *Varieties Weekly* III, 29 (April 23, 1933): 5–10, 12; "The State and Film Industry—A Review," *Indian Talkie 1931–56: Silver Jubilee Souvenir* (Bombay: Film Federation of India, 1956), 175–96.

25 See Ashish Rajadhyaksha's essay "The 'Bollywoodization' of the Indian Cinema" for an astute analysis of the differences between the structure and aesthetics of Indian cinema in relation to the state before and after "Bollywood" emerged as a globalized enterprise in the 1990s in response to the state's interest in formalizing the industry and its encouragement of investment capital.

26 NAI, *Home (Political)*, 80/XXI/1928, "Subject: Supply to the Cinema Committee of Papers Relating to the Measures Taken in Foreign Countries to Encourage the Production and Exhibition of Their Own Films: Report of the Royal Commission on the Moving Picture Industry in Australia."

27 Representative examples of such studies include Baskaran, *The Message Bearers*; Bernstein and Studlar, *Visions of the East*; Bhowmik, *Indian Cinema, Colonial Contours*; Curran and Porter, *British Cinema History*; Chowdhry, *Colonial India and the Making of Empire Cinema*; Friedman, *Fires Were Started*; Kaul, *Cinema and the Indian Freedom Struggle*; MacKenzie, *Imperialism and Popular Culture*; Smyth, "The Central African Film Unit's Images of Empire, 1948–1963," "The British Colonial Film Unit and Sub-Saharan Africa, 1939–1945," and "Movies and Mandarins"; Walsh, "The Empire of the Censors" and "Thinking the Unthinkable."

28 In addition to references above, consult Baskaran's *The Eye of the Serpent* and Kaul's *Cinema and the Indian Freedom Struggle* for titles of nationalist Indian films from the 1920s to the 1940s. Overtly nationalist films were produced during the "Congress interregnum," a period in which the Indian National Congress held political office at the provincial and national levels for twenty-eight months, starting in 1935.

29 Lisa Odham Stokes and Michael Hoover make a similar argument in *City on Fire*, their study of Hong Kong cinema. They note that British state censorship produced a "dialectical process whereby the dictates of state prohibitive power are circumvented" by films which anticipate censorship (259).

30 See Green, *Dreams of Adventure, Deeds of Empire* for an analysis of this literature.

31 "Following the E.M.B.'s Lead," *The Bioscope Service Supplement* (11 April 1927): British Film Institute, iii.

32 Landy, *British Genres*; Richards, "Patriotism with Profit."

33 I use the term *revulsion* in Martin Green's sense.

34 In "Patriotism with Profit" Richards argues that "none of the [empire] films sought to tackle the contemporary issues" (252). Despite our disagreement on this point, I remain influenced by Richards's larger body of work, which comprises the most extensive analysis of British imperial film and music to date. See *Visions*

of Yesterday, The Age of the Dream Palace, Films and British National Identity (particularly pt.1, 31–61), and *Imperialism and Music*.

35 As Jameson argues, both artistic and social forms are symptomatic of their dominant relations of production, where the "dominant" is itself a variegated field of pre-existing and emerging social and economic relations. At times of radical historical change, when the past and the present are "visibly antagonistic," these contradictions move to "the very center" of social life and aesthetic form. I connect policy and different kinds of cinemas (commercial, trade, and documentary made with public and private funding) through an "ideology of form" that can be read in the "contradiction of the specific messages emitted by the varied sign systems which coexist in a given artistic process as well as in its general social formation" (Jameson, *The Political Unconscious*, 98–99, 95). See also Raymond Williams's *Marxism and Culture* for his discussion of "Dominant, Residual, and Emergent" cultures (121–27).

36 See "Following the E.M.B.'s Lead," *The Bioscope Service Supplement* (11 April 1927): iii, British Film Institute, which also mentioned the Quota Act.

37 Stollery, *Alternative Empires*, 190.

38 Alexander Korda entered a profitable tie-up with United Artists (UA) following his film *The Private Life of Henry VIII* (1933). Korda's London Films was to produce between six and eight features for UA for approximately £100,000 a year, which allowed his films to find good distribution in the United States. The following accounts give information on Korda's inroads into Hollywood, his fluctuating career, and his influence on the economics of British film making: Kulik, *Alexander Korda*; Street, "Alexander Korda, Prudential Assurance and British Film Finance in the 1930s" and *Transatlantic Crossings*.

39 *The Times*, 20 March 1934, p. 11, emphasis added.

40 PRO, CO 323/974/1, "Colonial Office Conference 1927."

41 Richards, "Boys Own Empire," 154.

42 My analysis of British empire cinema could be productively related to Richard Dyer's *White* and Robyn Wiegman's *American Anatomies*. Tracking similar maneuvers in other contexts, Dyer examines the redefinition of racial hierarchies for the manufacture of apparent egalitarianism in the post–World War I era, and Wiegman does so for the post–Civil Rights period in America.

43 Said, *Culture and Imperialism*, 69.

44 Brooks, *The Melodramatic Imagination*.

45 As my later chapters should make clear, *Elephant Boy* falls between a realist text and a romance text in narrating the adventures of an orphaned Indian boy who is nevertheless firmly subordinated to his British commissioner. Similarly, *The Great Barrier* is something of a romance-modernist text, depicting an antisocial Englishman who goes to Canada to gamble and womanize, only to be transformed in the frontier land by love and a patriotic duty to protect the Canadian Pacific Railways for British investors.

46 Imperial modernism was rare in the cinema of the 1930s, compared to literary fiction of the same period. Early silent British shorts typically combined realist and romance modes, as in *With the Indian Troops at the Front*, *With the Kut Relief Force in Mesopotamia*, *With Our Territories at the Front* (all circa 1914–1918), and in *The Battle of Jutland* (1921), *Armageddon* (1923), *Zeebrugge* (1924), and *Ypres* (1925), several of which incorporated actuality footage with adventure plots. Silent expedition films such as *Pearls to Savage* (1924), *The Vast Sudan* (1924), *Kilimanjaro* (1924), and *To Lhasa in Disguise* (1924) were similar. (My thesis here is based on reading about these films rather than viewing them.) Following the success of British empire films in the United States, empire-themed productions proliferated in Hollywood. These were primarily in the adventure/romance mode, as in the case of *Trader Horn* (Van Dyke, 1931), *Lives of a Bengal Lancer* (Hathaway, 1935), *Stanley and Livingstone* (Brower and King, 1939), *Gunga Din* (Stevens, 1939), *The Charge of the Light Brigade* (Curtiz, 1936), *Clive of India* (Boleslawski, 1935), and *Lloyds of London* (King, 1936). Romance was and remains the most popular form of imperial cinema. It has made its appearance in technicolor melodramas, campy adventures, and science-fiction films like *Cobra Woman* (Siodmack, 1944), *She* (Day, 1965), the *Indiana Jones* series (Spielberg, 1981, 1984, 1989), and the *Star Wars* series (Lucas, 1977, 1999, 2002; Marquand, 1983).

47 Arendt, *The Origins of Totalitarianism*, 125.

48 See Bennett's "The Exhibitionary Complex."

49 Hobsbawm, *The Age of Empire*, 83.

50 This periodization runs contrary to Hardt's and Negri's thesis in *Empire*. The globalization of capitalism has drastically restructured notions of territoriality and power, but by using a (reductive) reading of Homi Bhabha's work to stand in for all "postcolonial" scholarship, the authors find ways to dismiss the reality of U.S. global power and ongoing structural underdevelopment or patterns of skewed development in the former colonies, detailed in Latin American, African, and postcolonial studies. My book examines a neocolonial moral discourse produced in British cinema in the early twentieth century so there is little occasion for me to elaborate on Hardt and Negri, but for more on my difference with them see chapter 3.

51 Excerpts of Tony Blair's speech from "Blair's Words: 'Our Job Is to Be There with You,' " *The New York Times*, 18 July 2003, sec. A, p. 8. When Denham studios closed down in 1953, many years after it left Korda's ownership, the British journal *Graphic* (8 March 1953) reminisced that its memory would "never be buried while people still talk of great British films like 'The Four Feathers' . . . made there in the days when Britain could still talk in terms of bidding for world supremacy" (BFI, Subject Cuttings: *Denham*). The romance mode conveys a wistful feeling that global supremacy is possible, though neither permanent nor fully attainable.

52 I am thinking of Homi K. Bhabha's essays in *The Location of Culture*.

53 Bhabha, ever self-conscious, raises this question of his own theory in *The Location of Culture* (57). I define "text" broadly in this sentence, in the manner best

elaborated by Tom Gunning in D. W. Griffith and the Origins of American Narrative Film, 10–30.

54 Debates among postcolonial scholars and political economists have been bogged down by the perception that the former group evacuates context, while the latter ignores culture. R. Radhakrishnan's postcolonial reading criticizes Bhabha for creating occasions where his "metropolitan theory rereads a postcolonial dilemma as a poststructuralist aporia" ("Postmodernism and the Rest of the World," 58). Arif Dirlik rejects postcolonialism, claiming that "the postcolonial rush to culture is an escape not only from the structures of political economy but more importantly from revolutionary radicalisms of the past" ("Is There History after Eurocentrism," 39). I believe that creating solidarity between these theoretical positions in their battle over interpretation involves understanding the significance of history and the complexity of culture, which is inseparable from political economy especially since culture's commercialization under modernity. For concise statements on both sides of the debate consult Parry, "Problems in Current Theories of Colonial Discourse"; essays in Afzal-Khan and Seshadri-Crooks, The Pre-occupation of Postcolonial Studies (particularly the introductions); and Shohat, "Notes on the 'Post-Colonial.' "

55 Jameson, Signatures of the Visible, 177. Jameson observes that Hollywood's classical "realism" is a "genre system" that is "parceled out among the specific genres [romantic comedies, gangster films, and so on], to whose distinct registers are then assigned its various dimensions and specialized segments" (176).

56 The term "genre memory" is from Mikhail Bakhtin. It is elaborated in the context of cinema and culture by Morson and Emerson, Mikhail Bakhtin; and Burgoyne, Film Nation.

57 Brooks, The Melodramatic Imagination, 202.

58 The Great Barrier, which takes place in Canada, is an exception.

59 The Film in Colonial Development, 21.

60 A case in point: the Hollywood films The African Queen (Huston, 1951), Snows of Kiliminjaro (King, 1952) and Mogambo (Ford, 1953) were censored at the request of India's first prime minister, Jawaharlal Nehru, for their demeaning portrayal of Africans. With newfound empathy for Africa as the object of representation, a British newspaper noted, "Why . . . do American producers patronize Africa so much? . . . They do not even try to understand the ideas and feelings of foreigners, especially those belonging to the East"; further, "not only have the Asians had to protest against the undue share of unscrupulousness, brutality and cunningness which is attributed to them in US films, even the British have not been able to appreciate their portraits as dull, conventional and unsocial people" (BFI, Subject Cuttings: India Cuttings up to 1959. The paper's name and page numbers are not recorded; it is dated 1 June 1956.)

61 Songs were an important medium of nationalist messages. Examples include Bandhan's "Chal chal re naujavan" (Keep Moving Ahead, Young Man), Brandy ki Botal's

"Jhanda ooncha rahe hamara" (May Our Flag Fly High), and Janmabhoomi's "Hai desh hamara hara-bhara, phir bhi har prani mara-mara" (Our Lands Are Lush and Green, and Yet Are People Listless). *Neecha Nagar*'s "Utho ki hamein vakt ki gardhish ne pukara" (Arise, for our destiny beckons) ends with the refrain "Azaad hain, azaad hain, azaad rahenge" (We are free, we are free, and free we shall remain). *Thyagabhoomi* contains songs about the *Charkha* (the spinning wheel, representing Gandhi's message of self-sufficiency, later a symbol on the Indian flag) and the land, like "Jaya Bharata Punya Bhoomi" (Hail to India's Sacred Land). For more examples consult Kaul, *Cinema and the Indian Freedom Struggle*, 91–109; and Baskaran, *The Message Bearers*, especially "Nationalist Songs Books Proscribed During the Civil Rights Movement" (62). Film sets also incorporated nationalist symbols directly or indirectly. Records reveal, for example, that Ranjit Film Company's *College Girl* (1935) was uncertified for showing an anti-Government poster in a scene (MSA, *Home Department* [Political] 1935, file no. 248, "Cinematograph Film 'College Girl' "). Film dialogues censored for nationalist content are too numerous to mention, but an example is the silent film *Patriot* (1930), also by Ranjit Film Company, which was uncertified for several intertitles like the following.

> PETITITIONERS: But Sire, is it a crime to make a demand for our Rights?
> REGENT: Rights? What Rights? Are you fit to acquire Rights? What are your sufferings? Is service of the King a suffering?

A later exchange:

> REGENT: You are young and inexperienced. I will give you riches and honour.
> REPLY [*Unknown warrior, who is in fact the rebelling Prince in disguise*]: I would prefer death in the cause of freedom for my country.
> REGENT: If you join my service, you will be rewarded.
> REPLY: I would rather starve and would live in my poor cave and fight for my poor country. (MSA, *Home Department* [Political], 1930, file #301, "Cinematograph Film 'Patriot.' ")

62 Ahmed, "Jameson's Rhetoric of Otherness and the 'National Allegory,' " 21.

63 Chatterjee, *The Nation and Its Fragments*, 116–57; Gupta, *Sexuality, Obscenity, Community*; Hasan, *Forging Identities*, particularly the essays by Metcalf and Devji; Mani, *Contentious Traditions*; Jayawardena, *Feminism and Nationalism in the Third World*.

64 Gupta, *Sexuality, Obscenity, Community*, 24.

65 Ibid., 23.

66 Chatterjee, *The Nation and Its Fragments*, 130.

67 Scholars of Indian cinema tend to emphasize the underlying conservative neotraditionalism of women's apparent emancipation by nationalism. See Ashish Rajadhyaksha's reading of the *Diler Jigar* character Saranga in "India's Silent Cinema," and Neepa Majumdar's analysis of *Amar Jyoti*'s Queen Saudamini in "Female Star-

dom and Cinema in India, 1930 to 1950" (Ph.D. diss., Indiana University, 2002). See chapter 7 for my analysis of both films and for the debt my reading owes to Miriam Hansen's notion of the ambivalence of female figures ("Fallen Women, Rising Stars, New Horizons").

68 Social histories offer abundant evidence of this. In *Forging Identities*, for example, Zoya Hasan notes that the Indian Constitution's allowance for Muslim personal law is "resented by the majority as socially and culturally inferior because it allows multiple marriages and easy divorce" (xx). This "personal law is of no help to [Muslim] women; in fact, it undercuts and undermines their rights. Nonetheless it is seen as discriminatory by many people because it signifies the 'privileged' treatment of Muslims by the Indian State" (ibid.). Thus, secularism is defined by promoting an exceptionalism resented by the majority and by protecting an oppressive regulation of women among the minority.

69 See Premchand's *Yesterdays Melodies, Today's Memories* for details on the composers and singers.

70 Kesavan, "Urdu, Awadh and the *Tawaif*," 255.

71 Ibid., 249. Regarding Urdu alone, Kesavan argues persuasively that its linguistic "ability to find sonorous words for inflated emotions suited the purpose of stylized melodrama" better than a Sanskritized Hindi (255). "Urdu didn't simply give utterance to the narrative characteristics of Hindi cinema, it actually helped create them" (249).

72 Mufti, "A Greater Story-writer than God," 32. For a definition of the "social" as an early template of Indian cinema's dominant melodramatic narrative form see Rajadhyaksha and Willemen, *Encyclopaedia of Indian Cinema*, 219.

73 Appiah, *In My Father's House*.

74 Spivak, *A Critique of Postcolonial Reason*, 332.

75 Jameson, *The Political Unconscious*, 18.

76 Chakrabarty, *Provincializing Europe*.

two **ACTS OF TRANSITION**

The first epigraph is taken from a report on the second parliamentary reading of the Films Bill in *The Times*, 17 March 1927, p. 9 (BFI, Subject Cuttings: *Legislation: Cinematograph Films Act, 1927*).

1 "The Films Bill," *The Times*, 32 March 1927, p. 8. (BFI, Subject Cuttings: *Legislation: Cinematograph Films Act, 1927*).

2 PRO, CO 323/974/1, "1926 Imperial Conference Proceedings."

3 For historical debates on the impact of colonial markets on British economy consult Darwin, *The End of the British Empire*; Davis and Huttenback, *Mammon and the Pursuit of Empire*.

4 BFI, Subject Cuttings: British Films Abroad, "Co-operative Marketing Of British Em-

pire films: FBI Offer to Government," 10 November 1926, ref. no. 300/J/11, 1. (This cutting and *The Times* article referred to below were in the stated BFI file in 1995 but not on my subsequent research visits. I own copies of both documents.)

5   BFI, Subject Cuttings: *British Films Abroad*, article in *The Times*, 7 Oct 1926, n.p.

6   PRO, CO 323/974/1, "Imperial Conference, 1926: Economic Sub-Committee." Annex 1 of this document, "Cinema Films in the Dominions," offers detailed information on British films in Australia, Canada, India, New Zealand, South Africa, and the Irish Free State. Consult also NAI, *Home (Political)*, 80/XXI/1928 and BFI, Subject Cuttings: *British Films Abroad*.

7   These organizations are discussed further in chapter 3. Some examples include British Instructional Films Proprietors, founded in 1919 to produce and distribute films on educational, scientific, and nature subjects of national and imperial interest, including short films on naval battles and dramatic films; British Dominions Film, proposed in 1927 to launch a 50-percent British film program for Britain, New Zealand, Australia, India, Egypt, Canada, and the smaller colonies; and British United Film Producers, proposed in 1930 to distribute British films in the empire, with the recommendation of the Film Group of the FBI. For details see PRO, CO 323/974/1.

8   All quotes relating to the BEFI can be found in BFI, Subject Cuttings: B.E.F.I., including the clipping "Fight against American Stranglehold," *The Times*, 9 December 1928, n.p.

9   Despite claims (by Parry, Dirlik and others) that analyzing colonial discourse leads to a neglect of its enabling political and economic institutions, the institutional and discursive aspects of colonial film policy are inseparable, as this chapter shows.

10 The proportion of British films to be exhibited was calculated by multiplying "the total number of feet of each registered British film . . . by the number of times the film was exhibited within the period" and comparing this figure with "the total number of feet of each registered film" also multiplied by the times each of those films was exhibited ("Provisions as to Exhibitors Quota," provisions 19(1)(a) and (b) of the Quota Act, printed in "The Bill: Full Text of the Cinematograph Films Act, 1927," *The Bioscope* [17 March 1927]: 49). British Film Institute.

11 PRO, CO 323/994/4 provides the full text of the act. See clause 26.3 for the definition of a British film.

12 The Association of British Film Directors had suggested a six-point definition of a British picture at a meeting held on 31 January 1927. Mr. Sidney Rogerson of the FBI submitted this definition to the BOT for consideration at the 1926 Imperial Conference. For versions of the quota bill consult *The Bioscope* (17 March 1927): 50 and PRO, CO 323/974/1.

13 "Following the E.M.B.'s Lead," *The Bioscope Service Supplement* (11 August 1927): iii, British Film Institute.

14 PRO, CO 323/974/1.

15 Ibid.

16 The text of this two-page memorandum titled "To Revive Production: F.B.I's Summary of the Rival Plans" is reprinted in *Kinematograph Weekly* (6 August 1925): 30–31. For more on the FBI see Dickinson and Street, *Cinema and State*.

17 Germany's quota ratio was approximately 1:1, or one German film per import.

18 "To Revive Production," *Kinematograph Weekly*, 31.

19 PRO, CO 323/974/1, "Colonial Office Conference, 1927: Cinematograph Films: Memorandum on British Films, Prepared by The Federation of British Industries," annex 2. Other members of FBI's Film Group were Archibald Nettleford Productions, Astra National Productions, Brittania Films, British Instructional Pictures, British Projects, Burns-Scott Films, Ideal Films, New Era Productions, Stoll Picture Productions, Topical Film Company, and Welsh Pearson and Company.

20 BFI, Subject Cuttings: *British Films Abroad*, clipping from *The Times*, 7 October 1926, n.p.

21 See discussion in Hartog, "State Protection of a Beleaguered Industry."

22 *The Film in National Life*, 129.

23 Constantine, " 'Bringing the Empire Alive,' " 200.

24 Tallents, *The Projection of England*, 18, emphasis added. Tallents prefaced the publication with a note that he was writing in his personal rather than his official capacity. Nevertheless, his praise for Soviet films such as "Eisenstein's 'The Cruiser Potemkin,' Pudovkin's 'Storm over Asia,' Turin's 'Turk-Sib' and Dovjenko's [sic] 'Earth' " shows why he was able to realize John Grierson's vision for EMB's film unit: to make films that would enlighten British viewers about the heroism of colonial and domestic labor through a combination of propaganda and artistry (31).

25 Tallents, *The Projection of England*, 39.

26 Pronay and Spring, *Propaganda, Politics and Film 1918–45*, 53. For an analysis of the Empire and the BBC also consult MacKenzie, "In Touch with the Infinite."

27 "Rt. Hon. A. Creech Jones' Opening Address," *The Film in Colonial Development*, 4.

28 PRO, CO 323/974/1.

29 PRO, BT 64/1, "Cinematograph Films Bill."

30 Consult Harvey, *The Condition of Postmodernity*; Jameson and Miyoshi, eds. *The Cultures of Globalization*; Sassen, *Globalization and Its Discontents*; Wilson and Dissanayake, *Global/Local*.

31 PRO, CO 323/974/1, "Colonial Office Conference Proceedings of 1927," 2, 5. In a private letter, members of the BT requested Cunliffe-Lister to provide "an authoritative explanation" at the conference "of the policy we are pursuing at home," as it "would be most helpful in getting Colonial Governments to follow our lead in spite of local difficulties." Handwritten letter in file PRO CO 323/974/1, stamped 30 March, n.p.

32 The Canadian market was too precious to the United States for them to permit Britain to secure any percentage of it through regulations. For details consult Pendakur, *Canadian Dreams and American Control*, 78–89, 134.

33 NFAI, *Report of the Indian Cinematograph Committee 1927–1928* (henceforth, ICC Report), 27. (The ICC *Report* is also available at the NML.) Historians of the Australian film industry argue that the New South Wales quota for local films was marginal, and the passage of an empire quota after the Australian Royal Commission's 1927–28 report primarily supported the entry of British films into Australia (Baxter, *The Australian Cinema*, 40–53).

34 Along with the ICC *Report*, four volumes of "evidence" are available at the NFAI.

35 ICC *Report*, 102.

36 *Indian Cinematograph Committee 1927–1928: Evidence Volume I* (Calcutta: Government of India publication, 1928), 138–40.

37 The individual films are difficult to date accurately, given that their year of production in India must be accessed through incomplete government gazettes. They are mentioned, respectively, in *Film Report* (18 January 1930): 568; (15 February 1930): 571; (26 April 1930): 581; and (7 June 1930): 587. British Film Institute.

38 *Film Report* (18 January 1930): 568. British Film Insitute.

39 *Film Report* (15 February 1930): 571. British Film Institute.

40 *Parliamentary Debates*, Commons, 5th ser., vol. 203 (1927), col. 2103. The same concern was raised in the House of Lords by Earl Beauchamp in 1925 (*Parliamentary Debates*, Lords, 5th ser., vol. 61 [1925], col. 291).

41 A detailed discussion of the reasons for Hollywood's apparent universality are beyond the scope of this book, but consider the arguments in Miller et al., *Global Hollywood*, and Stephen Crofts's statement that "Hollywood is hardly ever spoken of as a national cinema, perhaps indicating its transnational reach" ("Reconceptualizing National Cinema/s," 50).

42 *The Film in National Life*, 126.

43 As Jeffrey Richards notes, Balcon was production chief of Gaumont-British at the time ("Patriotism with Profit," 249).

44 Refer to Barr, *Ealing Studios*.

45 Balcon, "Rationalise!" 62–63.

46 *The Film in National Life*, 17.

47 "The British Commonwealth," 49. The 9th Earl De La Warr is best remembered for supporting competitive commercial broadcasting against the BBC's monopoly.

48 Churchill, *India*, 81.

49 *Parliamentary Debates*, Commons, 5th ser., vol. 203 (1927), col. 2050.

50 *Parliamentary Debates*, Commons, 5th ser., vol. 203 (1927), col. 2042.

51 The film producers were well aware that there were a variety of pressing issues competing for the government's attention, particularly before World War II. So they argued that the need to attend to film was particularly significant at a time of national crisis. "There is . . . a risk that if we report prematurely to a public concerned with graver matters, we may lose an opportunity. On the other hand, if action is not soon taken by responsible authority, there is a very real danger lest the development of the film as an instrument of education and culture get into

the wrong hands, and the new medium be turned to our disadvantage" (*The Film in National Life*, 3).

52 "To Revive Production," 30.

53 Dickinson and Street describe the reciprocity talks prepared in Britain on April 1926 to persuade the Americans to distribute more British films (*Cinema and State*, 24–25).

54 Lapworth, "Production and the Exhibitor," 32.

55 In the 1930s the Latin American market was a major importer of American films, but this changed over the next decade. See Street, "The Hays Office and the Defence of the British Market in the 1930s," and Jarvie, "International Film Trade."

56 Lapworth, "Rival Remedies," 27.

57 Milton, *Concerning Legislation to Encourage Empire Films*, 6.

58 Ibid., 9.

59 Hobsbawm, *The Age of Extremes*, 94.

60 BFI, Subject Cuttings: *Legislations—Cinematograph Films Act, 1927*, "Cinematograph Films Bill: Reasons Against, by the Manchester and District Branch of the C.E.A. of Great Britain and Ireland," n.p.

61 Ibid.

62 United Artists was the only major American company that did not create temporary production houses in Britain merely to fulfill a quota as the others had done. Instead, they chose to enter into partnerships with reputable British production houses and gave British films first billing. From April 1933 to the end of 1935, UA distributed films by independent British producers, including Korda's Denham films and Wilcox's British and Dominion films in the British and American market (Richards, *The Age of the Dream Palace*, 39; Low, *Film Making in 1930s Britain*, 146). Sarah Street suggests that UA's amenability to entering into partnerships with high-quality British filmmakers was due in part to the lackluster box-office performance of films by D. W. Griffith, Howard Hughes, and the "dwindling output" of Mary Pickford, Charlie Chaplin, and Douglas Fairbanks in the Depression years ("Alexander Korda, Prudential Assurance and British Film Finance in the 1930s," 162).

63 Richards, *The Age of the Dream Palace*, 39.

64 Low, *Filmmaking in 1930s Britain*, 50. The exhibition sector had anticipated that substandard British films might be produced to meet the quota and had insisted on a "quality clause" in 1927, which was ultimately neglected (Dickinson and Street, *Cinema and State*, 22).

65 Street, *British National Cinema*, 9.

66 Hartog, "State Protection of a Beleaguered Industry," 65–66. The government and the FBI hoped that protective legislation would push the industry toward vertical integration, following the model of Hollywood's major studios or Germany's Universum Film Aktiengesellschaft (UFA).

67 Richards, *Dream Palace*, 36.

68 Bond, *Monopoly*, 18.
69 According to Rachael Low, after 1938 dominion films were made ineligible for the film quota (*Filmmaking in 1930s Britain*, 50). My research indicates that dominion films were excluded from the renter's quota.
70 ICC Report, 27.
71 PRO, BT 64/91, letter dated 13 December 1937, n.p.
72 PRO, BT 64/91, letter from E. J. Harding, secretary of state's office, to Hon. Vincent Massey, Canadian high commissioner (16 February 1938), n.p.
73 PRO, BT 64/91.
74 PRO, BT 64/91, letter from R. D. Fennelly at the BT to R. A. Wiseman, Dominions Office (17 February 1938), n.p.
75 Nevertheless, the BT guaranteed that "the situation [of excluding dominion and Indian films] would of course be altered if *effective* reciprocity were offered on a Dominion-wide basis" (PRO, BT 64/91, letter from the office of the secretary of state to Hon. Vincent Massey, Canadian high commissioner [16 February 1938], n.p.).
76 PRO, BT 64/1, "Cinematograph Films Bill," emphasis added.
77 "Cinematograph Films Act 1927, As Amended and Passed in the Third Reading," pt. 4, 26(5).
78 In the House of Commons "representations were made from all quarters against the unchanged continuance of the quota provisions of the 1927 Act" because "producers in Canada, India and Australia had been able to sell their films in this country for the purpose of renters quota, thus ousting a considerable number of United Kingdom films which would otherwise have been made" (PRO, BT 64/91).
79 PRO, BT 64/91.
80 Ibid.
81 Harvey, *The Condition of Postmodernity*, 216.

three **EMPIRE AND EMBARRASSMENT**

The first epigraph can be found in IOR, L/E/8/137, handwritten note dated May 9 on Economic and Overseas Register No. E & O 2607/34. The second epigraph is from *Indian Cinematograph Committee 1927–1928: Evidence*, vol. 1 (Calcutta: Government of India publication, 1928), 99.

1 Cohn, *Colonialism and Its Forms of Knowledge*; see in particular the foreword by Nicholas B. Dirks, the introduction, and chapter 3. "Investigative modalities" is Cohn's phrase.
2 NAI, Home (Political), 134/36.
3 Hobsbawm, *Nations and Nationalism since 1780*, 163.
4 "The traditional concept of just war [*bellum justum*] involves the banalization of war and the celebration of it as an ethical instrument, both of which were ideas

that modern political thought and the international community of nation-states had resolutely refused" (Hardt and Negri, *Empire*, 12).

5 The British economist John A. Hobson's cost-benefit analysis of imperialism in 1902 repudiated what he called "the moral and sentimental factors" of British jingoism to present a discussion of the "economics taproots" of empire. The text presents a convenient marker of change in Britain's discourse on imperialism, dividing those who supported empire (like Churchill) from those who (like Hobson) were concerned with the diminishing returns of imperial expansion. Hobson is also significant because he provided a point of departure for Lenin's later study of imperialism as the decay of capitalism. Hobson argued *against* Ricardian economics, which proposed that under British capitalism, there was a Malthussian growth in population, necessitating an import of goods and an export of people to other territories in order to prevent a domestic scarcity of resource and space. Proponents for the colonization of Australia and New Zealand shared this belief. (See De Schweinitz Jr., *The Rise and Fall of British India*; Hobson, *Imperialism*; Lenin, *Imperialism*.)

6 To extend the argument: if the political defense of economic domination was not ethically sustainable in the democratic West after World War II, neither was it entirely necessary after the overdetermined induction of postcolonial nations into capitalism by the late twentieth century. The coercive state apparatus of colonialism was replaced by a "civil society" in the postcolonies, where class-based principles of consumption, pleasure, leisure, and profit corroborated to maintain global hierarchies. Global finance capitalism became the mode of neo-imperial power structures.

7 Myths have always accompanied the practice of political imperialism, obstructing easy identifications of imperialism's financial sine qua non. In *Dreams of Adventure, Deeds of Empire*, the literary theorist Martin Green observes that since the sixteenth century, Western adventure narratives provided "energizing myths" for imperial politics (7).

8 Arora, " 'Imperilling the Prestige of the White Woman.' "

9 Chowdhry, *Colonial India*.

10 IOR, L/P&J/6/1995, file #372, handwritten page no. 430.

11 In many ways, the British image of African film audiences satisfied both fantasies: of naïve, insatiable hyperconsumers (see chapter 4). The mention of colonial and eastern markets lingers like an inconvenience in FBI memoranda and popular journals through the 1920s to the 1940s. In 1937 the BBC director and television producer Dallas Bower stated, "The British film industry has paid comparatively little attention to the marketing and distribution of its production in the East. Obviously, the reason cannot be lack of awareness of the huge potential revenue awaiting carefully handled exploitation; most producers are fully alive to the possibility of making the vast millions of the East cinema conscious" ("British Films in the Orient," 909). Here, Bower imagines the East as simultaneously teeming

with people yet empty of the technological or cultural advances required for a prosperous film industry, making invisible indigenous traditions of filmmaking.

12 *Indian Cinematograph Committee 1927–1928: Evidence*, vol. 1 (hereafter, ICC *Evidence* 1), 97.

13 Chowdhry, *Colonial India and the Making of Empire Cinema*, 5–6.

14 For the idea of a "coauthorship" of colonial-nationalist ideology see the discussion of the native intellectual in Chatterjee, *Nationalist Thought and the Colonial World*, and the idea's development by Lydia Liu ("The Female Body and Nationalist Discourse," 39). I am not suggesting an absence of opposition between imperialism and colonial nationalism, merely that assuming self-contained coherence in imperial and anticolonial positions manufactures a contest prior to analyzing it. Here I join other scholars who caution against producing a hagiography of the Indian nation-state and re-reading 1947 as a triumphant culmination of colonial nationalism. See Gyanendra Pandey's critique of the retrospective "biography of the [Indian] nation-state" frequently imposed on the colonial context, and Ashish Rajadhyaksha's extension of this critique to historical work in cinema studies (Pandey, "In Defence of the Fragment"; Rajadhyaskha, "Indian Cinema").

15 ICC *Report*, xii, 10.

16 On 22 January 1925 the Hon. Sir Ebrahim Haroon Jaffer (subsequently a member of the ICC) expressed dissatisfaction in the Council of State about the lack of centralization of censor boards. He also called attention to the fact that subordinate police inspectors (instead of police commissioners) conducted inspections of films in Bombay and Calcutta. On 15 September 1925 Jaffe asked for the number of films produced in India and the amount of capital invested in the industry, to which the government had no answer. This question had also been asked 30 August 1927 by Khan Bahadur Sarfaraz Hussain Khan in the Indian Legislative Assembly, to which the home member Hon. J. Crerar answered that the government was considering an examination into the industry's condition (ICC *Report*, 8–9).

17 NAI, Home (Political), 48/VIII/1927, and ICC *Report*, 10. Someswar Bhowmik also recounts some of these debates in *Indian Cinema, Colonial Contours* (71–74).

18 ICC *Report*, 10–11.

19 After the Government of India Act of 1919, 33 of a total of fifty members in the Council of State were elected, while the remaining twenty-seven members were nominated by the Governor General of India. The Legislative Assembly had 104 elected members, with the Governor General nominating 41 members. Thus, some scope was given to Indian representation in the legislature via elections, though at the time Indians elected to Parliament could not stand on behalf of a political party, and the Secretary of State for India (representing the British parliament and Crown) had final power to legislate for India or repeal legislation. (Eggar and Rajagopaul, *The Laws of India and Burma*, 63–75; Chandra et al., *India's Struggle for Independence*, 241.) Regarding the Simon Commission, Bipan Chandra

notes that 1927 was the year that "the Conservative Government of Britain, faced with the prospect of electoral defeat at the hands of the Labour Party, suddenly decided that it could not leave an issue which concerned the future of the British Empire in the irresponsible hands of an inexperienced Labour Government" and appointed the all-white Indian Statutory Commission later known as the Simon Commission (262; also 260–63).

20 ICC Report, 12.

21 Ibid.

22 B. D. Garga, So Many Cinemas, 68.

23 ICC Evidence 1, 80.

24 Ibid., 10.

25 For these links consult ICC Report (3) and the reprint of a speech by B. V. Jadhav (M.L.A. [Member of Legislative Assembly]) at the Indian Legislative Assembly ("Indian Film Industry," 5).

26 Occasionally to amusing effect: when Crawford asked Rustom C. N. Barucha, a Bombay film distributor, "Have you been to the west?" Barucha answered, "Not yet, Sir. I narrowly escaped going there." Crawford bristled with, "You can only give an opinion." Chairman Rangachariar added, "You have strong views. Quite right. Nothing like expressing them." (ICC Evidence 1, 141.)

27 ICC Evidence 1, 10–11, 79, 98, 141. The state maintained that film was a luxury item that would acquire a market if the films were salable. In his interview with the ICC D. Healy, who was both the British commissioner of police and president of the Bombay Board of Film Censors, pointed out elliptically that intervening on behalf of empire films would require a reversal of this position, or a selective application of it. If Indian films were not worthy of state support, he argued, empire films shared the same nonessential commodity status. If Indian films were to earn audiences on their own merit, it followed that American films attracted audiences because they intrinsically merited them. Otherwise the state's position was riddled with logical inconsistencies. (ICC Evidence 1, 98.)

28 ICC Report, 13–14.

29 The total receipts from Empire, Pathé, and Wellington Cinemas, which screened Western films, were Rs. 2,42,061, while the receipts from the Imperial, Majestic, and Krishna, which screened Indian films, amounted to Rs. 2,83,580 (ICC Evidence 1, 23, 45; ICC Evidence 3, 304). Both Britain and India were on the predecimal system, and in general the following conversion rate applied for the 1930s. 1 rupee = 1 shilling 6 pence, where 1 pound = 20 shillings and 1 shilling = 12 pennies.

30 I'm drawing on Foucault and Habermas here. Consult Barry, Osborne, and Rose, Foucault and Political Reason, 8; Habermas, "The Public Sphere," 49–55.

31 A fourth volume collates written statements from witnesses not examined orally. My particular argument about Indian responses to British Empire film schemes far from exhausts the wealth of the ICC interviews, particularly as I limit myself to volume 1 for the sake of concision. Another caveat to the following discussion is

that ICC witnesses spoke of broad trends within the industry rather than of particular films, and my analysis reflects this tendency. For a more textured sense of specific Indian films and film personalities, I direct the reader to the concluding section of this chapter and to chapter 7.

32 ICC Evidence 1, vi–vii.

33 B. D. Garga, "A New Look at an Old Report," 67.

34 Bhowmik, Indian Cinema, Colonial Contours, 84.

35 Ibid., 73.

36 Barnouw and Krishnaswamy, Indian Film, 44; particularly the chapter "Empire" (39–58). The authors state, "Great Britain's careful approach to this problem and the delicate wording of the resolution [of the Imperial Conference] reflected the nature of the relationship that existed in 1927 between Great Britain and British India" (43). Beyond this, the authors do not examine the imperial encounter in detail.

37 ICC Evidence 1, 141.

38 Ibid., 130, emphasis added.

39 Ibid., 383.

40 Ibid., 140.

41 Ibid., 1, 24.

42 These titles were mentioned in various interviews (see, for example, ibid., 1, 24, 327, 339). Madan Theaters touted Savitri as their co-production in Rome, using Italian actors in Indian dresses, but according to Ashish Rajadhyaksha and Paul Willemen, the film was an Italian import originally made by Giorgio Mannini for Cines in Rome (Encyclopaedia of Indian Cinema, 139).

43 ICC Evidence 1, 1.

44 Ibid., 121. Engineer was of the opinion that Hindus preferred Indian films and "Parsis, Mohammadans and Europeans and Anglo-Indians" saw "foreign pictures" (123). Most data points to the fact that both Hindus and Muslims liked Indian films, though the upper classes of both communities favored American films.

45 Ibid., 16.

46 Ibid., 1–10.

47 Ibid., 214–16. For more on Yajnik see Rajadhyaksha and Willeman, Encyclopaedia of Indian Cinema, 239–40. Others such as Mohan Dayaram Bhavnani, director, Imperial Studio, and Ardeshir Irani demanded the abolition of duties on raw materials needed for film production, including heavy machinery and transport (165). Several witnesses were also in favor of the government offering incentives to Indian filmmakers, such as removing taxes on raw film stock or offering concessions for the use of equipment, railways, troops, horses, and public resources utilized by Indian filmmakers in their productions. (More about the cost of Indian films can be found in ICC Evidence 1, 28, 334.)

48 Prior to the adoption of a decimal-based monetary system where 100 paise were

equivalent to 1 rupee, a rupee was made up of 16 Indian annas. Each anna was further divisible into 4 pice. The consensus was that an 8,000-foot film cost approximately Rs. 2,000 to import, including Rs. 300 in customs tax. A film of similar
length in India cost about Rs. 20,000 to produce. The cost of renting these films
varied proportionately for the exhibitor. (ICC *Evidence* 1, 165.)

49 Ibid., 348.

50 Ibid., 179.

51 ICC *Evidence* 3, 1011.

52 ICC *Evidence* I, 181.

53 Ibid., 338.

54 Ibid., 140.

55 Ibid., 364.

56 Ibid., 144.

57 Wadia, "I Remember, I Remember," 93.

58 ICC *Evidence* 1, 439–48.

59 Ibid., 382.

60 Ibid., 332, 339.

61 Ibid., 539.

62 Ibid., 503–511.

63 Ibid., 17.

64 ICC *Report*, 104. See "The Resolution of the Imperial Conference Concerning the
    Exhibition within the Empire of Empire Films," 99–104.

65 ICC *Report*, 99.

66 ICC *Evidence* 1, 98. On the same topic see also IOR, L/E/8/137, draft of a letter from
    R. Peel, secretary, Public and Judicial Department, India Office, dated 25 April
    1934.

67 ICC *Report*, 100

68 Ibid., 103.

69 Ibid., 101.

70 ICC *Evidence* 1, 165.

71 ICC *Report*, 103.

72 ICC *Evidence* 1, vi.

73 ICC *Report*, 166.

74 Ibid., 164.

75 Ibid.

76 Comments on the ICC *Report* can be found in the section "The Cinema and the
    Empire" in *The Film in National Life* (particularly 131–33).

77 BFI, Subject Cuttings: *India Cuttings up to 1959*, clipping from *The Times*, 9 August
    1928, n.p.

78 Mehta, *Liberalism and Empire*, 8.

79 MSA, *Home Department (Political)*, 1928, file no. 208, "Information Regarding Film

Producing Companies in the Bombay Presidency," letters from the BT, 8 December 1927; Ganguly, 23 March, 1928; and the commissioner of police, 28 April 1928.

80 For a brief discussion of the relationship between the production of knowledge and its assumption of norms refer to Foucault's "History of Systems of Thought."

81 Garga, *So Many Cinemas*, 60; Kaul, *Cinema and the Indian Freedom Struggle*, 26.

82 "Indian Circuit for British Group?" *The Bioscope* (21 March 1927): 27.

83 *ICC Evidence* 1, 138–39.

84 Ibid., 141; repeated on 143.

85 Ibid., 331. Bilimoria managed Excelsior Cinema, Empress Cinema, Empire Cinema, and Edward Cinema for Madan Theaters, which attracted educated Indians, Anglo Indians, and British audiences (322).

86 *ICC Evidence* 3, 972. The imported film was a Hepworth Production, unidentified by the witness.

87 For examples, refer to NFAI, *The Bombay Government Gazette* 1 (1929–1938), especially (9 May 1929): 1063; (6 February 1930): 244; and (29 August 1935): 1627.

88 "Co-operative Marketing of British Empire Films: F.B.I. Offer to Government," 10 November 1926, ref. no. 300/J/11, 1, British Film Institute.

89 Ibid., 2. The company was to purchase dominion rights for the distribution of "British Empire made pictures," advancing the producer a sum agreed on between that producer and the renting company (3). Failing the scheme, the FBI Film Group wanted to send agents to the empire to market their films. Emphasizing the need for coordinated action, the Film Group argued that "the mobilisation of our overseas resources would greatly strengthen and lend variety to the Film industry of our Empire and thus enhance the efficiency of the distributing organisation" (2). The letter also makes an argument for regulatory state assistance to British film producers: "It would be advantageous if Dominion interests could participate in the scheme financially and otherwise. It will, however, be extremely difficult to obtain money through ordinary channels unless protective legislation is introduced for the home market and the leading Dominion markets and the industry thus be put upon a stable basis" (2).

90 *The Film in National Life*, 134.

91 In proposing a distribution organization in 1926, the FBI's Film Group noted that the British production *Alf's Button* was sold to Canada for £500; *Armageddon* generated the offer of a small sum from Australia but was later declined; *Britain's Birthright* was turned down by all dominions and colonies. None of these films are dated ("Co-operative Marketing of British Empire Films: F.B.I. Offer to Government," 10 November 1926, ref. no. 300/J/11, appendix 1, British Film Institute). Without mentioning film titles, *The Film in National Life* notes that the BUFP sent commercial features to the West Indies and to East and West Africa (134). I have not found many references to the BUFP in subsequent documents, though Sir Philip Cunliffe-Lister answered a question about it in the House of Commons on

15 May 1935, identifying an associate organization that was to assist the BUFP in selecting suitable films for the colonies (IOR, L/P&J/6/1995, file 372, "Parliamentary Notice: Session 1934–35.")

92 Guha, *Elementary Aspects of Peasant Insurgency in Colonial India*, 259.

93 Ibid.

94 IOR, L/PJ/6/30, "Move to Check Foreign Films in India: British Scheme in Preparation: Government to Be Asked for Subsidy," *The Morning Post*, 25 August 1937. The article quotes Britain's need to counteract America's hold in India as the rationale for a subsidy.

95 IOR, L/P&J/8/30.

96 Jha, *Indian Motion Picture Almanac*, 789.

97 Baskaran, *The Eye of the Serpent*.

98 IOR, L/P&J/8/30, Legislative Assembly debates of 20 September 1937; *filmindia* 4, no. 8 (December 1938): 9. As noted earlier, 1 anna equals 1/16th of a rupee.

99 To state the obvious, I have access to these rumors because they were tracked for their controversial status and filed by the Economic and Overseas Department of the India Office and the British Board of Trade.

100 IOR, L/PJ/6/30.

101 IOR. L/PJ/8/30. In a memorandum to the India Office on 19 April 1934 the FBI again proposed imperial preference in India "so as to counteract the influence of foreign films." In a memorandum sent a day earlier to the India Office, the FBI stated, "[It is] understood that British Government Departments as well as the Indian Government are anxious that British films should obtain more general exhibition in India than hitherto, so as to present the British rather than the foreign (or American) angle of things to the vast audiences which annually attend film pictures in India. To this end certain sections of the British film industry have recently made special efforts to facilitate production of films suitable for the India market, and also to increase the distribution in India of films produced in the United Kingdom for general exhibition."

102 IOR, L/P&J/8/30, letter dated 27 October 1937.

103 BFI, Subject Cuttings: *India Cuttings up to 1959*, *The Film Daily* (6 May 1938): n.p.

104 The editorial page of *Sound* 3, no. 5 (May 1944) declares it a "biting, fighting" journal. These journals, along with popular newspapers, launched a sustained attack on what they considered worldwide "Anti-Indian Propaganda" in American and British films. For a collation of this outcry consult MSA, *Home Department (Political)/71/1935*.

105 IOR, L/PJ/8/30.

106 IOR, L/PJ/8/30, "Cinematography: Financial Subsidies to British Film Industry in India." The same wording was repeated in different drafts of the letter, written by W. T. Amman and Peel (India Office) to Fennelly (BT) on 13 January 1938.

107 IOR, L/PJ/8/30, "Copy of Minutes Written in Department of Overseas Trade," 27 January 1938.

108 IOR, L/E/8/137, "Resolution re Indian Film Industry," 1431.

109 ICC *Evidence* 1, 5, 80, 86; IOR, L/E/8/137, "Indian Film Industry," 16.

110 Phalke's quote, originally in the popular magazine *Navyug* (September 1918), is reprinted in "Birth of a Film Industry," *Cinema Vision India* 1, no. 1 (January 1980): 19 (Siddharth Kak, ed., *Cinema Vision India* [4 volumes], Bombay: IBH, 1980). Rai's comments can be found in ICC *Evidence* 3, 1005. Also consult *Proceedings of the First Session of the Indian Motion Picture Congress and Other Sectional Conferences* for S. Satyamurthi's comments on cinema and swadeshi (173–79; 203–4), and Chandulal J. Shah's comments on Indian cinema's international and national character (158–64).

111 ICC *Evidence* 1, 141.

112 ICC *Evidence* 3, 998–1015.

113 Pal, "The Rise and Fall of Bombay Talkies," *Filmfare* (16–31 December 1983): 25.

114 Barnouw and Krishnaswamy, *Indian Cinema*, 45.

115 Rajadhyaksha and Willemen, *Encyclopaedia of Indian Cinema*, 169; Nadkarni, "A Painter Called Baburao," in *Cinema Vision India* I, no. 1 (January 1980): 40.

116 Rajadhyaksha and Willemen consider him the founder of the historical and social genre of Indian films. (*Encyclopaedia of Indian Cinema*, 169). Though he made mythologicals, Painter's films were highly visual, meticulously avoiding intertitles and incorporating trick photography that he had learned on his trips abroad. By all descriptions, Painters's films displayed a diachronic modernism through combining mythic content while exploiting cinema's facility for visual manipulation. He returned to painting after the introduction of sound film because he felt that sound compromised the medium's true aesthetic form. Rai, on the other hand, was more of a classical realist.

117 ICC *Evidence* 3, 1014.

118 See Dnyaneshwar Nadkarni's and J. B. H. Wadia's accounts in *Cinema Vision* 1, no. 1 (January 1980): 39–43 and 93–95, respectively.

119 Koch, *Frantz Osten's Indian Silent Films*, 25.

120 Pal, "The Rise and Fall of Bombay Talkies," 26.

121 ICC *Evidence* 3, 998.

122 Shantaram and Narwekar, *V. Shantaram*, 22. The Hindi- and Marathi-language filmmaker V. Shantaram started his career in the Gandharava Natak Mandali, with stalwarts of theater like Bal Gandharava, Govindrao Tembe, and Ganpatrao Bodas.

123 For a personal account of these actresses, see Manto, *Stars from Another Sky*, 85–102, 172–81.

124 Nadkarni, "A Painter Called Baburao," 40. By this account, the wrestler-turned-actor Balasaheb Yadev tried directing and eventually took to organizing mob scenes in films (43).

125 ICC *Evidence* 1, 364.

126 Dorabji noted in his written statement that "one who can read his own language only, finds other Indian languages to be as foreign as English" (349). According

to Ardeshir Bilimoria, Madan produced their own films in Bengal, but they didn't exhibit them in Bombay because the films had been made "according to the Bengali custom" (ICC Evidence 1, 327). Additionally, films made in Bengal had to be titled in Gujarati and Hindi to be comprehensible to Bombay audiences. The Bombay Board of Film Censors talked of the "differences between the large towns like Bombay, or Calcutta and the less enlightened country districts" (84), and Chunilal Munim, representative BCTTA, noted that translations "mar the beauty of the picture or story" (10). According to him, the difference between films popular in Bengal versus those in Bombay were among "the main difficulties we have to face in developing this industry in India" (11). Bilimoria similarly noted, "So far as history, customs and mythology is concerned, it is confined to each province" (341).

127 ICC Evidence 1, 347.

128 Proceedings of the First Session of the Indian Motion Picture Congress and Other Sectional Conferences, 158. In 1937 the interim Congress Party under C. Rajagopalachari attempted to make Hindi the official language of the Madras presidency (including modern Tamilnadu, parts of Karnataka, and Andhra Pradesh) to widespread protest in Tamilnadu.

129 Kesavan, "Urdu, Awadh and the Tawaif," 249.

130 See Desai's Beyond Bollywood for a filmography and analysis.

131 All statements by Wadia in this paragraph are taken from his recollections, reprinted as "I Remember, I Remember" in Cinema Vision I, no. 1 (January 1980): 92–93.

132 Chatterjee has argued that the colonial middle class "was simultaneously placed in a position of subordination in one relation and a position of dominance in the other," referring, of course, to its subordination to the colonizers and its "cultural leadership of the indigenous colonized people." (The Nation and Its Fragments, 36). As I discuss above, for Indian aspirants of the film industry battling social prejudices against their profession, the position of cultural leadership was less obvious.

133 IOR, L/E/8/137, Legislative Assembly Debates, "Resolution re Indian Film Industry," 1 March 1933, 1434.

134 IOR, L/E/8/137, Legislative Assembly Debates, "Resolution re Indian Film Industry," 1 March 1933, 1439, emphasis added.

135 IOR, L/E/8/137, Legislative Assembly Debates, "Resolution re Indian Film Industry," 1 March 1933, 1438–41. Several suggestions for the recuperation of state income through other sources were forthcoming but not accepted.

136 IOR, L/E/8/137, minute paper dated 23 April 1934.

137 IOR, L/P&J/8/30, letter from Amman and Peel (India Office) to Fennelly (BT), 13 January 1938.

four   **REALISM AND EMPIRE**

1   Christopher Williams, *Realism and the Cinema*, 12. In a review of Auerbach's *Mimesis*, Terry Eagleton offers a characteristically entertaining overview of different traditions of realism in fiction ("Pork Chops and Pineapples").

2   Gunning, *D. W. Griffith and the Origins of American Narrative Film*, 17.

3   Examples include Laura Mulvey's "Visual Pleasure and Narrative Cinema," Colin MacCabe's "Theory and Film" and his earlier "Realism and the Cinema," and Peter Wollen's "Godard and Counter-Cinema," which defines political cinema by its structural departures from realism. The anthologies *Narrative, Apparatus, Ideology*, edited by Philip Rosen, and *The Sexual Subject* collate much of this work, particularly of the screen theory that presented a sustained analysis of film texts in relation to ideology, subjectivity, sexuality, and gender.

4   Althusser, "Ideology and Ideological State Apparatus."

5   In "Falling Women, Rising Stars, New Horizons" Miriam Hansen suggests that conceptualizing Hollywood cinema in purely classical-realist terms fallaciously reserves modernist aesthetics for alternative experimental and avant-garde film practices, ignoring the extent to which Hollywood was associated with the modern. I concur that classical-realist fiction is best understood in relation to modernity, which refers to the triumph of Western capitalism, mass consumption, industrialization, urbanization, and changes in visual, social, and economic relations. But it is possible to maintain that realism contains narrative elisions of its own modernist impulses while also arguing that theoretical models (like Bordwell's and Thompson's, mentioned by Hansen) that conflate modernity or modernization with aesthetic modernism divorce classical realism from its historical moment. For nuanced distinctions between the "dialectics of modernization and modernism" consult Marshall Berman's *All That Is Solid Melts into Air* and a useful review by Perry Anderson, "Modernity and Revolution."

6   Lukács, *Essays on Realism*, 51–52.

7   Ibid., 53–54.

8   NFAI, *The Bombay Government Gazette Part 1* (1929–1938): 1627, *Sanders of the River* (ser. no. 14976), certified for exhibition in India on 29 August 1935.

9   Though all cinema relies on artifice, realist art exaggerates the paradox through its claims to realism. In André Bazin's words, "But realism in art can only be achieved in one way—through artifice" (*What Is Cinema?* 27). And in *Signatures of the Visible* Fredric Jameson notes, " 'Realism' is, however, a peculiarly unstable concept owing to its simultaneous, yet incompatible, aesthetic and epistemological claims, as the two terms of the slogan, 'representation of reality' suggest" (159).

10 For another discussion of realism and imperialism consult Shohat and Stam, on "The Question of Realism," in *Unthinking Eurocentrism*, 178–82.

11 Whissel, "Uncle Tom, Goldilocks, and the Rough Riders," 402. "Referential heterogeneity" is her term (398). See also Hansen, *Babel and Babylon*, 23–59.

12 *Rhodes* takes the heterogeneity a step further, using high-contrast lighting in indoor shots of the Boer leader to codify him as evil. Expressionist stylistics combine with narrative realism in the film.

13 Karol Kulik provides these accounts in his biography of the director, *Alexander Korda*. They are also excerpted in the National Film Theater's programming notes on the film (see BFI, Subject File: *Elephant Boy*). Quoting from the latter, "over fifty-five hours of film had been shot in India, all background material to a still non-existent story. This was a customary state of affairs on a Flaherty picture. Apparently in the last stages of production, Flaherty had no control on the film" (n.p).

14 Robeson, a radical leftist, political activist, and champion of racial equality accepted the role of Bosambo because of his interest in Africa. A linguist, he also learnt a few African languages during his visits to Africa for the film shoot. "I believe it would be a good thing for the American Negro to have more consciousness of his African tradition, to be proud of it," he said in an interview with Marguerite Tazelaar, "Robeson Finds a Natural Link to the Songs of African Tribes," *New York Herald-Tribune* (October 27, 1935). Reprinted in Foner's *Paul Robeson Speaks*, 103.

15 Comolli, "Historical Fiction." A vast body of literature theorizes the relationship of history to cinema. Some representative examples include Grindon, *Shadows on the Past*; *History and Theory* 36, no. 4, a theme issue that includes Ann-Louise Shapiro's "Whose (Which) History Is It Anyway?" Paula Rabinowitz's "Wreckage Upon Wreckage," and Shapiro in conversation with Jill Godmilow in "How Real is the Reality in Documentary Film"; Kaes, *From Hitler to Heimat*; Rollins, *Hollywood as Historian*; Rosenstone, *Revisioning History*; Sorlin, *The Film in History*; Toplin, *History by Hollywood*.

16 Mimi White, "An Extra Body of Reference," 50.

17 Churchill, *India*, 96.

18 See Roman Polanski's *Repulsion* (1965) as a modernist film that experiments with ruptures between the subjective and the objective (like *Black Narcissus*) in contrast to the operation of *Sanders*'s realist constructions of point of view.

19 Jeffrey Richards, "When East Meets West," *Daily Telegraph*, 19 October 1987, p. 13.

20 Fanon, *The Wretched of the Earth*, 38.

21 The introduction of alcohol into interactions between the British and African natives disrupts the hierarchy entirely, as when inebriated Africans in King Mofalaba's land forget their subordinate position and overstep behavioral boundaries. Representations of the British Empire make clear that mastery over the social codes of exchanging conversation and alcohol carry great significance with regard to inclusion in or exclusion from the ruler's exclusive coterie (see more on this in chapter 5). The last scene of *Sanders* that involves a private conversation between Sanders and Bosambo seems to break down this binary schema, but in fact the men are still not allowed spatial equivalence: Sanders sits as Bosambo stands.

22 Richards, "Korda's Empire," 127.

23 Physical violence also provides spectatorial pleasure in empire films, and in *Sanders* it erupts at unexpected moments, as in the war song that Bosambo teaches his young son.

> Off, Off, into Battle,
> Make the War-drums Rattle,
> Mow them Down like Cattle,
> Onward, On, On into Battle,
> Bite them into the Dust, Into the Dust.
> Charge, Cheer, Shoot, Spear, Smash, Smite, Slash, Fight, and Slay-ay-ay.

24 From Robeson's interview with Ben Davis Jr., "U.S.S.R.: The Land for Me," *Sunday Worker*, 10 May 1936, reprinted in *Paul Robeson Speaks* (108). By Communist Party Robeson is referring to the American delegation to the Sixth Congress of the Comintern (Third International) in 1928. The delegation defined African Americans as an oppressed nation rather than an oppressed minority of workers.

25 Ibid., 105–9.

26 Robeson in an interview with Sidney Cole, "Paul Robeson Tells Us Why," in London's *The Cine-Technician* (September–October 1938): 74–75, reprinted in *Paul Robeson Speaks* (121). For the controversial reception of *Sanders* among African Americans see "Paul Robeson: Crossing Over" in *Heavenly Bodies*, wherein Richard Dyer discusses the varying significance of Robeson's figure for black and white American audiences.

27 Details in Steward, *Paul Robeson*.

28 To the Africans, Sanders is known as "Sandi the Tiger. Sandi the Eater of Kings."

29 The British repeat the transmogrifying legends of "Sandi" with wry disdain, but in the absence of attributing a thousand eyes to Sanders, they are at a loss to explain his knowledge of the land. When Sanders claims to know the strange African found by Hamilton, the latter says incredulously, "You're not going to tell me that out of the two million souls here, you know that man I picked up an hour ago." "I might," says Sanders enigmatically.

30 Said, *Orientalism*, 72.

31 Bhabha, *The Location of Culture*, 71.

32 Bhabha sees the displacement of orientalism's fixity to be the result of an overdetermination of a manifest orientalism by a latent orientalism, the former being the site of historical articulation and the latter of unconscious repositories of fantasies, imaginative writings, and ideas (ibid.). I demur from conceptualizing the imperial unconscious in any form other than its historical particularity, not to fetishize the historical but to accept the manifest as the only legible discourse.

33 Fanon, *The Wretched of the Earth*, 37.

34 Realist films like *Sanders* and *Rhodes of Africa* are plentiful in their references to natives as children. In *Sanders* Father O'Leary advises Ferguson, "You must be quick and strong now like a father with his misguided children." When two men dis-

tribute gin and firearms to the natives, one of them says, "His [Sanders's] black children have become pretty civilized," so "it would be considerable pleasure to teach his black children a thing or two while he's cooing and billing in London." In *Rhodes* the following conversation transpires between Cecil B. Rhodes (Walter Huston) and Anna Carpenter (Peggy Ashcroft).

> RHODES: I always think of them—the natives I mean—as children. One has to be patient and understanding. Educate them.
>
> CARPENTER: Generations of these children in your hands—makes me happy.

35 Colin Beale, secretary of the Edinburgh House Bureau for Visual Aids, speaking at a conference (*The Film in Colonial Development*, 20).

36 Useful early discussions of Grierson's documentaries are included in Armes, *A Critical History of the British Cinema*; Ellis, *The Documentary Idea*; Swann, "John Grierson and the G.P.O. Film Unit, 1933–1939"; Winston, *Claiming the Real*.

37 This was Flaherty's second film, following *Nanook of the North*.

38 Private companies also funded documentary production. For accounts of Grierson's work for the oil company Shell International and Basil Wright's sponsorship by the Ceylon Tea Propaganda Board, consult Ellis, *The Documentary Idea*, especially "Institutionalization: Great Britain, 1929–1939" (58–77).

39 Flaherty was an influential figure for the entire movement, of course, and served as a mentor to several young British documentary filmmakers.

40 Stollery, *Alternative Empires*, 172–75. See also Ellis, *The Documentary Idea*, 61.

41 Aitken, *Film and Reform*; Stollery, *Alternative Empires*; Street, *British National Cinema*, 150–60. The assessment of the British documentary movement as modernist rather than realist points to a shift in film criticism as well. Only a few decades ago, in the 1980s, radical rereadings of British cinema distinguished the 1930s documentaries from modernist, avant-garde film production in Britain in order to redress an overemphasis on British documentaries and reclaim independent films as a part of British film history. See Don MacPherson's and Paul Willemen's *Traditions of Independence* and Anne Friedberg's discussion of this work in *Close Up*.

42 Stollery, *Alternative Empires*, 177–79, 189–96.

43 BFI, Microfiche: *Sanders of the River*, G. E. T. Grossmith, "With a Film Unit in Africa."

44 BFI, Microfiche: *Sanders of the River*, Zoltan Korda, "Filming in Africa."

45 In "Engendering the Nation," Kathryn Dodd and Philip Dodd describe nineteenth-century accounts of the bestial and depraved poor that documentarists aimed to rectify (42).

46 BFI, Microfiche: *Sanders of the River*.

47 Dodd and Dodd, "Engendering the Nation," 46–47.

48 MacCabe, "Theory and Film," 183.

49 Stollery, *Alternative Empires*, 180, 201. Rotha considered Korda a "facile producer." See Rotha, "Films of the Quarter," 116.

50 In a Lacanian sense, the imaginary prescribes a full relation between the word and the thing with a mysterious unity of sign and referent. According to psychoanalytic film theory, a text that breaks the imaginary relationship between sign and referent also participates in breaking down spectatorial identification, given that mechanisms of identification govern the organization of a realist text. Consequently the disruption of identification is posited as an essential criterion for subversive texts by MacCabe in "Theory and Film" (184, 194–95).

51 I agree with Miriam Hansen that "we seem to be faced with a gap between film theory and film history, between the spectator as a term of cinematic discourse and the empirical moviegoer in his or her demographic contingency. The question, then, is whether the two levels of inquiry can be mediated" (*Babel and Babylon*, 5). MacCabe voiced this concern earlier: "Realism is no longer a question of an exterior reality nor of the relation of reader to text, but one of the ways in which these two interact" ("Theory and Film," 194–95).

52 *World Film News* 1, no. 12 (March 1937): 5, British Film Institute.

53 Powell mentions this in an interview conducted by Martin Scorsese (*Black Narcissus*, CD, directed by Michael Powell and Emeric Pressburger [1947; Los Angeles: Criterion, 1998]).

54 Richards, "Korda's Empire," 123.

55 MacCabe, "Realism and the Cinema" 26.

56 Lyotard, *The Postmodern Condition*, 74.

57 Moore, *Savage Theory*, 40.

58 Ibid., 2.

59 Renov, "Towards a Poetics of Documentary."

five **ROMANCE AND EMPIRE**

1 Frye, *The Secular Scripture.*

2 Ibid., 15.

3 Ibid., 15. A good example of such sacralization is *The Projection of England*, a short book published by Sir Stephen Tallents, president of the Empire Marketing Board. Tallents declared that the fame of England broken up into its "primary colours" would consist of the following national institutions and virtues. "*The Monarchy* (with its growing scarcity value); *Parliamentary Institutions* (with all the values of a first edition); *The British Navy; The English Bible, Shakespeare, and Dickens . . .* ; In international affairs—*a reputation for disinterestedness*; In national affairs—*a tradition of justice, law, and order*; In national character—*a reputation for coolness*; In commerce— *a reputation for fair dealing*; In manufacture—*a reputation for quality . . .* ; In sport—*a reputation for fair play*." According to Roy Armes, Tallents also proposed these as appropriate topics for films by the EMB. Tallents, *The Projection of England*, 14; Armes, *A Critical History of British Cinema*, 133.

4 De Certeau, *The Writing of History*. Nicholas Dirks observes, "History is surely one

of the most important signs of the modern. We are modern not only because we have achieved this status historically, but because we have developed consciousness of our historical depths and trajectories, as also our historical transcendence of the traditional" ("History as a Sign of the Modern," 25).

5 Barthes, *Image-Music-Text*, 169. Also see Barthes, *Mythologies*. In *Tropics of Discourse* Hayden White discusses overlaps between history and fiction through shared semiotic structures embedded in dominant ideology. Also consult Hayden White's *The Content of the Form*.

6 The *amirs* agreed to give Britain exclusive navigational rights around the region in return for a peace treaty. The British broke their treaty by blowing up the Imam Garh fortress and butchering around five-thousand Sindis (the people of Sind).

7 Consult Hopkirk, *The Great Game*; Maley, *The Afghanistan Wars*; Wolpert, *A New History of India*, 219–56.

8 *The Four Feathers* is also set against the backdrop of fierce enemies of the British Empire, against whom the British accepted defeat at least once. The Haden Dowah tribes of *The Four Feathers* were much admired by the British for this reason. To quote Alex Waugh, who was responsible for making location arrangements in Sudan for the film, "As soon as I arrived at our desert location I had to go up to the Red Sea hills, and bring some other tribesman—the Haden Dowah or the Fuzzie Wuzzies as they are usually called. The people we had booked already were Arabs, of course. We wanted these chaps because they were the only tribesmen who ever had been known in British history to have broken the famous British square. They actually formed part of the Khalifa's attacking force on Kitchener's troops at the battle of Omdurman" (Waugh, "Filming 'The Four Feathers,'" 899). Rudyard Kipling includes a tribute to these fighters in his poem "Fuzzie Wuzzy: Sudan Expeditionary Force." The poem contains variations of the following verse, written in a mock cockney accent.

> So 'ere's to you, Fuzzy Wuzzy, at your 'ome in the Soudan;
> You're a pore benighted 'eathen but a first-class fightin' man;
> We gives you your certificate, an' if you want it signed
> We'll come an' 'ave a romp with you whenever you're inclined.
> (*Gunga Din and Other Favorite Poems*, 25–29)

Also see Churchill's *The River War*.

9 Though Korda's *Sanders* is based on Edgar Wallace's stories and *The Drum* on a novel by A. E. W. Mason, there's a cross-referential system in colonial adventure tales that gives this fiction its own dense reality. As the film historian Jeffrey Richards points out, Mason's novel depicts Carruthers as the younger brother of Sanders, who now ranks below the governor. In the exclusive world of Britain's aristomilitaristic diplomacy depicted in the film and the novel, Carruthers marries the governor's niece, Marjorie. (See Richards, "Korda's Empire," 131.)

10 For information related to Chitral consult the following government files: NAI, *Foreign (Political)*, 336-G/1928; 190-G/1928; 68-F/1929; 403-I/1932; 158-F/1935; 93-F/1935; 386-X/1935; 390-F/1935; 65-X/1935; 182-X(Secret)/1936; 235-G/1936. Also see *Foreign (Political)*, 294-F (Secret)/1934, "Soviet Propaganda: Enlistment of the Support of His Highness Agha Khan in Counteracting Soviet Propaganda in Gilgit and Chitral"; *Foreign (Political)*, 342-X (Secret)/1935, "Soviet Agents: Penetration of Soviet Agents into Chitral, Gilgit, and Ladakh and Measures Taken to Neutralize Their Efforts."

11 NAI, *Foreign (Political)*, 68-F/1928.

12 NAI, *Foreign (Political)*, 68-F/1928.

13 Technicolor technology came to Britain with the musical extravaganza *Wings of the Morning* (Schuster, 1937), under the cinematography of Jack Cardiff, who was also the cinematographer for *Black Narcissus*. Early examples of Technicolor include Disney's *Flowers and Trees* (Gillett, 1932); *La Cucaracha* (Corrigan, 1934); *Becky Sharp* (Mamoulian, 1935); *The Garden of Allah* (Boleslawski, 1936); *The Wizard of Oz* (Fleming, 1939); and *Gone with the Wind* (Fleming, 1939).

14 "The Drum," *The New Statesman and Nation*, 612.

15 "Two Reissues," *Kinematograph Weekly*, 21; and "The Drum," *Film Weekly*, 24.

16 The magazine added that "the use of color has given the interiors a tawny hue and sequences do not always match, but the mountain backgrounds are impressive" ("The Drum," *Motion Picture Herald*, 46).

17 "Two Reissues," 21.

18 "The Drum," *The Cinema*, 220.

19 Dallas Bower, "British Films in the Orient," *Great Britain and the East* (24 June 1937): 909.

20 Niranjana, *Siting Translation*, 3.

21 Street, *British National Cinema*, 41.

22 Makdisi, *Romantic Imperialism*; Sudan, *Fair Exotics*. See also Fulford and Kitson, *Romanticism and Colonialism*; Richardson and Hofkosh, *Romanticism, Race, and Imperial Culture*.

23 A "pure" form of the Gothic narrative does not exist, but I have culled the main tropes from Brooks's and Frye's analyses, as well as from the works of fiction named above. Anne Radcliffe's novels, Edgar Allen Poe's poetry and short stories, and Emily Brontë's *Wuthering Heights* are considered landmarks of the Gothic romance tradition. Brooks relates modern melodramas by Balzac and James to early Gothic novels as well.

24 Brooks, *The Melodramatic Imagination*, 4. According to Northrop Frye, the revolutionary quality of a romance lies in "the polarization between the two worlds, one desirable and the other hateful" (*The Secular Scripture*, 163). Though this may be hair-splitting, I'd suggest that as soon as the division permits a clear identification of the elements that need to be expunged, the polarization loses its revolutionary

aspect, as the text is no longer unsettled by the presence of its "abject" elements (more on this ambiguity in chapter 7).

25 Mulvey, "Notes on Sirk and Melodrama," 97.

26 Ibid., 75–76. See Elsaesser, "Tales of Sound and Fury," 78–79, for differences between westerns and melodramas (distinct from melodramatic westerns).

27 Gledhill, "The Melodramatic Field," 13.

28 In "Notes on Sirk and Melodrama," Mulvey notes that all films deal generously with male fantasy (76).

29 See Ella Shohat's and Robert Stam's chapter "The Western as Paradigm" (Unthinking Eurocentrism, especially 114–21). Also see Bazin's essays "The Western, or the American Film Par Excellence" and "The Evolution of the Western" (What Is Cinema?, 140–57). Other sources include Cawelti, Six Gun Mystique; Grant, Film Genre Reader 3; Kitses, Horizons West; Wright, Sixguns and Society; Slotkin, Regeneration through Violence; Tompkins, West of Everything; Walker, Westerns.

30 As Richard Abel argues in The Red Rooster Scare, the North made a poor template for tales of white Anglo-Saxon American masculinity when compared to the cinematic and ideological potential of the western frontier.

31 Shohat and Stam, Unthinking Eurocentrism, 115.

32 As Shohat and Stam argue, "Even within an already condensed spatiotemporality, these westerns privilege a period roughly fifty years, and return time and again to particular sites and events. Although historical Native Americans generally avoided direct confrontation with the White military—according to the Nation Parks Service, there were probably only six full-scale attacks on US cavalry forts between 1850 and 1890—the Indian raid on the fort, as the constructed bastion of settled civilization against nomadic savagery, nevertheless became a staple topos in American western" (ibid., 115–16).

33 Like Will Wright in Sixguns and Society (49–50), John Cawelti in Six Gun Mystique observes that simple differentiations between "good" and "bad" or "self" and "other" are impossible when the western is considered in all its variations from the 1930s to the early 1970s. Depending on the film, evil is shown to reside within society (corrupt authorities, oppressive community) as much as outside it (in the outlaws, "Indians"), and protagonists rarely integrate with a community given their affinities with an unfettered wilderness, which provides a viable alternative to civilization's degeneration. Cawelti does not incorporate the same nuanced level of differentiation into his analysis of British empire films. He notes that an imperial film's Manicheanism varies from a western's dialectical symbolic structure. In empire films, he argues, the wilderness remains alien and either affirms civilization or threatens it (40; see also Kitses, Horizon's West, 10–11). Wright agrees that imperial films are more binary than westerns and have an affinity to Icelandic sagas or Greek myths in which the hero is never challenged as an outsider to society but remains a man of aristocratic birth temporarily alienated from his exalted status through a predestined sequence of events (150–51). I believe a discussion

of the realist, romance, and modernist modes of empire cinema makes such distinctions between westerns and empire films untenable.

34 This is Peter Brooks's argument when he notes that the "Promethean search to illuminate man's quotidian existence by the reflected flame of the higher cosmic drama" followed the destruction of the institutions of church and monarchy after the French Revolution (The Melodramatic Imagination, 21).

35 Wright, Sixguns and Society, 130–84.

36 Of particular interest here is the debate on the role of the family in melodrama between Chuck Kleinhans ("Notes on Melodrama and the Family under Capitalism") and Christine Gledhill ("The Melodramatic Field"). Kleinhans proposes that the bourgeois domestic form's coincidence with the rise of Western capitalism can be traced to the simultaneous commodification of the domestic sphere (where self-gratification is defined in terms of a family's choices in consumption and lifestyle) and its distance from the productive base of an economy (suppressing the possibility of meaningful social action through the family). This produces the primary conflict of melodrama wherein the family is fraught because "people's personal needs are restricted to the sphere of the family, of personal life, and yet the family cannot meet the demands of being all that the rest of society is not" ("Notes on Melodrama and the Family under Capitalism," 200). Gledhill takes this reading to task because she sees it as positing a realm of real conflict against which the representation of the family in melodrama offers "a mystifying resolution," thus prioritizing "a set of socio-economic relations outside the domestic and personal sphere, to which issues of sexual relations, of fantasy and desire are secondary" ("The Melodramatic Field," 13).

37 Altman, Film/Genre, particularly "Why Are Genres Sometimes Mixed?" (123–43).

38 For an early critique of feminist film theory's color blindness, consult Gaines, "White Privilege and Looking Relations." My aim is to triangulate all the categories of analysis in play here, prominently race, gender, sexuality, and nation.

39 E. M. Forster, A Passage to India, 289. The novel was first published in 1924.

40 As an interesting biographical sidebar, the imperial heroes Baden-Powell, Rhodes, Gordon, and Kitchener were known in their time as misogynists, celibates, or to prefer the company of young boys (Judd, Empire, 174–78).

41 Elsaesser, "Tales of Sound and Fury" 69.

42 This is also true of David Lean's Lawrence of Arabia (1962). There, too, the eponymous Lawrence shares his story with other British and Arab men of power, gaining meaning through his interactions with them rather than radiating significance to all characters and aspects of the narrative, as in the case of the protagonist in Sanders. It was also Peter O'Toole's first major role, and he did not possess the star currency he was to acquire after the film.

43 "The Drum," The Cinema 48, no. 3610 (12 May 1937): 25. In many ways The Drum can be understood as Prince Azim's story. He is the heir-apparent, unseated by his uncle's evil machinations, who stoically survives his days as a pauper. Depictions

of Sabu visually anticipate the iconic image of the familiar street thief from *The Thief of Baghdad*, shirtless and living off his wit—an image retained in the Disney productions of the *Aladdin* films in the 1990s.

44 For a narrative of how Korda and Flaherty worked together in *The Elephant Boy*, consult Rotha, *Robert J. Flaherty*.

45 Compare "New Films at a Glance," 26 to "Two Reissues," 21.

46 Britmovie, "The Drum," http://www.britmovie.co.uk/genres/drama/filmography 01/033.html (accessed 17 April 2005).

47 Peters, "Exile, Nomadism, and Diaspora," 22–24, 29–31.

48 "The Drum," *Picturegoer Weekly*, 24.

49 Ghul, like the figure of the native ally Azim, complicates binaries. As Carruthers admits to his wife, "It's the old story of the mad dreamers of this world, who are half empire builders and half gangsters. If they succeed, history books call them great." By virtue of the fact that he will not stay in the place to which he has been assigned in the imperial order of things, Ghul becomes causal to the problems propelling the film's narrative.

50 J. A. Hobson, *Imperialism*, 93.

51 The dialogue is as follows.

> AZIM: Always [tell the truth]? That will be very hard!
> CARRUTHERS: Yes, I expect it will. But promise to try, will you?
> AZIM: Tell the truth! All right. I promise.
> CARRUTHERS: That's fine.
> AZIM: But nobody in Tokot ever does!

52 Shohat, "Gender and the Culture of Empire," 54.

53 Shohat and Hansen approach the film differently in part because Shohat is less mindful of periodizing cultural shifts, as she ambitiously traces the underlying operation of orientalism across a range of Western texts. Studying Valentino's films more historically, Hansen argues that the deliberate construction of an erotic male object for female spectators exposed contraditions in the shifting role of women in post–World War I U.S. society.

54 Hansen, *Babel and Babylon*, 292.

55 Holder is a leader among the drummer boys and conducts himself with boyish swagger; at his first appearance he receives a whipping for smoking. The sequence is shown though shots of another drummer boy wincing in pain as Holder is punished.

56 Butler, *Gender Trouble*, 136.

57 Creekmur and Doty, *Out in Culture*. Consult also Doty's *Making Things Perfectly Queer* and *Flaming Classics*.

58 Chowdhry, *Colonial India and the Making of Empire Cinema*, 89. See also her sociological reading of *The Drum* in relation to the acceptance of homosexuality in Pathan culture (70–72).

59 Justin's quote is from an episode in the BBC's *Rear Window* series, "Sabu: The Elephant Boy" (Channel 4 Television, 1993).

60 The vision of torture in a wooden cage is a recurrent one and reappears in Shekhar Kapur's *The Four Feathers*.

61 Versions of *The Four Feathers*, which was based on A. E. W. Mason's 1902 novel, were filmed in 1915, 1921, and 1928 (see Richards, "Korda's Empire" for details); the most recent screen adaptation was by the Indian film director Shekhar Kapur in 2002. Karol Kulik notes in *Alexander Korda* that *The Four Feathers* was an important film for the producer because he used it as collateral to get loans to the effect of $3,600,000 from U.S. banks, including Security National Bank of Los Angeles and Bankers Trust Company of New York.

62 The scenes of suffering include Durrance and Faversham struggling in the desert sand as the blind man flails around for a gun to shoot himself; Durrance's delirious talk of his love for Ethne when he is driven half mad by thirst; and Faversham's difficult incarceration at the Kalipha's fort, where he is crushed amid a thousand natives and slurps food and water from troughs.

63 NFAI. *The Bombay Government Gazette* (7 February 1946): 7, *The Four Feathers* (ser. no. 33286). Scenes of Arab natives being whipped by white men were also curtailed.

64 I call the bodily excesses potentially regenerative to represent Bakhtin's argument that the principle of degeneration is deeply positive in Rabelais. According to Bakhtin, "The body discloses its essence as a principle of growth which exceeds its own limits only in copulation, pregnancy, childbirth, the throes of death, eating, drinking, or defecation" (*Rabelais and His World*, 26).

65 Readers may be reminded of Linda Williams's analysis of women's melodramas. Examining *Stella Dallas*, Williams notes that the iconic and institutional notion of motherhood is reinstated when the woman submits herself to suffering and devaluation for her family's sake. Williams goes on to explore the mechanisms of pleasure embedded within this patriarchal narrative structure, arguing that "these melodramas also have reading positions structured into their texts that demand a female reading competence," which relates to the "social fact of female mothering." The notion that suffering is both a primary source of pleasure in women's melodramas and a socially gendered experience is relevant to my concluding observations. (Williams, "Something Else besides a Mother," 312.)

66 Jameson, *The Political Unconscious*, 271. Jameson's analysis of Conrad's *Lord Jim* as a heterogeneous combination of modernism and premodernism and of Conrad as perhaps a postmodernist ahead of his time can be revisited by thinking of the same text as divided between imperial romance and modernism in the ways discussed in this book.

67 Renan, "What Is a Nation?" 153.

68 Ibid.

69 The idea of seeking the infinite in the minute comes from Lillian R. Furst's *Roman-*

ticism, wherein she defines English literary romanticism as a tradition in which essences are sought or imagined within the real. See her discussion of Fairchild (2).

70 Robson and Robson, *The Film Answers Back*, 174–75.

71 Harvey, *The Condition of Postmodernity*, 31. Harvey is talking about the emergence, in the interwar years, of a modernism he witnesses as heroic but reactionary and fraught with danger, as exemplified by Italian futurism (with its faith in militarization and Mussolini), Nazi Germany (with its Bauhaus-style death camps), social realism (with its mythologizing of the proletariat), and Heidegger. In imperial romance's desperate search for a mythology I see a type of heroic modernism.

six MODERNISM AND EMPIRE

1 Peter Wollen's classic essay, "The Two Avant Gardes," may be related to this observation, as it identifies opposing tendencies in U.S. and European avant-gardes, one pulling toward "purist" formal experimentation and the other toward political agendas expressed through form.

2 Summarized from Lunn, *Marxism and Modernism*. See in particular the chapter "Modernism in Comparative Perspective" (33–71).

3 Jameson, "Modernism and Imperialism," 43–69; Said, *Culture and Imperialism*, particularly the chapter "Note on Modernism" (186–90).

4 The works of Alberto Giacometti, Amedeo Modigliani, and Pablo Picasso stand out as prominent examples of modern art influenced by primitivism. For different readings of the presence of the primitive within European avant-garde and modernist cinema and art, consult Burch, "Primitivism and the Avant-Gardes"; Moore, *Savage Theory*; Perloff, "Tolerance and Taboo"; Stollery, *Alternative Empires*; and Torgovnick, *Gone Primitive*.

5 Césaire, *Discourse on Colonialism*, 36.

6 From the chapter "Production of the Archers" in James Howard's *Michael Powell* (57). The element of fantasy and artifice in the film is underscored by the fact that it was shot primarily on set.

7 Michael Walker, "Black Narcissus." Walker's essay treats the film in terms of the Freudian syndrome "the return of the repressed," arguing that this syndrome structures the horror genre and that its manifestation leads to the film's melodrama. Throughout the film there is "the sense of something terrible and/or uncontrollable coming/returning to haunt or plague the 'helpless' protagonist(s)" (10). That "something" in *Black Narcissus* is primarily the sexually repressed, according to Walker. In *Damned If You Don't* (1987) video artist Su Friedrich uses excerpts from *Black Narcissus* in a manner that dissects the relationship between the nuns and presents them as repressed lesbians. In the video, an anonymous viewer watches *Black Narcissus* on television, and the 1947 feature is re-edited to expose

it as a male-oriented narrative working to repress passionate lesbian attractions between the female nuns (Gever, "Girl Crazy").

8 Shohat and Stam, *Unthinking Eurocentrism*, 166.

9 A. L. Vargas, "The Future of British Film Writing," 161–22; Arthur Vesselo, "British Films of the Quarter," 76.

10 Vesselo, "British Films of the Quarter," 76.

11 Review of *Black Narcissus* by "T.M.P.," *The New York Times Film Review* (14 August 1947): 2197. British Film Institute.

12 "Reviews for Showmen," *Kinematograph Weekly* (24 April 1947): 27.

13 Ibid.

14 Howard, *Michael Powell*, 60.

15 Peachment, *Time Out*, 57; Combs, "Under the Wimple," 29.

16 Hoberman, Review of *Black Narcissus*, 36. The article transposes Attenborough and Gandhi.

17 Thomson, "Michael Powell, 1905–1990," 28.

18 Christie, "In the Picture," 17.

19 Segal, "Political Paranoia," 35.

20 Combs, "Under the Wimple," 29.

21 In this chapter, rather than referring solely to the rich literature in film melodrama, I am choosing to formulate a semiotic definition of both melodrama and irony because I wish to raise a set of questions about the form of melodrama in relation to the imperial mode of address: here the melodramatic and the ironic aspects are mutually constitutive and their related but oppositional forms help reconcile a past of imperial affirmations with the imminence of imperial failure.

22 Brooks, *The Melodramatic Imagination*, 199.

23 Forster, *A Passage to India*, 144, 146.

24 "The term irony ... indicates a technique of appearing to be less than one is, which in literature becomes most commonly a technique of saying as little and meaning as much as possible," states Frye, positing irony or *eiron* (the one who deprecates self) as a tragic mode in literature that is opposed to stories of the *alazon* (the one who pretends or attempts to be more than she or he is) (*Anatomy of Criticism*, 40). Interestingly, he places Conrad's protagonist Lord Jim in the latter category. In light of potential axes of similarities between Sister Clodagh as a romantic heroine and Lord Jim as a romantic hero, explored in this essay in relation to the film's conclusion, it is provocative to think of Sister Clodagh's internal progression through this film as a move from the *alazon* to the *eiron*. In other words, we may consider whether her ability to deprecate herself to Mr. Dean at the conclusion of the film draws her closer to tragic irony than to melodrama.

25 Elsaesser, "Tales of Sound and Fury," 87.

26 Lyotard, *The Postmodern Condition*, 78.

27 One of the prominent groups against imperialism in the late nineteenth century

and early twentieth was a coalition of some liberals and radicals, the Low Church, Quaker millionaires, and missionary societies. These "ethical imperialists" disapproved of wars and land grabbing, but approved of "benevolent stewardship" (MacDonald, *The Language of Empire*, 6). I mention this group to note that dividing missionary work from militarism and mercantilism hardly captures the complexity of imperial politics.

28 Hobson, *Imperialism*, 201.

29 In his analysis of *The Jewel in the Crown* Richard Dyer links the television series' operation of gender with liberalism: "There is a further sense in which *Jewel* might be seen as addressing women. This is its liberalism. A liberal position is not necessarily or exclusively feminine, but it very often is and men espousing it are often thought, at the least, unmanly" (*White*, 193). Though not the same as my argument above, there is an overlapping interest in the work gender does for politics.

30 Conrad, *Heart of Darkness*, 31.

31 The paradox is somewhat similar to the Hegelian master-slave paradigm of two entities locked in a relationship where the master has no familiarity with the surrounding realities except through the slave. The master's position is one of subjective projection and practical dependence on the slave, while the slave develops a consciousness of his (her) materiality and situation through constant interactions with it. With the collapse of this relationship, the slave is able to consolidate the familiarity with surrounding realities while the master is left without a vocation or identity.

32 This is not far from *Old Bones of the River* (Varnel, 1938), mentioned previously for its spoofing of films like *Sanders of the River*. Tibbets, who is Sanders's assistant in *Sanders*, but a lifetime member of TWIRP or Teaching of Welfare Institution for the Reformation of Pagans in *Old Bones*, discovers that the missionaries who preceded him taught compound multiplication to his forest-dwelling community. Tibbets's own lessons are just as useless because the pupils are far more knowledgeable than their teacher.

33 Framing this film as a breakdown of imperial coherence allows one to elucidate Marcia Landy's distinction between British empire films as belonging to the "genre of order" (in that they deal with violent disequilibrium and its restitution) and "a woman's film" like *Black Narcissus*, which Landy notes "seems to be a variation on the films of empire" (*British Genres*, 138, 233). I would argue that as both an empire film and a woman's film, *Black Narcissus* uses women as subjects to explore the breakdown of the genre of order.

34 The argument that the "West" produced itself as rational in relation to a sensual "East" is discussed, of course, in Edward Said's *Orientalism* and books that have followed in its wake, like Rana Kabbani's *Europe's Myths of the Orient* and Robert G. Lee's *Orientals*.

35 At this level the film is readable as a horror story, anticipating the "plasmapsychosis" of David Cronenberg's *Brood* (1979). In *Black Narcissus* invisible forces of colo-

nial place produce corporeal disfigurements when they take their toll on the imperial conscience.

36 Conrad, *Heart of Darkness*, 15.

37 Ibid., 24.

38 Ibid., 57.

39 Ibid., 69.

40 The scenes between the whites and the nonwhites continue to be dramatically divided, but they are used to comment or instigate reflection on the Europeans. Thus, when Sister Clodagh and Mr. Dean examine Kanchi with her watermelon and flowers, the dark woman's untamed sexuality is exoticized, but Kanchi is less important qua Kanchi than as an element that brings out the subtext of Clodagh and Dean's flirtation. Similarly when the young general speaks to Sister Clodagh, his naïve questions about the convent and Christ make him a buffoon, clumsy in his attempts to emulate Western ways, but his remarks are also presented as ironic comments on Sister Clodagh's own attitude toward her faith.

41 Bhabha, *The Location of Culture*, 62.

42 Freud, "The Uncanny," 219–252; Todorov, *The Fantastic*.

43 Howard, *Michael Powell*, 59. David Farrar, who played Mr. Dean, felt that *Black Narcissus* had "the right form of expression" for a talkie film and that it made judicious and cinematic use of sound (58). Mr. Dean was his favorite character among the various roles of his career.

44 Sheehan, "Black Narcissus," 37. This dominance of music over dialogue in specific segments is characteristic of Powell's cinematic style and anticipates *The Red Shoes* (1948), where the choreographed sequences are literally ballet performances in addition to being symbolic reworkings of the film's plot.

45 Brooks, *The Melodramatic Imagination*, 49.

46 Ibid., 48.

47 Brooks proposes that each dramatic form has its corresponding sense deprivation. Thus tragedy, which deals with insight, finds meaning in figurative or literal blindness. Comedy, the realm of miscommunications, deploys characters that overhear, cannot hear, or pretend not to hear. And melodrama, a form about explicit expressions, finds symbolic value in muteness. (*The Melodramatic Imagination*, 57.)

48 Godden, *Black Narcissus*, 163.

49 See chapter 5 for full quote from Dallas Bower ("British Films in the Orient," 909).

50 Mulvey, "Notes on Sirk and Melodrama," 76.

51 The film is occasionally sensitive to this. Recall the memorable shot that dissolves from Clodagh's face in Ireland, as she says, with a faraway look, "I don't want to go away. I want to stay here like this for the rest of my life," to her face in a chapel in Mopu, miles away from home.

52 Pinkney, "Modernism and Cultural Theory," 14.

53 Bersani, *The Culture of Redemption*. According to Bersani, if we were to react to tragedy as primarily moral, it could appear to be an illustration of the inherently

sacrificial possibilities of a redemptive aesthetic. Bersani argues that the moment of death (or loss of worldly power) is also the moment of self-comprehension and cognition for tragic heroes like Oedipus, Lear, Othello, and Racine's Phedre. The awareness of defect absolves the catastrophe of the defect, and self-cognition at death redeems a life of error.

54 Conrad, Heart of Darkness, 70.

55 Thomson, "Michael Powell 1905–1990," 39.

56 Conrad, Lord Jim, 246.

57 Bersani, The Culture of Redemption, 2.

58 The 1930s debates in Marxist aesthetic theory (between Lukács and Bloch, Adorno and Benjamin) over the relationship between fascism/imperialism and modernism/expressionism are worth invoking here for their ratiocinations over the social functions of modernism in totalitarian and democratic societies (see Bloch et al., Aesthetics and Politics). My theorization of the multiple aesthetic modes of empire aims to describe some of the heterogeneity and contradictions of an empire in retreat, as discussed in the introduction.

59 In Present Past Terdiman makes a similar argument about modernity. He argues that the disruption of community life by the forces of urbanization, industrialism, and capitalism, and the breakdown of conventional modes of apprehending the world lead to a lack of transparency in interpreting one's past, vocation, and behavior. This may be read as the loss of a culture's sense of place within a continuous flow of time. Modernity, according to Terdiman, is characterized by the isolation of a culture from its own history, resulting in the active creation of history as a response to this rupture in memory. The "crisis in representation" associated with modernity is an aspect of its crisis in memory.

seven HISTORICAL ROMANCES AND MODERNIST MYTHS

1 Rajadhyaksha, "India's Silent Cinema," 26.

2 Rajadhyaksha, "The Phalke Era"; Geeta Kapur, "Mythic Material in Indian Cinema"; Anuradha Kapur, "The Representation of Gods and Heroes." Note also reference to this literature in Prasad, Ideology of the Hindi Film, 18.

3 Rajadhyaksha, "India's Silent Cinema," 26. Also consult Dwyer and Patel, Cinema India, 7–63.

4 Prasad, Ideology of the Hindi Film, 75–76. Also see Eck, Darsan; Vasudevan, "The Politics of Cultural Address in a 'Transitional Cinema.' "

5 Freitag, "Vision of the Nation," 34–49. I also thank an anonymous reviewer at Duke University Press for this observation.

6 Chakravarty, National Identity in Indian Popular Cinema, 82.

7 For other discussions of a foregrounded spatial code, as opposed to the production of realism through the cause-effect chain in cinema, see Burch, Theory of Film Practice; Thompson and Bordwell, "Space and Narrative in the Films of Ozu."

8 Consult Appadurai, *Modernity at Large.*

9 Huyssen, *After the Great Divide*, vii.

10 Chakravarty, *National Identity in Indian Popular Cinema*, 117.

11 Chakravarty argues that films of the 1950s mark a "metaphoric site of displaced intellectual anxiety" in their use of realism, particularly when village life, rather than urban space, is made a persistent symbol of Indian authenticity (ibid., 85).

12 Ibid., 238.

13 Prasad, *Ideology of the Hindi Film*, 60.

14 Ibid., 50.

15 Ibid., 62.

16 Ibid., 64.

17 Julien and Mercer, "De Margin and De Center," 4.

18 Mufti, "A Greater Story-writer than God," 11.

19 Prasad, *Ideology of the Hindi Film*, 65, 67, 69. Prasad periodizes changes within the dominant film form in relation to the postcolonial Indian state's relationship to capitalist development.

20 Prasad's theory offers a good heuristic device in that it (a) differentiates between melodrama as a generic mode as opposed to its specific presence in the dominant Indian film form; (b) considers realism as the aesthetic correlative of a middle-class cinema that, by its emergence, provokes a shift in the structure of populist cinema; and (c) periodizes form as responsive to sociopolitical shifts in state structure by theorizing the relationship between realism and melodrama in the development of a bourgeois nation-state. In some ways Prasad completes his project too well: his theoretical apparatus consumes films within a machinery of internal divisions and conceptual gravity, making culture all too rationalist. The impulse derives from a turn in Marxist formalist analysis that reads aesthetics as materially connected to state and economic structures. My sympathies with this move are evident, though I accept (with Spivak) that such an analysis remains circumscribed by its primary reference to "cultural dominants." The solution may lie in attending to textual details that demonstrate the manufacture of social compromise and consensus as well as antithetical pressures. Quoting Vasudevan, "Looking further afield from the overarching system of ideological coherence, we may simultaneously explore local moments and disaggregated elements for the different stances and resources mobilized in the accession of Indian fictional processes and spectator situations to the realm of modernity. These need not be dominant elements, but that does not make them negligible" (*Making Meaning in Indian Cinema*, 24).

21 According to Prasad, this predominantly melodramatic form emerged close to India's independence and experienced a crisis in the 1970s when the delegitimation of political consensus in India during the National Emergency broke the contract between state and citizen.

22 Rajadhyaksha, "Realism, Modernism and Post-colonial Theory," 415–16.

23 Appiah, "The Postcolonial and the Postmodern," 120.

24 Kapur, *When Was Modernism*; Vasudevan, "Nationhood, Authenticity, and Realism." In analyzing Satyajit Ray's work, Vasudevan insightfully extends Kapur's detailed arguments about modern Indian art and its modes of authentication.

25 Kapur, "When Was Modernism in Indian/Third World Art?" 477, 481, 480, 482 respectively. Modernism has also been discussed in relation to the West's recognition of modernist "auteur" cinemas from the Third World, or in the context of more recent experimental cinemas in the postcolonies, by Rajadhyaksha ("Realism, Modernism, and Post-colonial Theory," 416).

26 Kapur, "When Was Modernism in Indian/Third World Art?" 475. She expands her arguments in the book *When Was Modernism*.

27 Anderson, *Imagined Communities*, 25, 24. See in particular the chapter "Cultural Roots" (9–36).

28 Chatterjee, *The Nation and Its Fragments* (see the introduction and chapters 6 and 7).

29 In Chatterjee's words, "The world is a treacherous terrain of the pursuit of material interests, where practical considerations reign supreme. It is also typically the domain of the male. The home in its essence must remain unaffected by the profane activities of the material world—and woman is its representation" (*The Nation and Its Fragments*, 120). Matching this "new meaning of the home/world [*ghar/bahir*] dichotomy with the identification of social roles by gender, we get the ideological framework within which nationalism answered the women's question" and defined itself in the process (121). At the same time, Chatterjee invites an analysis of the "specific forms that have appeared, on the one hand, in the domain defined by the hegemonic project of nationalist modernity, and on the other, in the numerous fragmented resistances to that project" (13).

30 Mufti, "A Greater Story-writer than God," 4.

31 Ibid.

32 Kapur, "Mythic Material in Indian Cinema," 81. Kapur intricately draws out two opposing operations of realism in the pre-independence *Sant Tukaram* (Marathi, Damle and Fattelal, 1936) and post-independence *Devi* (Bengali, Ray, 1960). She argues that the historical and social representation of Saint Tukaram's life also serves an emblematic function, as it condenses reformist messages against caste discrimination into an iconic presentation of Tukaram in the manner of a Gandhian nationalist praxis. Myth and realism coexist here, as they do not under the post-independence mistrust of iconicity visible in *Devi*. For the rational, progressivist Satyajit Ray, realism becomes an occasion to show myth as a "bad object," in a film about the fatal consequences of the superstitious deification of a young woman by her father-in-law. As a synopsis, this is necessarily a simplification of Kapur's more textured argument.

33 Kapur, "Mythic Material in Indian Cinema," 80.

34 Hansen, "Fallen Women, Rising Stars, New Horizons," 16.

35 Ibid.

36 Chatterjee, *The Nation and Its Fragments*, 151.

37 Ibid., 156.

38 For descriptions of each genre, their overlaps and influences, consult Rajadhyaksha and Willemen, *Encyclopaedia of Indian Cinema*, 106, 155, 219.

39 NAI, *Home (Political)*, 27/II/1929, see Amba Prasad and Tilak's case.

40 Barnouw and Krishnaswamy, *Indian Film*, 111.

41 Rajadhyaksha, "India's Silent Cinema," 34.

42 A. K. Ramanujan, *A Flowering Tree and Other Oral Tales from India*, 218. In this uncom-
pleted work, Ramanujan collects South Indian stories in the Kannada language.

43 By the previous definition, for instance, the first all-Indian feature film *Raja Harishchandra* (Phalke, 1913) would be anomalous as a male-centric story as it is about
(religious) devotion and moral fortitude. Most narratives based in the *bhakti* (devotional) tradition, such as biographies of saints (like *Tukaram*), would be more
"feminine" than "masculine" as they involve spiritual battles fought at home
rather than external quests with an alien enemy. And this is precisely my point.
Male-centered tales that find their way to popular colonial cinema cannot always
be identified as popular masculinist quest narratives in Ramanujan's sense.

44 The last statement is not by or to Hameer, but he is associated with those who
cannot abide by tyranny.

45 "The liberation [of the woman] effectively inaugurates the hugely popular convention of demure women turning into masked Western challengers who simultaneously fight for independence and yes, in the end, are revealed to be as faithful
and chaste as they 'always' were" (Rajadhyaksha, "India's Silent Cinema," 35).

46 More historicals may have depicted women in a position of physical valor than we
are aware of, given our insufficient records. For instance, we know of a silent film
The Valiant Princess a.k.a. *Rajkuvarini Ranagarjana* (Kohinoor, 1930), because it attracted the attention of censors in India. Among other deletions, reel 5 was excised
for dialogues on patriotism and duty to the country. (NFAI, *The Bombay Government
Gazette 1929–1938* [9 October 1930]: 2532, ser. no. 9506.)

47 *Report of the Indian Cinematograph Committee 1927–1928* (hereafter, ICC Report), 22.

48 J. B. H. Wadia, "I Remember, I Remember," *Cinema Vision I*, no. 1 (January 1980): 93.
See Rajadhyaksha's and Willemen's discussion of the indigenous symbols in the
film *Diamond Queen* counterbalancing its Western influence (*Encylopaedia of Indian
Cinema*, 284).

49 Gupta, *Sexuality, Obscenity, Community*, particularly chapter 2; Mufti, "A Greater
Story-writer than God," 8.

50 Kesavan, "Urdu, Awadh and the Tawaif," 247–49.

51 In addition to the texts already mentioned, consult Jyotika Virdi's *The Cinematic
ImagiNation* for a recent analysis of the family as a symbolic notation of the nation
in independent India.

52 In the 1970s and beyond, the crisis of state authority was primary negotiated
through images of rebellious masculinity, with Hindi films like *Zanzeer* (Mehra,

1973), *Deewar* (Chopra, 1974), and *Sholay* (Sippy, 1975) laying the basis for the angry male proletariat hero in conflict with representatives of state law. As M. Madhava Prasad, Vijay Mishra, Ranjani Mazumdar, and others argue, the historical shift was epitomized by the rising stardom of Amitabh Bachhan as the masculine "subaltern hero" of the proletariat, whose films variously thematized the inefficacy, betrayal, and qualified redemption of the nation-state's authority. Femininity in these films manufactured a new consent between the rebelling protelariat and the delegitimated masculine law of the state, symbolically recuperating a qualified statist doctrine for the new order (Mishra, *Bollywood Cinema*; Mazumdar, "From Subjectification to Schizophrenia"). Though a detailed analysis of this historical moment is neither relevant nor necessary here, the seventies should be marked as the second significant misalignment between state and community, the first dating back to the colonial era when the definition of a modern and national state was still in process.

53 My appeal here is not to a formal determinism but to form's responsiveness to context. It would be ridiculous to claim that the mythological or historical genre intrinsically untethers female characters from their ideological positioning within a patriarchally defined nationalism; the television serializations of the *Ramayana* and the *Mahabharatha* clearly reveal otherwise.

54 Huyssen, *After the Great Divide*, 30.

55 For a discussion of the social hierarchy of genres see Prasad, *Ideology of the Hindi Film*, 135; Kakar, "The Ties that Bind."

56 NFAI, *Saar* [plot], *Bandhan* songbook.

57 Particularly memorable are arguments between Saudamini and her prisoner Durjaya (Chandramohan). He accuses her of being dependent on an entire galley of men instead of one man as a married woman might be. She in turn derides his love for Princess Nandini, because of his presumption that a woman may love a man irrespective of his appearance or condition. Durjaya, at this point, is unkempt and chained as a slave.

58 Neepa Majumdar, *Female Stardom and Cinema in India, 1930 to 1950*, 133.

59 Hansen, "Fallen Women, Rising Stars, New Horizons," 13.

60 Ibid.

61 From her autobiography *Mi Durga Khote* as reproduced in Watve, *V. Damle and S. Fattelal*, 7.

62 Ibid.

63 Ibid., 52.

64 Consult Bahadur and Vanarase, "The Personal and Professional Problems of a Woman Performer," 21.

65 Rajadhyaksha and Willemen note that Khote's class background and her feminism "allowed her to assume different images from the conventional Sangeet Natak stereotypes," and that her acting "recalled the Talmadge sisters or Mary Pickford" (*Encyclopaedia of Indian Cinema*, 125). Sangeet Natak style combined the traditions

of Sanskrit classics and Shakespearean theater with Parsi theater and Ravi Verma paintings to produce a template for Indian film images (ibid., 205).

66 See also the special issue on V. Shantaram in *South Asian Cinema* 1, nos. 3–4 (2002).

67 Shantaram and Narwekar, *V. Shantaram*, 9.

68 Kapur, "Mythic Material in Indian Cinema," 82.

69 Ibid., 84.

70 Ibid., 89. The unity of idea and image links this representational ethos to the tradition of bhakti saints, according to Kapur. The bhakti tradition, which Kapur analogizes to Gandhian spiritualism, was part of a devotional movement (800–1700 AD) that influenced Hinduism, Islam, Sikhism, and Jainism through its saint-composers of varying religions, classes, and castes. They achieved divinity through ecstatic songs and dances that made spirituality accessible to ordinary people. See Sharma, *Bhakti and Bhakti Movement*; Mullatti, *Bhakti Movement and the Status of Women*.

71 Hansen, "Fallen Women, Rising Stars, New Horizons," 11.

72 Personal conversation with A. V. Damle, Law College Road, Pune (6 August 2000). Also see Rajadhyaksha and Willemen, *Encyclopaedia of Indian Cinema*, 214.

73 Samik Bandyopadhyay, *Indian Cinema*, 12–13.

74 The influence of European cinema's modernist and realist traditions were evident in the films produced in the late 1940s and 1950s by the Indian People's Theater Association (IPTA), a progressive group of playwrights, artists, and filmmakers informally affiliated with the Communist Party of India. Their films combined Indian folk forms and neorealist and expressionist aesthetics with socially relevant themes to create alternatives to the commercial products generated by Indian and U.S. film industries. For details see Bhatia, "Staging Resistance."

75 Rajadhyaksha and Willemen, *Encyclopaedia of Indian Cinema*, 214.

76 Kaul, *Cinema and the Indian Freedom Struggle*, 66.

77 Baburao Patel, editor of *filmindia*, refuted the claim that *Admi* was based on *Waterloo Bridge*, arguing that MGM released the film in New York on 17 May 1940 and in Bombay on 23 August 1940. Prabhat's *Admi* had already been released by this time. However, MGM's film was apparently based on a Universal film by the same name released in Bombay on 21 October 1931. (*filmindia* 6, no. 10 [October 1940]: 37–40.)

78 Rajadhyaksha and Willemen, *Encyclopaedia of Indian Cinema*, 130, 88, respectively.

79 Pal, "The Rise and Fall of Bombay Talkies," *Filmfare* (16–31 December 1983): 27.

80 For more on Osten consult Schonfeld, "Franz Osten's 'The Light of Asia.'"

81 See the following accounts: Pal, "The Rise and Fall of Bombay Talkies," *Filmfare* (16–31 December 1983): 24–28 and (1–15 January 1984): 24, 26, 27, 29; Koch, *Franz Osten's Indian Silent Films*; Barnow and Krishnaswamy, *Indian Film*, 93–103; Rajadhyaksha and Willemen, *Encyclopaedia of Indian Cinema*, 68, 183, 192.

82 Rajadhyaksha and Willemen, *Encyclopaedia of Indian Cinema*, 265.

83 Film historians Barnow and Krishnaswamy argue that Shantaram abjures his fa-

miliar realities in *Amritmanthan* and *Admi*. "By necessity Shantaram, producing in Hindi, a language foreign to him, for a huge audience he did not know and whose entertainment requirements were made known to him via distributors, statistics, and trade press, was moving into a world of quasi-realistic fantasy" (*Indian Film*, 93). As must be clear from my discussion, I find it more productive to understand Shantaram's use of multiple styles as a sign of his aspiration to address local markets while creatively engaging global styles, rather than as an unwitting error on his part.

84 Elsaesser, "Tales of Sound and Fury," 43.

85 This echoes a sentiment underscored by Moti's neighbor in the preceding scene, in which he reminds the young man of the many kinds of love in the world (like maternal and paternal love) other than romantic.

86 *filmindia* 6, no. 10 (October 1940): 39–40. This review celebrates Indian cinema's realism by emphasizing Shantaram's message of social uplift, but is less articulate about the film's stylization. Expressionist experimentation in a later IPTA film, *Neecha Nagar* (1946), similar to Shantaram's work, was reportedly considered pretentious in retrospect by the film's director Chetan Anand (according to Chakravarty, *National Identity in Indian Popular Cinema*, 92).

87 Counterpoints to the expressionist scenes in *Amritmanthan* can be found in sequences in which the young hero Madhavgupt teaches Rani Mohini about the natural charms of life in a forest, mostly recreated in a studio but intercut with documentary shots of deer and rabbits. Though *Amritmanthan* cannot be characterized as realist, these sequences demarcate themselves as "natural" within the film. The young queen, who has been misled by Rajguru, learns lessons in simplicity, poverty, and humility once she steps out of the artificial life of the palace.

88 Ghosh, "Reminiscences of a Friend from Prison"; Anil Biswas, "My Journey into the World of Music," *Cinema Vision* II, no. II (January 1983): 54–57.

89 Wadia, "Experience in Jaswantlal's Office," *Cinema Vision* I, no. I (January 1980): 95–96.

BIBLIOGRAPHY

BFI   British Film Institute
BT   Board of Trade
CO   Colonial Office
FO   Foreign Office
IOR   India Office Records, United Kingdom
MSA   Maharashtra State Archive
NAI   National Archive of India
NFAI   National Film Archive of India, Pune
NML   Nehru Memorial Library, New Delhi
PRO   Public Records Office, United Kingdom

Abel, Richard. *The Red Rooster Scare: Making Cinema American, 1900–1910.* Berkeley: University of California Press, 1999.

Achebe, Chinua. *Hopes and Impediments: Selected Essays.* New York: Anchor Books, 1990.

Afzal-Khan, Fawzia, and Kalpana Seshadri-Crooks, eds. *The Pre-occupation of Postcolonial Studies.* Durham, N.C.: Duke University Press, 2000.

Ahmad, Aijaz. "Jameson's Rhetoric of Otherness and the 'National Allegory.'" *Social Text* no. 17 (fall 1987): 3–25.

Aitken, Ian. *Film and Reform: John Grierson and the Documentary Film Movement.* London: Routledge, 1990.

Althusser, Louis. "Ideology and Ideological State Apparatus." In *Lenin and Philosophy and other Essays*. Translated by Ben Brewster, 127–86. New York: Monthly Review Press, 1971.

Altman, Rick. *Film/Genre*. London: BFI, 1999.

Anderson, Benedict. *Imagined Communities*. Rev. ed. London: Verso, 1991.

Anderson, Perry. "Modernity and Revolution." *New Left Review* 144 (March–April 1984): 96–113.

Appadurai, Arjun. *Modernity at Large: Cultural Dimensions of Globalization*. Minneapolis: University of Minnesota Press, 1996.

Appiah, Kwame Anthony. "The Postcolonial and the Postmodern." In *The Postcolonial Studies Reader*, edited by Bill Ashcroft, Gareth Griffiths, Helen Tiffin, 119–24. London: Routledge, 1995.

Arendt, Hannah. *The Origins of Totalitarianism*. New York: Harcourt, Brace and World, 1966.

Armes, Roy. *A Critical History of the British Cinema*. New York: Oxford University Press, 1978.

Arora, Poonam. " 'Imperilling the Prestige of the White Woman': Colonial Anxiety and Film Censorship in British India." *Visual Anthropology Review* 11, no. 2 (fall 1995): 36–50.

Ashby, Justine, and Andrew Higson, eds. *British Cinema, Past and Present*. London: Routledge, 2000.

Auerbach, Erich. *Mimesis: The Representation of Reality in Western Literature*. Princeton, N.J.: Princeton University Press, 2003.

Bahadur, Satish, and Shyamala Vanarase. "The Personal and Professional Problems of a Woman Performer." *Cinema Vision India* 1, no. 1 (January 1980).

Bahl, Vinay. "Situating and Rethinking Subaltern Studies for Writing Working-Class History." In *History after the Three Worlds: Post-Eurocentric Historiographies*, edited by Arif Dirlik, Vinay Bahl, and Peter Gran, 85–124. Lanham, Md.: Rowman and Littlefield, 2000.

Bakhtin, Mikhail. *Rabelais and His World*. Bloomington: Indiana University Press, 1984.

Balcon, Michael. "Rationalise!" *Sight and Sound* 9, no. 36 (winter 1940–41): 62–63.

Bandyopadhyay, Samik, ed. *Indian Cinema: Contemporary Perceptions from the Thirties*. Selected by Dhruba Gupta and Biren Das Sharma. Jamshedpur, India: Celluloid Chapter, 1993.

Barkan, Elazar, and Ronald Bush, eds. *Prehistories of the Future: The Primitivist Project and the Culture of Modernism*. Stanford, Calif.: Stanford University Press, 1995.

Barnouw, Eric, and S. Krishnaswamy. *Indian Film*. New York: Oxford University Press, 1980.

Barr, Charles. *Ealing Studios*. Berkeley: University of California Press, 1998.

Barrier, N. Gerald. *Banned: Controversial Literature and Political Control in British India, 1907–1947*. Delhi: Manohar Book Service, 1976.

Barry, Andrew, Thomas Osborne, and Nikolas Rose. *Foucault and Political Reason: Liber-*

alism, Neo-liberalism and Rationalities of Government. Chicago: University of Chicago Press, 1996.

Barthes, Roland. *Image-Music-Text*. Selected and translated by Stephen Heath. New York: Noonday Press, 1977.

———. *Mythologies*. Translated by Annette Lavers. London: Paladin, 1973.

Baskaran, S. Theodore. *The Eye of the Serpent: An Introduction to Tamil Cinema*. Madras: East West Books, 1996.

———. *The Message Bearers: The Nationalist Politics and the Entertainment Media in South India, 1880–1945*. Madras: Cre-A Publishers, 1981.

Baxter, John. *The Australian Cinema*. Sydney: Pacific Books, 1970.

Bayly, C. A. *Empire and Information: Information Gathering and Social Communication in India, 1780–1870*. New York: Cambridge University Press, 1996.

Bazin, André. *What Is Cinema?* 2 vols. Selected and translated by Hugh Gray. Berkeley: University of California Press, 1971. [vol.2 cited]

Bennett, Tony. "The Exhibitionary Complex." In *Culture/Power/History: A Reader in Contemporary Social Theory*, edited by Nicholas B. Dirks, Geoff Eley, and Sherry B. Ortner, 123–54. Princeton, N.J.: Princeton University Press, 1994.

Berman, Marshall. *All That Is Solid Melts into Air: The Experience of Modernity*. Rev. ed. New York: Penguin, 1988.

Bernstein, Matthew, and Gaylyn Studlar, eds. *Visions of the East: Orientalism in Film*. New Brunswick, N.J.: Rutgers University Press, 1997.

Bersani, Leo. *The Culture of Redemption*. Cambridge, Mass.: Harvard University Press, 1990.

Bhabha, Homi K. *The Location of Culture*. London: Routledge, 1994.

Bhatia, Nandi. "Staging Resistance: The Indian People's Theater Association." In *The Politics of Culture in the Shadow of Capital*, edited by Lisa Lowe and David Lloyd, 432–60. Durham, N.C.: Duke University Press, 1997.

Bhowmik, Someswar. *Indian Cinema, Colonial Contours*. Calcutta: Papyrus, 1995.

Biswas, Anil. "My Journey into the World of Music." *Cinema Vision* 2, no. 2 (January 1983): 57.

Bloch, Ernst, et al. *Aesthetics and Politics*. Translation edited by Ronald Taylor. Afterword by Fredric Jameson. London: Verso, 1980.

Bond, Ralph. *Monopoly: The Future of British Films*. Watford: Watford Printers, 1946.

Bower, Dallas. "British Films in the Orient." *Great Britain and the East* (24 June 1937): 909.

Bratton, Jacky, Jim Cook, and Christine Gledhill, eds. *Melodrama: Stage, Picture, Screen*. London: BFI, 1994.

Brewer, Anthony. *Marxist Theories of Imperialism: A Critical Survey*. 2nd ed. London: Routledge, 1990.

"The British Commonwealth: Case of India." *Journal of the Parliaments of the Empire* 26, no. 1 (February 1945): 49.

Brooks, Peter. *The Melodramatic Imagination: Balzac, Henry James, Melodrama, and the Mode of Excess*. Rev. ed. New Haven, Conn.: Yale University Press, 1995.

Brydon, Diana, ed. *Postcolonialism: Critical Concepts in Literary and Cultural Studies*. 5 vols. London: Routledge, 2000.

Bukharin, Nikolai. *Imperialism and World Economy*. London: Merlin, 1972.

Burch, Noël. "Primitivism and the Avant-Gardes: A Dialectical Approach." In *Narrative, Apparatus, Ideology: A Film Theory Reader*, edited by Philip Rosen, 483–506. New York: Columbia University Press, 1986.

———. *Theory of Film Practice*. New York: Praeger, 1973.

Burgoyne, Robert. *Film Nation: Hollywood Looks at U.S. History*. Minneapolis: University of Minnesota Press, 1997.

Butler, Judith. *Gender Trouble: Feminism and the Subversion of Identity*. New York: Routledge, 1999.

Cawelti, John G. *Six Gun Mystique*. Bowling Green, Ind.: Bowling Green State University Popular Press, 1984.

Césaire, Aimé. *Discourse on Colonialism*. Translated by Joan Pinkham. New York: Monthly Review Press, 1972.

Chabria, Suresh, ed. *Light of Asia: Indian Silent Cinema 1912–1934*. New Delhi: Wiley Eastern, 1994.

Chakrabarty, Dipesh. *Provincializing Europe: Postcolonial Thought and Historical Difference*. Princeton, N.J.: Princeton University Press, 2000.

Chakravarty, Sumita S. *National Identity in Indian Popular Cinema, 1947–1987*. Delhi: Oxford University Press, 1993.

Chanan, Michael. "The Emergence of an Industry." In *British Cinema History*, edited by James Curran and Vincent Porter, 39–58. Totowa, N.J.: Barnes and Noble, 1983.

Chandra, Bipan, et al. *India's Struggle for Independence*. New Delhi: Penguin Books, 1989.

Chatterjee, Partha. *Nationalist Thought and the Colonial World: A Derivative Discourse?* London: Zed Books for the United Nations University, 1986.

———. *The Nation and Its Fragments: Colonial and Postcolonial Histories*. Princeton, N.J.: Princeton University Press, 1993.

Chatterjee, Partha, and Pradeep Jeganathan, eds. *Subaltern Studies 11: Community, Gender and Violence*. New York: Columbia University Press, 2000.

Chatterjee, Partha, and Gyanendra Pandey, eds. *Subaltern Studies 7: Writings on South Asian History and Society*. Delhi: Oxford University Press, 1992.

Chowdhry, Prem. *Colonial India and the Making of Empire Cinema: Image, Ideology and Identity*. Manchester, U.K.: Manchester University Press, 2000.

Christie, Ian. "In the Picture." *Radio Times* 250, no. 3272 (9 August 1986): 17.

Churchill, Winston. *India: Speeches and an Introduction*. London: Thornton Butterworth, 1931.

———. *The River War: An Historical Account of the Reconquest of the Soudan*. New York: Carroll and Graf, 2000.

Cinematograph Films Act, 1927: Report of a Committee Appointed by the Board of Trade, Presented by the President of the Board of Trade to Parliament by Command of His Majesty. HMSO, November 1936.

"Cinematograph Films Act 1927, As Amended and Passed in the Third Reading." *The Cinema: News and Property Gazette* (17 November 1927): i–viii.

Cohn, Bernard S. *An Anthropologist Among the Historians and Other Essays.* Delhi: Oxford University Press, 1987.

———. *Colonialism and Its Forms of Knowledge: The British in India.* Princeton, N.J.: Princeton University, 1996.

Combs, Richard. "Under the Wimple." *The Listener* 116, no. 2972 (7 August 1986): 29.

Commission on Educational and Cultural Films. *The Film in National Life: Being the Report of an Enquiry Conducted by the Commission on Educational and Cultural Films into the Service which the Cinematograph May Render to Education and Social Progress.* London: George Allen and Unwin, 1932.

Comolli, Jean-Louis. "Historical Fiction: A Body Too Much." Translated by Ben Brewster. *Screen* 19, no. 2 (summer 1978): 41–53.

Conrad, Joseph. *Heart of Darkness: An Authoritative Text, Backgrounds and Sources, Criticism.* Edited by Robert Kimbrough. 3rd ed. New York: W. W. Norton, 1988.

———. *Lord Jim: Authoritative Text, Backgrounds, Sources, Criticism.* Edited by Thomas C. Moser. 2nd ed. New York: W. W. Norton, 1996.

Constantine, Stephen. " 'Bringing the Empire Alive': The Empire Marketing Board and Imperial Propaganda, 1926–33." In *Imperialism and Popular Culture*, edited by John M. MacKenzie, 192–231. Manchester, U.K.: Manchester University Press, 1986.

Creekmur, Corey K., and Alexander Doty, eds. *Out in Culture: Gay, Lesbian, and Queer Essays in Popular Culture.* Durham, N.C.: Duke University Press, 1995.

Crofts, Stephen. "Reconceptualizing National Cinema/s." *Quarterly Review of Film and Video* 14, no. 3 (1993): 49–67.

Curran, James, and Vincent Porter, eds. *British Cinema History.* Totowa, N.J.: Barnes and Noble Books, 1983.

Dahbour, Omar, and Micheline R. Ishay, eds. *The Nationalism Reader.* Atlantic Highlands, N.J.: Humanities Press, 1995.

Darwin, John. *The End of the British Empire: The Historical Debate.* Oxford, U.K.: Basil Blackwell, 1991.

Davis, Lance E., and Robert E. Huttenback. *Mammon and the Pursuit of Empire: The Political Economy of British Imperialism, 1860–1912.* Cambridge, U.K.: Cambridge University Press, 1986.

De Certeau, Michel. *The Writing of History.* Translated by Tom Conley. New York: Columbia University Press, 1988.

De Schweinitz Jr., Karl. *The Rise and Fall of British India: Imperialism as Inequality.* London: Methuen, 1983.

Desai, Jigna. *Beyond Bollywood: The Cultural Politics of South Asian Diasporic Film.* New York: Routledge, 2004.

Dickinson, Margaret, and Sarah Street. *Cinema and State: The Film Industry and the British Government, 1927–1984.* London: BFI, 1985.

Dirks, Nicholas B. *Castes of Mind: Colonialism and the Making of Modern India*. Princeton, N.J.: Princeton University Press, 2001.

———. "History as a Sign of the Modern." *Public Culture* 2, no. 2 (spring 1990): 25–32.

Dirlik, Arif. "Is There History after Eurocentrism? Globalism, Postcolonialism, and the Disavowal of History." In *History after the Three Worlds: Post-Eurocentric Historiographies*, edited by Arif Dirlik, Vinay Bahl, and Peter Gran, 25–47. Lanham, Md.: Rowman and Littlefield, 2000.

Dirlik, Arif, Vinay Bahl, and Peter Gran, eds. *History after the Three Worlds: Post-Eurocentric Historiographies*. Lanham, Md.: Rowman and Littlefield, 2000.

Dodd, Kathryn, and Philip Dodd. "Engendering the Nation: British Documentary Film, 1930–39." In *Dissolving Views: Key Writings on British Cinema*, edited by Andrew Higson, 38–50. London: Cassell, 1996.

Donald, James, Anne Friedberg, and Laura Marcus, eds. *Close Up, 1927–1933: Cinema and Modernism*. Princeton, N.J.: Princeton University Press, 1998.

Donzelot, Jacques. *The Policing of Families*. Translated by Robert Hurley. New York: Pantheon, 1979.

Doty, Alexander. *Flaming Classics: Queering the Film Canon*. New York: Routledge, 2000.

———. *Making Things Perfectly Queer: Interpreting Mass Culture*. Minneapolis: University of Minnesota, 1993.

"The Drum." *The Cinema* 62, no. 4977 (5 January 1944): 220.

"The Drum." *Film Weekly* 20, no. 495 (9 April 1938): 24.

"The Drum." *Motion Picture Herald* 131, no. 5 (30 April 1938): 46.

"The Drum." *The New Statesman and Nation* 15 (9 April 1938): 612.

"The Drum." *Picturegoer Weekly* 8, no. 368 (11 June 1938): 24.

Dwyer, Rachel, and Divia Patel. *Cinema India: The Visual Culture of Hindi Film*. New Brunswick, N.J.: Rutgers University Press, 2002.

Dwyer, Rachel, and Christopher Pinney, eds. *Pleasure and the Nation: The History, Politics and Consumption of Public Culture in India*. Delhi: Oxford University Press, 2001.

Dyer, Richard. *Heavenly Bodies: Film Stars and Society*. London: BFI, 1986.

———. *White*. London: Routledge, 1997.

Eagleton, Terry. "Pork Chops and Pineapples." *London Review of Books* 25, no. 20 (23 October 2003): 17–19.

Eagleton, Terry, Fredric Jameson, and Edward W. Said, eds. *Nationalism, Colonialism, and Literature*. Minneapolis: University of Minnesota Press, 1990.

Eck, Diana L. *Darsan: Seeing the Divine Image in India*. 2nd ed. New York: Columbia University Press, 1996.

Eggar, Arthur, and G. R. Rajagopaul. *The Laws of India and Burma*. Calcutta: Butterworth, 1929.

Eisner, Lotte H. *The Haunted Screen*. Berkeley: University of California Press, 1973.

Ellis, Jack C. *The Documentary Idea: A Critical History of English-Language Documentary Film and Video*. Englewood Cliffs, N.J.: Prentice Hall, 1989.

Elsaesser, Thomas. "Tales of Sound and Fury: Observations on the Family Melodrama."

In *Imitations of Life: A Reader on Film and Television Melodrama*, edited by Marcia Landy, 68–91. Detroit: Wayne State University Press, 1991.

Fanon, Frantz. *The Wretched of the Earth*. Translated by Constance Farrington. New York: Grove Press, 1963.

The Film in Colonial Development: A Report of a Conference. London: BFI, 1948.

Foner, Philip S., ed. *Paul Robeson Speaks: Writings, Speeches, Interviews, 1918–1974*. New York: Brunner/Mazel Publishers, 1978.

Forster, E. M. *A Passage to India*. Rev. ed. Harmondsworth, U.K.: Penguin Books, 1984.

Foucault, Michel. *The Archaeology of Knowledge and The Discourse on Language*. Translated by A. M. Sheridan Smith. New York: Pantheon Books, 1972.

———. "Governmentality." In *The Foucault Effect: Studies in Governmentality with Two Lectures by and an Interview with Michel Foucault*, edited by Graham Burchell, Colin Gordon, and Peter Miller, 87–104. Chicago: University of Chicago Press, 1991.

———. *The History of Sexuality*. Translated by Robert Hurley. New York: Vintage, 1978.

———. "History of Systems of Thought." In *Language, Counter-Memory, Practice: Selected Essays and Interviews by Michel Foucault*, edited by Donald F. Bouchard, translated by Donald F. Bouchard and Sherry Simon, 199–204. Ithaca, N.Y.: Cornell University Press, 1977.

———. *Power*. Vol. 3 of *Essential Works of Foucault, 1954–1984*. Edited by James D. Faubion. New York: New Press, 2000.

Freitag, Sandria B. "Vision of the Nation." In *Pleasure and the Nation: The History, Politics and Consumption of Public Culture in India*, edited by Rachel Dwyer and Christopher Pinney. Delhi: Oxford University Press, 2001.

Freud, Sigmund. "The Uncanny." In *An Infantile Neurosis and Other Works (1917–1919)*, 219–52. Vol. 17 of *The Standard Edition of the Complete Psychological Works of Sigmund Freud*. Translated from the German under the general editorship of James Strachey, in collaboration with Anna Freud, assisted by Alix Strachey and Alan Tyson. London: Hogarth, 1953.

Friedberg, Anne. "Introduction: Reading *Close Up*, 1927–1933." In *Close Up, 1927–1933: Cinema and Modernism*, edited by James Donald, Anne Friedberg, and Laura Marcus, 1–26. Princeton, N.J.: Princeton University Press, 1998.

Friedman, Lester, ed. *Fires Were Started: British Cinema and Thatcherism*. Minneapolis: University of Minnesota Press, 1993.

Frye, Northrop. *Anatomy of Criticism: Four Essays*. Princeton, N.J.: Princeton University Press, 1957.

———. *The Secular Scripture: A Study of the Structure of Romance*. Cambridge, Mass.: Harvard University Press, 1976.

Fulford, Tim, and Peter J. Kitson, eds. *Romanticism and Colonialism: Writing and Empire, 1780–1830*. Cambridge, U.K.: Cambridge University Press, 1998.

Furst, Lilian R. *Romanticism*. London: Methuen, 1969.

Gaines, Jane. "White Privilege and Looking Relations: Race and Gender in Feminist Film Theory." *Screen* 29, no. 4 (autumn 1988): 12–27.

Garga, B. D. "A New Look at an Old Report." *Cinema Vision* 1, no. 1 (January 1980): 67–70.

————. *So Many Cinemas: The Motion Picture in India*. Bombay: Eminence Design, 1996.

Gellner, Ernest. *Nations and Nationalism*. Ithaca, N.Y.: Cornell University Press, 1983.

Gever, Martha. "Girl Crazy: Lesbian Narratives in *She Must be Seeing Things* and *Damned if You Don't*." *The Independent* 11, no. 6 (July 1988): 14–18.

Ghosh, Satyavrata. "Reminiscences of a Friend from Prison." *Cinema Vision* 2, no. 2 (January 1983): 54–56.

Gledhill, Christine. "The Melodramatic Field: An Investigation." In *Home Is Where the Heart Is: Studies in Melodrama and the Woman's Film*, edited by Christine Gledhill, 5–39. London: BFI, 1987.

————, ed. *Home Is Where the Heart Is: Studies in Melodrama and the Woman's Film*. London: BFI, 1987.

Gledhill, Christine, and Linda Williams, eds. *Reinventing Film Studies*. London: Arnold, 2000.

Godden, Rumer. *Black Narcissus*. Boston: Little, Brown, 1939.

Goswami, Manu. *Producing India: From Colonial Economy to National Space*. Chicago: University of Chicago Press, 2004.

Grant, Barry Keith. *Film Genre Reader 3*. Austin: University of Texas Press, 2003.

Green, Martin. *Dreams of Adventure, Deeds of Empire*. New York: Basic Books, 1979.

Grewal, Inderpal, and Caren Kaplan, eds. *Scattered Hegemonies: Postmodernity and Transnational Feminist Practices*. Minneapolis: University of Minnesota Press, 1994.

Grierson, John. "The Film and Primitive Peoples." *Film in Colonial Development*. Reprint, "The Film and the Commonwealth," *Sight and Sound* 17, no. 65 (spring 1948): 3.

Grindon, Leger. *Shadows on the Past: Studies in the Historical Fiction Film*. Philadelphia: Temple University Press, 1994.

Guha, Ranajit. *Elementary Aspects of Peasant Insurgency in Colonial India*. Delhi: Oxford University Press, 1983.

————. "On Some Aspects of the Historiography of Colonial India." In *Selected Subaltern Studies*, edited by Ranajit Guha and Gayatri Chakravorty Spivak. New York: Oxford University Press, 1988.

Guha, Ranajit, and Gayatri Chakravorty Spivak, eds. *Selected Subaltern Studies*. New York: Oxford University Press, 1988.

Gunning, Tom. *D. W. Griffith and the Origins of American Narrative Film: The Early Years at Biograph*. Urbana: University of Illinois Press, 1994.

Gupta, Charu. *Sexuality, Obscenity, Community: Women, Muslims, and the Hindu Public in Colonial India*. New York: Palgrave, 2002.

Habermas, Jürgen. "The Public Sphere: An Encyclopedia Article." *New German Critique* no. 3 (fall 1974): 49–55.

Hansen, Miriam. *Babel and Babylon: Spectatorship in American Silent Film*. Cambridge, Mass.: Harvard University Press, 1991.

————. "Fallen Women, Rising Stars, New Horizons: Shanghai Silent Film as Vernacular Modernism." *Film Quarterly* 54, no. 1 (fall 2000): 10–22.

Hardt, Michael, and Antonio Negri. *Empire*. Cambridge, Mass.: Harvard University Press, 2000.

Harlow, Barbara, and Mia Carter, eds. *Imperialism and Orientalism: A Documentary Sourcebook*. Malden, Mass.: Blackwell, 1999.

Hartog, Simon. "State Protection of a Beleaguered Industry." In *British Cinema History*, edited by James Curran and Vincent Porter, 59–73. Totowa, N.J.: Barnes and Noble, 1983.

Harvey, David. *The Condition of Postmodernity: An Enquiry into the Origins of Cultural Change*. Oxford: Blackwell, 1989.

———. *The New Imperialism*. Oxford: Oxford University Press, 2003.

Hasan, Zoya, ed. *Forging Identities: Gender, Communities and the State in India*. Boulder, Colo.: Westview Press, 1994.

Havighurst, Alfred F. *Britain in Transition: The Twentieth Century*. Chicago: University of Chicago Press, 1979.

Hayward, Susan. *French National Cinema*. New York: Routledge, 1993.

Hegel, G. W. F. "The Philosophy of Right." In *The Nationalism Reader*, edited by Omar Dahbour and Micheline R. Ishay, 71–78. Atlantic Highlands, N.J.: Humanities Press, 1995.

———. *Reason in History: A General Introduction to the Philosophy of History*. Translated by Robert S. Hartman. New York: Liberal Arts Press, 1953.

Higson, Andrew. *Waving the Flag: Constructing a National Cinema in Britain*. Oxford: Clarendon Press, 1995.

———, ed. *Dissolving Views: Key Writings on British Cinema*. London: Cassell, 1996.

Higson, Andrew, and Richard Maltby, eds. *"Film Europe" and "Film America": Cinema, Commerce and Cultural Exchange, 1920–1939*. Exeter, U.K.: University of Exeter Press, 1999.

Hill, John, and Pamela Church-Gibson, eds. *The Oxford Guide to Film Studies*. Oxford: Oxford University Press, 1998.

Hjort, Mette, and Scott MacKenzie, eds. *Cinema and Nation*. London: Routledge, 2000.

Hoberman, J. Review of *Black Narcissus*. *The Village Voice* (2 April 1985): 36.

Hobsbawm, Eric. *The Age of Empire: 1875–1914*. New York: Random House, 1989.

———. *The Age of Extremes: The Short Twentieth Century, 1914–1991*. London: Abacus, 1991.

———. *Nations and Nationalism since 1780: Programme, Myth, Reality*. 2nd ed. Cambridge, U.K.: Cambridge University Press, 1992.

Hobsbawm, Eric, and Terrance Ranger. *The Invention of Tradition*. Cambridge, U.K.: Cambridge University Press, 1992.

Hobson, John A. *Imperialism: A Study*. Ann Arbor: University of Michigan Press, 1965.

Holmes, Winifred. "British Films and the Empire." *Sight and Sound* 5, no. 19 (autumn 1936): 72–74.

Hopkirk, Peter. *The Great Game: On Secret Service in High Asia*. London: Oxford University Press, 2001.

Howard, James. *Michael Powell*. London: B.T. Batsford, 1996.

Hroch, Miroslav. *Social Preconditions of National Revival in Europe: A Comparative Analysis of* the Social Composition of Patriotic Groups among the Smaller European Nations. Cambridge, U.K.: Cambridge University Press, 1985.

Huyssen, Andreas. After the Great Divide: Modernism, Mass Culture, Postmodernism. Bloomington: Indiana University Press, 1986.

Jadhav, B. V. "Indian Film Industry: History of Its Growth: Government Inaction X-rayed." Varieties Weekly 3, no. 29 (23 April 1933): 5–13.

Jaikumar, Priya. "Hollywood and the Multiple Constituencies of Colonial India." In Hollywood Abroad: Audiences and Cultural Exchange, edited by Richard Maltby and Melvyn Stokes, 78–98. London: BFI, 2005.

Jameson, Fredric. The Geopolitical Aesthetic: Cinema and Space in the World System. Bloomington: Indiana University Press, 1995.

———. "Modernism and Imperialism." In Nationalism, Colonialism, and Literature, edited by Terry Eagleton, Fredric Jameson, and Edward W. Said, 43–66. Minneapolis: University of Minnesota Press, 1990.

———. The Political Unconscious: Narrative as a Socially Symbolic Act. Ithaca, N.Y.: Cornell University Press, 1981.

———. Signatures of the Visible. New York: Routledge, 1992.

Jameson, Fredric, and Masao Miyoshi, eds. The Cultures of Globalization. Durham, N.C.: Duke University Press, 1998.

Jarvie, Ian C. "International Film Trade: Hollywood and the British Market." Historical Journal of Film, Radio and Television 3, no. 2 (1983): 161–69.

Jayawardena, Kumari. Feminism and Nationalism in the Third World. London: Zed Books, 1986.

Jha, Bagishwar, ed. Indian Motion Picture Almanac. Calcutta: Shot Publications, 1986.

Judd, Denis. Empire: The British Imperial Experience from 1765 to the Present. London: Phoenix Press, 2001.

Julien, Isaac, and Kobena Mercer. "De Margin and De Center." Screen 29, no. 4 (autumn 1988): 2–10.

Kabbani, Rana. Europe's Myths of the Orient. Bloomington: Indiana University Press, 1986.

Kaes, Anton. From Hitler to Heimat: The Return of History as Film. Cambridge, Mass.: Harvard University Press, 1992.

Kakar, Sudhir. "The Ties that Bind: Family Relationships in the Mythology of Hindi Cinema." India International Center Quarterly 8, no. 1 (March 1980): 11–21.

Kapur, Anuradha. "The Representation of Gods and Heroes: Parsi Mythological Drama of the Early Twentieth Century." Journal of Arts and Ideas nos. 23/24 (January 1993): 85–107.

Kapur, Geeta. "Mythic Material in Indian Cinema." Journal of Arts and Ideas nos. 14/15 (July–December 1987): 79–108.

———. When Was Modernism: Essays on Contemporary Cultural Practice in India. Delhi: Tulika, 2000.

———. "When Was Modernism in Indian/Third World Art?" South Atlantic Quarterly 92, no. 3 (summer 1993): 473–514.

Kaul, Gautam. *Cinema and the Indian Freedom Struggle*. New Delhi: Sterling Publishers, 1998.

Kaviraj, Sudipto. "The Imaginary Institution of India." In *Subaltern Studies 7: Writings on South Asian History and Society*, edited by Partha Chatterjee and Gyanendra Pandey, 1–39. Delhi: Oxford University Press, 1992.

Kent, John. *British Imperial Strategy and the Origins of the Cold War, 1944–49*. Leicester, U.K.: Leicester University Press, 1993.

Kesavan, Mukul. "Urdu, Awadh and the *Tawaif*: The Islamicate Roots of Hindi Cinema." In *Forging Identities: Gender, Communities and the State in India*, edited by Zoya Hasan, 244–57. Boulder, Colo.: Westview Press, 1994.

Kipling, Rudyard. *Gunga Din and Other Favorite Poems*. New York: Dover Publications, 1990.

Kitses, Jim. *Horizons West*. Bloomington: Indiana University Press, 1969.

Klein, Christina. *Cold War Orientalism: Asia in the Middlebrow Imagination, 1945–1961*. Berkeley: University of California Press, 2003.

Kleinhans, Chuck. "Notes on Melodrama and the Family under Capitalism." In *Imitations of Life: A Reader on Film and Television*, edited by Marcia Landy, 197–204. Detroit: Wayne State University Press, 1991.

Koch, Gerhard, ed., comp., trans. *Franz Osten's Indian Silent Films*. New Delhi: Max Müller Bhavan, 1983.

Kulik, Karol. *Alexander Korda: The Man Who Could Work Miracles*. New Rochelle, New York: Arlington House, 1975.

Landy, Marcia. *British Genres: Cinema and Society, 1930–1960*. Princeton, N.J.: Princeton University Press, 1991.

———, ed. *Imitations of Life: A Reader on Film and Television Melodrama*. Detroit: Wayne State University Press, 1991.

Lapworth, Charles. "Production and the Exhibitor." *Kinematograph Weekly* (6 August 1925): 32.

———. "Rival Remedies: What Can the Trade Make of the FBI's Memorandum?" *Kinematograph Weekly* (6 August 1925): 27.

Lee, Robert G. *Orientals: Asian Americans in Popular Culture*. Philadelphia: Temple University Press, 2000.

Lenin, V. I. *Imperialism: The Highest Stage of Capitalism: A Popular Outline*. New York: International Publishers, 1939.

Lewis, Justin, and Toby Miller, ed. *Critical Cultural Policy Studies: A Reader*. Malden, Mass.: Blackwell, 2003.

Liu, Lydia. "The Female Body and Nationalist Discourse: The Field of Life and Death Revisted." In *Scattered Hegemonies*, edited by Inderpal Grewal and Caren Kaplan, 37–62. Minneapolis: University of Minnesota Press, 1991.

Lotringer, Sylvere, and Christian Marazzi, ed. *Italy: Autonomia. Post Political Politics*. New York: Semiotext(e), 1980.

Low, Rachael. *Film Making in 1930s Britain*. London: George Allen and Unwin, 1985.

Lowe, Lisa, and David Lloyd, eds. *The Politics of Culture in the Shadow of Capital.* Durham, N.C.: Duke University Press, 1997.

Lukács, Georg. *Essays on Realism.* Edited by Rodney Livingston. Translated by David Fernbach. Cambridge, Mass: MIT Press, 1981.

Lumley, Robert. *States of Emergency: Cultures of Revolt in Italy from 1968 to 1978.* New York: Verso, 1990.

Lunn, Eugene. *Marxism and Modernism: A Historical Study of Lukács, Brecht, Benjamin and Adorno.* Berkeley: University of California Press, 1982.

Lyotard, Jean-François. *The Postmodern Condition: A Report on Knowledge.* Translated by Geoff Bennington and Brian Massumi. Minneapolis: University of Minnesota Press, 1984.

MacCabe, Colin. "Realism and the Cinema: Notes on Some Brechtian Theses." *Screen* 15, no. 2 (1974): 7–27.

———. "Theory and Film: Principles of Realism and Pleasure." In *Narrative, Apparatus, Ideology: A Film Theory Reader,* edited by Philip Rosen, 179–97. New York: Columbia University Press, 1986.

MacCaulay, Thomas Babington. "Minute on Indian Education" (1835). In *Imperialism and Orientalism: A Documentary Sourcebook,* edited and introduced by Barbara Harlow and Mia Carter, 56–62. Malden, Mass.: Blackwell, 1999.

MacDonald, Robert H. *The Language of Empire: Myths and Metaphors of Popular Imperialism, 1880–1918.* Manchester, U.K.: Manchester University Press, 1994.

MacKenzie, John M. "In Touch with the Infinite." In *Imperialism and Popular Culture,* edited by John M. MacKenzie, 163–91. Manchester, U.K.: Manchester University Press, 1986.

———, ed. *Imperialism and Popular Culture.* Manchester, U.K.: Manchester University Press, 1986.

MacPherson, Don, and Paul Willemen, eds. *Traditions of Independence: British Cinema in the Thirties.* London: BFI, 1980.

Majumdar, Neepa. *Female Stardom and Cinema in India, 1930 to 1950.* Ph.D. diss., Indiana University, 2002.

Makdisi, Saree. *Romantic Imperialism: Universal Empire and the Culture of Modernity.* New York: Cambridge University Press, 1998.

Maley, William. *The Afghanistan Wars.* London: Palgrave MacMillian, 2002.

Maltby, Richard, and Melvyn Stokes, eds. *Hollywood Abroad: Audiences and Cultural Exchange.* London: BFI, 2005.

Mani, Lata. *Contentious Traditions: The Debate on Sati in Colonial India.* Berkeley: University of California Press, 1998.

Manto, Saadat Hasan. *Stars from Another Sky: The Bombay Film World of the 1940s.* New Delhi: Penguin Books, 1998.

Marx, Karl. "The British Rule in India." In *Karl Marx on Colonialism and Modernization: His Despatches and Other Writings on China, India, Mexico, the Middle East and North Africa,* ed. Shlomo Avineri, 88–95. New York: Anchor Books, 1969.

Mazumdar, Ranjani. "From Subjectification to Schizophrenia." In *Making Meaning in Indian Cinema*, edited by Ravi S. Vasudevan, 238–66. Delhi: Oxford University Press, 2001.

Mazzini, Giuseppe. "The Duties of Man." In *The Nationalism Reader*, edited by Omar Dahbour and Micheline R. Ishay, 87–97. Atlantic Highlands, N.J.: Humanities Press, 1995.

McClintock, Anne. *Imperial Leather: Race, Gender and Sexuality in the Colonial Contest.* New York: Routledge, 1995.

Mehta, Uday Singh. *Liberalism and Empire: A Study in Nineteenth-Century British Liberal Thought.* Chicago: University of Chicago Press, 1999.

Merck, Mandy, ed. *The Sexual Subject: A Screen Reader in Sexuality.* London: Routledge, 1992.

Mill, John Stuart. "Considerations on Representative Government." In *The Nationalism Reader*, edited by Omar Dahbour and Micheline R. Ishay, 98–107. Atlantic Highlands, N.J.: Humanities Press, 1995.

Miller, Toby, et al. *Global Hollywood.* London: BFI, 2001.

Milton, Meyrick. *Concerning Legislation to Encourage Empire Films.* London: Austin Leigh, 1927.

Mishra, Vijay. *Bollywood Cinema: Temples of Desire.* New York: Routledge University Press, 2001.

Miyoshi, Masao. "A Borderless World? From Colonialism to Transnationalism and the Decline of the Nation-State." In *Postcolonialism: Critical Concepts in Literary and Cultural Studies*, vol. 5, edited by Diana Brydon, 78–106. London: Routledge, 2000.

Moore, Rachel O. *Savage Theory: Cinema as Modern Magic.* Durham, N.C.: Duke University Press, 2000.

Morley, David. "EurAm, Modernity, Reason, and Alterity: Or, Postmodernism, the Highest Stage of Cultural Imperialism?" In *Stuart Hall: Critical Dialogues in Cultural Studies*, edited by David Morley and Kuan-Hsing Chen, 326–60. New York: Routledge, 1996.

Morley, David, and Kuan-Hsing Chen, eds. *Stuart Hall: Critical Dialogues in Cultural Studies.* New York: Routledge, 1996.

Morson, Gary Saul, and Caryl Emerson. *Mikhail Bakhtin: Creation of a Prosaics.* Stanford, Calif.: Stanford University Press, 1990.

Mufti, Aamir. "A Greater Story-writer than God: Genre, Gender and Minority in Late Colonial India." In *Community, Gender and Violence: Subaltern Studies 11*, edited by Partha Chatterjee and Pradeep Jeganathan, 1–36. New York: Columbia University Press, 2000.

Mullatti, Leela. *The Bhakti Movement and the Status of Women: A Case Study of Virasaivism.* New Delhi: Abhinav Publications, 1989.

Mulvey, Laura. "Notes on Sirk and Melodrama." In *Home Is Where the Heart Is: Studies in Melodrama and the Woman's Film*, edited by Christine Gledhill, 75–79. London: BFI, 1987.

————. "Visual Pleasure and Narrative Cinema." In *Narrative, Apparatus, Ideology: A Film Theory Reader*, edited Philip Rosen, 198–209. New York: Columbia, 1986.

Nadkarni, Dnyaneshwar. "A Painter Called Baburao." *Cinema Vision India* 1, no. 1 (January 1980): 39–43.

Naficy, Hamid, ed. *Home, Exile, Homeland: Film, Media, and the Politics of Place*. New York: Routledge, 1999.

Nairn, Tom. *The Break-up of Britain: Crisis and Neo-Nationalism*. London: NLB, 1977.

Negri, Antonio. *Marx beyond Marx: Lessons on the Grundrisse*. New York: Autonomedia, 1991.

"New Films at a Glance." *Kinematograph Weekly* (7 April 1938): 26.

Niranjana, Tejaswini. *Siting Translation: History, Post-structuralism, and the Colonial Context*. Berkeley: University of California Press, 1992.

Niranjana, Tejaswini, P. Sudhir, and Vivek Dhareshwar, eds. *Interrogating Modernity: Culture and Colonialism in India*. Calcutta: Seagull, 1993.

O'Regan, Tom. *Australian National Cinema*. London: Routledge, 1996.

O'Regan, Tom, and Brian Shoesmith, eds. *History on/and/in Film*. Perth: History and Film Association of Australia, 1987.

Pal, Colin. "The Rise and Fall of Bombay Talkies." *Filmfare* (16–31 December 1983): 24–28 and (1–15 January 1984): 24, 26–27, 29.

Palmer, Norman D., and Howard C. Perkins. *International Relations: The World Community in Transition*. Boston: Houghton Mifflin, 1969.

Pandey, Gyanendra. "In Defence of the Fragment: Writing about Hindu-Muslim Riots in India Today." *Economic and Political Weekly* 26, nos. 11–12 (March 1991): 559–72.

Parry, Benita. "Problems in Current Theories of Colonial Discourse." In *Postcolonialism: Critical Concepts in Literary and Cultural Studies*, vol. 2, edited by Diana Brydon, 66–81. London: Routledge, 2000.

Peachment, Chris. *Time Out* no. 802 (2 January 1986): 57.

Pendakur, Manjunath. *Canadian Dreams and American Control: The Political Economy of the Canadian Film Industry*. Detroit: Wayne State University Press, 1990.

Perloff, Marjorie. "Tolerance and Taboo: Modernist Primitivism and Postmodernist Pieties." In *Prehistories of the Future: The Primitivist Project and the Culture of Modernism*, edited by Elazar Barkan and Ronald Bush, 339–54. Stanford, Calif.: Stanford University Press, 1995.

Peters, John Durham. "Exile, Nomadism, and Diaspora: The Stakes of Mobility in the Western Canon." In *Home, Exile, Homeland: Film, Media, and the Politics of Place*, edited by Hamid Naficy, 17–41. New York: Routledge, 1999.

Pinkney, Tony. "Modernism and Cultural Theory." In *Politics of Modernism: Against the New Conformists*, by Raymond Williams, 1–29. London: Verso, 1989.

Polan, Dana. "Inexact Science: Complexity and Contradiction in Roland Barthes's 'Classic Semiology.'" *Yale Journal of Criticism* 14, no. 2 (2001): 453–62.

Prakash, Gyan. "Subaltern Studies as Postcolonial Criticism." *American Historical Review* 99, no. 5 (December 1994): 1475–90.

———. "Who's Afraid of Postcoloniality?" *Social Text* no. 49 (winter 1996): 187–203.

Prasad, M. Madhava. *Ideology of the Hindi Film: A Historical Construction*. Delhi: Oxford University Press, 1998.

Premchand, Manek. *Yesterday's Melodies, Today's Memories*. Mumbai, India: Jharna Books, 2003.

Proceedings of the First Session of the Indian Motion Picture Congress and Other Sectional Conferences. Bombay: H. Divakar, Bombay Radio Press, 1939.

Pronay, Nicholas, and D. W. Spring, eds. *Propaganda, Politics and Film 1918–45*. London: Macmillan, 1982.

Rabinowitz, Paula. "Wreckage upon Wreckage: History, Documentary and the Ruins of Memory." *History and Theory* 36, no. 4: 119–37.

Radhakrishnan, R. "Postmodernism and the Rest of the World." In *The Pre-Occupation of Postcolonial Studies*, edited by Fawzia Apzal-Khan and Kalpana Seshadri-Crooks, 37–70. Durham, N.C.: Duke University Press, 2000.

Rajadhyaksha, Ashish. "The 'Bollywoodization' of the Indian Cinema: Cultural Nationalism in a Global Arena." *Inter-Asia Cultural Studies* 4, no. 1 (2003): 25–39.

———. "Indian Cinema." In *The Oxford Guide to Film Studies*, edited by John Hill and Pamela Church-Gibson, 535–42. Oxford: Oxford University Press, 1998.

———. "India's Silent Cinema: A Viewer's View." In *Light of Asia: Indian Silent Cinema 1912–1934*, edited by Suresh Chabria, 25–40. New Delhi: Wiley Eastern, 1994.

———. "The Phalke Era: Conflict of Traditional Form and Modern Technology." In *Interrogating Modernity: Culture and Colonialism in India*, edited by Tejaswini Niranjana, P. Sudhir, and Vivek Dhareshwar, 47–82. Calcutta: Seagull, 1993.

———. "Realism, Modernism and Post-colonial Theory." In *The Oxford Guide to Film Studies*, edited by John Hill and Pamela Church-Gibson, 415–25. Oxford: Oxford University Press, 1998.

Rajadhyaksha, Ashish, and Paul Willemen. *Encyclopaedia of Indian Cinema*. New rev. ed. London: BFI, 1999.

Ramanujan, A. K. *A Flowering Tree and Other Oral Tales from India*. New Delhi: Penguin, 1997.

Renan, Ernest. "What Is a Nation?" In *The Nationalism Reader*, edited by Omar Dahbour and Micheline R. Ishay, 143–53. Atlantic Highlands, N.J.: Humanities Press, 1995.

Renov, Michael. "Towards a Poetics of Documentary." In *Theorizing Documentary*, edited by Michael Renov, 12–36. New York: Routledge, 1993.

Richards, Jeffrey. *The Age of the Dream Palace: Cinema and Society in Britain 1930–39*. London: Routledge and Kegan Paul, 1984.

———. "Boys Own Empire: Feature Films and Imperialism in the 1930s." In *Imperialism and Popular Culture*, edited by John M. MacKenzie, 140–64. Manchester, U.K.: Manchester University Press, 1986.

———. *Films and British National Identity: From Dickens to Dad's Army*. Manchester, U.K.: Manchester University Press, 1997.

———. *Imperialism and Music: Britain 1876–1953*. Manchester, U.K.: Manchester University Press, 2001.

————. "Korda's Empire: Politics and Film in *Sanders of the River*, *The Drum* and *The Four Feathers*." *Australian Journal of Screen Theory* nos. 5–6 (January–July 1979): 122–37.

————. "Patriotism with Profit: British Imperial Cinema in the 1930s." In *British Cinema History*, edited by James Curran and Vincent Porter, 245–56. Totowa, N.J.: Barnes and Noble, 1983.

————. *Visions of Yesterday*. London: Routledge and Kegan Paul, 1973.

Richardson, Alan, and Sonia Hofkosh, eds. *Romanticism, Race, and Imperial Culture, 1780–1834*. Bloomington: Indiana University Press, 1996.

Robeson, Paul. *Paul Robeson Speaks: Writings, Speeches, Interviews, 1918–1974*. Edited with an introduction and notes by Philip S. Foner. New York: Brunner/Mazel, 1978.

Robson, Emanuel W., and Mary Major Robson. *The Film Answers Back: An Historical Appreciation of the Cinema*. London: John Lane, 1939.

Rollins, Peter C., ed. *Hollywood as Historian: American Film in a Cultural Context*. Lexington: University Press of Kentucky, 1983.

Rosen, Philip, ed. *Narrative, Apparatus, Ideology: A Film Theory Reader*. New York: Columbia University Press, 1986.

Rosenstone, Robert A., ed. *Revisioning History: Film and the Construction of a New Past*. Princeton, N.J.: Princeton University Press, 1995.

Rotha, Paul. "Films of the Quarter." *Sight and Sound* 3, no. 11 (autumn 1934): 115–17.

————. *Robert J. Flaherty: A Biography*. Edited by Jay Ruby. Philadelphia: University of Pennsylvania Press, 1983.

"Rt. Hon. A. Creech Jones' Opening Address." In *The Film in Colonial Development: A Report of a Conference*. London: BFI, 1948.

Said, Edward W. *Culture and Imperialism*. New York: Vintage Books, 1994.

————. *Orientalism*. London: Routledge and Kegan Paul, 1978.

Sassen, Saskia. *Globalization and Its Discontents: Essays on the New Mobility of People and Money*, foreword by K. Anthony Appiah. New York: New Press, 1998.

Schlesinger, Philip. "On National Identity: Some Conceptions and Misconceptions Criticised." *Social Science Information* 26, no. 2 (June 1987): 219–64.

Schonfeld, Carl-Erdmann. "Franz Osten's 'The Light of Asia': A German-Indian Film of Prince Buddha—1926." *Historical Journal of Film, Radio and Television* 15, no. 4 (October 1995), 555–61.

Segal, Clancy. "Political Paranoia." *The Listener* 115, no. 2942 (9 January 1986): 35.

Shantaram, Kiran, with Sanjit Narwekar. *V. Shantaram: The Legacy of the Royal Lotus*. New Delhi: Rupa, 2003.

Shapiro, Ann-Louise. "How Real is the Reality in Documentary Film," a conversation with Jill Godmilow. *History and Theory* 36, no. 4: 80–101.

————. "Whose (Which) History Is It Anyway?" *History and Theory* 36, no. 4: 1–3.

Sharma, Krishna. *Bhakti and the Bhakti Movement: A New Perspective*. New Delhi: Munshiram Manoharlal, 2002.

Sheehan, Henry. "Black Narcissus, 1947." *Film Comment* 26, no. 3 (May/June 1990): 37.

Shoesmith, Brian. "From Monopoly to Commodity: The Bombay Studios in the 1930s."

In *History on/and/in Film*, edited by Tom O'Regan and Brian Shoesmith, 68–75. Perth: History and Film Association of Australia, 1987.

Shohat, Ella. "Gender and the Culture of Empire: Toward a Feminist Ethnography of the Cinema." In *Visions of the East: Orientalism in Film*, edited by Matthew Bernstein and Gaylyn Studlar, 19–66. New Brunswick, N.J.: Rutgers University Press, 1997.

———. "Notes on the 'Post-Colonial.' " In *The Pre-occupation of Postcolonial Studies*, edited by Fawzia Afzal-Khan and Kalpana Seshadri-Crooks, 126–39. Durham: Duke University Press, 2000.

Shohat, Ella, and Robert Stam. *Unthinking Eurocentrism: Multiculturalism and the Media*. London: Routledge, 1994.

Slotkin, Richard. *Regeneration through Violence: The Mythology of the American Frontier, 1600–1860*. Middletown, Conn: Wesleyan University Press, 1973.

Smith, Anthony D. *Theories of Nationalism*. 2nd ed. New York: Holmes and Meier, 1983.

Smyth, Rosaleen. "The British Colonial Film Unit and Sub-Saharan Africa, 1939–1945." *Historical Journal of Film, Radio and Television* 8, no. 3 (1988): 285–98.

———. "The Central African Film Unit's Images of Empire, 1948–1963." *Historical Journal of Film, Radio and Television* 3, no. 2 (1983): 131–47.

———. "Movies and Mandarins: The Official Film and British Colonial Africa." In *British Cinema History*, edited by James Curran and Vincent Porter, 129–43. Totowa, N.J.: Barnes and Noble Books, 1983.

Sorlin, Pierre. *The Film in History: Restaging the Past*. Totowa, N.J.: Barnes and Noble, 1980.

Spivak, Gayatri Chakravorty. *A Critique of Postcolonial Reason: Toward a History of the Vanishing Present*. Cambridge, Mass.: Harvard University Press, 1999.

"The State and Film Industry: A Review." In *Indian Talkie 1931–56: Silver Jubilee Souvenir*, 175–96. Bombay: Film Federation of India, 1956.

Steward, Jeffrey C., ed. *Paul Robeson: Artist and Citizen*. New Brunswick, N.J.: Rutgers University Press, 1998.

Stokes, Lisa Odham, and Michael Hoover. *City on Fire: Hong Kong Cinema*. London: Verso, 1999.

Stoler, Ann Laura, and Frederick Cooper, eds. *Tensions of Empire: Colonial Cultures in a Bourgeois World*. Berkeley: University of California Press, 1997.

Stollery, Martin. *Alternative Empires: European Modernist Cinemas and Cultures of Imperialism*. Exeter, U.K.: University of Exeter Press, 2000.

Street, Sarah. "Alexander Korda, Prudential Assurance and British Film Finance in the 1930s." *Historical Journal of Film, Radio and Television* 6, no. 2 (1986): 161–79.

———. *British Cinema in Documents*. London: Routledge, 2000.

———. *British National Cinema*. London: Routledge, 1997.

———. "The Hays Office and the Defence of the British Market in the 1930s." *Historical Journal of Film, Radio, and Television* 5, no. 1 (1985): 37–55.

———. *Transatlantic Crossings: British Feature Films in the United States*. New York: Continuum, 2002.

Sudan, Rajani. *Fair Exotics: Xenophobic Subjects in English Literature, 1719–1853*. Philadelphia: University of Pennsylvania Press, 2002.

Swann, Paul. "John Grierson and the G.P.O. Film Unit, 1933–1939." *Historical Journal of Film, Radio and Television* 3, no. 1 (1983): 19–34.

Tallents, Stephen G. *The Projection of England*. London: Faber and Faber, 1932.

Terdiman, Richard. *Present Past: Modernity and the Memory Crisis*. Ithaca, N.Y.: Cornell University Press, 1993.

Thomas, Rosie. "Indian Cinema: Pleasures and Popularity." *Screen* 26, nos. 3–4 (May–August 1985): 116–31.

Thompson, Kristin. *Exporting Entertainment: America in the World Film Market, 1907–34*. London: BFI, 1985.

Thompson, Kristin, and David Bordwell. "Space and Narrative in the Films of Ozu." *Screen* 17, no. 2 (summer 1976): 41–73.

Thomson, David. "Michael Powell, 1905–1990." *Film Comment* 26, no. 3 (May–June 1990): 28.

Todorov, Tzvetan. *The Fantastic*. Ithaca, N.Y.: Cornell University Press, 1975.

Tompkins, Jane. *West of Everything: The Inner Life of Westerns*. New York: Oxford University Press, 1993.

Toplin, Robert Brent. *History by Hollywood: The Use and Abuse of the American Past*. Urbana: University of Illinois Press, 1996.

"To Revive Production: F.B.I's Summary of the Rival Plans." *Kinematograph Weekly* (6 August 1925): 30–31.

Torgovnick, Marianna. *Gone Primitive: Savage Intellects, Modern Lives*. Chicago: University of Chicago Press, 1990.

Trumpener, Katie. *Bardic Nationalism: The Romantic Novel and the British Empire*. Princeton, N.J.: Princeton University Press, 1997.

"Two Reissues." *Kinematograph Weekly*, no. 1916 (6 January 1944): 21.

United Kingdom. *Parliamentary Debates*, Commons, 5th ser., vol. 203 (1927).

Vargas, A. L. "The Future of British Film Writing." *Sight and Sound* 16, no. 61 (spring 1947): 161–22.

Vasudevan, Ravi S. "The Melodramatic Mode and the Commercial Hindi Cinema: Notes on Film History, Narrative and Performance in the 1950s." *Screen* 30, no. 3 (summer 1989): 29–50.

———. "The Politics of Cultural Address in a 'Transitional Cinema': A Case Study of Indian Popular Cinema." In *Reinventing Film Studies*, edited by Christine Gledhill and Linda Williams, 130–64. London: Arnold, 2000.

———, ed. *Making Meaning in Indian Cinema*. Delhi: Oxford University Press, 2001.

———. "Nationhood, Authenticity, and Realism in Indian Cinema: The Double Take of Modernism in the Work of Satyajit Ray." http://www.sarai.net/mediacity/filmcity .htm (accessed 4 June 2005).

Vesselo, Arthur. "British Films of the Quarter." *Sight and Sound* 16, no. 61 (spring 1947): 76.

Virdi, Jyotika. *The Cinematic ImagiNation: Indian Popular Films as Social History.* New Brunswick, N.J.: Rutgers University Press, 2003.

Viswanathan, Gauri. *Masks of Conquest: Literary Study and British Rule in India.* New York: Columbia University Press, 1989.

Wadia, J. B. H. "Experience in Jaswantlal's Office." *Cinema Vision* 1, no. 1 (January 1980): 95–97.

———."I Remember, I Remember." *Cinema Vision* 1, no. 1 (January 1980): 93–95.

Walker, Janet, ed. *Westerns: Films through History.* New York: Routledge, 2001.

Walker, Michael. "Black Narcissus." *Framework* 9 (winter 1978–1979): 9–13.

Walsh, Mike. "The Empire of the Censors: Film Censorship in the Dominions." *Journal of Popular British Cinema* 3 (2000): 45–58.

———. "Fighting the American Invasion with Cricket, Roses, and Marmalade for Breakfast." *The Velvet Light Trap* no. 40 (fall 1997): 4–17.

———. "Thinking the Unthinkable: Coming to Terms with Northern Ireland in the 1980s and 1990s." In *British Cinema, Past and Present,* edited by Justine Ashby and Andrew Higson, 288–98. London: Routledge, 2000.

Watve, Bapu. *V. Damle and S. Fattelal: A Monograph.* Pune, India: National Film Archive of India, 1985.

Waugh, Alex. "Filming *The Four Feathers,*" *The Listener* (27 April 1939): 898–900.

Whissel, Kristen. "Uncle Tom, Goldilocks, and the Rough Riders: Early Cinema's Encounter with Empire." *Screen* 40, no. 4 (winter 1999): 384–404.

White, Hayden. *The Content of the Form: Narrative Discourse and Historical Representation.* Baltimore: Johns Hopkins University Press, 1990.

———. *Tropics of Discourse: Essays in Cultural Criticism.* Baltimore: Johns Hopkins University Press, 1985.

White, Mimi. "An Extra Body of Reference." Ph.D. diss., University of Iowa, 1980.

Wiegman, Robyn. *American Anatomies: Theorizing Race and Gender.* Durham, N.C.: Duke University Press, 1995.

Williams, Christopher, ed. *Realism and the Cinema: A Reader.* London: RKP and BFI, 1980.

Williams, Linda. "Something Else besides a Mother: Stella Dallas and the Maternal Melodrama." In *Imitations of Life: A Reader on Film and Television Melodrama,* edited by Marcia Landy, 307–30. Detroit: Wayne State University Press, 1991.

Williams, Raymond. *Marxism and Literature.* Oxford: Oxford University Press, 1977.

———. *Politics of Modernism: Against the New Conformists.* Edited and introduced by Tony Pinkney. London: Verso, 1989.

Wilson, Rob, and Wimal Dissanayake, eds. *Global/Local: Cultural Production and the Transnational Imaginary.* Durham, N.C.: Duke University Press, 1996.

Winston, Brian. *Claiming the Real: The Griersonian Documentary and Its Legitimations.* London: BFI, 1995.

Wollen, Peter. "Godard and Counter-Cinema: Vent d'Est." In *Narrative, Apparatus, Ideology: A Film Theory Reader,* edited by Philip Rosen, 198–209. New York: Columbia University Press, 1986.

————. "The Two Avant Gardes." *Studio International* 190, no. 978 (November/December 1975): 171–75.

Wolpert, Stanley A. *A New History of India.* 4th ed. New York: Oxford University Press, 1993.

Wright, Will. *Sixguns and Society: A Structural Study of the Western.* Berkeley: University of California Press, 1975.

INDEX OF FILMS

GENERAL INDEX

Priya Jaikumar is an assistant professor in the School
of Cinema-Television at the University of Southern
California.

*

An earlier version of chapter 6 appeared as " 'Place' and
the Modernist Redemption of Empire in Black Narcissus
(1947)" Cinema Journal 40, no. 2 (2001): 55–57. © 2001
University of Texas Press. Reprinted with permission. A
typographical error ("an unproblematic relationship of a
nation to its imperial past," 72, which should have read
"problematic relationship") is amended in this book.

Chapter 2 expands on arguments first presented in
"An Act of Transition: Empire and the Making of a
National British Film Industry, 1927," Screen 43, no. 2
(summer 2002): 119–38. © 2002. Reprinted with
permission.

Chapter 3 expands on the essay "More than Morality:
The Indian Cinematograph Committee Interviews (1927),"
The Moving Image 3, no. 1 (spring 2003): 82–109. © 2003.
Reprinted with permission.

*

Library of Congress Cataloging-in-Publication Data
Jaikumar, Priya, 1967–
Cinema at the end of empire : a politics of transition in
Britain and India / Priya Jaikumar.
p. cm.
Includes bibliographical references and index.
ISBN 0-8223-3780-0 (cloth : alk. paper)
ISBN 0-8223-3793-2 (pbk. : alk. paper)
1. Motion picture industry—India—History. 2. Motion
picture industry—Great Britain—History. 3. Motion
pictures, British—India. I. Title.
PN1993.5.18J28 2006
384′.80954—dc22   2005029787